THE COLD WAR AT HOME

PHILIP JENKINS

THE COLD WAR

AT HOME

THE RED SCARE IN PENNSYLVANIA, 1945–1960

The
University
of North
Carolina
Press

Chapel Hill
and London

Designed by April Leidig-Higgins
Set in Minion type by Running Feet Books
Manufactured in the United States of America

The paper in this book meets the guidelines for
permanence and durability of the Committee on
Production Guidelines for Book Longevity of the
Council on Library Resources.

Library of Congress Cataloging-in-Publication Data
Jenkins, Philip, 1952– The Cold War at home :
the Red Scare in Pennsylvania, 1945–1960 /
by Philip Jenkins. p. cm. Includes bibliographical
references (p.) and index.
ISBN 0-8078-2498-4 (cloth : alk. paper).—
ISBN 0-8078-4781-x (pbk. : alk. paper)
1. Anti-communist movements—Pennsylvania
—History—20th century. 2. Communism—
Pennsylvania—History—20th century.
3. Pennsylvania—Politics and government—
1865–1950. 4. Internal security—Pennsylvania
—History—20th century. 5. Anti-communist
movements—United States—History—20th
century—Case studies. 6. Communism—United
States—History—20th century—Case studies.
7. United States—Politics and government—
1933–1953—Case studies. 8. Internal security—
United States—History—20th century—Case
studies. 9. Cold War—Case studies. I. Title.
F154.J46 1999   974.8'043—dc21   99-17969 CIP

03 02 01 00 99   5 4 3 2 1

TO LIZ

CONTENTS

TABLES

ACKNOWLEDGMENTS

In undertaking the research for this book, I have been greatly assisted by support from several institutions. The Balch Institute for Ethnic Studies, in Philadelphia, gave me a one-month residential fellowship; I also received travel grants from the Institute for the Study of American Evangelicals, at Wheaton College, Illinois, and from the Harry S. Truman Presidential Library in Independence, Missouri. To all of these, my heartfelt thanks.

ABBREVIATIONS USED IN THE TEXT

ABC   Americans Battling Communism

ACLU   American Civil Liberties Union

ACTU   Association of Catholic Trade Unionists

ADA   Americans for Democratic Action

AFL   American Federation of Labor

AJC   American Jewish Congress

ASC   American Slav Congress

CAP   Civil Air Patrol

CFU   Croatian Fraternal Union

CIO   Congress of Industrial Organizations

CIO-PAC   Congress of Industrial Organizations Political Action Committee

CPAC   Citizens' Political Action Committee

CPUSA   Communist Party of the United States of America

CRC   Civil Rights Congress

DAR   Daughters of the American Revolution

FBI   Federal Bureau of Investigation

HUAC   House Un-American Activities Committee

ICCASP   Independent Citizens' Council of the Arts and Sciences and Professions

IUE   International Union of Electrical Workers

IWO   International Workers' Order

NAACP   National Association for the Advancement of Colored People

NCC National Council of Churches

OGPU Ob"edinennoe Gosudarstvennoe Politicheskoe Upravlenie
(Unified State Political Administration, i.e., Soviet secret
police, 1923–34)

PCA Progressive Citizens of America

PMA Pennsylvania Manufacturers' Association

PNA Polish National Alliance

SANS Slovenski Amerishki Narodni Svet (Slovenian American
National Council)

SISS Senate Internal Security Subcommittee, Committee
on the Judiciary

SNPJ Slovenska Narodna Podporna Jednota (Slovene Mutual
Benefit Union)

UE United Electrical, Radio and Machine Workers of America

USWA United Steelworkers of America

VFW Veterans of Foreign Wars

THE COLD WAR AT HOME

1

INTRODUCTION

During the decade after the Second World War, one of the leading figures of Pennsylvania's Republican politics was James H. Duff, who successively served as governor and U.S. senator. Duff was distinctly progressive by the standards of contemporary Republicanism, presiding over an enlightened reformist administration in the state and taking a politically unpopular position against Senator Joseph McCarthy long before most members of his party would dare take such a step. Duff seems like a classic moderate or even liberal, which makes it surprising that on the issue of Communism he was more extreme than most of the visible Red-hunters in public life. In 1950 he declared that members of the Communist Party were ipso facto traitors deserving the penalties of treason, which meant hanging. Furthermore, he believed, "if people put themselves in a position where their activities are doubtful, we are going to treat them if they are doubtful the way they are if they are wrong, because the time has come in America where we can't continue to make mistakes with the people who are trying to destroy our Way of Life."[1] Such were the views of a moderate Republican in a politically moderate state.

Duff's position on Communism raises important questions about what exactly constituted extremism in these years. Specifically, it is a useful comment on what has come to be known as McCarthyism, a word that is often used in a far broader sense than it deserves. The term has come to be synonymous with the official movement to seek out and remove Communists from American life, a theme that became a national phenomenon in 1947 and remained in vogue at least through the mid-1950s. Accurately reflecting popular usage, Ellen Schrecker writes of "McCarthyism, the anti-Communist political repression of the late 1940s and 1950s," while Albert Fried's book on McCarthyism is subtitled *The Great American Red Scare*.[2] Governor Duff's views suggest a problem with this approach: while he yielded to nobody in his anti-Communist zeal, he was categorically not a McCarthyite in the sense in which that word was used in his day. For Duff, as for many of his contemporaries who would have described themselves as liberals, McCarthyism was an unacceptable form of extremism. It was an irresponsible and dangerous tactic characterized by vague and unsubstantiated accusations for political ends, the exploitation of hysterical public fears, the reckless persecution of innocent or relatively harmless dissidents, and the practice of using loose connections between suspected individuals in order to construct "a conspiracy so immense." Critics used the term essentially synonymously with witch-hunting or demagoguery, and, as such, it deserved utter repudiation. Worse, it distracted public attention from the urgent need to discover authentic Communists, who should at the least be removed from any office of trust. McCarthyism did not, in these years, refer to the use of quite intrusive or inquisitorial means to discover and root out genuine Communists or subversives, potential spies and saboteurs, a process that had sustained the support of a broad bipartisan consensus for several years before Senator McCarthy himself became a figure of national consequence. McCarthyism did not emerge until after many of the most important inquiries and purges had already occurred.

Criticizing the McCarthyite label would be pedantic if the widespread identification of the anti-Communist movement with Senator McCarthy had not done so much to shape popular historical understanding of these years. The word diverts attention from the other protagonists of this era, to the extent that the senator is popularly associated with the House Un-American Activities Committee (HUAC), which long predated him, and he attracts blame for acts that in fact occurred under the Democratic administration of Harry Truman. In folk memory, the voice of Joseph McCarthy may be indelibly associated with the notorious question of "Are you now, or have you ever been, a member of the Communist Party?," but the phrase was a cliché before he ever used it. Conversely, the fall of McCarthy in 1954 is often taken as marking the end of the movement of hysterical anti-Communism that he symbolized, when in fact the basic system of anti-Communist investigations, loyalty oaths, and deportations continued for years afterward. David Caute's history, *The Great Fear*, avoids the McCarthy label in its subtitle; he prefers to write of *The Anti-Communist Purge under Truman and Eisenhower*.[3] McCarthyism was extreme, while the Red Scare arose from the political mainstream.

Politically, the historical emphasis on McCarthyism places responsibility for the postwar Red Scare on those conservatives, mainly Republicans, who used the movement as a flank attack on New Deal policies, which could be tainted by association with "twenty years of treason." As Albert Fried has written, "McCarthyism may also be defined as the Cold War's revenge on liberal Democrats."[4] While the anti-Communist purges did cause a traumatic split within the New Deal coalition, it would be equally fair to see liberals as the motivators rather than the victims in seeking to drive Communists and other progressives out of the Democratic camp and the labor unions. McCarthyism may have been a desperate ploy of the Republican Right, but the anti-Communist movement itself was thoroughly bipartisan. In a sense, identifying the whole movement as McCarthyism allowed the campaign to be depoliticized, to be seen not as a social or political movement in which both parties had been involved, but as the criminal ambition of one dubious character and the band of irresponsible adventurers around him: everything could be blamed on "a one man party called McCarthyism."[5] Once the senator was discredited, his political eclipse served to bury the worst extremes of the previous decade, which henceforward were conventionally associated with him.

Finally, to speak of McCarthyism places undue emphasis on the role of the federal government, of congressional investigation, and of the element of "high" politics, as McCarthy's prime issue was not so much Communism as Communism within the U.S. government. Whatever we call it, inquisition or purge, the practical effects of the anti-Communist movement were felt across the nation, and the vast majority of the victims were relatively humble individuals, factory workers and clerks, teachers and minor civil servants, rather than officeholders or celebrities, but once again, popular memory has focused on the great national causes célèbres. Scholarship on the domestic front of the Cold War has paid enormous attention to cases like those of Alger Hiss, the Rosenbergs, and the Hollywood Ten, together with the abundantly publicized attack upon show business personalities, but far less is available on the "ordinary" aspect of the persecutions.

This approach is well reflected in popular culture treatments of the Cold War era, which became numerous in the decade after the Watergate scandal. With the lifting of old restrictions and the collapse of blacklisting, the "McCarthy years" became a flourishing genre in film and literature, and the emphasis was firmly upon the major national events. Inevitably, given the interests of writers and producers in the visual media, conditions in the entertainment industry were prominently depicted in fictionalized films like *The*

Way We Were (1973), *Fear on Trial* (1975), *The Front* and *Bound for Glory* (both 1976), *Guilty by Suspicion* (1991), and the documentary *Hollywood on Trial* (1979), while the McCarthy hearings formed the subject of *Tail Gunner Joe* (1977) and *Citizen Cohn* (1992).[6] The Rosenberg case in particular has attracted later authors and was treated in E. L. Doctorow's *The Book of Daniel* (1971; filmed as *Daniel*, 1983), and Robert Coover's *The Public Burning* (1977). In contrast, the plight of relatively ordinary citizens caught up in McCarthyite suspicions has been the subject of only a few minor and forgettable features.[7]

To understand the impact of national events on everyday life, historians often use case studies that examine the experience of a particular city or state, and the number of books dealing with the local impact of the Red Scare years has been steadily growing since the mid-1980s. Recent examples include T. Michael Holmes' *The Specter of Communism in Hawaii* and M. J. Heale's account of several diverse states in *McCarthy's Americans*.[8] Much still remains to be done on these models, particularly in some of the major states or regions where Communism was said to be particularly rampant and where the resulting purges were peculiarly intense. In this context, Pennsylvania offers a valuable example. One of the most significant industrial states, with a powerful radical tradition, by the early 1950s it was the scene of some of the fiercest anti-Red activism to be found anywhere in the country. David Caute's *The Great Fear* includes a chapter entitled "Hell in Pittsburgh," describing the testimony of one long-term infiltrator into the Communist Party, Matt Cvetic, and how his allegations initiated a period of purges and trials. Pittsburgh became "that Mecca of the inquisition."[9] Philadelphia was equally subjected to major loyalty purges in 1952–53, and these events had ramifications in many smaller communities.

Pennsylvania's experience with anti-Communism raises many important questions for understanding events nationwide. One immediate point is the irrelevance of McCarthy himself, if not of McCarthyism: events would probably not have happened too differently if the senator had never come to public attention. Though his example influenced the hearings in both Philadelphia and Pittsburgh in 1953, these occurred very much at the tail end of five years or more of investigation and suppression of Communist activities in the state. Pennsylvania's Red hunt proceeded according to a regional dynamic that can be traced back to 1946, and arguably to 1939. We will often find that the "little Red Scare" between 1939 and 1941 set the stage for later conflicts. If there was a single detonator for the 1940s Red Scare, perhaps it was not the case of the "atom spies," nor the conviction of Alger Hiss, nor Senator McCarthy's celebrated speech in Wheeling, West Virginia: it may rather have been the Nazi-Soviet pact of 1939, which set off a two-year period of judicial and political repression of Communists that foreshadowed the events of a decade later, often targeting the same individuals and groups. From this perspective, the era of good feelings that the Communist Party enjoyed through the Second World War looks like a truce in a long-term struggle under way from the late 1930s through the early 1960s.

The case of Pennsylvania also raises the question of why anti-Communist politics and rhetoric should have been so extremely vigorous, why in fact there should have been hell in Pittsburgh, or in Philadelphia, or any one of a dozen other cities. Pennsylvania politics did not generally lend itself to extremism. Though the state was politically Republican through most of the twentieth century, it had a distinctly moderate tradition in areas like civil rights and racial issues and was in the midst of a historic shift to the Democrats. In 1951, at the height of anti-Red sentiment, the city of Philadelphia broke a century of tradition by voting in a new administration that was not merely Democratic but definitely liberal in persuasion. On Communism, though, the political consensus remained implacable. The state was the home of some of the fiercest Red-hunters in the country and the scene of some of the most sweeping public exposés and denunciations.

We repeatedly find that liberalism in one area did not transfer to attitudes toward the far Left. The state's best-known anti-Communist was probably Judge Michael Angelo Musmanno, whose pro-labor credentials were wonderful. he had personally defended Sacco and Vanzetti, he campaigned to abolish the employers' private Coal and Iron Police, and in the mid-1960s he attracted the ire of the far Right when he supported civil rights marchers in Mississippi. His anti-Communist rhetoric was utterly intemperate, however, and he viewed Communist Party members as traitors deserving lengthy prison sentences at the least. One of the state's great liberals was Father Charles Owen Rice, a labor activist who was a devoted supporter of civil rights and passionately opposed the Vietnam War, yet who waged his own personal decade-long war against Red influences in the labor unions. An odd member of this "liberal" group was Francis "Tad" Walter, who chaired HUAC from 1954 to 1963 and was a dedicated enemy of all things Communist, yet whose own voting record on social and labor issues was the despair of his conservative admirers.

Musmanno, Rice, and Walter were all New Deal supporters, and this list underlines the extent to which the anti-Red movement was a product of the

Democratic Party rather than a Republican riposte to the Roosevelt inheritance. Activism in the late 1940s was launched by powerful Democratic factions and was usually directed against groups and individuals who claimed a foothold within the same party. In 1950, for example, progressives within the United Electrical, Radio and Machine Workers of America (UE) described the deadly rightist challenge to their existence as coming from an unholy alliance between the Democratic Party, the Congress of Industrial Organizations (CIO), and the Federal Bureau of Investigation (FBI). That Communism could expect to provoke a violent response from business groups, veterans, and the Catholic Church was scarcely surprising; what was new after 1945 was the anti-Communist activism of the Democratic Party and of major unions like the steelworkers.

This internecine quality reflected the fundamental fact that the state's Democratic Party was fighting for its existence. Democratic power in this region was very new, and the potent coalition of the mid-1940s was a still-young artifact of the New Deal years. The 1946 elections showed that this coalition was on the verge of fragmenting, with the most acute tension evident in the labor movement and the ethnic components, so that unless Communists and fellow travelers were purged thoroughly, and publicly, Democrats faced obliteration. Democratic anti-Communism was a matter of self-preservation. Similar factors explain why anti-Communism found such fervent support in the state's labor unions, as the CIO was likewise fighting to preserve the gains of the previous decade. For both the Democratic Party and the CIO, the 1948 campaign of Henry Wallace on the Progressive ticket was the last straw; the Left was in danger of splitting the New Deal coalition for its own sectarian purposes, even if this meant returning conservative Republicans to national power.

Anti-Communist zeal must be understood in terms of the religious and ethnic makeup of the state's population. Pennsylvania had a sizable Catholic minority that had gained enormous social and political influence as a result of the New Deal, though ideologically Catholics found themselves ill at ease with the leftists that formed part of the Roosevelt coalition. After 1946 the deteriorating international situation provided justification for the purge of leftist forces. Furthermore, in a state with a strong heritage from the nations of southern and eastern Europe, religion was closely related to ethnicity. In the decade after 1945, the Communist threat became much more immediate in the European countries with which many Pennsylvanians had ethnic ties. Prior to 1939, Communist rule was an established fact for Russians and Ukrainians, but during the next decade, this fate also befell the Baltic republics, as well as citizens of several other eastern European nations. Most of the newly "captive nations" were either predominantly Catholic or, like Yugoslavia, included substantial Catholic minorities. Between 1946 and 1950 it was a serious possibility that several other nations would be "lost to Communism," and the Communist coup in Czechoslovakia in early 1948 showed the vulnerability of advanced industrial states like France and Italy. Many (though not all) Catholic Poles, Slovaks, Croats, and Italians thus had powerful and multifaceted reasons for opposing Communism, or any ideas that seemed vaguely pink.

Throughout the Red Scare years, militantly anti-Communist politicians reflected the deeply held views of a large section of the public, including the working and middle classes. The extent of these feelings is suggested by the extreme difficulty of holding public meetings for Henry Wallace's Progressives during his 1948 campaign, or by the frequent incidents in which individual Communists were subjected to random attack or vilification (FBI undercover informants often told of such incidents after they had surfaced). Communists found it difficult to organize rallies or even closed-door meetings after 1948, the year that the traditional May Day celebrations largely died, and this did not result from official suppression by police or government. When a mob attacked a major Communist meeting in Pittsburgh's North Side in 1949, victims had a hard time escaping because cab drivers would not assist them. Some street-level anti-Communists may have been Catholics or eastern Europeans, but all evidence suggests that such attitudes traversed the religious and ethnic spectrum, affecting Jews and Protestants as well as Catholics, and extended to members of all classes. Of course, there was still much room for disagreement about specific policies to combat Communism, and firebrands like Musmanno often adopted stances much more extreme than other leaders, but there was little conflict about the overall goals. The Red Scare arose from a genuinely comprehensive social movement.

Though it is no adequate excuse for the hysteria of these years, the popular consensus can best be understood against a background of imminent war. Emergency measures could be justified because the nation might at any time face a military conflict of unprecedented savagery, and it became an urgent necessity to seek out and suppress potential spies and saboteurs. A clear and present danger to national security might arguably justify the suspension of some civil liberties. If there was a subversive threat, then all logic suggested that a primary target would be the defense-related industries of Pennsylvania, its steelworks and coal mines, electrical plants and shipyards. Concerns about a global war were not unfounded: such an outbreak was a real possibility at several points between, say, 1947 and 1962, and had it occurred, both superpowers would have exploited whatever assets they had behind enemy lines to cause maximum disruption. Both sides would likely have used front organizations to undermine the other side's will to fight. As it would be suicidal to speak openly on behalf of a military enemy during wartime, antiwar propaganda would have to be carried on in the guise of other ideologies, such as humanitarian calls for world peace. Americans were influenced here by memories of the thoroughly discredited isolationist movement that had been such a powerful voice before Pearl Harbor but in retrospect was regarded (unfairly) as a naive puppet of the Axis governments. If the United States might now be facing a nuclear Pearl Harbor, then the nation was justified in using the harshest measures against subversives and their dupes as a necessary part of the broader civil defense effort.[10]

Even before a Soviet nuclear attack was conceivable, the experience of European states in the Second World War suggested the likely dangers for a key industrial state such as Pennsylvania if war broke out. While war industries and population centers would be targeted by long-range bombers, initial strikes would come from clandestine forces, either domestic guerrillas or Soviet special forces operating along the lines of the United States's own wartime Office of Strategic Services or its British counterparts. In this perspective, Pennsylvania's Communist Party took on a sinister appearance as an organized conspiracy that specifically targeted the leading industries for recruitment and propaganda; several of its leaders even had significant experience in clandestine warfare. In reality, evidence of actual or planned sabotage was next to none. Neither state nor federal authorities were able to produce substantiated charges at the time; between 1945 and 1955 the FBI had a dozen known agents in place in the state's Communist apparatus, and if any of them had encountered serious military or conspiratorial plans, these would presumably have come to light in trials for sedition, treason, or espionage. None did; instead, Party leaders were tried on unconvincing charges of seeking to overthrow the U.S. government by distributing Communist propaganda works. Nevertheless, the hatred of Communists can only be understood in this fifth-column context: they were viewed as potential enemy agents in a "next war" that might be only days or weeks away.

The Communist Party suffered from the current state of Marxist terminology and thought, in which the interests of the Soviet Union and its allies were depicted as identical with those of progressive peoples and working-class power worldwide. When, in 1946, western Pennsylvania Party leader Roy Hudson was asked which side he would support in the event of a war between the United States and USSR, he replied deftly that "the Communists and the Communist Party owe allegiance to only one power—that power is the American people. We will be on the side of our people fighting for what is in the true national interests of our country."[11] But such a political statement of class loyalty and identification was all too easily transformed into an assertion of support for a foreign state. Hudson's successor as regional Party chief, Steve Nelson, was reported to have celebrated the Soviet acquisition of the nuclear bomb, an event lamented by most Americans as an undiluted catastrophe. For Nelson, the event promoted peace by restoring a global balance: "We have the atom bomb now and the enemy won't be in such a goddamned hurry to start a war."[12] "We," in this context, meant the Communist world and the international working class, and "the enemy" meant the forces of reaction, but it was all too easy to read the statement as a simple assertion that it was the American government and people who were "the enemy," while "we" meant the Soviet government. This thinking was close to treason, and one can only imagine the effect of contemporary headlines claiming "Nelson Hailed Red Bomb." The often-repeated charge that Communists were "atom spies" was the most effective single weapon in the arsenal of Red-baiting.

Treason charges became a real likelihood following the outbreak of the Korean War in 1950, when Communist sympathy for foreign powers was potentially transformed into support for an enemy power with which the United States was in armed conflict. When Pittsburgh's Communist Party headquarters was raided in 1950, for example, documents opposing the war were seized and quoted as showing the Party's allegedly treacherous positions: "The document does state in part its hope and wishes that the American forces fighting in South Korea take a shellacking."[13] By raising fears of an imminent Soviet military move against western Europe, Korean events had a double resonance for Catholics and many ethnic groups. The invasion of South Korea on June 25, 1950, a second day of infamy, fundamentally changed the whole political environment for dissent within the United States. The intensified antisubversive quest of the next three years is conventionally known as McCarthyism, but it might with more justice be termed the Korean War Red Scare. No account of this movement can afford to ignore the impact of living in "pre-war" conditions, or the fact that regions like Pennsylvania already regarded themselves as a critical home front in the emerging global struggle.

A regional study in an area like Pennsylvania provides a useful balanced perspective in the continuing debate over the anti-Communist movement and, specifically, the motivations of the anti-Communist campaigners: How far were they pursuing a serious or realistic national danger? Was there a genuine "Red menace," or was it all a "Red scare"?[14] This question has been subject to radically different interpretations over the years. From the 1960s through the 1980s, historians generally accepted a liberal consensus that saw the so-called McCarthy era in terms of a straightforward battle between vice and virtue in which persecuted leftists were depicted as martyrs and their persecutors were either fanatics or ruthless political adventurers. The Red-hunters of mid-century suffered an abysmal reputation: McCarthy himself had dropped into general disfavor shortly after his spectacular fall in 1954, while events of the Watergate era suggested that men such as Richard Nixon, J. Edgar Hoover, and Roy Cohn had been villains quite as squalid as their victims and detractors claimed. Few doubted that the early 1950s had indeed been "scoundrel time," the "American inquisition," the age of "the great fear," "a study in national hysteria," another manifestation of "the paranoid style in American politics."[15] It was considered far more disgraceful to have been an informer than to have been informed against. After all, any movement so detested by Hoover and Nixon must have had some redeeming features.

These perceptions affected both academic and popular culture treatments of the Red Scare years: inquisitors were damned not only by their unscrupulous tactics, but also by their underlying assumption that domestic leftists might be linked to authentic subversion. The idea seemed self-evidently absurd, and the image of, say, Philadelphia Communists sabotaging defense installations appeared as ill-founded as the notion of Jews poisoning the wells of medieval villages. Charges made against the American Communists of the early 1950s were now viewed as skeptically as those directed against black militants, antiwar protesters, or antinuclear activists in later days. No rational person believed that these latter-day protesters were tools of Moscow, members of so-called Communist front groups, so why should such charges be accepted in an earlier context? Films and documentaries of the new era explicitly linked the older Communist concerns with modern issues, as when the 1983 film *Daniel* intercut reconstructions of protests against the Rosenberg executions with news film of Reagan-era antinuclear rallies. The suppression of the Left in the McCarthy years was now commonly seen as an episode in the construction of the national security state, part of the militarist trend in American history that culminated in the Vietnam disaster.

In the last decade, anti-Communist politics have been treated more respectfully, partly as a result of the conservative political trends of the 1980s, but also because of the uncovering of documents that would hitherto have been thought unavailable, particularly those from the intelligence services of the former Communist states. In the revisionist view, Red-hunters were correct more frequently than their enemies gave them credit for; a plausible case can be made, for example, that figures like Alger Hiss and the Rosenbergs were in fact involved in espionage, or at least were in contact with agents of Communist powers, and that American Communists were being financed secretly, and generously, by the Soviet Union, which was treating its American followers with all the cynical brutality that it used toward its own subjects.[16] The continuing exposure of Communist misdeeds lends more credibility to democratic critics of the extreme Left, who emerge as prophets "not without honor," while even the maligned informers are seen to have performed a valuable service. In this light, the concept of a Red menace appears less of a bad joke than it might have seemed some years ago.[17]

Although the liberal perspective on the "American inquisition" has in no sense been invalidated, any assessment of anti-Communist politics now must take account of the new abundance of information about the American Communist Left. Put another way, the rival interpretations of the "Red menace" and the "Red scare" are not mutually incompatible, in that we can agree both that an authentic Communist threat existed and that the reaction to it was excessive, and often misplaced. Ideally, we are now far enough away from the conflicts to begin to see them more objectively, though it may be many years yet before any kind of balanced view finds its way into popular culture.

Attitudes toward American anti-Communism are profoundly influenced by the terminology we decide to use. For forty years, the McCarthy years were discussed in terms of a purge, an inquisition, and, above all, a witch-hunt, all of which imply the irrational persecution of innocent victims, with Arthur Miller's play *The Crucible* offering a classic model of a disturbed community wreaking vengeance on imaginary demon figures.[18] Once again, it is perilous to confuse anti-Communism with McCarthyism: McCarthy often did act like the stereotypical witch-hunter, finding evidence of evil in words or acts that others would consider harmless, but this does not mean that the witch-hunt analogy should be applied to all phases of the movement. When a moderate governor like James Duff alleged that a Communist presence in a strategic industry was a threat to national security, he may have been utterly misreading Communist intentions, but he was not fabricating the presence of real Party members and sympathizers in those locations. In this sense, the witches really did exist, whether or not that fact should arouse concern.

The word "Red-baiting" is equally loaded. Historically, bear-baiting referred to the maltreatment of a chained animal, and in the late nineteenth century, the term "Jew-baiting" was coined to suggest malicious sadism toward innocent human victims. This idea gained currency in the early days of the Nazi regime, and within a few years, the notion of Red-baiting emerged, implying a similar cruelty inflicted on a harmless scapegoat; the linkage was made plausible by the anti-Semitism often found on the radical Right. In 1940 the popular leftist writer George Seldes published a book with the doubly significant title *Witch Hunt: The Technique and Profits of Redbaiting*, and the term became widespread in 1947 at the time of HUAC's Hollywood hearings. "Red-baiting" is a useful way of describing a common type of extreme anti-Communist rhetoric, but like "witch-hunt," the word is misleading if used to imply that targets were always innocuous and opposition to them invariably irrational.[19]

The case of Pennsylvania is valuable in showing the role of Communism in the wider political environment. Hell broke forth in Pittsburgh, as in Philadelphia or Reading or Johnstown, because Communism there was not perceived simply as a distant demon-figure threatening American ideologies and interests, but as a very present local reality posing a serious threat of controlling or influencing some key areas of life. Between 1936 and 1948 a vigorous conflict was in progress between Communists and their enemies for the control of important social and economic institutions, including labor unions, the educational system, and major ethnic organizations; during the Second World War particularly, Communist advances had been impressive. By taking control of these institutions, Communists would be in a position to exercise real influence within the state's political life. The Red Scare was so intense locally because the national climate of fervent anti-Communism provided a unique opportunity for politicians to uproot these local rivals and to purge the institutions of all vestiges of Red influence. Communist strength was potentially greatest in those areas that would be critical in a future war, and it is difficult to imagine many political systems sufficiently easygoing to tolerate such a network of influence in a military-industrial heartland like western Pennsylvania. It was not simply a matter of groundless Red-baiting.

Having said this, it is difficult to sympathize with many tactics of the anti-Communist movement, which generally operated according to quite draconian state and federal laws and even then went considerably beyond those measures. In consequence, civil liberties were dramatically curtailed, with the worst effects generally being felt not by any likely subversives, but by people with consciences too scrupulous to take the necessary oaths of loyalty. In this environment, it was all too easy for unsubstantiated charges to be thrown cynically at rivals: Red smears were used by newspapers against commercial competitors, politicians against their electoral rivals, political parties against their enemies, and union faction against union faction.

Throughout the process, courts and congressional committees permitted investigative tactics that violated elementary principles of justice, including something as basic as the concept that conduct cannot be criminalized ex post facto, or retroactively. Nobody in the early 1950s was technically punished for having been a member of the entirely legal Communist Party a decade previously, but many former Communists did suffer ruinous consequences for this past behavior. During congressional hearings, such a heinous past could only be expiated if one was prepared to name and stigmatize past friends and colleagues, an act of moral betrayal that became the touchstone of anti-Communist principle. This was the era of naming names, in which the dubious figure of the informer was all but canonized. Lacking the experience of foreign occupation, Americans never acquired the postwar European revulsion against infiltrators, moles, and provocateurs and were slow to learn the full danger of creating an underworld of career informers.

The consequences of "naming" could be a kind of vigilantism, another equally troubling resort to extralegal sanctions. When, in both 1940 and 1948, the *Pittsburgh Press* published the names and addresses of individuals signing the nominating petitions for leftist parties (Communist and Progressive, respectively), the paper's proprietors must have known that they were exposing those signers to the threat of ostracism, dismissal, or physical violence and that the potential victims were mostly very ordinary people: factory workers, small merchants, teachers, and housewives. When the paper received indignant letters protesting this practice, it duly printed the names and addresses of protesters, again with the same likely results.[20] As in the case of congressional committees relentlessly pressing witnesses to name their former friends and contacts, the fact that investigators were doing such things is less shocking than their lack of any sense that they were doing something reprehensible. That anti-Communists were dealing with a sophisticated Communist apparatus scarcely justifies their tactics or the conduct that they held out as public example. Many accused "subversives" may have been authentic Communists, rather than the misunderstood liberals of media mythology, but their pursuers often were cynical demagogues who deserve no vindication. There were witch-hunters as well as witches.

Because understanding the objective reality of the Communist presence is fundamental to understanding the official response, Chapter 2 will analyze the Communist specter in the years leading up to its post-1948 cataclysm. Though the Party was well established in major cities and industrial regions, its real significance lay in its outreach to a broader progressive community to which it could appeal on issues like civil rights and lynching, free speech and workers' rights. Communism did gain broad influence in these years, but the very strengths of the pre-1948 Party all lent themselves to the most sinister interpretation by investigators. If the Party of the Popular Front era had been admirably catholic and inclusive, that openness provided ammunition for those seeking to stigmatize liberals, progressives, and socialists for collaborating with Communism. If the Party despised national and ethnic differences, that internationalism gave rise to charges that the organization was controlled by wide-ranging cosmopolitan radicals owing allegiance to no state or law other than that of Moscow, for whom the United States was an arena of potential revolutionary action no different from Spain or China. By the 1940s the Party's rich traditions of revolutionary commitment, activism, and organization were portrayed as the techniques of expert spies and masters of deceit. Following the disastrous Progressive Party campaign of 1948, Communists were left isolated, vulnerable to a repression that would all but destroy the Party.

Chapter 3 suggests why the progressive wing of the New Deal coalition should have been so thoroughly excommunicated and subjected to persecution from both conservatives and liberals. Traditional anti-Communism remained a vigorous force, advocated forcefully by the veterans' and business groups that enjoyed so much influence in the state, but the vital new factor was the split within the Democratic Party following the disastrous 1946 elections. In reaction, Democrats adopted a much tougher line against the Left at both the national and regional levels, which in turn permitted the party's relative recovery in 1948. By 1950 Democrats yielded nothing to the Republicans in the competition to prove which party could offer the more solid anti-Communist front.

Chapter 4 explores the period of intense hostility to Communists and any suspected subversives that was precipitated by the Korean conflict and other events of 1950. Pittsburgh was now the scene of dramatic anti-Communist exposés, culminating in what can only be described as the great show trials of these years. Public exasperation with Communism resulted in a package of severe state legislation, which gave Pennsylvania a code of anti-Communist laws and loyalty investigations as strict as those of any jurisdiction. Throughout, antisubversive campaigns were viewed as part of a larger civil defense effort, on the grounds that Communist Party members or sympathizers were automatically supporters of the enemy superpower and were only awaiting their opportunity to begin clandestine operations on its behalf.

This perception was uniquely perilous in industry, where Communists had developed significant influence in certain labor unions. From the late 1930s, anti-Communist and, especially, Catholic forces had been engaged in a war to purge these influences, which reached its height in the late 1940s with the expulsion or withdrawal of Left-led unions from the CIO. Chapter 5 examines the struggle for control of the unions. By far the most important battlefront was UE, one of the nation's largest labor organizations, and the fight to organize the electrical industry raged in Pittsburgh and western Pennsylvania; indeed, the war for the electrical workers set the stage for the city's Red nightmare during the tense year of 1950.

The prospect of subtler forms of subversion created alarm about the leftist presence in the teaching profession, through which the minds of America's children and teenagers could be turned against their country. Chapter 6 discusses the effort to eliminate Communist influences from the schools and colleges that resulted in a harsh purge of the teaching profession in Philadelphia during 1953. This led to a much-feared HUAC visit to Philadelphia, an encounter that demonstrates the tactics and legal powers of the investigators and the near impossibility that any witness could emerge unscathed without making a groveling submission. The colleges suffered similarly as part of the general assault on "eggheads," otherworldly intellectuals whose foolish idealism blinded them to the grim reality of Communist plots.

Contemporary writers on Communism in Pennsylvania often discussed its strength in "labor and fraternal organizations," though the latter "fraternal" dimension rarely receives as much historical attention as do the unions. Though a majority of the eastern and southern European ethnic groups were firm supporters of the anti-Communist consensus, they did not constitute a monolithic bloc, as Left and Communist groups had been quite successful in securing a foothold in the ethnic organizations, a process that is discussed in Chapter 7. As with the labor unions, the intensity of anti-Red activism in the ethnic organizations owed much to a sense of fighting for survival and seeking to expel what had become an enemy within. Conservative ethnic leaders had good reason to fear failure: if Communists remained, then whole communities could be denounced as part of a pro-Soviet Trojan horse, with dire consequences in terms of renewed xenophobia. Jews had much to lose in this regard, which helps to explain the ferocious attitudes of Jewish anti-Communists across the state in these years.

The struggle against Communism was all the more intense given the presence of a powerful countervailing ideology in the form of religion. Chapter 8 focuses chiefly on Catholic attitudes but also notes the influence of the evangelical Right. Purely secular factors undoubtedly played their part in mobilizing Catholic anti-Communist militancy, but we must also give due credit to apocalyptic elements of the faith, which merged so readily with the nuclear fears of the age. In consequence, American Catholics were deeply hostile toward Communism far earlier than their compatriots, and for better or worse they led the way in demanding the harshest possible measures against those suspected of disloyalty. Their absolute religious dualism placed Catholics well to the Right in terms of contemporary political divisions, with important consequences for partisan politics when they were so firmly entrenched in the Democratic Party.

By the mid-1950s Communist power had been smashed in all its traditional strongholds, but anti-Communist ideology was kept alive by the continuing foreign threat. Moreover, anti-Communism had become thoroughly institutionalized within Pennsylvania and provided the political raison d'être of some activist groups and individuals. The slow process of decompression is the subject of Chapter 9, which describes the regrouping of political life around new issues that reflected the demographic and economic changes in these years. By far the most significant change was in matters of race, which came to be a crucial dividing line in Pennsylvania politics by the mid-1960s. The Red era was followed by a crisis in black and white.

Chapter 10 explores some of the long-term effects of the Red Scare years. Though the removal of the Communist presence may not of itself have changed the American political system to any great degree, the Red Scare contributed to a fundamental shift in American political structure by accelerating the New Deal and wartime trend toward growing federal power. The judicial reaction to the suppression of radicalism would also ensure a new determination to safeguard the rights of political minorities. In both cases, the issues raised by the anti-Communist movement would have enduring consequences throughout the 1960s and beyond.

HAUNTING PENNSYLVANIA

THE COMMUNIST TRADITION

> It was explained to me that the Communist Party was very liberal, and
> very much the same kind of a sociological and political program as the
> Roosevelt administration, and so far as I could see, it didn't seem to be
> too different. . . . [T]he aims, apparently, were in line with the 1934, 1935
> and 1936 political situation.
> —Dr. Wilbur Lee Mahaney, 1954[1]

The Communist threat was a pervasive issue in Pennsylvania's political life in
the decade after 1945, yet at no time in this period did the number of actual
Communist Party members in the state exceed 6,000, out of a state population of 11 million. In 1948 only 55,000 people were prepared to vote for the
Communist-backed presidential ticket of the Progressive Party, a paltry 1.5 percent of the Pennsylvania ballot. While these figures would seem to suggest that
the anti-Communist movement was chasing a phantom, such a conclusion
would be misleading. Though Communists never became a major party in the
state, they did succeed in becoming a recognized third force on the left of the
Democratic Party and the labor movement, with a rich network of institutions
and affiliated groups through which they could project their distinctive point
of view. Communists were a well-established political presence, not only in
great cities like Philadelphia and Pittsburgh, but also in smaller industrial and
suburban areas.

Moreover, Communists in 1945 could look back on a period of vigorous
growth; they had come a very long way from their near-invisibility of fifteen

years before. Theirs was still largely a party of new, energetic, and idealistic members. It was not unreasonable that they could hope for still greater things in the future, particularly if the Party was right in its predictions that more moderates would be drawn into its ranks by the pressures of economic crisis and the threat of Fascism and warmongering. Why should Communists not repeat what Pennsylvania's Democrats had already done, graduating from the status of a political joke to electing a majority of the state's congressional representatives, all in the space of a decade or two? In its heady early days, the Progressive movement seemed to be a potential vehicle to such success. In retrospect we know that the Communist Party of the mid-1940s was on the verge of calamity, but it was not unreasonable at the time to see it as a serious political force, especially given its successful record of cooperating with and influencing established groups and supporting a broad Left-liberal Popular Front. The Communist reality was sufficiently impressive to give some validity to the fears of its enemies.

In an advanced industrial state like Pennsylvania, both Communism and anti-Communism rested on well-established foundations. Charges that the state was being threatened by sinister activists of the radical Left had been commonplace throughout the labor conflicts of the nineteenth and early twentieth centuries. Such charges built a vast superstructure of innuendo and speculation upon a foundation of reality, but as in the 1940s, there was usually some objective core, some militant or revolutionary tradition. In the early twentieth century, Red nightmares focused on the Socialist Party, which was strong in Philadelphia and Reading, and the Industrial Workers of the World. Both groups were targeted by the antiforeign movement of 1917–18, a time when any hint of opposition to the war was taken as proof of treacherous pro-German sentiment. This antisubversive movement, which continued into the anti-Bolshevik panic of 1919 and 1920, established a rhetoric that would become familiar in coming decades: radicals were viewed as alien in sentiment and ideology, and they were suspected of secretly working for a foreign power as spies and saboteurs.[2]

After a difficult start, the Communist Party in Pennsylvania enjoyed explosive growth during the Depression years. In the 1920s it had been a fringe movement concentrated in mining communities in both the anthracite and the bituminous regions, along with a largely immigrant following in Philadelphia. Matters completely changed after the stock market crash in 1929, and the Party won nearly 6,000 votes statewide in the 1932 presidential election.[3] Domestic and foreign events appeared to confirm the Communist worldview and led to a radicalization of middle-class groups far removed from the Party's older ethnic and industrial constituencies. Capitalism seemed to be in a state of collapse quite as disastrous as the Marxists had predicted; between 1932 and 1936 there was daily evidence of the desperate lengths to which capitalists would go to maintain their power in this terminal crisis. At the time of the new Nazi regime in Germany, violent attacks upon the working class in Austria, and military repression in Spain, the Soviet Union stood in heroic isolation against the capitalist states, gaining immense prestige as the only major nation to offer significant material and military support to the threatened Spanish republic. Within the United States, the forces of capitalism, racism, and militarism were seemingly arrayed together against any attempt by the common people to escape from the horrors of the Depression. Communists emerged as energetic leaders of the unemployed workers movements in the cities and industrial areas—and were blamed for inciting the riots that were so frequent in the early 1930s.[4]

In the Marxist analysis, racism and repression could only be ended by developing the power of the organized working class. With legislation in the mid-1930s that permitted and encouraged unionization, the federal government offered an unprecedented opportunity to organize the American working class. Labor battles nationwide reached a climax in 1937, a year in which struggles in the steel and automobile industries were just the most visible aspects of a hugely enhanced labor consciousness. In Pennsylvania this was the year of spectacular industrial conflicts in the Johnstown steelworks, the chocolate factories at Hershey, and textile plants in Philadelphia and the Reading area. By the outbreak of war in 1941, the power and prestige of the labor unions stood higher than ever before, and by 1946 the Pennsylvania CIO represented some 600,000 members.[5]

The mid-1930s were a time of great danger as well as potentially historic social change. Studying a sample of older Philadelphia Communists in the 1970s, Paul Lyons found that "the mean year of radicalization is 1936, the year of Roosevelt's second election victory, of the beginning of the Spanish civil war, and of the rise of the ... CIO. These Philadelphia Communists began as a youth movement in a particular period of historical and cultural upheaval." Most were around twenty years old when radicalized.[6] By 1938 the young activists had the sense of sharing in an international movement of historic proportions, symbolized by the anti-Fascist parades and protests in Philadelphia and other cities that might draw tens of thousands of supporters. Philadelphia's May Day parade in that year included representatives of 200 organizations, including uniformed veterans from the Abraham Lincoln Brigade, the mainly Communist unit of American volunteers for the Spanish Civil War.[7]

The Party's growth was made possible by its changed attitude toward the political mainstream. In the early 1930s the American Communist Party had been pessimistic and confrontational, regarding all other strands of left-wing and liberal opinion as social Fascism beyond the pale of possible collaboration. From about 1935, however, following the shock of Nazi successes in Europe, the Party moved into its Popular Front phase, in which members were told to collaborate with all liberal and progressive forces in order to stop Fascist advances. Young and optimistic recruits of these years might criticize the liberal administrations of Roosevelt in Washington and liberal allies like Governor Earle in Pennsylvania, but they did not have to believe that such leaders were effectively indistinguishable from Hitler or Mussolini. Communists could now form tactical fighting alliances with liberals, reformers, and religious activists. This open attitude drew potential recruits into the orbit of the Party and won some over to full membership. By the late 1930s Communists were portraying themselves as a purely American movement, as in the frequently quoted words of Party leader Earl Browder: "Communism is the Americanism of the Twentieth Century." Traditional national symbols and rhetoric were appropriated in events like Lincoln-Lenin Day celebrations. At a Communist-sponsored Lincoln's Birthday celebration held in Pittsburgh in 1943, portraits of Lincoln and FDR flanked a life-size picture of Stalin, and May Day rallies often included a rendition of "The Star-Spangled Banner."[8]

Efforts to pose as a purely patriotic Americanist movement took a grievous blow from the 1939 Nazi-Soviet pact. In the embarrassing two years that followed, the Communist Party urged isolationism, and pro-Fascist groups made copious use of Communist flyers warning "The Yanks are NOT coming," a slogan that would often return to haunt Party members. The Party found itself the victim of its own rhetoric, having sensitized the public to the scale of the fifth-column danger of spies and saboteurs, yet now standing in a de facto alliance with those same forces. Between August 1939 and mid-1941, the Communist Party suffered a series of investigations and trials that closely prefigured the better-known events of a decade later, with the main venom coming not from the traditional Republican Right, but from Roosevelt followers in the unions and the Democratic Party. There were anti-Red purges in major unions, like the Philadelphia Teachers' Union, and abortive calls for Communist officials to be excluded from their stronghold in UE. The severity of this crackdown should have taught the Party a dreadful lesson about the extremes to which repression could be taken if an already unpopular radical party could plausibly be linked to foreign intrigues: Communists were welcomed within the New Deal coalition, but only so long as they did not develop ambitions at variance with those of the administration or its key supporters.

Pennsylvania shared in the "little Red Scare" of these years, when several states established investigative committees that foreshadowed the more celebrated bodies of the late 1940s. By early 1942 Pennsylvania's commonwealth counsel was creating a pioneering official list of Communist front groups, giving an official stigma to later notorious organizations like the American League for Peace and Democracy, the American Youth Congress, the Consumers Union, and the Spanish Refugee Relief Campaign.[9] Also of disastrous long-term significance, the FBI now planted agents within the western Pennsylvania Party, notably Matt Cvetic, who would wreak such havoc when he surfaced a decade later, as well as George Dietze and Joseph Mazzei; infiltration of the American Party became an important aspect of the broader effort against the Axis, long before the USSR itself became a pressing concern of American policy. The Philadelphia Party was also targeted at this time, though the extent of penetration was never as widely publicized as that in the Pittsburgh area; nevertheless, the FBI had no shortage of informants to report on every aspect of Party affairs in Philadelphia, including its industrial strongholds.[10] The Party was also infiltrated by journalists, one of whom, from the conservative *Pittsburgh Post-Gazette*, attended the Workers' School on Grant Street and wrote an embarrassing exposé, "The Red, Red Schoolhouse." Philadelphia papers now targeted Communists as well as Nazi sympathizers in their investigations of potential fifth-column and sabotage activities.[11]

Congressional investigations were also damaging. By early 1940 the Un-American Activities Committee headed by Martin Dies was investigating Communist activities and propaganda, with arrests and raids on Party offices in Philadelphia and Pittsburgh. Dies's investigators secured a massive haul of documents from the Philadelphia headquarters of the Communist Party as well as from the International Workers' Order (IWO), the network of Party-affiliated ethnic and fraternal societies. The papers were potentially very embarrassing, showing the close ties between the Party and myriad nominally independent front groups, but a federal court ordered the papers returned on the grounds that the search had been illegal.[12]

The official assault was more successful, and more sweeping, in Pittsburgh and the western parts of the state. The best-known target here was Communist veteran James Dolsen, who was described in the Pittsburgh-area press as an agent of OGPU, the Soviet secret police. Because he had lectured for the Works Progress Administration, local enemies of the Roosevelt administration were also able to associate this suspicious Red character with the New Deal.[13] In March the Dies Committee interrogated Dolsen, Party district secretary George Powers, and Richard H. Lawry, president of Pittsburgh's IWO, and Party leaders were investigated for an alleged racket in selling Soviet citizenship papers.[14] All the more humiliating, left-wing leaders were interviewed as part of a wider investigation into pro-Nazi and Fascist militants, suggesting that they were equally connected with international totalitarianism. Meanwhile, the Party's main investigative journalist, John L. Spivak, was jailed in Pittsburgh on charges of having committed criminal libel in his exposé of pro-Nazi activism in the United States.[15] The political repression of Communism in western Pennsylvania in the spring of 1940 looked very much like what would occur exactly a decade later, and in both eras the media suggested that the suppression of Communists was essential to national security: when dozens of Communists were indicted in an election fraud case in July 1940, the *Post-Gazette* crowed about "a smashing attack against leftist activists in this important national defense area."[16]

The federal offensive was followed by the petitions scandal. In 1940 Communists tried to capitalize on their recent popularity by running for office in the forthcoming state and national elections, for which purpose candidates required nominating petitions. These petitions would produce much agony for Party members and associates, as the act of signing gave material proof of political sympathies and lists of signatories were published by local newspapers.[17] The fact that supporters were willing to publicize their Communist sympathies shows the relative comfort the Left felt in the Roosevelt years, but the ensuing scandal indicates how tenuous this position was. As late as 1954, the petitions were again in the public eye when the commonwealth secretary promised to make public all 59,000 signatories, giving the FBI and state police a useful tool to detect radical and subversive sympathizers.[18]

The nominating petitions provoked calls for dismissals and other sanctions, especially for civil servants and teachers, and some important precedents emerged from the ensuing law cases. In 1942 a school board dismissed a Pittsburgh-area teacher who had signed a nominating petition for an old Communist friend; the teacher himself was not a Communist but signed because of his belief in the rights of political minorities to be heard. A lower court refused to reinstate him, but his appeal was upheld by the state supreme court.[19] Other cases were more ominous for the Left. In 1941 Pennsylvania's Superior Court heard the case of employees dismissed by the Unemployment Compensation Board of Review for giving false answers to questionnaires about Communist Party membership or whether they had ever signed Communist nominating petitions. The dismissals were technically for misconduct, in that employees had lied to superiors, but the court held that the state did not have to wait for overt acts of disloyalty before dismissing suspected subversives.[20] The court took judicial notice of the fact that "Communism, as a political movement, is dedicated to the overthrow of the government of the United States . . . by force and violence." This ruling accepted the fundamental grounds later used against Pennsylvania Communists, that their activities automatically violated state sedition laws.[21]

Other disasters were to come. When the *Pittsburgh Press* began publishing petitions in full, many alleged signatories denied having participated, and there was soon massive evidence of electoral fraud: uneducated people, often with a poor command of English, had been tricked into signing some official-looking document, while others assumed they were signing a petition to keep the nation out of war. An investigation by state authorities resulted in the indictment of forty-three Communist leaders and the conviction of twenty-seven, in what was incidentally a much bigger single trial than any in the region in the early 1950s, and which led to even more generous use of penal sanctions and prison terms. George Powers received nine months in the county workhouse and Dolsen ten months; on release both faced congressional contempt citations. In contrast to later events, these charges were upheld by superior courts. This scandal explains the poor Communist showing in the 1940 election, when the Party won only 4,500 votes statewide, up slightly from 1936, but down from 1932.[22]

Pearl Harbor may well have saved the American Communist Party. From its low ebb in the previous two years, Communist prestige reached a new height during the Second World War. Between 1942 and 1945 the Soviet Union was the esteemed ally of the United States and Great Britain, and America's mainstream media regularly offered tribute to Russian fighting prowess, symbolized by the heroic events at Stalingrad. In the words of a faculty member at Jefferson Medical College in Philadelphia, "At one time we were allied with the Soviet Union. I was brought up in very difficult circumstances; never had a sense of security in my life; I was a young man during the Depression. For years we had nothing.... Certainly during the war there was a real feeling of friendship with the Soviet Union, and for a little while after the war I felt that this perhaps might be what I was looking for." Nationwide, Party membership had risen from 7,500 in 1930 to over 20,000 in 1933, and it was briefly around 80,000–100,000 by about 1945.[23] The FBI field office in Philadelphia claimed that Party membership in that region rose by an astonishing 39 percent during the year 1942 alone. In 1945 the *Philadelphia Inquirer* reported that the local Party was "deeply rooted, represented in the labor movement, engaged in stirring up minorities, and busy with plans for expanding membership."[24]

Through the war years, Communists were among the most enthusiastic supporters of the administration, using all their resources to boost production and suppress labor disputes, while calling for vigilance against spies. Within the labor movement, Communists were the firmest enemies of radical excesses: they struggled to prevent other unions from challenging the wartime no-strike pledge or raising the slightest opposition to the Roosevelt administration, and they adamantly opposed any suggestion of a pro-labor third party.[25] After all, the causes of the United States and the Soviet Union were, briefly, indistinguishable, so that Communists could see themselves as the leading edge of a broad national and international coalition. In a move that would later come back to haunt them, Communist writers used their new superpatriotic stance to denounce leading right-wing politicians as Nazi sympathizers who should be sought out and prosecuted by the full force of the federal government. While this effort culminated in the sedition trial of some Fascist extremists in 1944, it never achieved the propaganda victory the Communists hoped that it would, though the affair did help condition the public to the notion of traitors in high places within the U.S. government. The Left-induced spy scare of the war years shaped the thought world of postwar countersubversion, in which, of course, the main villains were Communists themselves.[26]

The Communist Party's new role as standard-bearer of a new leftist Americanism was evident during the crisis that developed in Philadelphia in August 1944, when the local mass-transit company attempted to hire black workers. The action precipitated a citywide strike by whites and raised fears of race riots comparable to those that had occurred in New York and Detroit during the previous year. Communist and IWO leaders took the lead in the interracial community meetings that protested the racist industrial action and demanded official intervention to end it, using the armed forces if necessary. Communists were now in the unusual position of calling for state or federal action to end a working-class protest. The Left called on the Democratic administration to unite the country in a supreme national war effort, stressing the fundamental need for racial unity to promote social progress. In a mass meeting in West Philadelphia, the antistrike effort was supported by leaders of the local Communist Party and affiliated organizations, as well as by sympathetic leftist unions; these activists were joined by a cross-section of community leaders and religious groups. As a labor leader stated, "If the people stick together they will not only be successful, but will be united under one front, under the leadership of our Commander in Chief, Franklin Delano Roosevelt, and the CIO." Speakers agreed that white strikers were tools of Fascism and that the whole affair "was not a strike, but was an insurrection."[27] Communists supported the United People's Action Committee, which combated the strike and gave the FBI evidence that it hoped would incriminate Fascist or Klan agitators.

In 1944 Communist leader Earl Browder carried the Popular Front policy to what was for many an unacceptable extreme when, in an abortive attempt to become part of the mainstream, the Party officially transformed itself into a Communist Political Association. This proved too much for the faithful either at home or abroad, and at Soviet direction, Browder was ousted the following year. While these feuds cost the loyalty of some members, the Party now stood at its height of popularity, and there were short-lived hopes of consolidating a broad progressive front with liberals, labor militants, and other opponents of racism and militarism.

PENNSYLVANIA COMMUNISTS

By this time the Communist Party had a solid infrastructure in Pennsylvania. The Party was a hierarchical and bureaucratic organization, with a chain of command that descended from national headquarters to regional districts, which might include one or more states, and thence down to sections, branches, and clubs. Within each district, key officials included a district organizer, a crucial figure who transmitted orders and policies from the national level to the regions, an organizational secretary, and a district chairman. The state of Pennsylvania contained all or part of two districts, one in the eastern part of the state, centered on Philadelphia, and another based in Pittsburgh in the west, each in its own different way a significant component of national Party organization. That the two neighboring districts varied so widely in their composition, appeal, and activities illustrates the diversity of American Communism.

Though boundaries varied over time, in the 1940s District 3 comprised eastern Pennsylvania and Delaware and was firmly based in the Greater Philadelphia area. This was an important region in terms of numbers and fundraising, though it received less attention than other areas associated with the heavy industry that Party thought and rhetoric viewed as critical. In 1938 the district probably mobilized 3,500 members, and although the number of active adherents fluctuated over time, membership probably remained between 2,500 and 3,000 for the period 1936–48. In 1948 the district had nineteen sections, thirteen of which were in metropolitan Philadelphia; five were located elsewhere in the state, while one section covered the whole state of Delaware. Each section included from three to seven clubs.

The geography of Party strength is indicated by voting patterns in the 1948 presidential election, specifically the support for Henry Wallace's Progressives (see Table 1). Wallace polled 21,000 votes in Philadelphia, some 2.5 percent of the total, and over half of these votes came from just eight of the city's fifty-two wards, those located in "West Philadelphia, particularly the 24th ward, the Strawberry Mansion neighborhood in North Philadelphia, some Jewish pockets in South Philadelphia, and some downtown areas."[28] The Progressives ran two congressional candidates in the city, one of whom picked up 5,600 votes in the Fourth District, 4.4 percent of the ballot. The counties surrounding Philadelphia (Bucks, Delaware, Montgomery) also included significant centers of Wallace support.

Outside the greater Philadelphia area, Wallace support was concentrated in certain industrial regions. In the anthracite mining counties (Lackawanna, Luzerne, Schuylkill), Communists had a foothold in cities like Scranton and Wilkes-Barre. The Progressive vote also reflects the Communist presence in the Lehigh Valley cities of Allentown, Bethlehem, and Easton (in the counties of Northampton and Lehigh). However, there were some anomalies, such as the strong showing in cities like Harrisburg and York. Progressives took 864 votes in York, some 3.5 percent of the total, and the York County total of 3.7 percent was better than the party's showing in either Philadelphia or Pittsburgh; this resulted less from Communist support than from Wallace's enthusiastic endorsement by the local newspaper, the *York Gazette and Daily*. Conversely, Progressives did surprisingly poorly in the major industrial center of Reading, given the powerful radical traditions in Berks County; this is explained by the

Table 1. Major Centers of Henry Wallace's Support in Pennsylvania, 1948

Eastern Pennsylvania		Western Pennsylvania	
County	Votes	County	Votes
Berks	665	Allegheny	11,164
Bucks	619	Beaver	1,588
Delaware	1,562	Cambria	959
Lackawanna	738	Erie	660
Lehigh	594	Fayette	468
Luzerne	977	Lawrence	421
Montgomery	1,089	Mercer	540
Northampton	721	Washington	1,688
Philadelphia	20,745	Westmoreland	2,585
Schuylkill	842		
York	2,555		

Source: Pennsylvania Manual.
Note: Only counties producing 400 or more votes are included.

rival presence of the more established Socialist Party, which took three times as many votes here as the Progressives. At the opposite extreme, Progressives had no presence in most rural regions: sixteen Pennsylvania counties were Progressive-free, producing no Wallace votes at all.

In western Pennsylvania, the Communist Party's District 5, the leftist vote was concentrated in the Greater Pittsburgh region. By way of comparison with Philadelphia, the Wallace campaign polled 11,000 votes in Allegheny County, less than 2 percent of the total number cast. Even so, some local centers of leftist strength do emerge—for example, in the city's Fourth, Fifth, Eleventh, and Fourteenth Wards—which broadly reflect the Communist Party presence. There was also a significant Progressive showing in the steel and coal communities in several neighboring counties, where Wallace typically gained between 2 and 3 percent of the ballot. Other outlying centers of support lay as far afield as Erie and Johnstown (Cambria County), a pattern that again indicates the Communist presence. Johnstown was sufficiently important to have its own full-time Party organizer in the mid-1940s.[29] By 1948 Communist organization in District 5 was based on five sections—Pittsburgh City (fourteen clubs), Monongahela (eight clubs), Allegheny Valley (five clubs), East Pittsburgh (three clubs), and Washington (seven clubs)—in addition to seven or so unattached clubs in various western cities. Typical Pittsburgh units of this era included a North Side club, a South Side club, a Squirrel Hill club, a Hazelwood club, a Hill group, an Oakland group, and a West Pittsburgh/UE group, as well as a professional group.[30]

The scale of Communist membership for the whole western district is hard to gauge. In 1940 George Powers told HUAC that a total of 130 branches had some 2,500 members in all, which is at least double what we would expect from other sources; on the other hand, Powers had every interest in making his numbers seem as small and nonthreatening as possible.[31] Later media estimates are bedeviled by a failure to distinguish between Party strength for the whole district and that for the metropolitan region, but a consensus would suggest a figure of 800 members in 1948, falling to only 550 by the start of 1950.[32]

Communists were also active outside the two main urban regions. Evidence for this comes from two FBI infiltrators from eastern Pennsylvania who surfaced in 1954 and reported to a Senate committee gathering evidence of Red "infiltration" in some of the other major industrial centers that formed part of District 3. According to these accounts, Communists were indeed involved in steel and other industries in centers like Allentown and Bethlehem, but the membership included a broad section of occupations and backgrounds. The Allentown Club of the late 1940s included a delicatessen clerk, a textile weaver, an office employee, a trolleyman, a UE organizer, and a business agent for the Roofers' Union.[33] One member owned a furniture store in the small town of Souderton; another was a farmer. Small business people and farmers were also found among the fifty or more members of Reading's Debs Club, an assortment of Communist adherents drawn mainly from the greater Reading area, but also from nearby cities like Lancaster and Harrisburg, with a scattering from tiny communities like Shoemakersville, West Leesport, and Robesonia. Rural West Oley was home to Nature's Friend, "a camp for the Communist people to gather and to hold meetings and to go to schools and relax through the weekend, reading books, enjoying swimming, and many other activities." Investigators were suspicious that these farms and small businesses might have been operated with ulterior motives on behalf of the "Communist conspiracy" ("Do you know whether or not his peanut stand is a mail drop?"), but it is more likely that the Party was simply exerting a more varied appeal far outside its traditional centers.[34]

In summary, the two districts combined might have mustered 6,000–7,000 members at the zenith of Party popularity in the early 1940s, but that number fell to 3,400 by 1948 and to only 2,000 statewide during the worst of the McCarthy years. Though the overall figure is scarcely impressive, Communists were by no means as politically isolated during the 1936–48 period as at other times in their history, and the Party regularly cooperated with progressives in the Democratic Party as well as in labor organizations and in community groups mobilized for specific issues. In addition, a numerous body of former Communists, who had joined briefly but had dropped out for various reasons, retained varying degrees of attachment to the Party and its ideology. The 55,000 Wallace votes in 1948 represent the outer limits of the Party's influence by that point. While Pennsylvania was nowhere near "going Red" at any time in the 1940s, neither was Communism wholly an imaginary specter.

Communism exercised a similar emotional and intellectual appeal in both regions, though their specific constituencies differed. To its members and sympathizers in the 1940s, the Party provided a coherent philosophical and political worldview that offered a greater chance of achieving social justice than any competing ideology and appeared to be the only reliable vehicle for social progress, racial equality, and global peace. The familiar choice between socialism and barbarism was made all the more urgent by the revelations of the Holocaust and the beginnings of the nuclear age. Enemies of the movement were perceived in the most pernicious terms as tools, conscious or otherwise, of the forces of reaction, big business, racism, obscurantist religion, and, ultimately, Fascism.

In the language used by later scholars to describe the appeal of fringe religious movements, Communism was a greedy group, demanding a high investment of time and resources but offering rich rewards in emotional and intellectual satisfaction. While the belief system required absolute adherence, the Party also provided a complete and fulfilling life, with its own social circles, its familiar rituals, customs, and celebrations, even its distinctive vocabulary. Philadelphia's Party was a complete subculture in itself, with "its two fraternal groups among ethnic minorities, its choral groups, sports clubs, nature clubs, lecture clubs, dance and art classes and performances, picnics and summer camps."[35]

Communist political activity was extremely varied in terms of the causes and issues addressed, and the Party's flexible response to local circumstances goes far toward explaining its success. Communist efforts were characterized by extraordinary energy and by the tough discipline demanded by "Bolshevik work-habits." In Pittsburgh the North Side section in the late 1940s incorporated a North Side club, a Lawrenceville club, a Croatian club, and a club for workers in the Hotel and Restaurant Employees Union.[36] Characteristically, this range of groups included community, ethnic, and labor interests, as it was intended to replicate the mainstream organizations that provided the social life in most industrial towns and urban neighborhoods. Where feasible, clubs concentrated on organizing within industrial plants and unions, and the North Side club focused on the Heinz plants in Manchester. In contrast, the East End club "functioned on a community level. There were no industries there. It was a residential area and most of the work out there was distributing Communist party literature, distributing and selling the *Daily* and *Sunday Worker*, and so on, raising funds for the Communist Party."[37] Lawrenceville was similarly "a community club." Regular club meetings usually consisted of "discussion groups about current problems, about political problems that were taking place, either in Harrisburg or in Washington or whatever international crisis if such was occurring and we spent usually about an hour and a half discussing things and expressing our opinions pro and con."[38]

The range of Communist activity in western Pennsylvania was suggested by the organizational breakdown provided by FBI infiltrator Matt Cvetic. Testifying to HUAC in 1950, he listed the chief Party leaders and their responsibilities.[39] Under District Organizer Steve Nelson, other individuals took responsibility for steel organizing, "Negro work," the Civil Rights Congress (CRC), youth organizing, the American Slav Congress, and nationality work, with at least ten nationality commissions operating within the district; other militants were charged with organizing in specific plants or corporations, including Westinghouse, the General Electric plant in Erie, and the Hotel and Restaurant Employees Union. The emphasis on ethnic work and nationality questions was distinctive to Pittsburgh, with its wide range of ethnic groups, whose members were often first- and second-generation immigrants who maintained their traditional languages as well as close links with their homelands. This gave added significance to the work of the IWO, which had some 39,000 policyholders in western Pennsylvania, mainly working families attracted by its cheap and nondiscriminatory insurance system, though the fraternal societies also had a range of social groups that even included a bugle and drum corps.[40] The Philadelphia-based Party was less diverse ethnically, as Jews accounted for perhaps 75 percent of the membership, but an equally broad range of meetings and activities was available.

The energy of Party activists was remarkable. In one instance, HUAC investigators claimed that between 1947 and 1949, Louis Ivens, a Philadelphia member of the American Youth for Democracy, had participated in frequent Communist street meetings as well as major functions like May Day rallies in Reyburn Plaza and district conventions.[41] In 1949 alone, he was accused of participating in a picket at the U.S. Courthouse to protest the trial of the Communist Party national leadership (May); a charter meeting of the Labor Youth League (June); a picket of City Hall, jointly organized with the National Association for the Advancement of Colored People (NAACP) and the CRC (July); a rally to commemorate the thirtieth anniversary of the Communist Party of the United States of America (CPUSA) (September); and a People's Rally to celebrate the thirty-second anniversary of the Soviet Union and Stalin's birthday (November). A Lenin Memorial Rally in February 1948 drew between 1,500 and 1,800 of the faithful. In February 1950 the Philadelphia Party held a peace festival to commemorate Lenin and Stalin, and throughout the first half of that year, the Party was heavily engaged in collecting signatures for its World Peace Appeal, which aspired to eliminate nuclear warfare.[42] In February 1951 the Philadelphia CRC sponsored a Negro Freedom Rally, which was addressed by Paul Robeson. The following August, a Peace and Brotherhood Festival was held in Bucks County; in December, the CRC organized a Bill of Rights Rally at Philadelphia's Reynolds Hall, in response to new laws intended to ban the Party and introduce loyalty oaths for public employees. In considering this lively schedule, we should recall that the Party by this point was in deep public disfavor, running the constant risk of mob action and under intense official surveillance. Nevertheless, Philadelphia Communists continued to hold regular meetings and extraordinary festivals, usually orchestrated through affiliated groups like the American Peace Cruade, the CRC, and the Philadelphia Council of the Arts, Sciences and Professions. As late as June 1953, the Philadelphia Committee to Secure Justice for the Rosenbergs sent 120 people to Washington, D.C.[43]

Communism had something to offer to many groups, from ethnic minorities and industrial workers to students and idealists to peace activists and tenants' groups. Of course, the reality was usually less than the ideal, in that these different elements often were manipulated cynically for the broader goals of the Party and were arbitrarily subjected to bizarre policy shifts caused by internal controversies and foreign interests. But to borrow a phrase from the 1980s, the American Communist Party appeared for a decade or so to be a flourishing rainbow coalition.

Congressional investigations into Communist activities made damning use of lengthy lists of leftist organizations and front groups, association with any one of which could potentially blight a career. The use of such fronts ("mass orga-nizations") had been a well-known tactic at least since the 1920s, when Com-intern activists realized how useful it was to persuade visible non-Communist celebrities to endorse statements supporting Communist causes; this might mean signing a petition supporting the release of some political prisoner or demanding that a government reverse some controversial policy. Many people who would be reluctant to ally themselves openly with a specifically Commu-nist cause would have no qualms about signing a statement ostensibly pro-duced by a civil rights or humanitarian pressure group. It was an open secret that many such institutions were Communist fronts, with only a token repre-sentation of non-Communist officials or board members. In propaganda terms, a demand issued by a dozen or more apparently independent groups speaking in roughly one voice was far more useful than one emanating solely from a local Communist branch.

During the peak years of Communist activity between 1936 and 1948, the Party was exceptionally creative in generating such fronts, both long-term organizations and ad hoc pressure groups. Party fronts in the late 1940s in-cluded the American Peace Mobilization, the National Negro Congress, the Labor Press Committee, the American Committee for the Defense of the For-eign Born, the IWO, the CRC, and the Language Press. The value of such fronts was demonstrated when ethnic allies put out Communist-influenced radio programs on stations that would have declined material stemming from the Party itself; Cvetic described the use of Braddock station WLOA in presenting materials in Croat, Ukrainian, Polish, and Slovak. Finally, a host of transient or issue-oriented structures included support groups for political prisoners or for victims of racial injustice, like the Trenton Six or Martinsville Seven. Philadelphia had its Committee for the Defense of the Pittsburgh Six, as well as a Committee for Repeal of the Walter-McCarran Act and to Defend Its Victims.

The process of creating a front group was plausibly described by Matt Cvetic. He portrayed a well-practiced art of cultivating "this reverend or this doctor" so that they could become unwitting arms of Party policy: "Steve Nelson or Roy Hudson [the District Organizers] would make a list of people to invite. We would call them up or visit them and represent ourselves as citizens committees. You can go to anybody and tell them you are starting a peace cam-paign: everybody is for peace. We would sit down and say 'Let's make a list of names.' We would set up a peace committee against the war-makers."[44] A series of personal networks would generate a storm of telegrams and letters, and at best, "this would have a tremendous impact upon the public, the publication of the list of names of 1,000 or 500 college professors all across the country."[45]

Front groups proper, wholly owned subsidiaries of the Party, must be distinguished from organizations in which the Communists had established a foothold through a process known by its enemies as infiltration, and in which a Communist presence was counterbalanced by rival interests (the distinction was properly drawn by Cvetic himself, though the difference was often lost on later investigators).[46] Communists became compulsive joiners, seeking to spread influence through an ever-widening network of groups. The process was explained in 1953 by a former Party member, who was by that time an embittered critic of Communism:

> It is the Communist teacher's duty to join as many organizations as we possibly can in order to influence and to bring the line of the party into those organizations. And this is particularly true of her professional organizations. Thus a teacher might be a member of the Communist Party, of her union, then of a broad professional organization like the Association of Mathematics Teachers or the Association of Social Science Teachers or the Association of English Teachers. Then into as many of the political organizations to which teachers might belong and if they are women, into as many women's organizations as they can. Thus one Communist Party teacher gets the equivalent of ten or twelve memberships and becomes not one person but ten or twelve different people because she operates in ten or twelve different organizations. . . . [I]f they are going to support certain legislation, they will bring this thing into ten different organizations at one time and you have the feeling that this is a spontaneous merger [sic] of public feeling.[47]

Some sense of perspective is essential for understanding such an account. Anti-Communist investigators in these years often made wild charges about the supposed infiltration of all manner of groups, which had typically committed the sin of espousing some liberal position or condemning McCarthyite excesses; as a result, the whole notion of front groups has attracted skepticism. Infiltration did take place during this period, however, sometimes successfully and sometimes not. A Communist takeover certainly occurred in groups like the Philadelphia Teachers' Union of the 1930s or the Croatian Fraternal Union in the mid-1940s (in both cases, the organization became an organ of Party policy), and the Philadelphia Citizens' Political Action Committee was repeatedly torn over charges of Left infiltration.[48] The phenomenon could and did happen, though not nearly as frequently as critics charged.

The Rosenberg campaign of 1952 offers a case study of the mobilization of support. Of course, the Rosenberg verdict excited outrage well beyond Communist circles, but the far Left took the lead in the national mobilization to petition courts and legislators. That October a meeting at Philadelphia's Town Hall coordinated activities of the new Committee to Save the Rosenbergs, and the secretary orchestrated a letter-writing campaign in association with established groups like the CRC and Left-dominated locals of UE.[49] The Philadelphia movement helped establish its counterparts in other regions, like the Lehigh Valley; according to an FBI infiltrator, "members of the Allentown branch of the Philadelphia American Jewish Congress were instructed by the Party to enlist support for the Rosenbergs within that organization."[50] Winning support from even a local chapter of a mainstream organization like the American Jewish Congress (AJC) would carry much greater weight than statements from familiar and largely discredited names like the CRC. It also carried the danger that the mainstream organization would itself acquire a subversive taint. Hearing a listing of Lehigh Valley activists who served in groups like the NAACP, one congressional investigator asked a witness, "That NAACP, is that on the list too, as a Communist-inclined organization?" The witness, an FBI informant, was "not sure."[51]

The rhetoric of this broad front activity was useful whenever the Communist Party was under attack, as protests appeared to come from across the political spectrum. In September 1948 a CRC complaint against anti-Red violence was signed by an impressive range of groups purporting to represent Serbian, Croat, Ukrainian, Polish, Slovene, and Slovak communities.[52] The Party typically presented its predicament in a way likely to appeal to other interest groups with whom it had cooperated on various issues, so that defense against official persecution could be portrayed as a black issue, a labor issue, a Jewish issue, or an immigrant issue rather than merely the self-interest of one fringe group. We can see this rhetorical process at work in the 1948 campaign against the proposed federal subversive control law, the Mundt bill, which would effectively have prohibited the Communist Party without naming it (the measure died with the Eightieth Congress in June 1948). The bill attracted fire from all the expected sources: the CRC warned that the subversive or Communist label might be applied to those who "want an FEPC law . . . work for abolition of Poll Tax . . . work for an end to lynching and lynch law . . . work for higher wages and better working conditions . . . work against segregation of American citizens . . . oppose US betrayal of the Jewish people in the United Nations."[53] In Philadelphia, the campaign claimed the support of "Quakers, Zionists, Communists, trade unionists, professionals, ministers, and dozens of other groups [who] rallied to defeat the Bill. Members of more than sixty Philadelphia organizations attended." The movement generated 200 telegrams and 5,000 individual letters from all parts of the state.[54] Through 1948 and 1949 the same tactic was used to attack the trial of twelve Communist Party leaders in New York, an event compared to the Reichstag fire and the establishment of the Nazi police state.[55] The show trial was contextualized with acts suh as Klan cross-burnings, violence against strikers, and police killings of young black men: "This is the way it happened in Germany and Italy. First the 'Reds' . . . next the unions, liberals, Catholics, Negroes, and Jewish people! That is the logic of events."[56]

One valuable source for understanding the diversity of Communist interests and activities in the late 1940s comes from the *Congressional Record*, as HUAC found itself in the odd position of reprinting an impressive range of ephemeral Communist propaganda materials. Following the Cvetic defection in February 1950, Party activists associated with the Labor Youth League tried to dispose of embarrassing papers, but these materials fell into the hands of federal authorities and were published in the HUAC exposé of Communism in western Pennsylvania.[57] The result is a fascinating snapshot of Communist concerns and activities in the late 1940s, particularly its racial attitudes.

Cvetic described the Labor Youth League as a straightforward front group, established in 1949 as an instrument for Party influence in colleges and high schools; he claimed that it was effectively under the direction of the Party's youth organizer for western Pennsylvania. Still a relatively small group, it had 143 members in eastern Pennsylvania and 43 in the western district.[58] In retrospect, one is most struck by the ordinariness of the group's materials, their lack of any subversive or even controversial quality. In fact, they look remarkably like standard educational materials on diversity generated by any number of school boards and community institutions over the last two decades, especially in the common visual images of ethnically diverse young people linked arm in arm: young men and women are depicted as allies in the struggle, carrying banners bearing slogans demanding peace, jobs, and freedom.[59] The interracial theme was pervasive. In early 1950, for instance, the economic outlook in western Pennsylvania was reported to be dismal: "Unemployment is increasing. Many plants like Westinghouse have already reached the eight year seniority mark in layoffs. This means the laying off of mainly young workers, veterans, young women and especially Negro workers." Conditions for African Americans were said to be notoriously bad in western Pennsylvania, and the league proposed to demand "the employment of Negro youth in certain lily-white establishments."[60] The national league called for the commemoration of Negro History Week in February 1950.[61]

The racial emphasis was partly in response to the centrality of segregation issues in the mainstream politics of the Truman years. The CRC was a critical area of Party activism in these years, and we are repeatedly struck by how flawless this body's statements appear in terms of later political orthodoxies. In October 1948 a CRC meeting at the Fort Pitt Hotel in Pittsburgh adopted a statement denouncing "the shame of white supremacy. . . . It is time to wipe the scourge of Jim Crow from the face of America!" Signers called on the federal government to use its full police powers to suppress the "mob violence, lynching and police terror" deployed against black voters.[62] The main Communist paper, *The Worker*, regularly reported instances of police brutality and frame-ups directed against African Americans in Philadelphia and Pittsburgh, usually cases that would never be noted by the mainstream press. Militants also struggled persistently against "white chauvinism" within the ranks of the Party itself.[63]

Communists made dedicated efforts to recruit African Americans. By 1943 blacks already made up about a sixth of the Party membership in the Philadelphia region, and heavy recruitment meant that that proportion increased over the next few years.[64] In the 1950s the Philadelphia Party leadership noted that "the Negro people are the staunchest and best workers in the block committees."[65] African American Thomas Nabried was one of the main Party leaders in the Philadelphia area, and Pittsburgh Party leader Ben Careathers was a well-known figure in the black community of Wylie Avenue, respected for his work on behalf of a state fair employment practices law to prohibit job discrimination; both men would be among the defendants in the federal Smith Act trials of the early 1950s. The Communist Party's ability to cross racial lines was a particular advantage in the era when segregation was being challenged in Pittsburgh as elsewhere; in a typical protest, in 1948 the Party led an effort to force the admittance of blacks to the Highland Park swimming pool, an action led by leftist militants from UE.

The record of Communist civil rights activities may explain the relative success of the African American community in avoiding the worst excesses of the Red Scare era. Black Communists like Careathers and Nabried were not subjected to the kind of ostracism that other leftists experienced in their communities, and when Careathers was arrested on state sedition charges in 1950, leaflets issued on his behalf made great play of his work against racial discrimination and lynching.[66] The leading black newspaper, the *Pittsburgh Courier*, was one of the few relatively mainstream publications to pay serious attention to the 1948 Progressive Party campaign, in which segregation issues played so central a role. Meanwhile, the CRC had attracted some respected non-Communist African American leaders: in 1947 the Philadelphia chapter listed among its sponsors not only well-known Communists like Anna Pennypacker and David Davis, but also several members of the city's black political, legal, and religious elite, including later judges and congressmen like Raymond Pace Alexander and Robert Nix.

PROGRESSIVES

In racial matters, as in so much else, Communists aligned themselves with liberal and progressive opinion. The need for consolidating and advancing alliances with more mainstream groups became all the more pressing given what seemed to be a deteriorating postwar situation: the Party adopted an apocalyptic view of American history, wrongly predicting a savage economic downturn in 1945–46 and again in 1949.[67] They imagined a desperate ruling class that would seek its salvation in outright Fascist policies at home and in foreign confrontations that would inevitably lead to a third world war; as Eugene Dennis argued, America was "a few minutes before midnight." This nightmare scenario found easy confirmation in developments like the Taft-Hartley labor laws, the anti-Communist purges, and the almost daily news of East-West conflicts in Europe and Asia. In response, Communists pinned their hopes on developing a broad front organization that could act as a brake on Cold War policies at home and abroad. In 1947 and 1948 American Communists increasingly looked to Henry Wallace, whose views on major issues seemed congenial to their own. As Franklin Roosevelt's vice president from 1941 through 1945, Wallace had represented the Left of the New Deal coalition, and he later became the standard-bearer of those who opposed the Cold War and favored radical social reform at home. In 1948 Wallace was the presidential candidate of the Progressive Party.[68]

Whatever its later history, the Wallace movement did not originate with the Communist Left. Its main backer in Pennsylvania was Josiah W. Gitt, the quirky publisher of the *York Gazette and Daily*, "just a stubborn Pennsylvania Dutchman" who believed in an old-fashioned, near-pacifist liberalism. Describing himself proudly as "cantankerous," Gitt boasted of running "about the most liberal newspaper in the United States," and by 1948 he was printing leftist work that few other outlets would consider, including columns from novelist Howard Fast, who was contemplating the prospect of his imminent imprisonment.[69] Though far from being a Communist himself, Gitt largely agreed with the Party's pessimistic view about the prospects for civil liberties.[70] Like Wallace, Gitt believed in a strong state role in the domestic economy, coupled with international peace secured through the United Nations; this ideological package appealed to many non-Communist liberals appalled at what they saw as President Truman's warlike policies. The decisive split with Truman came with Wallace's speech at Madison Square Garden in September 1946, which provoked the president into demanding his resignation as commerce secretary. Thereafter, Wallace was identified as the national leader of the New Deal Left, whose supporters were mobilized through the group Progressive Citizens of America (PCA). In March 1948 Wallace was in York for a People's Convention, organized to launch the third party in Pennsylvania. The event attracted 3,000 supporters, over a third of whom arrived on a special train from Philadelphia; Wallace expressed surprise at "how many people there were in Pennsylvania who have their hearts in the 'left place' where it ought to be."[71] Several of the leading Progressive figures were respected liberals and internationalists, such as Gitt himself, academic Marion Hathaway, or former U.S. attorney Francis Fisher Kane, and the state party's treasurer was a Philadelphia Baptist clergyman.

Other activists, though, were well to the Left. Prominent in this group was Thomas Fitzpatrick, a leader of UE Local 601 in the East Pittsburgh Westinghouse plant, who was often the target of anti-Communist investigations. The working committee to place Wallace's name on the Pennsylvania ballot was chaired by Jess Gitt, but its vice presidents included a powerful sampling of the leadership of UE and the CIO Left.[72] The two Pennsylvania members of the party's national committee were Gitt himself and Goldie Watson, who would later be one of the main targets of the anti-Communist purge in the Philadelphia school system. The Wallace campaign in Pennsylvania was effectively in the hands of two major groups, namely, the Left-led unions, above all UE, and the leftist ethnic groups concentrated in the ASC. As in 1940, the *Pittsburgh Press* published lists of those signing nominating petitions, noting, accurately enough, that "the list includes leaders of the Progressive Citizens of America, the Communist-line American Slav Congress, a couple of branches of the subversive International Workers Order, and several labor unions."[73] Apart from Gitt's own paper, by far the most sympathetic coverage of the York meeting came from the Communist paper, *The Worker*, which presented the new party as "a people's organization that will smash the Democratic and Republican machines and present the people of Pennsylvania with a chance to vote for peace and security next November."[74]

Wallace was often active in Pennsylvania through 1947 and 1948, and his speeches regularly denounced the familiar targets of militarism, segregation, and Wall Street dominance of national and international policy; throughout, his rhetoric was closely akin to that of contemporary American Communism. In Pittsburgh in November 1947, he drew the familiar contrast between the revered figure of Franklin Roosevelt and President Truman, who he claimed was a puppet of the militarists.[75] At York in March 1948, he declared that "less than three years after the end of a war against Fascism, the civil liberties of Americans are in graver peril than when Nazi armies were on the march"; Tom Fitzpatrick agreed that "the ghost of Hitler is all over this country." Speaking at Reading in October, Wallace claimed that "military men occupy the State Department like termites in the beams of a house." At Wilkes-Barre shortly afterward, the candidate's themes included preserving the rights of coal miners, repealing the Taft-Hartley Act, and defeating the Marshall Plan.[76]

The radicalism of the Wallace movement was evident at the Progressive Party's national convention held in Philadelphia in July 1948, just a week after the conclusion of the Democratic gathering in the same city. An audience of 30,000 was said to be "near hysteria" as Wallace proclaimed that "the party Jefferson founded 150 years ago was buried here in Philadelphia last week. . . . A party founded by Jefferson died in the arms of a Truman."[77] The Progressives supported a platform that demanded the enforcement of civil rights and deseg-regation together with repeal of the Taft-Hartley Act and abolition of HUAC.[78] Progressives promised to withdraw U.S. troops from China and end aid to Chiang Kai-Shek, and they opposed the Marshall Plan. The party also pledged to increase black representation in political life, and the main thrust of the Progressive campaign in Pennsylvania went to supporting the congressional candidacy of NAACP leader Joseph Rainey in Philadelphia's Fourth District.[79] With only one dissenting vote, the 220 members of the Pennsylvania delegation advocated the nationalization of the entire coal and steel industries in the United States, though this measure was ultimately defeated in the convention.[80] Throughout, the Progressive Party rejected attacks that it was Communist-dominated, and the final platform denounced "anti-Soviet hysteria as a mask for monopoly, militarism and reaction."[81] Progressives presented themselves as "liberals" opposing "reaction."[82]

It was an article of faith on the Right that the whole Wallace movement was Communist-sponsored. Matt Cvetic claimed that as far back as 1946, Communist leader William Z. Foster had spoken in Pittsburgh of the need to create a broad progressive front and that "blanket instructions were issued to all Communist Party members to join the Progressive Party. . . . [T]he Progressive Party is one of our big concentration points." Cvetic also argued that by 1950 Pittsburgh Progressives were subservient to Communist interests and that highly placed local Communists operated a political commission specifically to determine Progressive policy.[83] Such a conspiratorial view underestimated the complex dynamics of the movement, but some local branches were in fact heavily influenced by Communists and had little compunction about cooperating with Communists or Party associates. Both Gitt and Wallace worked closely with leftist writer Louis Adamic, Gitt's "very good friend," who roamed eastern Europe as an accredited correspondent of the York paper at a time when it could not even afford a full-time Washington correspondent.[84]

Other infiltrators agreed with this portrait of manipulation, and one, Herman Thomas, claimed to have been a leading figure in the state's Progressive movement at a time when he was apparently an active Communist. In his account, the Lehigh Valley Progressive Party was thoroughly dominated by Communists, and like Cvetic, he identified the Progressive Party's state director, Zalmon A. Garfield, as a Communist.[85] FBI informant Ralph Heltzinger agreed with this general picture in his description of Reading Communism: "All the Communist Party members were Progressive Party members also. We had two or three members of the Progressive party that said they would never join the Communist Party, but every Communist Party meeting I attended, they were there."[86] Though these infiltrators were portraying matters in their most sinister colors, Paul Lyons's sympathetic account of Philadelphia likewise reports heavy Communist involvement in the Wallace campaign: there were "regular one to one clandestine meetings between Party functionaries and Progressive Party leaders who were secret Communists."[87] The vision of an infiltrated Progressive Party was particularly frightening because over the previous two years, the "people's democracies" of eastern Europe had been created by broad front groups that masked a Communist core, as in the 1948 putsch that destroyed Czechoslovak democracy.[88]

Wallace's movement provoked a violent anti-Left reaction, from Democratic sources scarcely less than from Republican. In November 1947, following a major Wallace appearance in Pittsburgh, the local press was uniformly hostile, describing him as a Communist puppet: the *Post-Gazette* called his constituency a mixture of "sincere and progressive citizens, along with a lot of Pinks and chronic malcontents," who threatened to provoke undesirable class conflict.[89] In one incident in this city, two young actresses touring with *A Streetcar Named Desire* accepted an invitation to appear at a UE-sponsored rally for Wallace. According to a Communist pamphlet, "The next day, drama critics of two local newspapers launched an attack on them. They urged purchasers of advance tickets to storm the box office and demand their money back. They publicized the name of the hotel, telephone and room number in which the actresses were staying, which left them open to harassment at all hours."[90]

Bitter street confrontations greeted Progressive rallies, and the ensuing violence all but ended the period in which Communist groups and their allies could organize major public demonstrations and rallies. Since the mid-1930s, Communists had been granted relative tolerance, and large gatherings like May Day celebrations were recognized, if controversial; in May 1947, for example, 700 people crowded Pittsburgh's Carnegie Library Lyceum to hear a speech by District Organizer Roy Hudson.[91] Some months later, rightists would literally drive the Progressives off the streets. In November the PCA organized a meeting in Philadelphia's Independence Hall Square to protest the HUAC investigation of Hollywood leftists; the speakers would include several of the purged Hollywood Ten, those facing contempt charges for refusing to answer questions about their political affiliations.[92] The city protested that the venue was reserved for events of a patriotic character and that the loyalty of PCA members was distinctly questionable, but a federal court permitted the rally to proceed. It was a fiasco. Some 1,500 people attended, about a third of whom were veterans present for the purpose of heckling. From the American Legion and both the Jewish and Catholic War Veterans, they were armed with "stench bombs, [and] noise from a siren on a Voiture No. 1 Forty and Eight Engine and boxcar." Following numerous fistfights and frequent shouts of "Go Back to Russia," missiles were thrown at one of the speakers, Francis Fisher Kane, and the event was abruptly terminated.[93] In March 1948 speakers at a Wallace rally in Oakland (Pittsburgh) were driven off the stage by violent heckling, and shortly before the election, a Philadelphia rally for congressional candidate Joseph Rainey was barraged with eggs.[94]

Communists hoped that Wallace would gain at least 5 million votes, perhaps as many as 10 million, thus identifying an authentic progressive constituency from which they could draw support.[95] He received only a fraction of this, however, a mere 1.16 million. The campaign in Pennsylvania took 55,000 votes out of some 3.73 million cast. The Progressive Party survived a little longer, but

Wallace himself resigned following the party's refusal to condemn the Korean invasion of 1950. Gitt's paper denounced the invasion, which he assumed to have been Soviet-inspired, though "just what is responsible for so stupid and reckless a policy on the part of the Russians is difficult to understand."[96] Both Gitt and Marion Hathaway resigned from the Progressive Party shortly afterward; by this point, even Gitt had renounced hope of "any outside chance that [the Progressive Party] could be kept free of Communist domination." He felt that "the party was taking positions that were dictated by those who were more interested in furthering ends other than those of American progressivism, with which those of us who were not willing to be agents of any foreign group could not go along." The Pennsylvania Progressive Party reappeared as a shadowy force in the 1952 elections, but by this time its positions were scarcely distinguishable from those of the Communists.[97]

The 1948 campaign marked the end of the Communist Party's effective presence in the American political system, as shortly afterward, it was crippled by official investigations and sanctions. Post-Wallace schisms further intensified anti-Communist activism within the Democratic Party, especially from the CIO. Nationwide, Communist Party membership fell sharply to pre–New Deal levels, back below 25,000 by 1953, and we can only speculate what proportion of even that apparent hard core were themselves infiltrators or informants serving the FBI and related law-enforcement agencies. Nor could Communist groups or allies hope to appear on the streets after the violence of the campaign, even in the form of an apparently neutral front group.

The declining fortunes of the Communist Left are illustrated by the collapse of May Day celebrations in these years, after the inspiring revolutionary pageantry of the late 1930s. Even then, conservative and Catholic groups tried to combat the popularity of May Day by developing rival attractions. In 1938 the Philadelphia archdiocese began an annual series of masses for Catholic officeholders on that day, urging judges and lawyers to combat anarchy and atheism, and two years later, 5,000 Communist demonstrators may have been outnumbered by an "antidote" parade sponsored by the American Legion.[98] May Day 1946 was marked a small but confident event for the Communists, galvanized by an ongoing UE strike, but later May Day celebrations dwindled rapidly in numbers and were increasingly likely to attract disruption or physical assault. The last of the old-style efforts occurred during the Wallace campaign, under threat from "hoodlums, reactionaries" on the fringes of the crowd.[99] About this time, however, Left events were being dwarfed by the Loyalty Day events sponsored by veterans' and patriotic groups like the Veterans of Foreign Wars (vfw). In 1951 Philadelphia's Loyalty Parade was some 5,000 strong, representing all the major veterans' groups "as well as Boy Scouts, fraternal and labor organizations, and a number of volunteer corps and community organizations."[100] By 1953 a Philadelphia meeting of the Communist-linked Freedom of the Press Association was observed by "a large vfw truck parked across from the . . . entrance of the meeting hall. A powerful searchlight mounted on the truck was focused on the entrance and a cameraman took movies of all persons as they walked from the building."[101] Western Pennsylvania Communists were a little more successful than their Philadelphia counterparts in maintaining their right to public expression, but in Pittsburgh, too, riots in early 1949 made even closed-door meetings a risky venture.

The Wallace campaign was the high-water mark of the Communist Party's quest for legitimacy within the American political system, but the debacle achieved precisely the opposite result. By the end of 1948 Communists were both marginalized and demonized, cast out from the New Deal coalition in which they had once hoped to flourish.

THE NEW AMERICANISM, 1944–1950

> We condemn the Republican Party, in power for so long in Pennsylvania, for its failure to pass legislation to meet the threat of Communism in the Commonwealth.—Statement from the Nationalities Division of the Pennsylvania Democratic Committee, 1950[1]

American conservatives had long employed antiradical rhetoric as a means of discrediting their liberal rivals. This was a recurrent theme in the politics of the 1920s, and the image of a Democratic Party tainted by Soviet Communism was a mainstay of Republican attacks on the New Deal. Because Communism on the international stage in the 1930s did not pose as imminent a danger as Fascism, liberals tended either to ignore such charges or to portray them as a ploy to divert attention from social injustice. The anti-Communist crusades of the twenties and thirties could be dismissed as a reactionary refusal to concede progress on domestic issues involving organized labor, civil rights, or individual liberties.

A dramatic change occurred after 1945, however, as the hostility to Communism that had once been the prerogative of the Right now became a bipartisan consensus, largely under the influence of foreign developments. While conservative Republicans remained firmly anti-Communist, this perspective now crossed factional boundaries and profoundly affected some of the most liberal members of that party. The Democratic Party also became militantly anti-Red, partly through a sincere recognition of the real perils posed by the Soviet Union and its allies, but also, as the experience of Pennsylvania illustrates, out of a domestic political agenda. Throughout the early twentieth century, the

Democratic Party had been a cipher in the state's politics, until its fortunes were transformed by the building of a powerful new coalition in the New Deal years that included organized labor and liberal groups as well as Jews, African Americans, and the traditionally excluded ethnic communities from eastern and southern Europe, who were largely Catholic. With this broad foundation, the Democrats enjoyed a brief hegemony in state politics, but the issue of Communism threatened to destroy these hard-won achievements. Charges that the Democratic Party and its allied labor unions were soft on Communism resonated with ethnic and Catholic constituencies, who threatened to desert to the more trustworthy Republicans. By 1947 it was politically essential for the Democrats to become "sound" on Communism, beginning a period in which the two parties competed enthusiastically in Red-baiting.

As in most northern industrial states, the Republican Party enjoyed a long dominance in Pennsylvania after the Civil War.[2] Unlike other regions, however, control at state level was not counterbalanced by Democratic strength in the big cities, and both Philadelphia and Pittsburgh were run by powerful Republican machines into the 1930s. Between 1909 and 1930, Democrats rarely commanded as many as a quarter of the seats in the state legislature. Matters changed dramatically following the Great Depression, which devastated the state's heavy industries, and Franklin Roosevelt's policies soon became very popular in the state. Pennsylvania suddenly acquired a genuine two-party system, in which Democrats had the dual advantage of support from the federal government and a crucial alliance with organized labor. In 1934 George Earle was the first Democratic governor to be elected since 1891, and Joseph Guffey won a seat in the U.S. Senate. Guffey was associated with the Left of the New Deal coalition, and his rhetoric regularly drew on the hallowed memories of organized labor, harking back to events like the Homestead massacre, while denouncing the systematic evils of the large employers.[3] Democrats took control of Pittsburgh in 1936. Philadelphia went for Roosevelt by 150,000 votes in 1944, suggesting that this city too might soon fall; though the Republican machine succeeded in retaining its grip through the 1940s, Democrats could be optimistic that Republican power there would eventually be destroyed by the recurring cycle of scandals involving graft and gangsterism.[4]

The changing fortunes of the parties are suggested by the numbers of U.S. representatives that each succeeded in electing in different periods (see Table 2). Prior to 1932, Democrats could only count on one or two congressmen, usu-

Table 2. The Shifting Partisan Balance in Pennsylvania, 1926–1964

| Election | Number of U.S. Representatives* | |
	Republican	Democrat
1926	34	2
1928	36	0
1930	33	3
1932	22	11**
1934	11	23
1936	7	27
1938	19	15
1940	15	18
1942	18	15
1944	18	15
1946	28	5
1948	18	15
1950	20	13
1952	19	11
1954	16	14
1956	17	13
1958	14	16
1960	16	14
1962	12	14**
1964	12	15

Source: Pennsylvania Manual.
*Under successive redistricting, the state's congressional representation fell from 36 in the 1920s to 34 in the 1930s, 33 in the 1940s, and 30 in the 1950s.
**In these years, one district was vacant at the time of recording.

ally from a heavily industrialized region like Luzerne County, and Republicans occasionally managed a clean sweep of the state. Matters changed dramatically under Roosevelt, and in 1936 Republicans won only seven out of thirty-four districts. Though Democrats suffered some setbacks in the late 1930s, their continuing congressional strength showed that the New Deal had effected permanent changes: in 1944 Pennsylvania Democrats achieved an unheard-of feat when they briefly held both seats in the U.S. Senate (see Table 3).

In response to this crisis, Republicans swung far to the Right, and most abandoned the liberal and reformist traditions associated with former governor Gifford Pinchot. Anti-Communist rhetoric reached a new height between about 1939 and 1941, during the gubernatorial administration of Repub-

Table 3. Pennsylvania Senators and Governors, 1938–1968

Year of Election	Senator 1	Senator 2	Governor
1938	James J. Davis (R)		Arthur James (R)
1940		Joseph Guffey (D)	
1942			Edward Martin (R)
1944	Francis J. Myers (D)		
1946		Edward Martin (R)	James H. Duff (R)
1948	—	—	—
1950	James H. Duff (R)		John Fine (R)
1952		Edward Martin (R)	
1954			George Leader (D)
1956	Joseph S. Clark (D)		
1958		Hugh Scott (R)	David L. Lawrence (D)
1960	—	—	—
1962	Joseph S. Clark (D)		W. W. Scranton (R)
1964		Hugh Scott (R)	
1966			Raymond P. Shafer (R)
1968	Richard S. Schweiker (R)		

Source: Pennsylvania Manual.

lican Arthur James. Attacks on the far Left found a ready audience because of the strongly right-wing tone of the Pennsylvania media. The newspapers were overwhelmingly Republican, with the exception of some important liberal and pro-labor organs like the *Pittsburgh Press*, the *York Gazette and Daily*, and the *Philadelphia Record*, and even the last perished in 1946.

In keeping with a familiar Marxist interpretation of class conflict underlying political change, contemporary leftist critics placed great stress on the role of business groups in mobilizing anti-Communist sentiment, and the Right in Pennsylvania was indeed closely linked to industrial wealth. The state's Republican Party was for many years dominated by powerful business interests, including the Pennsylvania Railroad, the anthracite and bituminous coal industry, and the family business empires of the Pews and the Mellons. Joseph N. Pew was "Mr. Moneybags," a supporter of countless radical right-wing sects, and the financial angel of Philadelphia Republicanism. Business money naturally exercised key influence in state politics: in 1944 Republican state organizations spent some $2.4 million, outspending the Democrats by roughly four to one. Democrats complained about the large donations from "the multimillionaires" and the "oily fat cats" ("oil" being the source of wealth of both the Pews and the Mellons, in the Sun and Gulf corporations, respectively). Republicans, on the other hand, resented the money that Democrats received from the CIO unions through the CIO-PAC, the political action committee initiated by Sidney Hillman, which was attacked as a channel for leftist influence. Attacks on the CIO-PAC were central to Republican campaigns in 1944 and 1946: in 1944, for instance, Republican governor Edward Martin charged that "the Hillman-Browder-Roosevelt axis has taken over the Democratic Party."[5]

The most potent force in the state's Republican politics was the Pennsylvania Manufacturers' Association (PMA), headed by Joseph R. Grundy and G. Mason Owlett. Grundy himself was "dictator of Pennsylvania" due to his fund-raising skills, which had been honed in a lobbying career that dated back to 1909.[6] In 1950 the *New York Times* claimed hyperbolically that "the Grundy group . . . openly and proudly operates the Republican party of this state from the headquarters of the Pennsylvania Manufacturers' Association."[7] The PMA tended to grow when Democratic or reformist administrations were in power (as a defensive measure against government intervention), and it was undergoing an impressive expansion in membership in the Truman years, with a 23 percent growth rate between 1946 and 1954. The organization coordinated the local efforts of dozens of county-based manufacturers' associations as well as local groups that represented particular trades or industries; the PMA was also affiliated with the National Association of Manufacturers, another bogeyman for the Left.

Despite its purported lack of partisanship, the political tone of the PMA was far to the Right, and by the 1940s the group was regularly protesting against "the disaster-bound Communistic trend of the New Deal." In its papers and speeches the PMA viewed organized labor and recent social reforms as manifestations of the ultimate evil of Communism; in 1945, for instance, Owlett summarized recent American history as a simple struggle between democracy and Marxist state socialism.[8] Richard M. Simpson, Republican congressman from the midstate Seventeenth District, summarized the PMA creed that "what is good for business is good for all." The PMA's political coloring is suggested by its choice of speakers at successive annual dinners: between 1949 and 1954 this roster of solid conservatives included Robert Taft, Richard Nixon, John T. Flynn, and Senator William F. Knowland.[9] At the state level, PMA support ensured that most of Pennsylvania's Republican congressmen and senators remained close to the organization, even after the Grundy machine was crippled in internecine Republican feuding in 1950.[10] In 1954 the PMA's legislative director listed fifteen of the state's nineteen Republican congressmen as friendly, with two independents; just two others were viewed as "unfriendly," in light of their association with the more liberal faction of U.S. senator James Duff. One of the organization's best friends was Edward Martin, governor from 1943 to 1947 and U.S. senator until 1959, a man who has been described as both a "PMA Senator" and a "Mellon errand boy."[11]

Business interests played an important role in raising doubts about the loyalty of officials within the federal government: apart from the PMA, the national U.S. Chamber of Commerce did much to define the anti-Communist issue in the early years of the Red Scare through a series of widely circulated pamphlets produced in 1946–47 on *Communists within the Government* and *Communism within the Labor Movement*. Operating from Philadelphia, leftist journalist John L. Spivak claimed to have found specific evidence linking the national Chamber of Commerce to local anti-Communist activities in the unions. He also claimed a direct link between the Chamber of Commerce and the activities of HUAC through committee members like western Pennsylvania Republican and newspaper publisher John McDowell.[12] Leftist union members directly blamed Chamber of Commerce pressure for the 1947 decision by the state's CIO council to exclude Communist labor officials from membership.[13]

As international tensions grew steadily after 1945, Republican anti-Communism was reinvigorated by the growing hold of the Soviet Union on the nations of eastern and central Europe.[14] Foreign trends also raised fears about possible Communist penetration at home. As evidence accumulated after early 1946 of Soviet spy rings in the West, espionage was soon directly blamed for the transfer of nuclear technology: the "atom spy" became the ultimate villain of the period. Equally threatening in the long term was the prospect of Communist agents entrenched within the U.S. government, subtly perverting American policies for Soviet purposes.[15] Such infiltrators were blamed for the spread of Soviet influence in Europe, the collapse of anti-Communist forces in China, and the failure of the West to win a decisive victory over the Communists in the Korean War.

By appearing to justify the warnings that the Republicans had been issuing for years, these new fears of Communism had a major impact on domestic politics. The revived potential of anti-Red rhetoric became apparent during the pivotal 1946 congressional elections, as Republicans hammered at the themes of international Communist aggression, pink sympathies within the administration, and the state Democratic Party's alliance with fellow-traveling groups. This final charge generally referred to the CIO and its well-known "PAC slush fund"; tainting the CIO-PAC as Red also had the great advantage, of course, of sabotaging the Democrats' prime funding source.[16] When the state Republican Party adopted its platform at Pittsburgh in September, "Communism" was the third item out of twenty-three listed; this clause announced that "the insidious poison of communism has been injected into the blood and sinew of the Democratic Party. The leadership of the Democratic Party now traffics openly for votes with those agents of Moscow who deny God and seek to destroy the American system of government."[17]

Over the next two months, the subversion of the Democratic Party was a core theme of the speeches of Edward Martin as he campaigned for the U.S. Senate against incumbent Joe Guffey, whom state Republican chairman M. Harvey Taylor described as "the eager bedfellow of the Reds."[18] At Harrisburg on September 14, Martin warned of the creation of a regime in Pennsylvania "dominated by the Communistic PAC. I am proud that the Communists of Pennsylvania have singled me out as their number one enemy." At Lewistown on September 18, he damned the Democrats for their failure to condemn Henry Wallace's speech at Madison Square Garden: "The Wallace speech had the blessing of the president. Later this was partially withdrawn, but the damage had been done. Secretary Wallace in his utterances is following the textbook of the Communist Party. . . . He was talking to a meeting dominated by the PAC-Communists, fellow travelers and their radical elements." The following day, in Clearfield, Martin claimed that "we are fighting that radical and subversive element when we oppose the PAC leaders in their attempt to dominate our state government by their open alliance with the remnants of the Little New Deal gang." On October 11, at Somerset, Martin warned that "sinister and subversive forces have infiltrated our government, our press and radio; even our churches and schools." Time and again, Martin stigmatized the Democrats as part of a leftist Popular Front, referring to "the fraudulent promises of the Democratic-PAC alliance" (Ephrata, September 28) and "the Truman, Wallace, Guffey type of government" (Montrose, October 24). In statewide radio broadcasts in October, Martin claimed that "Communists, under the New Deal, have been appointed to high public offices of influence and power. . . . Communism no longer walks on tiptoe in America. It is thundering at your door. . . . A victory for the Democratic Party would be a victory for the PAC. A victory for the PAC would be a victory for Communism." Though state politis was not noted for restraint, the open accusations of Communist sympathies in this election were particularly harrowing and even resulted in libel charges.[19]

Communist infiltration was by no means the only issue in the 1946 elections, which served to focus widespread discontent over many grievances, especially shortages and inflation: this was a "beefsteak election." However, since these problems were customarily blamed on the heavy-handed incompetence of the federal government and its price control administration, the bread and butter issues, too, were ultimately linked to the ills of big government and New Deal state socialism—and thus to the Red threat. Republicans also made use of the strike wave that had caused disruption over the previous year, notably the crippling power strike in Pittsburgh in September. As the *Philadelphia Inquirer*, the "Bible of Republicanism," claimed, "1946 Strikes Planned to Sabotage US."[20] One Republican statement claimed that "these strikes bear the hallmarks of Communism. Probably more than one is being engineered by Communists. . . . These strikes are identical in pattern with those which a few years ago prostrated France to the Nazi army."[21] Such statements had their impact: the *Chicago Tribune* believed that "tens of thousands of [Pennsylvania] Democrats, notably wives of union workingmen, had voted Republican in revulsion against the strikes." A crushing Republican victory briefly raised hopes that the GOP would be restored to its pre-1932 hegemony. Harvey Taylor described the victory simply as "a victory of Americanism over Communism."[22]

Republican leaders long continued to deploy the rhetoric that had enjoyed such success in 1946. Martin's 1948 campaign again focused on the subversive issue: "Let Harry Truman tell you and the country the true facts about Communist infiltration into places of trust and importance in his administration. Let him tell who opened the doors to those who dealt with Soviet spies."[23] "Subversive" themes reached new heights with the dismissal of General Douglas MacArthur in April 1951, following which Republican newspapers were contemplating Truman's imminent impeachment. Senator Martin claimed to have received 30,000 letters and telegrams of protest, many demanding impeachment: "I have never witnessed such a tremendous outburst of public indignation." This opinion was confirmed that fall when MacArthur's visit to the Lehigh Valley became something like a royal progress, attracting a quarter of a million adoring fans.[24] For the state commander of the vfw, the general's dismissal "proves that those people who have been attempting to appease the Communists are still in control."[25] Joe Pew urged the state's Republican delegation to support MacArthur for president in 1952 (he actually misspoke and nominated Ulysses S. Grant, but he was too rich to correct).[26]

Some within the state's Republican establishment moved far to the Right. Pennsylvania's most visible representative in the Eightieth Congress was John McDowell of Wilkinsburg, a HUAC member who in 1948 figured in some of that body's most spectacular moments; his eye for publicity is not surprising given his own background as a newspaper editor and publisher.[27] He was prominent in the Hollywood Ten hearings, and it was McDowell, an amateur ornithologist, who asked Alger Hiss the critical, though seemingly trivial, question about whether he had ever seen a bird known as a prothonotary warbler. Hiss eagerly answered that he had, not knowing that by so doing, he was confirming the background information about his interests provided by informant Whittaker Chambers and thus beginning the process that would result in his conviction for perjury.[28] Throughout 1948 McDowell constantly returned to the theme that espionage and subversion in high places were the central issue in the coming elections: he singled out Steve Nelson as the symbol of Soviet plotting in the United States and pressed to have him charged with espionage or treason.[29]

McDowell's sense of the melodramatic foreshadows McCarthy's, as do his charges about official conspiracies. In October 1948 McDowell claimed that the government's Smith Act prosecutions of Communist Party leaders were deliberately flawed so that they would fail in court. The *Pittsburgh Post-Gazette* attacked his "indiscriminate application of the tarbrush to suspected subversives, whatever the evidence or lack of evidence."[30] His election materials concentrated entirely on the Communist threat: "The Red Terror is spreading East and West and South in Europe and Asia and is now firmly entrenched in our country; in our government, in our political systems; in our labor movement, in our colleges, and is almost daily sweeping across our borders."[31] By the fall of 1948, McDowell was the best-known member of HUAC apart from committee chairman Parnell Thomas, and it is intriguing to speculate how McDowell's career might have developed had he been reelected; his colleague Richard Nixon certainly used his committee service to good effect. Pennsylvania Communists saw McDowell as a "pint sized Hitler," but he attracted enemies well beyond his ultra-Left foes; he was marked for special criticism by organized labor as well as the *Post-Gazette*.[32] His political life ended when he was defeated by the Democrats that November.

McDowell was no anomaly in the passion of his anti-Communism. Another powerful Republican congressman was James E. Van Zandt from the Twenty-second District, which included cities like Altoona. Van Zandt, a strong friend of the PMA interest, reacted so sharply to what he viewed as Red rhetoric that he even urged the exclusion of the word "democracy" from the American political lexicon, as the term was so often used by Communists.[33] The United States, he insisted, was a republic rather than a democracy, and this latter term had only been imported with the alien philosophies of the Roosevelt administration in 1933. In 1955 he argued that the United States had deliberately forfeited victory in Korea as a consequence of a secret Communist plot at the highest levels of the Democratic administration: "It was a war rigged against victory from the very start." The conspiracy to create "America's First Military Defeat" culminated with MacArthur's removal, and thus "the Owen Lattimore Plan of 1947, to deliver China to Communism, was now a *fait accompli.*"[34] The speech was given to the McCarthyite pressure group For America, founded by Colonel Robert McCormick, but even more remarkable, this presentation was reprinted in full in the anti-Semitic paper *The Cross and the Flag*, published by Gerald L. K. Smith.

Strident anti-Communism extended across the political spectrum of the state's Republican Party. In the late 1940s the party was deeply divided by issues and factions, with conservatives like Martin and Grundy opposed to the relatively liberal James Duff, who served as governor from 1947 to 1951 and U.S. senator from 1951 to 1957. Duff himself was quite progressive on many points, speaking vigorously for the Marshall Plan, while his administration liberalized workman's compensation and unemployment laws, increased state aid to education, and tried to control river pollution, funding all these activities by higher taxes.[35] In 1950 he called on his party to smash reactionary Grundyism, declaring that "mossbacked Republicanism must go," and President Truman semiseriously invited him to defect to the Democrats.[36] As early as 1951, he attacked Senator McCarthy for making "random blanket charges without specific data to back them up," and when McCarthy appeared at a state Republican gathering in 1955, PMA supporters in the audience booed loudly whenever Duff's name was mentioned.[37] One might think that Duff would be equally moderate on Communism, but in fact he was not, even by the standards of an intemperate age. As early as October 1947, he raised a storm among civil libertarians by suggesting that American Communists were in essence traitors and did not deserve the free speech granted to loyal citizens. He joined Martin in advocating the prohibition of the Communist Party in the state.[38]

Duff's views remained consistent. At the state's American Legion convention in August 1950, he spoke in terms indistinguishable from the hardest of the hard Right, praising the legion for its Americanism activities and warning of the imminent likelihood of nuclear war and massive sabotage. In this context, treason must be suppressed harshly: "As long as I am the Chief Executive of this state we will treat Communists in Pennsylvania as they ought to be treated— and that is as traitors to America [cheers]."[39] Federal and state lawmakers should be pressured "to make Communism what it is, treason, punishable as treason; and instead of putting some of these guys in jail for five, ten and twenty years, if they are found guilty they ought to be hanged like any other treasonable person should be [applause and cheers]." Citing the recent case of Philadelphia "atom spy" Harry Gold, Duff asked, "Why should a creature of that kind be allowed to live at a time that our boys are dying in Korea, because of the thing that men of his type have made it possible for the Russians to have this secret?" In summary, he continued, we must "rid ourselves of these snakes in our midst everywhere in Pennsylvania and in America [applause]." In 1953 he demanded that the Communist presence in the United States be utterly eradicated: "It ought to be done now. It ought to be done finally."[40] It was Duff's more conservative rival, Senator Martin, who was left to make the point that the quest to fight Communists should not lead the country to tolerate the opposite extreme, and Martin stressed the need to root out the Ku Klux Klan, whether in northern or southern states.

Throughout these years, anti-Communist campaigns were supported by well-established political constituencies, and veterans' organizations took the lead as the most visible militants in the domestic war against subversion. Pennsylvania's veterans' groups had often cooperated with networks of rightist citizens and employers' paramilitary forces in time of crisis, notably to combat the industrial militancy of the late 1930s. The American Legion was the most prominent veterans' organization. Though attacked by the Left as a Fascist militia, the legion was a genuine mass movement representing a wide range of ethnic and political viewpoints, with some 275,000 members in the state in the 1950s. An impressive local structure of regions coincided more or less with congressional districts, while local posts played a vital part in the social life of communities of all sizes and types. The Pennsylvania department was the largest of all the state units, and its annual conventions were a major speaking venue for state and national politicians. After World War II and Korea, the mass influx of younger veterans with recent combat experience made the group acutely sensitive to the likelihood of renewed war and overwhelmingly opposed to domestic leftism in any form. An outpouring of generous federal benefits reinforced loyalty to the veterans' organizations that had done so much to win approval of measures like the GI Bill.

Veterans' groups emerged as a political force on the Right during 1946, shortly after the mass demobilization, and successive legion conventions demonstrated the increasingly forceful tone of the anti-Communist rhetoric. The deteriorating situation was evident in the resolutions passed by the annual conventions, which by 1948 were expressing a consistently hard anti-Communist line. The legion resolved, for example, that "only loyal Americans be employed by the federal, state and local governments" and urged the continuation of the loyalty check system, which "has disclosed many individuals who profess to be American citizens but are definitely anti-American, Communists and others." This was a call for the expansion of the federal loyalty security system to the states, which actually occurred a few years later under the state's Pechan Act.[41] Another 1948 resolution denounced Communism as "supported by an organized government dedicated to imperialistic domination of the entire world, and its focal objective is the destruction of the American form of democracy, using every subversive means."[42] Anti-Communist activism became overwhelming during the Korean conflict, and each meeting from 1950 through 1953 was marked by urgent calls for patriotic vigilance, "one hundred percent Americanism," the exposure of highly placed pinks, and blood-curdling threats against Communist traitors. The Pennsylvania legion regularly spoke out in favor of both HUAC and the McCarran Act, the 1950 federal law that called for the registration of all "subversives."[43] The legion was by no means the only active veterans' organization in these years, however. The Catholic War Veterans were at least as militant in their anti-Communism, and their units sprang up rapidly across the state following demobilization in 1946. The group soon became involved in politics, organizing the mass anti-Communist demonstrations in Philadelphia in December 1946 to protest the repression of the Catholic Church in the new "people's democracies" of eastern Europe.

Besides physical confrontations, veterans undertook long-term propaganda and educational activities through groups such as the legion's Americanism Committee and other kindred bodies. During the late 1940s the VFW took the lead in sponsoring Loyalty Day, a patriotic celebration on or near May 1 that was explicitly intended as a challenge to the leftist May Day. In 1950 the VFW adopted this commemoration nationwide as a time "when all loyal Americans could stand up and be counted," and in 1958 President Eisenhower gave the event federal recognition.[44] Such gatherings provided an opportunity for militant anti-Communist pronouncements. In 1955 the VFW's anti–May Day parade in Lawrenceville had as its speaker Judge Michael Angelo Musmanno, who was celebrated for the passion of his oratory; at a recent American Legion event in Sunbury, he noted, "I addressed myself with such vocal fury to the subject of the menace of the Communist Party that I did a little damage to my vocal chords."[45] In 1961 Pittsburgh's celebration was addressed by Samuel Shoemaker, an evangelical clergyman who was "an outspoken foe of Communism."[46] In 1955, also, communities throughout Pennsylvania participated in May Day Takeovers of towns like Chambersburg, in which legionnaires posed as Communist troops, arresting civic officials, trampling civil liberties, destroying religion, and trying dissidents, all to give a "vivid lesson in the brutalities to which people behind the Iron Curtain were subjected every day." Memorial Day parades provided yet another annual affirmation of strictly defined patriotic values and Americanism.[47]

This hard line was important politically because veterans now represented a large component of the state's electorate. Of thirty-three U.S. congressmen from the state in 1950, no less than twelve recorded membership in at least one veterans' organization—all in the American Legion, and most also in at least one other group, such as the VFW, Amvets, or Catholic War Veterans. For some, this affiliation was a very important matter, both in their personal lives and in their political appeal. Paul B. Dague, for example, long-serving U.S. representative from Chester and Lancaster Counties and a solid conservative, was a leading figure in the Pennsylvania legion. James Van Zandt made his wartime Pacific naval service the centerpiece of his campaign biography, and he boasted that he was "twice Commander of the Department of Pennsylvania VFW, and three times Commander in Chief of the Veterans of Foreign Wars of the United States." Senior officials of the veterans' organizations were influential in their own right, and in 1948 the legion's Paul Griffith and the VFW's Van Zandt attempted to win the Republican presidential nomination for Edward Martin.[48]

Another enduring figure in state politics was Walter Alessandroni, who in 1949 became the first World War II veteran to head the Pennsylvania department.[49] Alessandroni believed firmly in the notion of Communist subversion throughout the higher reaches of American life and quoted the statement from J. Edgar Hoover that a mere 80,000 Communist revolutionaries had been able to transform Russia into a Communist state. Today, he claimed, "our fear in America is not that Russia will take America by Russian soldiers but our fear is that history will repeat itself and that America could be taken by Americans.

And we ought to be concerned that there are people in high places who are daily striving for that purpose." He was convinced that many thousands of Communists "are daily operating under the guise of patriotic Americans but taking their orders from the Kremlin."[50] In 1950–51 Alessandroni chaired the legion's National Committee on Un-American Activities.

The increasing centrality of the Red issue caused grave difficulties for the state's Democratic Party. Through the New Deal years, the party represented a broad constituency, and many Democrats were prepared to cooperate with progressive causes, even those associated with Communist front groups. At the same time, other Democrats active in social reform and labor organization were vigorously opposed to Communism and sought to exclude Communist influence from the party and the unions. Militant anti-Communism affected even radical New Deal leaders like former governor George Earle, who grew increasingly concerned about Soviet expansion by the latter days of World War II; by 1947 it was said that he "gets apoplectic even at the mention of Communists." In 1950 Earle contacted his Republican successor, Duff, offering "his services in conjunction with the overall internal security program in Pennsylvania. Earle has had a lot of experience with the methods and infiltration of Communism at first hand by his foreign experience, and feels he could be of great service."[51]

Catholic and ethnic Democrats came to the fore as deadly enemies of Communism. In the Pittsburgh area, the anti-Communist movement was by no means the preserve of the traditional far Right; it clearly included former New Deal supporters and pro-labor Democrats as well. In Philadelphia this tradition was represented by Frank Myers, the state's first Catholic senator, who in August 1946 was already complaining of numerous provocations by the Soviet Union and its allies, warning veterans that "American servicemen did not set the rising sun of Japan to have a red star rise as a potential menace to world peace."[52] He also appeared on the platforms of Catholic and eastern European ethnic groups demanding a tough line against Soviet provocations in eastern Europe. The following year, he was discussing Soviet behavior in terms of the psychology of the bully and urging the need for Marshall Plan aid to save Europe.[53] By 1948 Myers was bemoaning Czechoslovakia's fall to "totalitarian pressures and internal treachery," while "Russian aggression" had reached intolerable levels in Berlin, and the world situation was "explosive." Communism, he argued, was founded on "dreary materialism and ... spiritual bankruptcy."[54]

Catholic anti-Communism within the Democratic Party is personified by

Francis "Tad" Walter, an attorney and banker, who in 1933 was elected U.S. representative from the Twentieth District, which centered on the Allentown/Bethlehem/Easton industrial region. Leftist critics charged that he retained his seat in Congress through three decades "by the simple means of iron-fisted control through his dictatorial machine. No opposition to his seat has been observed within his party in the area for years. Nor has the GOP offered any vigorous and substantial opposition. Politicos have it that Walter has his fingers deep in the GOP pie as well." He was also "known for his friendliness to the Bethlehem Steel interests." Left and liberal groups in his district made periodic efforts to remove him, but to no avail.[55] In 1949 Walter joined HUAC, where he became known for his moderation, at least in comparison to the demagoguery of some of his predecessors: disliking both Joseph McCarthy and Martin Dies, he became "the committee's voice of reason." This moderation was strictly relative, however, as he personally harangued and bullied witnesses. Walter was increasingly convinced that the subversive presence in the United States was predominantly the result of too many aliens being admitted, and he became steadily more xenophobic. He drafted the McCarran-Walter Immigration and Nationality Act, which was bitterly criticized by liberals, and in response to these attacks, he swung still further to the Right. In 1954 he took over the chairmanship of HUAC, which became very much the Walter Committee over the next decade. He was ultimately praised by House Speaker Rayburn as one who had "dug out more dens of disloyalty than any man who has ever lived in the United States."[56]

Leaders like Walter and Myers were impervious to Red-baiting, but much of the Democratic Party was not so fortunate, and the alliance with the CIO-PAC and some of the Left-led CIO unions created a dangerous situation. Left-Right tensions became acute following the 1946 elections, which offered the grim prospect that the New Deal victories would be altogether lost; indeed, the Democrats' electoral disaster was actually worse than what they had inflicted on the Republicans at the height of Roosevelt's prestige in 1936. The loss was particularly marked in the race for U.S. Senate. In 1944 Frank Myers had won his seat with a razor-thin majority over his Republican rival; in 1946 Republicans won with almost exactly the same number of votes that they had received two years before, but Democratic support plummeted, with the party losing a third of its previous total. Joe Guffey managed the worst showing for a Democratic Senate race since 1930, and Republicans took the governorship by an almost identical margin, with 59 percent of the ballot. While many voters shifted to the Republicans, some 600,000 Democratic voters simply stayed home.

In the House, Pennsylvania Democrats elected fifteen U.S. representatives in 1944, but only five in 1946, proportionally a far worse decline than the party experienced at the national level.[57] Democrats suffered their greatest losses in the Philadelphia area, where they had previously held six seats and seemed poised to take the city in the next mayoral election in 1947; now they were obliterated in this region. In the six Philadelphia districts combined, Democrats outpolled Republicans in 1944 by 484,000 to 348,000; in 1946 Republicans won by a margin of 438,000 votes to 335,000. Democrats lost their old strongholds in the industrial counties of Lackawanna (Scranton) and Luzerne (Wilkes-Barre), while Berks (Reading) also fell. In Lackawanna County, Democrats had trounced the Republicans in 1944; in 1946, however, Republicans maintained their 1944 support, while the Democrats lost almost a quarter of theirs, resulting in a narrow GOP victory. Through the middle and eastern sections of the state, the Democrats had a single congressman, Francis Walter.

The only remaining Democratic power base was in the southwestern industrial counties, where the party still clung to four districts; survival here owed everything to the enduring power of key labor unions like UE. All of the Pittsburgh-area Democrats were firmly pro-labor: namely, Thomas Morgan (Twenty-fourth District), Augustine Kelley (Twenty-seventh District), Herman Eberharter (Thirty-second District) and Frank Buchanan (Thirty-third District). The last two had been close allies of UE during its bitter strike against Westinghouse earlier in the year and now benefited from that union's strength in the region.[58] Unlike their eastern counterparts, these pro-labor representatives could afford the luxury of maintaining a progressive voting record through the darkest years of conservative ascendancy; in 1947 Eberharter and Morgan were two of the handful of congressmen who voted against the contempt citations of the Hollywood Ten (Buchanan was absent). Nevertheless, Republicans made some advances even in the west, electing John McDowell over concerted labor opposition. GOP senatorial and gubernatorial candidates carried Pittsburgh, despite the Democrats' overwhelming registration majority there.

The statewide collapse in 1946 followed a series of painful defections—by working-class women and conservative upstate Democrats, but above all by Catholic and ethnic voters.[59] The New Deal coalition was founded upon an alliance of the ethnic groups most heavily concentrated in major cities and industrial areas, which gave rise to the unsavory but enduring Republican charge that northern Democrats were in the pockets of the "KKK": the "Kikes, Koons and Kat'lics." Since the mid-1930s national Democratic leaders, fearful of attracting an anti-Catholic backlash, had been disturbed at the strong Catholic coloring of the party leadership in Pennsylvania, and the Catholic element in state Democratic leadership remained important in the postwar years.[60] Catholic, and particularly Irish, Democrats were critical to the party's hopes in Philadelphia: by 1952 three of the five Democratic representatives from the city would be Irish American Catholics. Any loss of Catholic electoral support was therefore deeply troubling. Losses among the ethnic voters of eastern and southern European origin were also damaging for the Democrats. Though there certainly were leftist elements in the ethnic constituencies, these were generally in a minority, especially in large and influential groups like the Poles and Italians. Many of these ethnic communities stemmed from countries that had either fallen under Communist control or, like Italy, threatened to do so shortly, and there was consternation at any signs of Democratic willingness to appease the Soviets.

Republican support came from ethnic activists who would have been astonished only a few years earlier to find themselves breaching Democratic solidarity, and who had previously denounced the Republicans for their anti-immigrant bias. One example of this shift comes from Scranton newspaper publisher and Polish American activist Henry J. Dende, normally a firm Democrat. Shortly before the 1946 elections, he gave a blistering radio broadcast denouncing the Democrats as little better than Communists. He warned against "un-American radicals trying to overthrow our form and system of government. . . . [I]n this great country of ours, we do find extreme radicals imported from and of the same political thoughts as Communist Russia—that great enemy of our form of government! . . . Yes, ladies and gentlemen, Communists and Communist-thinking people are even holding very important government positions in this country—thus abling to influence present administration heads to use systems in our government offices, *à la* Communist Russia style!" Citing Democratic betrayal of Poland at Yalta and Potsdam, he declared that "the Democrats are still carrying on their program of appeasement . . . still giving in to Communist Russia. . . . When the Republicans get hold of all state and national government, they will immediately get rid of all Communist-thinking jobholders . . . and decrease the influence of Communists in this country almost to nothing!"[61]

The Democratic dilemma was at its most acute between 1946 and 1948. The state party reflected the national division between the progressive Left, which upheld the old idea of the Popular Front, and the anti-Communist liberals. In Lehigh County, for instance, the Democratic cause was deeply divided between mainstream party supporters and the progressive Wallaceites based in the unions, and liberals feared an outright Left takeover of the organization. Though he vastly exaggerated the influence of the far Left, the Democratic county chairman sincerely believed that "there are over two hundred card-carrying members of the Communist Party in the county and . . . 'it can happen here.'"[62] This suspicion made it difficult for some Democrats to collaborate with union leaders, who should have been natural allies.

The political division was particularly sharp in Philadelphia, where Left-liberal opinion was mobilized through the Citizens' Political Action Committee (CPAC), founded in 1944 as a local branch of the National Citizens' Political Action Committee (this group was in turn a middle-class analog to Sidney Hillman's CIO-PAC). The Philadelphia CPAC rapidly became a powerful force in the city's Democratic Party, with a well-established structure in each congressional district and a booming youth branch; by 1946 it was developing a presence in each ward. However, the Philadelphia CPAC disintegrated as liberal members worried that the group was being dominated by a pro-Communist caucus. In September 1946 a Conference of Progressives was sponsored by the National Citizens' Political Action Committee and the Independent Citizens' Council of the Arts and Sciences and Professions (ICCASP). This gathering produced a controversial anti-Truman manifesto demanding the reinstatement of Henry Wallace in government and an end to atomic-bomb testing.[63] Republican critics were overjoyed at the propaganda opportunity. Responding to Harold Ickes's speech at this event, Edward Martin commented that "Ickes is one of that group of habitual renegades who, along with Henry Wallace, was removed from the Cabinet because he could not be loyal to his country, his party, or in fact to anything. . . . [The ICCASP] of which he is national Chairman, has a membership of parlor pinks, so-called intellectuals, fellow travelers and radicals. It is dominated by Communists who follow the Moscow party line." In December the National Citizens' Political Action Committee merged with the ICCASP and other groups to form the new Progressive Citizens of America (PCA), which developed a network of local chapters in Philadelphia and other communities like Pittsburgh and York.[64]

Seeking to restrain the progressives, CPAC's anti-Communists sought the support of like-minded labor leaders, including Michael Harris, of the steelworkers union and the CIO's Industrial Union Council, and Johannes Hoeber, who was currently engaged in a struggle against the Left in the United Office and Professional Workers Union. Another recruit was William L. Batt Jr., the son of a leading Philadelphia industrialist, who was then fighting against a

Communist takeover in the American Veterans Committee. Batt and Hoeber became friendly while working on a liberal congressional campaign in suburban Montgomery County and subsequently collaborated in the fight for CPAC. In September 1946 the organization's liberals mounted a coup against the Left and introduced a rule excluding supporters of totalitarianism. The new regime purged the director of the youth branch, demanding to know "how many dues-paying members you have got into Youth PAC, apart from previously organized Communist groups." Philadelphia's CPAC was the only branch of the national organization to support President Truman's dismissal of Henry Wallace. By early 1947 most of the liberals from CPAC moved en masse to the newly formed Americans for Democratic Action (ADA), leaving the parent organization to leftist progressives like Joseph Myerson. Myerson and his allies founded the local chapter of PCA and subsequently became the prime movers for Henry Wallace's presidential campaign in Pennsylvania: it was Myerson who organized the 1947 anti-HUAC rally that was disrupted by rightist protesters.[65]

Philadelphia possessed "the largest, the politically most experienced and most influential single chapter of ADA," which included some individuals who would go on to occupy important positions in the Democratic Party at both state and national levels. It was Batt who in 1948 brought several Philadelphia associates into the policy-making circles of the Democratic National Committee, where they formed its influential research division.[66] ADA also provided a focus around which liberal and pro-labor Democrats could organize in Philadelphia proper. One critical figure was Harry Block, anti-Communist director of the Philadelphia UE and president of the state CIO council. Over the next year, "the politically active AFL moved into ADA," and labor leaders made up a third of the new board.[67] Ethnically, the ADA provided a meeting point for Philadelphia's old-line Protestant elite and reform-minded Jews. Several of the new leaders were "Philadelphia gentlemen" from the social register, like John F. Lewis, owner of the Academy of Music and president of the Academy of Fine Arts. Other establishment figures included Richardson Dilworth and Joseph S. Clark, the latter from a wealthy and traditionally Republican family; both men boasted impressive military records. Over the next fifteen years, Clark and Dilworth would play key roles in the politics of both the city and the state, and the ADA would be at the core of the renascent Pennsylvania Democratic Party of the 1950s. In 1948 the ADA held its first national convention in Philadelphia, in the distinguished presence of Eleanor Roosevelt.

A decisive shift in Democratic policies occurred in the spring of 1947, when

President Truman proclaimed his doctrine of supporting countries threatened by Communism and, at the same time, created a loyalty program for federal employees.[68] Pennsylvania Democrats now adopted an anti-Communist rhetoric scarcely less vigorous than that of the Republicans, so that anti-Communism could be freely used as a partisan weapon against Republicans themselves. In the 1947 mayoral elections in Philadelphia, the Italian Democratic newspaper *Libera Parola* urged its readers to turn out the totalitarian clique that dominated the city from "the Philadelphia Kremlin," namely, the Republican machine.[69] The anti-Communist trend became even more noticeable during the 1948 Henry Wallace campaign, a movement condemned throughout by the ADA. At the Progressive Party's Philadelphia convention in July 1948, ADA spokesman James Loeb berated the platform committee for ignoring obvious Communist domination, claiming that authority in the party "is vested in the hands of men and women, many of whom followed the dictates of totalitarianism in the period of the Nazi-Soviet pact." He advised Progressives to declare opposition to dictatorship wherever it should appear, whether in Mississippi or the Soviet Union, and to pledge support for European Socialists in their struggle against "ruthless totalitarianism." Though the Progressives obviously accepted none of these suggestions, ADA established its own credentials as a firm opponent of Communist or totalitarian sentiment; the protest even achieved respectful reporting in the Republican *Inquirer*, which normally had few good words to say for Democrats of any shade.[70] If the Democratic crisis of 1946 had been precipitated by Henry Wallace, then it is equally certain that Wallace saved the party two years later by siphoning off Progressive support, allowing mainstream Democrats to distance themselves from the Left.

Pennsylvania in 1948 gave Thomas Dewey a larger plurality than any other state, and while the Republicans remained the dominant party, the scale of Democratic recovery was striking. After the massacre of 1946, the party had controlled a mere five of the state's thirty-three congressional districts, but this figure now increased to fifteen, with the main improvement in urban and industrial sections. The party reclaimed populous industrial counties like Lackawanna, Luzerne, Berks, and Fayette and made a crucial breakthrough in the Philadelphia area. In 1946 Republicans still held all six of Philadelphia's congressional districts; in 1948 they were reduced to two, and in 1952 they lost all but one. In Pittsburgh, too, this was an outstanding year, with McDowell ejected and Eberharter and Buchanan returned with, respectively, 73 and 69 percent of the vote in their districts. The Democrats had thus assured that they remained in the game.

The realignment of 1947–48 placed Democrats in a much stronger position to criticize the more extreme suggestions now emanating from the Right about the best means to contain and defeat Communism. Though Democrats still had to walk a political tightrope, the assurance that the party was solid on the Red issue made it possible to reassert traditionally liberal positions without arousing fears of crypto-Communism. Having proved his democratic record in the struggle against the Philadelphia Left, William Batt of ADA could afford to raise doubts about the Truman Doctrine: while standing up to Communist aggression was appropriate and necessary, this should not imply uncritical support for right-wing dictatorships.[71] Though the Right leapt upon such liberal qualms as evidence of pinkness, the Red smear was difficult to imply against a group with such a record.

The city of Philadelphia offered a crucial test of ADA's redefined liberalism. In 1949 Richardson Dilworth and Joe Clark ran for the offices of treasurer and controller in the city, in a decisive challenge to the old machine. Republicans counterattacked on the Red issue: Republican city chairman Bill Meade denounced a dozen of the ADA leaders as former members of Communist-linked organizations, attacking even union leaders like Harry Block who had since emerged as the fiercest enemies of Red influence in the labor movement. Meade concluded that "when Dilworth tied himself in with the Communist-infiltrated ADA, he joined the company not only of sinister and dangerous crackpots, but still worse, of the associates of convicted subversive criminals." Dilworth's defense was prompt and convincing, and appropriately dressed in the language of anti-Communism: "The ADA acted and struck hard against Communism while Mr. Meade and his gang created by their corruption the very conditions which breed Communism." The ADA itself took legal action against its detractors and won the support of distinguished public figures like Eleanor Roosevelt and former U.S. Supreme Court justice Owen Roberts; in consequence, the affair scarcely damaged the group's prestige or, still less, its appeal to moderate and independent voters. This particular Red smear proved a disaster for the Republicans. Even the *Philadelphia Inquirer* supported the reform movement, and Dilworth and Clark, the "hardboiled eggheads," won handsomely. Escaping the Red label meant that Philadelphia Democrats could now reassert their earlier hopes of a total political realignment in the city. In 1951 Clark won the office of mayor, with Dilworth as district attorney, again with the support of the *Inquirer*; the Democrats thus acquired an electoral stranglehold that endured for a generation. As former Communist leader Sherman Labovitz notes, "At the apex of McCarthyism, as if in defiance, a kind of paradoxical Philadelphia progressive reaction was underway," a contrarian trend that has been attributed to "the aristocrat and the Quaker influence."[72]

A current of liberal and libertarian opinion would continue to express concern about the perils of false accusations of Communism, though these critics did not for a moment challenge the general goal of combating subversion. In 1947 the American Civil Liberties Union (ACLU) attacked Governor Duff's suggestion that Communists should be denied free speech. The following year, liberals of the Philadelphia Fellowship Commission recorded a protest against the federal Subversive Activities Control Act: "The propriety of an end does not justify employment of improper means. American democracy should not—indeed, cannot—be preserved by un-American and undemocratic means. Agreeing therefore with the declared objective of the Mundt-Nixon Bill, we nevertheless urge its defeat because its enactment would penalize opinions and associations contrary to the basic principles of American democracy."[73] In 1951 the Pechan loyalty bill was opposed by a broad coalition of educational, religious, labor, and libertarian groups, including many with solid anti-Communist credentials, like ADA. As Philadelphia district attorney, Dilworth could get away with remarks that would have ended the careers of other politicians, such as his alleged statement that "one McCarthy is worse than a thousand Alger Hisses."[74]

By 1950 both international and domestic tensions were reaching frightening proportions. Between October 1949 and June 1950, American media reported a series of shocking overseas events: the detonation of the Soviet atom bomb, the fall of China, and then the invasion of South Korea. At least until the Inchon landing of mid-September 1950, it seemed all too likely that the Korean intervention would result in a bloody defeat for U.S. forces and their allies, a specter raised once more following the Chinese intervention of early November. Given the universal idea that all the Communist powers were united in a monolithic bloc, the outbreak of hostilities could plausibly be seen as proof that a third world war actually was in progress. At home, during the first half of the year, the conviction of Alger Hiss set the stage for Senator McCarthy's notorious Wheeling speech, which warned of highly placed traitors in the State Department, and the FBI uncovered a network of alleged "atom spies." Cumulatively, these incidents suggested that the United States had been placed at a perilous strategic disadvantage through the misdeeds of American traitors.[75] Meanwhile, Pennsylvania was deeply involved in its own local Red Scare. The state's labor movement was embroiled in charges of leftist infiltration as left- and right-wing unions fought for the support of the state's electrical workers, and in February, Matt Cvetic purported to reveal the inner workings of the state's Communist apparatus (see Chapter 4).

These events set the tone for a critical election that fall, in which Republicans made full use of both Korea and the Red issue. The state party's platform stated that "what the president has been calling 'the red herring of communism' has been changed into a red trail of American blood across Korea. . . . The Democratic administration repeatedly, has stubbornly refused to alert the country to the real danger of subversive activities within our borders." In an appeal to ethnic voters, the platform declared that "the Democratic party's secret agreements entered into at Yalta, Teheran and Potsdam gave Soviet Russia vast territories in Manchuria, Poland, Yugoslavia, Czechoslovakia, Lithuania, Latvia, Estonia and Hungary, and enslaved more than 200 million people."[76] Senator Martin claimed that "the blundering foreign policy of the Truman administration that led to the crisis in Korea must be held responsible for the 30,000 American casualties on the Far Eastern battlefront."[77] Martin again reflected his party's mood when he demanded, "Let us have this as a country for one hundred percent Americanism. There are almost three thousand registered Communists in Pennsylvania. They are in industries." Citing a recent patriotic demonstration, he warned that "Communists were in that crowd of forty thousand without question. They are every place reporting on what we are doing. Communists have no part in America. When our forefathers laid this form of government down . . . they gave us free speech but they never expected to have infiltration of enemies to destroy the government they fought eight years to build and then all of those years of trying effort to put that government into effect. They did not expect free speech to men who would destroy our country."[78] The theme of denying civil rights to Communists was echoed by gubernatorial candidate John S. Fine, a McCarthy supporter, who argued that "he who gives loyalty and comfort to the Communist state is a traitor to America."[79] It was during the summer of 1950 as well that Governor Duff was attracting headlines for his even starker call to hang Communists.

But the Democrats were now on much firmer ground over the Red issue, with Dilworth running for governor and the fanatically anti-Communist judge Michael Angelo Musmanno running for lieutenant governor. Democrats showed how thoroughly they had learned the lessons of 1946 when they themselves smeared their Republican rivals: the Democratic State Committee issued a statement entitled "Fellow-Travelling Pennsylvania GOP Congressmen Follow

Red Party Line."[80] Senator Myers accused Republicans of "using Communist tactics and techniques" and found the Republicans weak on the defense of South Korea. He declared that the Marshall Plan had produced American victory in the Cold War in Europe and prevented the "Iron Curtain from moving forward"; why, then, had most Republicans opposed it?[81] Musmanno reiterated his familiar themes about subversion and the need for anti-Red vigilance, warning that "every Communist in [the] US is a Soviet paratrooper already landed here."[82]

This rhetoric was valuable in appealing to the ethnic constituencies who had felt so nervous about the Democrats a few years before, and Musmanno was explicitly added to the ticket to appeal to labor and ethnic voters. The Nationalities Division of the state Democratic Committee now issued a statement declaring that

> many of our sons and brothers are fighting and dying in Korea in the crusade to stop communism. And because we are natives or the sons and daughters of nations now imprisoned behind the Iron Curtain and of countries threatened by Communism, we are inevitably and acutely conscious of the evils and dangers of this loathsome ideology which would enslave mankind.... And because we know first hand the ruthlessness, the brutality, the murderous intent of those who would dominate the free world, we commend President Truman who, in the face of bitter opposition, successfully saved Italy, Persia, Greece and Turkey from Soviet infiltration and aggression with the Truman doctrine and the Interim Aid program, and who rescued the rest of free Europe from Communist enslavement with the Marshall Plan and the North Atlantic Defense Pact.[83]

Henry Dende, who had bolted to the Republicans in 1946, by 1952 led the Polish Nationality Division of the state Democratic Party.

Ultimately, Democratic efforts were blighted by disastrous Korean news in the last days of the campaign, and the election resulted in a clear Republican victory.[84] Duff defeated Myers for the U.S. Senate seat, so that Republicans now held both Senate seats for the first time since 1934. The party also placed John S. Fine in the governor's mansion, while reinforcing their hold on the state legislature. However, the election was not a complete disaster for the Democrats, who held on to thirteen congressional districts, and though Myers was defeated, he did far better than Guffey had managed to in 1946, taking some 48 percent of the vote. Party leaders felt that he had "made a brilliant run and lost in a close fight."[85] In a promising note for the future, Dilworth was the first

Democratic gubernatorial candidate since the Civil War to carry Philadelphia. Pennsylvania still had a two-party system, but it was conditional on both sides remaining firm on the Communist issue.

The Fine administration entered office in January 1951 with a mandate to fight Communism within the state—and perhaps to prepare Pennsylvania for imminent war. This sense of national emergency explains the general support for sweeping measures to suppress Communism, from demanding loyalty oaths of public officials to banning the Communist Party outright. In only five years, Communists had come to be seen as loathed outsiders, against whom almost no sanctions were too severe.

4

RED SCARE RAMPANT, 1950–1953

> We are a nation at war. . . . The force that is killing our loved ones, the
> power that is fighting against our democracy, is Communist, Godless
> Russia. It is fantastic to fight Communism with all our strength abroad,
> and to ignore it here at home.—State Senator Albert R. Pechan, 1953[1]

In retrospect, it seems remarkable that the suppression of a national political
movement aroused so little opposition, but the virulence of anti-Communist
feeling arose from general fears of a new world war in which American Communists might become an alien fifth column. The new Red Scare had its roots
in events of the late 1930s, when the Roosevelt administration had exaggerated
the threat of domestic traitors in order to make Americans more willing to
confront the Axis powers, portraying native Fascist sympathizers as the allies of
foreign intelligence services. Between 1938 and 1942, popular media often reported on the likely dangers of espionage and sabotage, and some genuine incidents of both did occur. In their struggles against Fascism and militarism,
Americans were subjected to constant propaganda about the absolute evil of
the Nazi and Japanese regimes, charges that had been confirmed by the exposure of the atrocities committed by those totalitarian states.[2] The hatred stirred
in the early 1940s was soon redirected against international Communism—
Red Fascism—a menace made still more threatening by its capacity to devastate the American homeland with nuclear weapons.[3]

This international context is essential to understanding the escalation of the
Red Scare into a perceived threat of clandestine warfare on American soil. An
official campaign to uncover potential enemy sympathizers did much to shape

public attitudes to domestic Communism, and the anti-Communist movement was repeatedly galvanized by the events of this underground war. The appearance of FBI infiltrators before congressional committees, the trials of real or alleged subversives, and the arrest of spies all intensified fears of a fifth column within the state and promoted the sense of living in a prewar, or even wartime, society.

APOCALYPSE SOON?

Concern about a new war became intense in 1948–49, when Pennsylvania followed a federal directive to revive its wartime civil defense apparatus; not surprisingly, militant anti-Communists were prominent in this endeavor.[4] By late 1949 the state civil defense committee was headed by Judge Vincent Carroll, a former chairman of the American Legion's state committee on national defense; as far back as 1940, Carroll had argued that Communists had no place in the American electoral system, as "the right of free speech is only for those who deserve it."[5] In 1950 Governor James Duff fulfilled the worst liberal fears about the rightist connotations of the civil defense movement when he appointed Major General Richard King Mellon to head the commonwealth's Military and Civilian Defense Commission: the Mellon name was synonymous with plutocracy and with business domination of the political life of western Pennsylvania.[6]

By 1950 the threat of open hostilities had become a prime concern of Pennsylvania's state government. In July Governor Duff alerted the three fighter squadrons of the state's Air National Guard for immediate combat duty, and a few days later, the governor wrote to warn local government authorities that "the rapid deterioration recently of the foreign situation has resulted in need for precaution, if not alarm."[7] The desperate mood of the time is indicated by Duff's speech to the state American Legion convention in Philadelphia that August, just at the time when United Nations forces in Korea were fighting off savage attacks against the Pusan perimeter. The governor warned that "Pennsylvania is bound to be one of the prime objectives of the Soviet Union not only by Communism but by major attack in the event of world war III" and that the state must consider the danger of Soviet bombers flying over the North Pole. Pennsylvanians must be prepared "to have some of our principal cities bombed and bombed by the most terrible type of explosive that has ever been known to the human race. And therefore that would be the kind of occasion in which the subversive elements will await like some hidden bears to jump out and cause confusion."

Duff stressed the linkage between direct Soviet attack and fifth-column activities. He claimed that "in the event that the difficulty in Korea breaks out and explodes into world war III . . . one of the great fronts we must defend is the front here at home. And unless we make this home front secure it makes very little difference what happens anywhere else in the far flung corners of the world." Pennsylvania was uniquely vulnerable to subversion: "No other community anywhere in the whole country has the concentration of industry that there is in Pennsylvania," and therefore, "in this city, in Pittsburgh, in every large industrial community, there is a tremendous problem this very hour of sabotage." He warned legionnaires that "no one knows better than you the widespread activities of Communism in this country. There are many large industrial establishments that have been infiltrated by those who do not believe in our Way of Life, and all they are awaiting is a favorable opportunity in order to do their dirty work."[8]

Governor Duff hoped to meet the challenge by reviving the civil defense system created during the Second World War. Potential sabotage would be combated by enforcing the emergency legislation introduced in 1941 and 1943.[9] With the state's National Guard unit called up for federal service, defensive policies would be implemented through state forces, which would coordinate with the State Police, home guard units, rifle clubs, and veterans' organizations. This was a return to the idea of the State Guard, which was originally formed as an antisabotage force in 1940, but which following Pearl Harbor was mobilized as a Reserve Defense Corps, armed with military weaponry. Duff also created a network of county defense councils that would prepare "precautionary and remedial measures for the prompt detection and neutralizing of any sudden and unexpected invasion, such as from air attack against our vital industries."[10] Veterans and other volunteers would be critical to the revived ground observer corps, the first line of defense against air attack.

Industrial Pittsburgh was believed to be the key target. Judge Musmanno claimed that "the steel city of America is reportedly listed in Moscow as the number one target of Russian aerial invasion." Apart from the steelworks, "the huge Westinghouse and other electrical plants manufacture the delicate equipment and machinery for submarines, radar and air engines."[11] In May 1950, Pittsburgh's chairman of civil defense agreed that "metropolitan Pittsburgh, the workshop of the world, is high on the list of strategic cities vital to the national defense. We are very vulnerable, and in the event of war, we could expect to be among the first to be bombed." Accordingly, he was examining the likely consequences of a nuclear strike on the city, though he cautioned against "an unreasoning fear of radiation." Pittsburgh's preparations reached feverish intensity that August, when a volunteer army of 7,000 was requested to come forward to staff positions on a twenty-four-hour-a-day basis. It would have the task of transmitting warnings of enemy threats and getting help to devastated areas.[12]

Defense against the fifth column implied an intelligence response that was, of its nature, covert, but a surprising public statement at this time casts some light on the means by which Duff's hidden bears were to be hunted. In 1948 Pennsylvania's Civil Air Patrol (CAP) issued a press release describing an ambitious plan to meet the "possibilities of an attack on the peace of United States through fifth column subversive activities." Individuals would be selected for intensive training in clandestine warfare, counterinsurgency, Communist methods and ideology, and the Russian language; training would be coordinated through the army counterintelligence school at Fort Holabird in Baltimore. Because the CAP was a part-time organization, this plan would require the support of the state's private corporations and businesses, each of which was asked to enlist at least one member of their firm in the CAP to take the countersubversion course. Businesses would "report via this enlistee all persons in their organization known to have Communistic or subversive tendencies." Private industry was also asked to subsidize the scheme. The military link with industry was sensitive in a state that had less than twenty years ago rid itself of its loathed Coal and Iron Police, an employers' militia that now appeared to be coming back under a different guise. The *York Gazette and Daily* saw the proposal as "the frank bid of CAP to constitute itself as a form of loyalty police," while *The Worker* headline proclaimed "Industry Backs Labor Spy Ring in Pennsylvania Factories."[13] Presumably the CAP was not the only agency in the state contemplating such internal security operations at this time, but it was the only one naive enough to discuss them openly.

Duff's concerns were wholeheartedly shared by the new governor, John S. Fine, who may, if anything, have been even more sensitive to the need for implacably anti-Communist politics: his political base was in Luzerne County, with its strong concentration of eastern and southern European ethnic groups. Taking office in 1951, Fine announced that Pennsylvania was being placed on a war footing in expectation of imminent international hostilities that would "make our familiar backyards, the Turnpike, our suburbs and cities of today, the potential frontlines of tomorrow."[14] Speaking to the Amvets convention at Harrisburg in July, he warned that "if and when the Communists decide to attack us, some of their bombs will reach home. Because they have atom bombs, eleven million Pennsylvanians for their own individual good will have to learn what to do if a bomb strikes."[15] He continued the civil defense bureaucracy established by Duff, so that by 1951 Pennsylvania had 624 ground observation posts located at eight-mile intervals over the entire state. Fine also expanded intelligence efforts. Pennsylvania had a well-established political surveillance system orchestrated through the State Police, but there now appeared "a new program integrating the work of the State Police and Justice Department against subversives. Our state now works closely with the FBI and with other progressive states to prevent any Communist infiltration."[16] The state's Sabotage Prevention Act provided heavy penalties for the destruction of property affecting national defense facilities at a time of national emergency, and such acts would represent first-degree murder if death resulted.[17]

Meanwhile, the State Council of Civil Defense alerted the public to possible dangers through training programs, films, and pamphlets with titles like *Protect Your Family—Keep It Safe from Biological Warfare*. The council advertised and distributed films like *Biological Warfare for Farmers*, *A Tale of Two Cities* (Hiroshima and Nagasaki), *You Can Beat the A-Bomb*, *Our Cities Must Fight*, and the notorious *Duck and Cover*, which told schoolchildren how to minimize nuclear damage by hiding under their desks.[18] The new civil defense bureaucracy published a monthly newsletter, with articles like "Suppose the Enemy Uses Gas?," "Coal Mines Studied for Shelter," "Block Wardens the Key to Panic Control," and "8,000 Nurses Take Atomic Nursing Course." Public awareness of nuclear and other dangers was enhanced by state and local preparedness days and by training in schools and churches, Granges and community groups. In a typical training drill in Bucks and Chester Counties in 1952, the CAP initiated the imaginary raid by dropping leaflets that announced "This might have been a bomb."[19]

The nuclear war scare reached its height in the first year of the Fine administration. In October 1951, "Defense" was the theme of the state's Pennsylvania Week, and shortly afterward the director of Philadelphia's Civil Defense Council asserted that the civil defense network would "be called upon to perform under fire very soon, possibly before the Spring of 1952 has passed."[20] This constant emphasis on sabotage, air raids, and civil defense served, of course, to fuel anti-Communist sentiment, and leftists protested the "hysteria" generated by school drills.[21] Talk of sabotage encouraged the rumors that buzzed in these years, like the charge that the Communists had poisoned the Pittsburgh reservoirs, or the report that a hoard of sabotage manuals (unaccountably written in Spanish) had been unloaded from a ship at the Philadelphia docks. The press tended to sensationalize such stories, as when dynamite was discovered at a McKeesport steelworks, but paid little attention when the incident was explained innocently.[22]

The defense of Pennsylvania's cities and industries was obviously a priority for the federal government. Apart from its economic significance, Pennsylvania also possessed other key strategic targets. Raven Rock, for example, a remote location near the Maryland line, was the site of the secret underground headquarters of the Joint Chiefs of Staff, to be occupied in the event of nuclear catastrophe; York was earmarked as a possible national capital if and when Washington ceased to exist.[23] Through the 1950s, the military planned to defend American cities from air attack, and Pittsburgh was prepared to resist bomber raids with the tactics used by London and other European cities during the Second World War. By 1952 a fighter wing was based at the Greater Pittsburgh airport, its efforts supported by a "ring of steel" around the city, namely, a network of anti-aircraft artillery positions in the surrounding hills, supported by the civil defense observer corps. Each battery was equipped with ninety-millimeter guns and radar, with a detachment of fifty-five soldiers.[24]

As the nuclear threat grew, the emphasis shifted from staving off air attack by shooting down bombers to preserving the population through shelters and evacuation procedures, and periodic air-raid exercises gave an opportunity to test sirens and civil defense mobilization.[25] Material goods also required safeguarding. By 1951 major corporations like U.S. Steel were taking the precaution of microfilming crucial records and burying the film in disused deep quarries in the hope that these would survive the loss of the Pittsburgh area. One site near Saxonburg in Butler County initially proved ideal, though other more remote locations were favored in later years as the destructive power of nuclear weaponry grew.[26] These records would provide the basis for postnuclear industrial reconstruction, for which executives of major corporations like Westinghouse, Alcoa, and U.S. Steel already had their assigned roles.[27]

CVETIC

The threat of war made it essential to know the intentions of potential subversive groups. The American Communist movement was subject to repeated exposés by an interminable series of informers, deep-cover agents, and defectors, who became a central component of the popular culture of the Cold War era. Public events at which infiltrators surfaced were dramatic and newsworthy, at least in the early years when the agents really had enjoyed some access to

Communist Party policy-making. The mere existence of such clandestine operations tended to confirm the worst expectations about the enemy within: if Communists were not engaged in hostile or criminal activities, why would the infiltrators need to maintain such elaborate security and sacrifice so many years of their lives in a dangerous charade? Infiltrators themselves had a vested interest in justifying their careers by portraying the activities they had uncovered in the most sinister terms. Here again, the investigations of the early 1950s were following a well-established formula that dated back to the Roosevelt years. The classic infiltrator was the pseudonymous John Roy Carlson, who had spent several years penetrating American Fascist and ultra-Right groups, and whose 1943 book *Under Cover* became a runaway best-seller. More recently, Communist misdeeds had been described from within by defectors like Whittaker Chambers and Elizabeth Bentley.

Pennsylvania's most significant mole was Matthew Cvetic, "undercover agent," who spent several years in place as a member of the Communist Party in the western parts of the state prior to his public description of his activities at a HUAC hearing in February 1950. His appearance gained impact from the timing, just ten days after Senator McCarthy's Wheeling speech. Cvetic's interest in cloak-and-dagger work dated to 1939, when he applied, unsuccessfully, to join U.S. Army Intelligence. In 1941 Cvetic was a low-level federal employee when he was approached by the FBI and asked to join the Party as an informant.[28] He was allegedly told to "concentrate on convincing the reds of your Communistic inclinations. Walk, talk and eat Communism. In other words, be a Red to all intent and purposes."[29] Following instructions, he befriended a number of leftists in his place of work in the U.S. Employment Service, and in 1943 he formally joined the Party following a Pittsburgh speech by the legendary Elizabeth Gurley Flynn. His Slovene ethnicity stood him in good stead as he became active in "nationality work" with the Party's Slovene Commission, which brought him into contact with activists in New York City, Detroit, Cleveland, and Chicago, as well as other Pennsylvania communities like Johnstown. By 1947 he was executive secretary of the American Slav Congress (ASC), a pressure group claiming to speak for the millions of Americans of Slav descent. Though Cvetic was not a negligible figure, he vastly exaggerated his role within the western Pennsylvania Communist Party; in reality, his usefulness either to the Party or the FBI was fading by at least 1948, and the Cvetic of early 1950 was a burnt-out case.[30]

Cvetic named some 300 leftists in the Pittsburgh region, described the workings of the local Party, and suggested how thoroughly Communists had penetrated institutions like the Progressive Party, the ASC, and various labor unions, above all UE. The evidence gained its power from its first-hand quality, in that Cvetic had actually dealt with important Party leaders, if never as intimately as he claimed, and the sheer volume of detailed information gave the press a daily cornucopia from which to select their headlines. Within just the first week of the story's breaking, on February 19, a sample of Pittsburgh-area headlines included the following: "Henry Wallace Met Commie Leaders Here, Cvetic Tells Probers"; "Plan Told for War on US"; "FBI Agent Lists Reds for Spy Probers"; and "Infiltrate Mines, Mills, Party Told." The Hearst *Sun-Telegraph* presented this last headline over a photograph of Henry Wallace.[31] The subversion theme recurs throughout the press coverage, with HUAC depicted as the "spy probers" and "the House spy hunting group."[32] Cvetic's critics, in contrast, were a fifth column.[33]

One potentially explosive topic surfaced early, but the lead died out quite early in the story. On February 25, under the headline "25 in Congress in Red Front Donation List," the *Pittsburgh Press* quoted Cvetic's statement that his ASC files contained folders of correspondence labeled "Congressmen and Senators."[34] This in itself was not remarkable, as the ASC in its early days had operated with the blessing of the federal government, and its meetings had been greeted with telegrams and speeches from cabinet officials and President Roosevelt himself. However, the documents now in question were dated much more recently, when the ASC was regarded as an outright arm of the Communist Party, a "red front." Republicans sniffed a scandal that might well taint pro-labor Democrats. Conservatives were both angry and alarmed at reports in April that these potentially incriminating papers were missing, but a major cover-up scandal failed to materialize.[35]

Lacking the supposed clique of Red congressmen, newspapers searched for alleged Communists in government employment, but the results were disappointing. The most visible casualty purged from local government in the aftermath of Cvetic's revelations was a deputy sheriff in neighboring Washington County.[36] In fact, for all the excitement in February and March, the new evidence of subversion presented by Cvetic was strictly limited. The propaganda materials produced by the committee on this occasion gave a fair sampling of the Party's activities, proving, for example, that Communists were trying to recruit black members, but that was scarcely a secret. Nor, by 1950, was it any surprise that groups like the ASC were essentially Communist fronts, as this group and others like it had often been denounced over the previous two years, and there was little new in revelations of Red influence in UE or the Progressive

Party. Also, virtually all of the Party figures of any substance whom Cvetic named were, or should have been, thoroughly familiar to any observer who had followed recent congressional investigations — or, indeed, had read the *Pittsburgh Press*'s lists of senior officers in the Wallace campaign or in the Left-run ethnic organizations.[37] HUAC and the *Press* had already made folk villains of Left and liberal leaders like Steve Nelson, George Wuchinich, James Dolsen, Thomas Fitzpatrick, and Alexander Wright, who all starred in Cvetic's accounts.

Nevertheless, Cvetic now became a potent symbol for anti-Communist crusaders. In July 1950 the *Saturday Evening Post* produced a serial entitled "I Posed as a Communist for the FBI," and the story was broadcast on Pittsburgh radio station KDKA and dramatized on television on NBC's *We The People*.[38] The following year the story was also transformed into a tendentious film, *I Was a Communist for the FBI*; scarcely less amazing than its subsequent Oscar nomination was the fact that the nomination was in the category of documentary rather than fiction. The film had a glitzy premiere in Pittsburgh in April 1951, when Mayor David Lawrence declared Matt Cvetic Day, and it would be seen by over 100,000 people in Allegheny County alone.[39]

Cvetic himself won Americanism awards from both the Amvets and the American Legion, and in 1952 he addressed the legion's convention in Philadelphia, where he was introduced as "our comrade . . . our colleague . . . our buddy in the fight against Communism."[40] He enjoyed a career as an anti-Communist pamphleteer, using his writings to argue his essential belief that Communism was marked by its "systematic brain-washing, thought control, enforced communal living, mass enslavement, and mass murder."[41] His speaking tours included over sixty cities, and he addressed more than 150,000 people. By the mid-1950s he was making a decent $15,000 a year from professional anti-Communism, though the big money always eluded him; even for the film of *I Was a Communist for the FBI*, 30 percent of his proceeds were taken by his "manager," anti-Communist attorney Harry Sherman.[42]

Cvetic's HUAC appearance was orchestrated by Harry Sherman and his allies in the pressure group Americans Battling Communism (ABC), which first brought Cvetic to the attention of HUAC. ABC exploited the fallout from the appearance and ably handled the informer's public relations throughout the coming months. Arguably, the group may also have scripted much of the testimony that Cvetic delivered in these months.[43] ABC is a mysterious organization, not least in its original inspiration. Most later sources rely on Steve

Nelson's account of the group, in which Judge Musmanno is portrayed as "the main culprit," but Nelson himself was a relatively new arrival in the region in 1950 and had little sense of the deeper roots of the movement.[44] In reality, Musmanno was the public face of an organization founded by two fanatical anti-Communists, Harry Sherman and Republican judge Blair F. Gunther, each of whom had been acting independently for several years before merging their interests. Sherman owed his interest in the Red issue to struggles in the Pittsburgh labor movement, and Gunther to activism in ethnic and fraternal organizations like the Polish National Alliance. (Sherman will be discussed further in Chapter 5, and Gunther in Chapter 7.) The two apparently combined forces in 1944 in order to expose the ASC, then planning a major national meeting in Pittsburgh, and the nucleus of Americans Battling Communism was formed. The group incorporated in 1947.[45]

Left-wing critics denounced ABC as a "small but well financed redbaiting organization" made up of "courthouse judges and political associates of the Mellons," but in fact this was a diverse and strikingly powerful group, by no means a gang of puppets. Apart from Gunther and Sherman, its founders included Court of Common Pleas judge Harry Montgomery; state senator Joseph M. Barr, secretary of the Allegheny County Democratic Party; Republican Party figure Curtis Haines; radio station executive William M. Burns; and Deputy Attorney General Raymond D. Evans.[46] One critical supporter was James Malone, Republican chairman for Allegheny County and lawyer for Westinghouse and the PMA, which he would serve as president from 1957 to 1971.[47] These were individuals of political substance: Gunther was the state's leading Republican vote-getter, and Montgomery would later join him on the state's Superior Court, while Malone would serve as district attorney. Barr is an intriguing figure in this context. He often acted as Mayor Lawrence's handpicked representative, and it was in this capacity that he would serve as state Democratic chairman in the 1950s and as Lawrence's successor as mayor of Pittsburgh.[48] Lawrence himself was not associated with radical anti-Communism, but it is difficult to imagine that Barr would have been active in ABC without Lawrence's knowledge and consent. In addition, ABC was rooted in the anti-Communist ethnic organizations, groups like the Sons of Italy and the Slovak societies, and the group worked closely with Walter Alessandroni of the American Legion. It also drew support from anti-Communist factions within the labor unions, notably the group currently at war with the leftist leadership of UE; both Sherman and Evans had been involved in the electrical workers' war since the mid-1940s.

As Nelson's remark suggests, Judge Musmanno was the group's most visible figure. The judge had a remarkably diverse political record, including a spell in the 1920s when he made some ardently pro-Mussolini remarks that would haunt his later career; as early as 1929, he had tried to introduce a bill in the Pennsylvania state legislature that would outlaw the Communist Party.[49] At the same time, he earned a record as a loyal Democrat and a solid friend of the labor movement in western Pennsylvania. He became a judge in Allegheny County in 1931, joining the Court of Common Pleas in 1933. As the Communist menace came to the fore around 1950, Musmanno showed himself to be one of the most devoted opponents of subversion in any form. He drafted the 1951 legislation prohibiting the Communist Party in Pennsylvania and boasted part authorship of the 1954 federal Communist Control Act, and his devoted support for McCarthy survived the notorious army hearings of 1954. Musmanno's zeal owed much to partisan politics, as his well-publicized Red hunt began shortly after he was defeated in his bid for the Democratic gubernatorial nomination. Though he claimed a thorough acquaintance with Marxist thought based on long study, Musmanno seems to have owed most of his knowledge to a crash course from Harry Sherman. Anti-Communism helped reestablish a struggling political career, so that he gained the nomination for lieutenant governor that fall and won election to the state supreme court the following year. His ambitions were boundless. As Democratic leader Hiram Andrews remarked, "He is now apparently nursing the ambition to become the Senator McCarthy of the Democratic party. He is a victim of exhibitionism in its advanced state."[50] Musmanno, an authentic demagogue, now emerged as the public face of anti-Communism in western Pennsylvania.

Unwittingly, Cvetic named as Communists several individuals who were themselves fellow FBI informants and would in turn surface over the coming years. One was George Dietze, who had in fact been recruited even before Cvetic himself, and who now found that public exposure as a Communist made life intolerable for himself and his family. He therefore came forward in March 1950, presenting the local Communist Party with yet another disaster. Dietze had been paying the rent on an office at 943 Liberty Avenue, which had often served as a venue for Communist meetings and which had been thoroughly bugged by the FBI.[51] A raid on these premises produced large quantities of Communist and ASC propaganda material, including radio broadcasts by George Wuchinich destined for the local Slavic-language stations. The plethora of peace-oriented materials by Paul Robeson and others helped stigmatize the whole peace and antinuclear movements as Communist fronts.[52] Publicity from the Dietze revelations maintained a high level of public interest in Communist plots until Cvetic began his second wave of testimony in mid-March.

The new anti-Communist outbreak had a massive impact on the lives of the individuals named, and perhaps 100 individuals lost their livelihoods over the next year or so: Steve Nelson estimated that seventy or eighty families simply fled the Pittsburgh area.[53] Early casualties, dismissed in the immediate aftermath of Cvetic's surfacing, included a violinist with the Pittsburgh symphony orchestra, a laborer in the local parks department, and a craneman employed at a steelworks.[54] The Glen Hazel Mothers Guild removed its leader because of her Communist sympathies, and another victim was the public relations director of the Laborers District Council of the American Federation of Labor (AFL), whose father had been named as a Communist.[55] It was all but impossible for anyone named in one of the investigations to gain employment. As one local institution asserted, when charged with employing a statistician with subversive connections, "Carnegie Tech doesn't want to hire any member of the Communist Party for anything—not even to mow the grass."[56]

Most such cases attracted little media attention after the initial dismissal, but a couple of individuals enjoyed greater notoriety. One was Charles M. Kerns, former Progressive Party leader and director of the Pittsburgh PCA chapter, who was fired from McKeesport radio station WMCK, where he had produced Left-oriented programs for the UE Local 601.[57] The American Federation of Radio Artists also attempted to expel Kerns from membership, though the union's board narrowly failed to carry this resolution.[58] Local radio stations became nervous about broadcasting anything that might be regarded as subversive, and a *Pittsburgh Press* critic led a movement to "kick Commies off the air and keep them off."[59] Dorothy Alberts, publicity director for the CRC (and sister of prominent UE leftist Nathan Alberts), was dismissed as a schoolteacher after a long-running legal battle.[60]

Individuals targeted included not only overt Communists, but also allies or perceived fellow travelers like Kerns, and the tactic of guilt by association produced glaring injustices. As left-wing attorney Hymen Schlesinger wrote in May 1950, "A new formula has been devised, namely the application of the clean hands doctrine, for denying civil rights to progressive and liberal people."[61] Schlesinger was appalled at the political consequences, especially in matters like civil rights. There was now tremendous pressure to abandon Left causes, and as one local newspaper remarked, "There's a strange sound heard in the Valley these days ever since the Cvetic hearings. . . . It resembles the noise when one is tearing paper. . . . Some say it is the Commies tearing up their Party membership cards."[62] In this atmosphere mere suspicion could be devastating, and the papers regularly presented the pleas of nonpolitical individuals that they not be mistaken for Communists with like-sounding names. A nonpolitical Andy Onda was afraid that he would be confused with his namesake, the local Party leader, and William Schultz of Dormont wished it to be known that he was a quite different person from another, Communist Schultz.

Cvetic and Dietze now began a career of testifying in courts to establish the Communist Party affiliations of people or groups, as judges acted on the assumption that Communists were not entitled to conventional legal or constitutional protections. Judge Musmanno began one of the first such quasi-legal attempts to strip Communists of civil rights when he found that the March grand jury included Alice Roth, secretary of the East Pittsburgh branch of the Communist Party, who had been active in the leftist UE faction at the Westinghouse plant. Having her identity confirmed by Cvetic and some members of the rightist UE faction, Musmanno interrogated Roth on her political beliefs; when she refused to answer, he excluded her from the jury, thereby earning the first of many rebukes from the state supreme court.[63] The Roth pattern was followed several times that spring, as the Red issue was dragged to the forefront of cases in which political loyalties had little to do with the specific charges. In one instance, Cvetic testified about the Communist ties of Nathan Alberts, who had led the 1948 desegregation protest at the Highland Park swimming pool.[64] The judge in this case was ABC's Harry Montgomery, who sentenced Alberts to a severe twenty-three months. In another instance, pickets from a Left-dominated union in New Kensington were involved in an assault on a police officer. In court, defendants were interrogated about their political sympathies, and the prosecution brought in Cvetic to prove that protesters were in fact Communists; one, Harry Truitt, was secretary of the Allegheny Valley branch of the ASC and was also active in the Progressive Party. Both convictions were upheld by the Superior Court, in which Judge Gunther was now such a potent voice, but the state supreme court overturned the picket case on the grounds that the evidence had been improperly admitted and prejudicial.[65]

Judge Musmanno once again attracted the wrath of the state's highest court when he targeted lawyer Hymen Schlesinger, whom he jailed for contempt in 1951 for refusing to answer direct questions about alleged Communist Party membership. Musmanno achieved limited vindication when the Allegheny County Bar Association began a lengthy attempt to prevent Schlesinger from practicing law.[66] The incident epitomized the attitude of the state supreme court, which was willing to support draconian anti-Communist legislation but drew the line at extralegal vigilantism.

Apart from the brakes placed on Musmanno, the court also intervened in the Marjorie Matson case, an incident that reveals the partisan agendas often underlying Red-baiting campaigns. This affair originated when state attorney general Charles Margiotti tried to establish a special loyalty investigation of Matson, an Allegheny County assistant district attorney, to determine her competence to hold office. Matson's record of Left-liberal activism dated back to the early 1930s, but more recently, as chair of the Pittsburgh ACLU, she protested Governor Duff's call to deny free speech rights to American Communists. In 1950 she denounced Musmanno's attempt to exclude Alice Roth from the grand jury, and she attacked post-Cvetic "hysteria."[67] This attracted the attention of Musmanno's old friend Margiotti, who was, like the judge, a political enemy of Mayor Lawrence. As Lawrence was Matson's patron, it was politically valuable to stigmatize her as an indirect means of attacking the mayor. Special hearings into Matson's politics were held in September 1951, with Harry Sherman as unofficial prosecutor and perennial expert on Communist theory. In this rare instance, the smear attempt failed, due to Lawrence's courageous decision to speak out publicly for Matson, whom he called "thoroughly American and a mighty good Democrat"; he even had a good word for Hy Schlesinger. Shortly afterward, the state supreme court determined that the loyalty review had no legal authority and termed Margiotti's attempt "absurd."[68]

These incidents were skirmishes compared to the major rightist offensive now under way, which aimed at nothing less than the trial of the whole leadership of the western Pennsylvania Communist Party. The chief target was District Organizer Steve Nelson, a legendary figure in Party circles, who occupied center stage in Cvetic's testimony. A Croat (his original surname was Mesarosh), Nelson was the model of a dedicated international revolutionary, who had served with distinction in the Spanish Civil War.[69] Anti-Communists saw him as a key agent of the Comintern or the Soviet secret police, or both, so that his presence in the industrial regions around Pittsburgh seemed a likely prelude to a campaign of sabotage in the event of war. The *Pittsburgh Press* greeted his arrival in 1948 with the description of Nelson as "inspector general for the Soviet underground."[70] Nelson himself had also been accused of involvement in atomic espionage, having allegedly used as intermediary a woman he knew from the Spanish conflict: she subsequently married J. Robert Oppenheimer, then a Berkeley scientist active in atomic research; this connection was said to explain Nelson's Communist activities in northern California, where he organized a cell at Berkeley. In 1943 the FBI observed him meeting clandestinely with a Soviet intelligence officer.[71] These activities attracted congressional attention; in a notorious appearance before HUAC in June 1949, Nelson refused to answer a question concerning which side he would support in the event of war between the United States and the USSR, a reply that would often be quoted as proof of his political depravity. For Musmanno, Nelson was "a world revolutionary bent on bloody mischief, he is the eye and prowling hand of aggressive Russia in our midst, he is a terrorist, a ruffian and an atomic spy—the most dangerous man in America."[72]

Nelson's role as "atomic spy" appeared in the first news stories reporting Cvetic's defection, and the Pittsburgh papers continued throughout the coverage to depict Nelson as a ruthless spymaster. In one *Sun-Telegraph* story that announced "Plot to Cripple Nation Headed by Steve Nelson," columnist Howard Rushmore spoke of "Stalin's Fifth Column in this country," which operated through "red fascist cells."[73] The *Pittsburgh Press* claimed "Nelson Gave M-Day Orders to Reds Here," reporting that he gave local Communists instructions on how to act in the event of a war between the USSR and the American "enemy," an event that had apparently been thought imminent in the spring of 1948.[74] The "atom spy" tag gained added significance over the coming months, as nuclear espionage was very much in the news. One figure in the alleged Rosenberg network was Harry Gold, who was arrested in Philadelphia in May 1950.[75] Though Gold had no direct links with the Pennsylvania Communist Party, the publicity accorded his case could not fail to carry the taint of treason to local Communists. Addressing workers at the Westinghouse plant, Musmanno declared, "That industrial strength the Philadelphia scientist [i.e., Gold] spoke of is [the] dropping of an atom bomb which would level all of Pittsburgh like a finger crushing a grape. Do we have any of those people around here?"[76]

In March, Gunther, Musmanno, and ABC were demanding that the state charge Nelson and other Red leaders—ideally, with treason or, failing that, with sedition. At first, Allegheny County district attorney William Rahauser was reluctant to oblige, a stance that certainly did not reflect any sympathy toward Communism, as he was a loyal member of both the American Legion and the VFW. He simply saw no evidence of overt criminal acts in either the Cvetic testimony or the available printed propaganda materials, and he feared, correctly, that a trial would have to focus on unpopular beliefs. Rahauser did fall into line, though, following pressure by Attorney General Margiotti, who threatened to include him in an ongoing investigation of official collusion with gambling and organized crime activities. Though this account originates with leftist critics of the investigation, it is quite plausible: the general tolerance of organized gambling by public officials in the region exposed virtually all of them to selective prosecution during a vice crackdown like that under way in these years.[77] Margiotti had already demonstrated his ability to use such charges to bring down political opponents, having virtually crippled the state's Democratic leadership through corruption charges in the late 1930s.[78]

Whatever the reason, Rahauser was now prepared to contemplate sedition charges, and Musmanno played the leading role in gathering evidence, demonstrating a bewildering blending of his roles as investigator and judge (he was also a political candidate, blithely ignoring the prohibition on campaigning by serving judges). On July 19 the judge crossed the street from his Court of Common Pleas on Pittsburgh's Grant Street and entered the Communist Party bookstore that represented such a continuing affront to his patriotic zeal. Following a civil encounter with Jim Dolsen, the judge spent $5.75 on a number of standard texts on Marxist-Leninist doctrine, which he proceeded to comb for language that might prove seditious intent. Later trips to Party offices in Philadelphia and New York were equally rewarding, and the trawl promised to find abundant evidence of the Communist advocacy of revolution. At exactly this time, he issued a public call for U.S. attorney general Howard McGrath to intern eleven local Communist leaders, a demand that he repeated on a radio broadcast. At the end of August, Musmanno, Cvetic, and some detectives raided Party headquarters, which the judge described as "the equivalent of an advance post of the Red Army."[79] Acting on information sworn out by the judge in his capacity as private citizen, the group seized large quantities of documents that would be used for a sedition prosecution against Nelson, Andy Onda, and Dolsen. The action may be better understood when we note that it occurred in the last two days of August 1950, at a time when the news media were grimly reporting the desperate plight of United Nations forces trapped within the Pusan perimeter and the likelihood of a final Communist offensive within days or hours. For Musmanno, a move in Pittsburgh was his only way of striking a blow in the growing world conflict.

The bizarre sedition trial began in January 1951, though a car accident in May meant that Nelson's case was severed from the others. Musmanno and his allies were on shaky legal grounds in these proceedings, and the state supreme court often had cause to strike down his actions; the court denounced the astronomical bail imposed on Steve Nelson, reducing the figure from $100,000 to $10,000, and also reversed Musmanno's attempt to padlock Party headquarters.[80] The trial itself also had some highly unconventional aspects. Though the entire scheme was chiefly Musmanno's endeavor, he was neither judge nor prosecutor; the assistant prosecutor, however, was Musmanno's nephew, William F. Cercone, while the judge in the Nelson trial was his ABC colleague, Harry Montgomery, who was appointed by the presiding judge of the Allegheny County Court of Common Pleas, Musmanno himself. In both instances, there was at least a strong suggestion of conflict of interest, or, put more directly, the trial "set new standards of inquisitorial justice."[81] Musmanno's professed role was that of private citizen and prosecution witness, who testified for thirty straight days, in what may have been a legal record, as he demonstrated his newfound acquaintance with Marxist literature; the court's other expert witness on the evils of Communism was Harry Sherman. Nelson himself was left without a lawyer for most of his trial, and in April 1951, he had to cope with the dreadful publicity from the film *I Was a Communist for the FBI*, then premiering only blocks away from the courthouse, which depicted a Red villain, clearly based on Nelson, as a ruthless murderer.

This was explicitly a trial of ideas and ideologies. The charges themselves were questionable, in that under state law, sedition consisted of advocating the overthrow of the United States or of the Commonwealth of Pennsylvania, but the materials discussed were generally Marxist classics that could easily be found in many libraries of unquestioned integrity, including the city's distinguished Carnegie Library. Despite this, Musmanno and his allies believed quite simply that the mere presentation of such ideas constituted a grave crime. As the judge remarked of Lenin's famous text *The State and Revolution*, "It can only be illegal to circulate this book which outrightly calls upon its readers to forcibly seize the government of the United States."[82] In court, the prosecution spent a good deal of time attacking Nelson's opposition to the Korean War.

The Pittsburgh prosecutions began a series of cases that ultimately dragged on for several years and became a cause célèbre for both Left and Right. For the Left, the Cvetic testimony and its aftermath was part of a conspiracy: "It was this moment that the Mellon, Jones and Laughlin, and Frick interests chose for their experiment. The experiment was to be a cold-blooded attempt to provoke a red scare, to panic the people, to crush the Left-led unions and whip up the cold war."[83] "The Pittsburgh Frame-Up Victims" were on trial because "they fought against the insanity and horror of a new world atomic war" and condemned MacArthur's attempts to spread the Korean War: "The hands of the Mellons are seen and felt in this courtroom today in the trial of the men who demanded the withdrawal of American troops from Korea."[84] For the Right, Nelson provided a visible face for global Communist conspiracy, and his political activities in the previous two decades all served to prove his anti-American intent, including his support for the Spanish Republic.

At first, ABC seemed to have won a clear victory: when Onda and Dolsen were convicted in August 1951, the *Sun-Telegraph* trumpeted "Guilt of Two Here Death Blow to Pennsylvania Reds."[85] Following health-related delays, Steve Nelson himself was ultimately convicted in January 1952, and Judge Montgomery sentenced him to the maximum twenty years imprisonment. The final outcome was decided when the lone juror with doubts about Nelson's guilt was beaten by "goons" who told him "This'll teach you how to vote."[86] While the three Party leaders were facing long prison terms, their adversaries had all won political prizes: Musmanno was on the state supreme court, Gunther on the Superior Court, and prosecutor Loran Lewis and District Attorney Rahauser were both county judges. Legally, too, the Red-hunters had made their point. When teacher Dorothy Alberts protested her dismissal to the state supreme court, the justices firmly accepted the view of the criminality of Communism: Justice John C. Bell warned her attorney, "I don't think you'll get any member of this court—certainly not the majority—to argue that Communism is not dedicated to the overthrow of the United States and each of its states. I suggest you don't bother arguing that point."[87]

Matters were now complicated by the federal decision to prosecute regional Communist Party leaders under the 1940 Smith Act. This measure, which made it a crime "to knowingly or willfully advocate, abet, advise or teach the duty, necessity, desirability or propriety of overthrowing or destroying any government in the United States by force or violence," had been the basis for the trial and conviction of the national Communist leadership in 1948–49. Crucially, this latter case also removed the necessity for the government to show that any further "clear and present danger" was required before sedition could be proven. As the U.S. Supreme Court decided in the 1951 *Dennis v. United States* case, "The words cannot mean that before the government may act, it must wait until the *putsch* is about to be executed, the plans have been laid, and the signal is awaited."[88] In practice, this meant that Communists would be tried for the rather intangible offense of "conspiring to teach to advocate."

Over the next four years, a series of local cases (see Table 4) unraveled the local Party structure in cities across the country; several Pittsburgh leaders

Table 4. Defendants in the Smith Act Trials in Pennsylvania

Pittsburgh*	
Steve Nelson	National Board Member; District Organizer
William Albertson	District Board Member
Irving Weissman	State Organizer
James Dolsen	District Committee Member
Benjamin Careathers	District Committee Member
Andrew Onda	County Chairman; District Steel Organizer
Philadelphia**	
Joseph Kuzma	District Committee Member; Trade Union Secretary
David Davis	National Committee Member
Sherman Labovitz	District Press Director
Walter Lowenfels	Editor, Pennsylvania edition of the *Daily Worker;* District Committee Member
Thomas Nabried	District Committee Member
Benjamin Weiss	Public Affairs Director; Treasurer; District Committee Member
Joe Roberts	District Organizer
Irvin Katz	District Committee Member
Robert Klonsky	Organizational Secretary; District Board Member

Source: *Digest of the Public Record of Communism in the United States* (New York: Fund for the Republic, 1955), 196–205.
*All were convicted except Onda, whose case was severed.
**All were convicted.

were indicted in August 1951, and their trial began in November 1952. Their Philadelphia counterparts were seized in July 1953. Like the state prosecution in Pittsburgh, the federal prosecutors in both cities encountered great difficulty in locating overt acts of sedition and were forced to concentrate on proving attendance at meetings, the organization of conferences, the circulation of letters and petitions, and so on. Philadelphia experienced its own "trial of the books," with seditious intent being proved by a series of ex-Communist informers like Louis Budenz and Paul Crouch. Although they had no specific knowledge of conditions or events in Pennsylvania, their testimony was nevertheless permitted by courts. Eventually, all nine of the Philadelphia defendants would be convicted and receive sentences of two or three years imprisonment apiece.[89]

Oddly, the Smith Act cases proved to be excellent news for the original Pittsburgh defendants, as the Pennsylvania Supreme Court now invalidated the state convictions on the grounds that they were preempted by federal jurisdiction, and this interpretation was ultimately upheld by the U.S. Supreme Court. The collapse of the state cases caused outrage on the Right, and the state's American Legion convention was one of many bodies to protest what seemed to be a soft approach to dangerous spies and agitators.[90] This was, however, a harbinger of even worse legal news for the "patriotic" lobby, in that the federal cases would likewise collapse in the long run. Though they were tied up in legal wrangling for several years, the Party leaders would suffer far less than ABC would have liked.

Though the Communist Party was on the run, federal law enforcement agencies continued their pressure, and infiltrators surfaced periodically. In fact, there were so many informants that the government was seemingly able to summon a new one every time it needed a surprise witness for a congressional hearing or a trial. Within the Communist Party, this encouraged the often accurate suspicion that any apparently reliable comrade could be a traitor, thus creating a demoralizing mood of paranoia and internal conflict.[91] In Philadelphia, the gallows humor of the surviving Party members held that informers could easily be identified, as they were the only ones who paid their dues on time.

The Smith Act trials were especially productive of moles, and in the years 1953–55 several figures emerged who were taken very seriously at the time, though in most cases subsequent interpretations were not so charitable. As we shall see, most of the major defectors would later be discredited because they were either exaggerating their testimony or largely fabricating it. One of the most dubious was Joseph Mazzei, who appeared as a witness in the federal trial of Jim Dolsen and Ben Careathers in March 1953. Mazzei had been underground since 1941 and appeared to be a new Cvetic, portraying Dolsen as a potentially violent fanatic and describing the Communist strong-arm squads that trained under cover of the Jewish Cultural Center in Pittsburgh's Squirrel Hill. Here "a district Communist taught red strongarm brigades how to make bombs and hand-grenades in the basement of the Center."[92] Mazzei even alleged that the Party had plotted McCarthy's assassination; the senator soberly confirmed that he had indeed heard of such a plot, while his colleagues agreed that they knew the personal risk they were running in their crusade.[93] Following these revelations, Harry Sherman and his brother Samuel secured a warrant permitting a well-publicized raid on the Cultural Center, which they termed "A Communist *Cheder*," and they sought the revocation of the charter of its parent organization, the Yiddisher Kultur Farband. The Pennsylvania Supreme Court refused to grant the latter request, despite a flowery dissent from Justice Musmanno, who depicted the members of the Kultur Farband as "ghouls sneering at the ineffable coffins" of the 25,000 American soldiers returning in "flag draped caskets," each killed by "a Communist bullet or the fragment of a Communist shell or grenade."[94]

Other western Pennsylvania moles now came to light: R. J. Hardin, whom Cvetic had identified as a leading Red in Cambria County; Mary Stella Beynon of Brushton, who had worked within the UE Left in the 1940s, until she was found out and expelled; and, remarkably, Alexander Wright, the union boss and old Progressive Party leader.[95] Also playing a double game was Harry Truitt, who had been at the center of the earlier political case involving union picketers.[96] The proliferation of agents meant that the FBI must have been thoroughly informed of the inner workings of the western Pennsylvania Party, at least since the early 1940s. It also showed how often agents had been investigating and denouncing each other, as the *Pittsburgh Press* noted in a late 1955 article, "Can't Tell Commie from FBI Aide Here."[97] These undercover agents became fixtures of anti-Communist politics and regularly spoke as expert witnesses.

Nor were other regions any more secure. In 1954 Herman Thomas of Bethlehem came forward to testify against the Philadelphia Smith Act defendants: he had been underground since 1944 and had become a trusted local functionary in the Lehigh Valley area. Thomas now provided abundant testimony on Party doings, matters that received even more publicity than usual because this was Tad Walter's backyard, and Walter never lost an opportunity to show that Communists regarded him as one of their greatest foes.[98] Thomas's Senate testimony was followed immediately by that of yet another mole named Ralph K. Heltzinger, of West Reading, who had also been recruited a decade previously.[99]

With the Party apparatus in ruins, Communists tried to maintain their organization by resorting to a clandestine structure, "a shadow underground organization that could survive the terror of fascism."[100] In a sense, the policy of moving underground was initiated spontaneously by the Party rank and file. As early as 1947, an alarmed membership secretary told the western Pennsylvania Communist leadership that "quite a number of CP members have been stricken with the jitters, and were so frightened over the recent redbaiting that they voluntarily destroyed their dues books and every bit of Communist literature they had in their possession, others hid their dues books. The pertinent fact is that the Party has lost control, to some extent, of its members."[101] The following year, the Party officially ordered the destruction of membership records and Party cards, and in the tense situation of August 1950, the Pennsylvania leadership split up its section leaders into cells of three or four members each. Herman Thomas described how he was given control of the Allentown area, in the Lehigh Valley/Bucks County section, while other supposedly trustworthy officials were left as organizers for Bethlehem/Northampton and for Bucks County, all working under a section organizer and a secretary.[102] Leaders would meet once a month, in cars or other out-of-the-way places, maintaining contact by courier and avoiding the telephone. In western Pennsylvania the core of survivors included Alexander Wright, who participated in clandestine meetings of the Party establishment in a Soho tavern or in a car near the Greater Pittsburgh airport. In Philadelphia some members were in hiding to avoid prison, while others remained "frozen" underground, ready to take over command once Party leaders were arrested.[103] Ordinary Party members were in cells of five each: "One person would act as chairman, collect the dues and then turn them in to your representative from the City Central Committee. Those cells, you didn't know from your cell who was in the next cell for security purposes."[104]

A shift to clandestine arrangements confirmed the worst suspicions about Communist behavior and intentions, as Party activists moved into a sinister-seeming world of secret meetings, dead drops, cutouts, and coded instructions, making them look for all the world like the spies their enemies claimed them to be. Members now had to deal with hitherto insignificant problems such as finding meeting places, and farms owned by rural members proved useful for this purpose. As Ralph Heltzinger reported in 1954, "Most all of these farms were used for secret party meetings, and we always had a security man out watching to see if anyone would come around and check on us or pass by with a car, and we would find out whom he was before we continued these meetings."[105] Transferring membership from one geographical region to another became a nightmare, as it was vital to ensure that a new member was not a spy. In the above-ground days, members moving into a new area would simply have received written "transfers" permitting them to enter a new club, but now evidence of good standing was provided by the device of tearing a dollar bill in half, so the candidate could match his part with the other half in the hands of his new Party secretary.[106] Such subterfuges made wonderful tidbits for press exposés. The new emphasis on underground membership also made it easier for followers of Musmanno or McCarthy to charge the existence of legions of covert Communists masquerading as regular citizens.

LEGISLATING LOYALTY

Legislative measures now taken against Communists represented another arm of the general movement toward effective civil defense, which acquired new urgency as "atom spies" and other conspirators stood trial in Pittsburgh and Philadelphia. In the name of political security, a series of radical new laws fundamentally transformed rights of expression and association, but these were enthusiastically upheld by both legislators and judges. In addition, some potentially devastating old statutes were now revived. The most important was the state's fearsome sedition law, originally passed in 1919 but dormant since its use in an industrial dispute in 1926; this was the measure now deployed against the Pittsburgh Party leadership. The law had long been opposed by radicals and liberals, as its terms could technically be extended to cover almost any form of social protest or direct action.[107] As reenacted in 1945, the law defined sedition as any writing, utterance, or other conduct that would cause an "outbreak or demonstration of violence against this state or against the US" or that might "encourage any person to take any measures or engage in any conduct with a view to overthrowing or attempting to overthrow or destroy by any force or show of threat or force, the government." Sedition included "any writing, publication, . . . or utterance which advocates or teaches the duty, necessity or propriety of engaging in crime, violence or any form of terrorism as a means of accomplishing political reform or change in government."[108]

If the aim was to suppress the Left, the state sedition law seemed quite adequate, but legislators were anxious to go on record as absolute opponents of Communism in all its forms, and this explains the support for Musmanno's 1951 bill to prohibit the Communist Party. The measure was introduced with the sponsorship of three Republican representatives and three Democrats, but it was equally passionately attacked from across the political spectrum as being unworkable as well as dangerous to civil liberties. Even with anti-Red fears at their height in mid-1951, several leading newspapers denounced the measure. An editorial in the *Pittsburgh Post-Gazette* was headlined "Kill This Ridiculous Bill," and the *Philadelphia Evening Bulletin* described the "hysteria" surrounding the legislative debate.[109] The *Harrisburg Evening News* warned of the law's overly broad scope: "Ever sign a petition? Ever put your name down for an honorary committee? Ever join an organization doing something about foreign affairs? Are you so sure now you never knowingly did something that would assist the communist purpose? The bill would make that kind of law."[110] Even Deputy Attorney General Robert Kunzig, normally the most fervent of anti-Communists, thought the measure was probably unconstitutional.[111] But the law proved to be a juggernaut: only eight state representatives were willing to vote against the measure at any stage of its passage, though a stubborn rearguard action was fought by two legislators, Harry E. Seyler of York and minority leader Hiram G. Andrews of Johnstown. The final vote in the state house that August was 206–0, and in December 1951, the measure passed the state senate by a vote of 46–0.[112]

The Musmanno Act had far-reaching legal implications, which went well beyond the specific attack on Communism. The law began by declaring that "there exists an international revolutionary Communist conspiracy which is committed to the overthrow by force and violence of the government of the US and of the several states . . . such conspiracy including the Communist Party of the United States of America, its local components in Pennsylvania, and the members thereof." This came close to Governor Duff's position that each individual Party member was guilty of participation in the global conspiracy, which if taken literally meant that each and every member was liable under the state's treason law, which made it a criminal offense to be "a member of the Communist Party of the United States of America or any other organization, no matter how named, whose object or purpose is to overthrow the federal or state government by force and violence, knowing the revolutionary object or purpose thereof, or whoever participates in the revolutionary activities of the Communist Party or any other organization with the same revolutionary purpose." The legal language was necessary to keep the Communist Party from merely adopting a convenient change of guise, by becoming a "Progressive People's Party" or something similar, but the clause had the effect of proscribing all future revolutionary organizations: the participation clause could in theory have been used not only against actual members, but against anyone seen as a fellow traveler of the Party. Copying the state sedition law, the banning measure carried a penalty of twenty years imprisonment and a $10,000 fine.

The state legislature's 1951 session debated other anti-Communist measures. A "Little McCarran Act" sought to register subversives, and another proposed bill would impose the death penalty for sabotage, but most attention focused on a loyalty act known as the Pechan law.[113] Albert R. Pechan, state senator for Armstrong and Butler Counties, was legislative director for the American

Legion, and his bill was upheld by veterans groups, including the legion, the VFW, and Amvets.[114] As originally introduced that January, it was a straightforward loyalty oath for public employees, requiring every employee of the commonwealth or its subdivisions to file a written statement under oath or affirmation that he or she was not a subversive.[115] This original bill attracted both vigorous support and fervent opposition. Supporters tried to make it more potent, amending it frequently until the original two sections had grown to seventeen, and creating elaborate procedures for the state's educational system.

Opponents were equally dedicated. The bill was criticized by an impressive range of groups representing labor and religious denominations, the Greater Philadelphia ACLU and other civil liberties interests, and the ADA. Joe Clark, now mayor of Philadelphia, was a severe critic. Much of the mobilization of local liberal and religious groups was undertaken by the leftist Teachers' Union of Philadelphia and its president, Francis Jennings (this group is not to be confused with the much larger Philadelphia affiliate of the mainstream teachers' union).[116] Large sections of the press were hostile, even conservative outlets like the *Philadelphia Inquirer* and the *Evening Bulletin*. Philadelphia's *Sunday Bulletin* bracketed the Pechan measure with the bill to suppress the Communist Party: "Both bills are loaded with buckshot, and have sights so bad that they are apt to miss the Communists and hit totally innocent persons."[117] One Democratic opponent called the loyalty measure the "asafetida Bill" after the pungent herb used to prevent influenza during the 1918 pandemic; like asafetida, the Bill would not keep the disease away, but it would assuredly stink. Nevertheless, the "stinking" bill also became law in December, a striking tribute to the legislative strength of the organized veterans' groups and their "rowdy steamroller lobby": the measure passed the state senate by a vote of 35−9, and the state house by 168−8.[118]

State laws of this type had become commonplace in recent years, but the Pennsylvania measure was draconian even by the standards of the time. "Subversion" was defined as all acts directed toward "the overthrow, destruction or alteration of the constitutional form of the United States or of the Commonwealth of Pennsylvania . . . by force or violence." It was an offense to be "knowingly a member of a subversive organization or a foreign subversive organization as defined in this act." Public employment in Pennsylvania was open to "no subversive person, . . . nor any person as to whom on all the evidence there is reasonable doubt concerning his loyalty to the government of the United States or the Commonwealth of Pennsylvania." This allowed the stigma of disloyalty to be based on "reasonable doubt" rather than requiring the customary proof of subversive character; even Musmanno thought this was going too far.[119] The act went on to specify the loyalty oaths or affirmations required of public officials, concentrating particularly on public schools and state-funded institutions of higher learning. Candidates for elective office were required to file with their nominating petition a sworn statement that they could not be considered subversive persons. The loyalty oath was sworn subject to penalty of perjury, which could mean heavy fines and prison terms.

Though the loyalty act was the state's main legislative response to subversion, other measures were adopted as well, including a state prohibition on public assistance for any grounds except blindness if the recipient advocated unconstitutional change in the form of government of the United States or acted in any way that promoted such change.[120] Below the state level, several municipalities also acted to express their patriotic detestation of the Left; these measures were concentrated in the early months of the Korean War. In 1950 York's city council passed an ordinance declaring it unlawful for anyone to distribute or sell any book, pamphlet, or any other object "which advocates disloyalty to or the overthrow of the Government of the US or of the Commonwealth of Pennsylvania . . . or encourages or tends to encourage a breach of the public peace or good order of the community." Nearby Lancaster required Communists or radicals to register with the police and to keep them informed of changes of address, subject to a fine of $100.[121] Once again, the law was entirely symbolic, as nobody had registered by 1954, and registration laws in communities like McKeesport were equally ineffective.[122] Also in 1950, the city council of Wilkes-Barre, likewise expressing community outrage, ordered that all departments of the city government "be alerted to be on constant lookout for the activities or propaganda of persons suspected of being members of the Communist Party and upon discovery of any such persons activities or propaganda to report the same immediately through the proper channels to the FBI." In October, Philadelphia faced an abortive attempt to prohibit the employment of subversives in state or city government, a measure introduced by Councilman David Jamieson with the strong support of the VFW and the American Legion.[123]

The ferocious laws of the early 1950s were enthusiastically upheld by the state's courts, which showed themselves to be militant enemies of subversion, broadly defined. The vehemence of the Pennsylvania judges was not surprising, given the long record of state courts as deadly enemies of organized labor, but they had not always been as implacable as they now appeared. Somewhat more liberal judges had been elected or appointed during the liberal Republican regimes of the 1920s and early 1930s, as well as the Democratic years of the mid-1930s. During the early 1940s, when various state and local authorities had attempted to take measures against Communists, especially state employees and teachers, courts had sometimes favored the accused individuals. In the decade after 1945, however, both state and federal courts became much less sympathetic to the rights of accused political defendants, not only upholding controversial laws, but doing so in language that suggested a wish that the legislature had gone still further.

One factor here was the increasing number of highly ideological anti-Communists who now occupied senior judicial positions. Though Gunther, Montgomery, and Musmanno were unusually visible, many other members of the state judiciary were responsible for some remarkable political invective from the bench. In 1947, for instance, the Left-dominated American Communications Association sought the lifting of an injunction against picketing in a Scranton labor dispute. The common pleas court of Lackawanna County refused the request on the grounds of the union's failure to comply adequately with the provisions of the Taft-Hartley Act excluding Communist officials. The court further took judicial notice that "the Soviet government is an enemy of the Christian religion and is patterned on the idea of a termite den," citing scholarly works on the life of the white ant.[124]

As the courts saw themselves on the front line of the anti-Communist crusade, they were especially sensitive to any infiltration within the legal profession itself, and any hint of leftist sympathies was likely to trigger inquiries about a given lawyer's fitness for the bar. This issue surfaced when attorneys who agreed to defend accused leftists were themselves charged with subversive conduct, thus placing their whole practice in jeopardy. Steve Nelson failed to find a lawyer either among the twenty-five he approached in western Pennsylvania or from over fifty contacted in other cities, but some less notorious defendants also faced difficulties in finding legal representation, including some of the Philadelphia teachers.[125] That the fears cited by nervous attorneys were quite genuine is suggested by the long-running attempt to disbar Hymen Schlesinger, and HUAC and its counterparts were quite capable of subpoenaing the lawyers representing witnesses called to testify. In 1956 Philadelphia's Harry Levitan, counsel for so many Left defendants, was himself placed on the witness stand while Herman Thomas identified him as a Communist.[126] In this context, it is impressive that some of the best-respected attorneys in Philadelphia mobilized such a strong defense for the Smith Act defendants in 1953–54.

Far from protesting excesses, bar associations themselves generally undertook rigorous self-policing in an effort to exclude Left-leaning attorneys. In one case in 1953–54, a young law school graduate named Jack Sirott applied for entrance to the Bucks County Bar, which rejected him on the strength of his earlier involvement with the NAACP and the Progressive Party and his supposed association with a Marxist fellow student at the Pennsylvania State University; he was also said to have participated in an antisegregation protest while at college.[127] Sirott was able to muster a powerful range of character references who vouched for his loyalty, despite having to face the "familiar sickening pattern" of intrusive questions about his associations, and following a year of appeals, he was eventually allowed to practice law in the state.[128]

Even granting the urgency of the war scare, the venom directed at individual leftists can still shock. One such case involved Antoinette "Toni" Nuss, whom Cvetic named as a Communist. Noting that she lived in a county-funded housing project in Pittsburgh, Deputy Attorney General Robert Kunzig argued that she should immediately forfeit all state benefits, asserting that the repression of Communists did not have to wait until the federal courthouse on Grant Street was actually blown up (he was, of course, echoing the U.S. Supreme Court's *Dennis* decision).[129] The news media agreed, and the *Pittsburgh Press* began its story on the question with the emotive lines, "The state demanded today that the courts tighten up on the freedom allowed Communists in this country while Americans are dying in Korea in a war brought on by the reds."[130] The state's position seems incomprehensible in the disproportion between the likely threat posed by the woman, the ludicrously nicknamed "Red Queen," and the ferocity of the response. This not untypical statement can only be understood in the context of war measures, and the thorough identification that now prevailed in the public mind between Communist sympathies and likely involvement in espionage or treachery. One would not have allowed a known agent of Nazi Germany to operate at large on American soil in 1942, still less to do so on public assistance, and the analogy seemed to apply to Communists a decade later. The identification between Communists and saboteurs was uniquely perilous in an industrial heartland like Pittsburgh, which seemed so vulnerable to the clandestine work of spies and saboteurs. This concern goes far toward explaining why heavy industry and organized labor should have been so central to the anti-Communist movement of the Truman years, and why conflict should have reached its peak in the uniquely dangerous circumstances of 1949–50.

SAVING LABOR

I don't see how we can have a successful revolution in this country
without getting control of the basic industries.
—Attributed to James Dolsen, 1948[1]

Marxist ideology placed a premium on the organization of the industrial
working class, and in the triumphant years of the 1930s, Communists shared in
the advances won through labor militancy. However, their successes in targeting workers in key industries like steel, energy, transportation, communications, and electrical power inspired alarm. With war threatening between the
United States and the Soviet Union, this very strength seemed to indicate that
Moscow-trained agitators were focusing on those economic sectors so crucial
to military preparedness. In 1950 the HUAC was inquiring how far the Party "has
infiltrated the basic industries of our country," declaring that "Pittsburgh is a
nerve center of our industrial production area."[2] A few years later, an informant
was asked if the Party has "any designs upon heavy industry in the United
States in the event of armed conflict between the United States and the Soviet
Union?"[3] As the state's civil defense magazine warned, "The Communists are
concentrated in our most vital positions—steel installations; transportation
centers like Chicago, Philadelphia and St. Louis; and key centers of aviation and
motors. Let us not get the idea that this is accidental. The Party has poured
large sums of money and organizers only into the area of greatest strategic
value."[4] Why else would Communists seek to organize industrial workers? One
person's "solid industrial base" was another's "economic infiltration." The link
with subversion and espionage was aggravated by the familiar Party termi-

nology, in which a group of members was a club or branch in the general community, but a cell in an industrial facility. Even if the CPUSA had been an entirely American movement with no foreign ties whatever, it would have excited intense suspicion by its very nature. Of course, the Party was not an autonomous entity; it was, proudly, one facet of a global revolutionary movement.

During the New Deal years, Communist labor leaders were insulated from Red-baiting as long as fellow unionists tended to view an attack on the Left as a move against organized labor itself. Later, however, the different environment of the Truman era posed a critical challenge to the Left in the labor movement, as Communists were increasingly isolated from the mainstream and were denounced by labor leaders of impeccable radical credentials, especially from militant groups like the steelworkers. In industrial Pennsylvania the labor movement became the most active front of the Red Scare, and the main leaders of the anti-Communist offensive tended to be Democrats who depended on labor for their political survival.

The Communist presence in the labor movement was not imagined. Communists neither initiated nor guided the labor movement of the 1930s, but many of the emerging unions were grateful for the dedicated work of Communist officials, and other workers were prepared to disregard their Party affiliations. Communists gained a foothold in various unions far beyond what their raw numbers would suggest, and they did so by dint of hard work, long hours, and careful caucus organization. Often a core of key supporters in a given local was able to sway its policies, without the necessity to win over a majority of the membership, and a Left presence in a group of locals could mean developing a voice in union activities at the city or regional level.

Communist activity throughout Pennsylvania was impressively diverse. In the Philadelphia area the Left had solid representation in unions like UE, especially in Local 155, and locals at General Electric and RCA; its Westinghouse Local 107 had a particularly radical tradition that dated back to the days of the Industrial Workers of the World (IWW).[5] Communist activity was also marked in the Food, Tobacco and Agricultural Workers Union in neighboring Camden; the Transport Workers Union; the State, County and Municipal Workers Union (later the United Public Workers); and the Philadelphia Teachers' Union. There was a Communist presence in the wartime shipyards at Chester and Camden and on the Philadelphia docks. However, as Communists met strong opposition in other important unions, the Party never dominated Philadelphia's CIO council.[6] Anti-Communist labor leaders were at the core of the ADA, which played so critical a role in the Democratic Party of the late 1940s.

Communists were equally well represented in the major industries of the Pittsburgh region, which was so crucial to the American economy. Hymen Schlesinger was quoted as declaring, "I don't see how we can wage a successful revolution unless we build the party in Pittsburgh. It stands to reason that we must get control of the basic industries and the industrial workers before we can even think of a revolution"; moreover, "if we can move Pittsburgh an inch, we can move the country a mile."[7] The source for each remark was Matt Cvetic, but the sentiments are not implausible, even if nuances have been mangled in the process of reporting. Communist strength in the 1920s and early 1930s "was in the soft-coal towns surrounding the city, and among the electrical workers of the East Pittsburgh, Turtle Creek, and Swissvale Westinghouse plants in the Monongahela Valley."[8] In 1948 Steve Nelson found that "progressive ideas still retained currency in the United Electrical Workers, the Hotel and Restaurant local, some steelworkers locals, and a few mine locals," as well as in some ethnic fraternal organizations. This gave the Party a foothold in "the working class ethnic communities of Homestead, Duquesne, Etna, Braddock and New Kensington."[9] The presence in the coalfields was moribund, however. Communist strength in the mines had been declining steadily since the great strike of 1927–28, and the strongly unionized mineworkers were generally hostile to the Communist Party. Cvetic recalled serious difficulties when he and Elizabeth Gurley Flynn attempted to address a miners' audience: "I had to run for my life. . . . It isn't safe to make a Communist speech to the coalminers." What Left strength remained in the coalfields "centered in Washington county, Allegheny Valley, and around the Johnstown area."[10]

The steel industry was a tempting yet dangerous target, a critical sector of the economy that had been a hotbed of militancy in the previous decade. Also, while older Pennsylvania industries like coal, textiles, and railroads were all in semipermanent crisis by the late 1940s, steel was booming, and Pennsylvania seemed likely to retain its role of world leadership for the foreseeable future. At the same time, any Communist successes here could not fail to provoke the wrath of the powerful steelworkers' union, the United Steelworkers of America (USWA). The Party made an explicit national decision in 1945 to develop a "steel concentration," and from that year Communists focused their efforts on key western Pennsylvania facilities: the U.S. Steel plants at Homestead, Braddock,

Duquesne, and McKeesport; Crucible Steel at Lawrenceville; and the Jones and Laughlin plants in Pittsburgh's South Side and Hazelwood.[11] These were the years of the Party's steel industry-oriented newspaper, *The High Carbon Truth*. Still, progress in recruitment was slow, given the deteriorating political situation and the solid anti-Communist line of the USWA under President Philip Murray. Left radicals were on the defensive in much of the region, and "in only a few locals were Communists, by dint of their ties with the rank and file, able to withstand the tide."[12] In August 1948 the Party undertook an urgent reorganization. Steve Nelson was dispatched to Pittsburgh as district organizer, with Andy Onda as steel organizer; Onda, a Pittsburgh native, had a long record of activism in the CIO drive to organize the steelworkers in the 1930s.[13]

Communist activity elsewhere in the state was concentrated on a range of industries similar to those in the two major cities. FBI infiltrator Herman Thomas described the important role of steelworkers in the Bethlehem City Club, which during the 1946 strike spun off a separate Bethlehem Steel Club. In these years the Communist Party's steel commission targeted workers at several Bethlehem steel plants, and national steel conventions were held periodically. While undercover as a supposedly dedicated Communist official, Thomas had been involved with clubs representing members of other unions, including the Fur and Leather Workers and, of course, UE; Easton alone had three Communist clubs, namely, the Easton City club, the Fur club and the UE club. Thomas also served on the CIO's Industrial Union Council for Northampton County.[14]

Left-wing union strength was pivotal to the 1948 Progressive Party campaign in Pennsylvania, and the roster of Wallace support provides a good sense of Left activism in these years. UE president Albert Fitzgerald served as cochairman of the Wallace for President Committee, while the core group of Wallace supporters in western Pennsylvania included Thomas Fitzpatrick of UE and Alexander Wright, business manager of the United Stone and Allied Products Workers, CIO.[15] Other UE figures included Stanley Loney, president of District 6; Thomas Delaney; and radio scriptwriter Charles M. Kerns, who later broadcast for the program *Voice of the UE*. During the 1948 campaign Wallace drew his friendliest audiences at UE venues, as when an appearance at the huge East Pittsburgh Westinghouse plant drew 5,000 supporters.[16] Other CIO supporters included a leader of the Food, Tobacco and Agricultural Workers in Philadelphia, as well as the Williamsport district representative for the Fur and Leather Workers.[17] Wallace was endorsed by representatives of the CIO Rubber Workers and Paperhangers and the AFL Store Employees, as well as Montgomery County's Industrial Union Council.[18] From Erie County alone, we find the presidents of the Industrial Union Council and the CIO-PAC, as well as a representative of the CIO Rubber Workers. Though not all of these groups were Communist in color, the progressive Left had a solid industrial base distributed across the state.

Communist activism in the labor movement stirred opposition, not least from established union leaders themselves. The older craft unions had a solid anti-Communist tradition, and in 1939 Herman Thomas was warned that his association with Communists would cost him not only his position as secretary-treasurer of his Brewery Workers local, but also his union card.[19] CIO unions also became increasingly hostile to Communists, partly out of fear of losing control to the far Left and partly from genuine concerns for the future of democracy; indeed, the sharpest conflicts between Left and Right were fought out within the CIO itself.[20] Anti-Communist activism was intensified by organized labor's strong Catholic element, which found a militant voice in 1937 with the new Association of Catholic Trade Unionists (ACTU), led by Father Charles Owen Rice.[21]

UE itself provided the setting for Pennsylvania's longest and bitterest battle for control of the labor movement. By the 1940s the union was a remarkable success story, in an industry that had grown rapidly over the previous two decades. Electrical manufacturing was the fastest growing industry in America in the 1920s, with employment doubling between 1921 and 1929.[22] Union organization grew dramatically from 1933, and throughout, Pennsylvania was a critical base for the new union. A strike at Philadelphia's Philco plant in 1933 gave UE its first major triumph and also gave prominence to a generation of leaders who would long dominate the organization. Also in the Philadelphia region, the union developed important bases in the Westinghouse plants at Lester and Essington. In the western parts of the state, the union's District 6, UE had key locals at New Kensington, Sharon, Erie, and at several plants in the Pittsburgh area. The crown jewel was Local 601 at the Westinghouse facility at East Pittsburgh; by 1944 the membership in plants represented by this local stood at 22,000, and it was UE's largest single local. By 1948 the 400 locals of UE nationwide had bargaining rights at plants employing 600,000 workers, and it was the third largest union in the CIO, one of the trinity that also included the steelworkers and autoworkers.[23]

Politically, too, the union enjoyed real power, which naturally enough was concentrated in the Democratic Party. In the Pittsburgh area alone, it counted among its close friends Pittsburgh mayor Cornelius Scully and U.S. congressmen Eberharter and Buchanan, as well as U.S. senators Guffey and Myers, and we have seen how local Democratic congressmen weathered the political storm that claimed so many of their colleagues in 1946.[24] Besides the direct influence of union leaders and officials, the UE Left disseminated its opinions in the greater Pittsburgh area through newspapers and leaflets and through nightly commentary on McKeesport radio station WMCK. In a typical week in the late 1940s, program titles included "An Answer to the Red-baiters," "The National Attack on Civil Liberties," and "The Fight against the Mundt Bill."[25]

The leftist presence in the union was controversial from the late 1930s, and there certainly were overt Communists in both the local and national apparatus: David Davis, for example, business agent for Philadelphia's Local 155, served on the national committee of the Communist Party. The existence of other clandestine Communists was hotly debated, but suspicions centered on two of UE's national leaders, Julius Emspak and James Matles. Steve Nelson considered UE "as progressive a union as existed."[26] Left-Right battles recurred in UE's national leadership from 1940 onward, and an unsuccessful attempt to purge Communist officers resulted in the fall of one union president and his replacement by Albert Fitzgerald, who was more sympathetic to the Left.[27] During the Second World War, charges of Communist sympathies in Local 601 focused on the Fitzpatrick brothers, Thomas and Michael, but by 1945 the brothers were fighting against each other for the local's presidency, with Mike alleging that he was facing an orchestrated Communist campaign. Tom went on to head District 6, while Mike allied with Father Rice and the Right.[28] Whatever the truth of specific accusations, UE's policies did tend to reflect Communist thinking at several critical points: after the Nazi-Soviet pact of 1939, the union moved suddenly from its earlier anti-Fascist militancy to a new policy favoring American isolationism, while Hitler's invasion of the USSR converted UE into a fervent advocate of total war.[29] UE leaders now "became superpatriots and would order people to work under any and all conditions and speed-ups."[30]

The isolationist period from 1939 through 1941 was damaging for the Left in UE, as in other unions. From 1940 various CIO locals tried to establish rules barring from union office anyone holding totalitarian views, a formula that in practice was aimed strictly at the Left. UE was tainted by the forged nomination papers scandal that hit western Pennsylvania Communists so hard in 1940;

coupled with the isolationist movement, it cost the progressive slate the Local 601 elections at Westinghouse in 1941.[31] In a polemic that would later become familiar, anti-Red campaigners now claimed that excluding Communists was imperative as "this country of America is seriously menaced by the operation of international dictatorships . . . [and] the Westinghouse company has been placed on the list of firms doing essential work for the national defense."[32] The ACTU made UE a primary target in its assault on Red influences among the working class, and a vigorous religious agenda now entered the debates: during union controversies in Pittsburgh, local Catholic clergy painted the UE Left as puppets of Moscow, allies of "Communists who shot down the priests and sisters in Spain." John McDowell's columns in the *Wilkinsburg Gazette* blamed Steve Nelson personally for the mass murder of Spanish priests.[33]

One key leader for the UE Right was Harry A. Sherman, who would later manage Matt Cvetic, and whose recruitment into the anti-Communist cause can be dated precisely to the struggles of 1940. Sherman was active through the later 1930s in fighting labor racketeers, and in later testimony before Senate investigators, he provided a startlingly frank recollection of the origins of what became an obsession: "We had some very serious fights that were not all legal. We had met up with the goon squads and the terrorists and the bomb squads and so forth, and we were trying to clean out some of those racketeer leaders in organized labor and had to do a little extra-legal work to do it sometimes, including setting up our own strongarm squads. So in the Pittsburgh area I was perhaps the spearhead of the group in labor that was attempting to get rid of the hangover or holdover thugs who were in charge of many of the leading unions."[34] Sherman cooperated with the local AFL leadership in resisting mob attempts to take over the city's Central Labor Union. Already possessing a tough reputation, he became involved with UE affairs in the fall of 1940, following discussions with Philip Murray, Allan Haywood, and other local CIO leaders. This time, Sherman's enemies were Communists rather than racketeers, and he led the struggle against the Left in UE Local 615, in the courts as well as the meeting halls.[35] His enemies attempted to expel him as a troublemaker after he publicly asserted that the leaders of the union's District 6 were engaged in treasonable and subversive activities. Communists brought in one of their ablest propagandists, Allan McNeil, who had handled public relations for the Abraham Lincoln Brigade, and a pamphlet war ensued. Sherman was incensed at what he saw as Communist anti-Semitism and the cynical manipulation of Jewish problems; he denounced the leftist Kultur Farband as "the headquarters for people who would privately be very anti-semitic themselves.

They are not or never were any members of the faith or interested in the faith except to use them to project the racial prejudice line."[36]

At every stage of his tempestuous career, there are indications of Sherman's close ties with powerful allies, above all with the FBI, and with like-minded friends in labor and business (though he consistently exaggerated his own importance). When faced with expulsion from UE, he noted, "I devised the means, with the help of the local FBI office, of becoming a business agent to be employed in the local, so I could hold a card and get into participation in their meetings."[37] About 1941, he recalled, "I was working in close collaboration with the FBI office in Pittsburgh, and they were very much concerned about the infiltration of communism into the trade union movement. I was projected into it in a labor fight with the international in behalf of a local [615] and our interests were concurrent, and from that moment on we compared notes and I gave them reports on a number of agents."[38] This permitted him to become a delegate to UE's District 6, as well as to the CIO council. "I tried to build up an anti-communist slate, working with a couple of FBI agents for the purpose of testing the strength of the Communist organization in the CIO council, which is known as the Steel City Industrial Union Council at that time, '41–'42."[39] The FBI also tried to inform Westinghouse directly about Communist infiltration into its facilities, but Sherman alleged that the advice was rejected, presumably because Communists were themselves doing such an outstanding job of suppressing labor unrest in the war years. Sherman had now formed the close association with city and federal law enforcement agencies that would stand him in excellent stead in coming conflicts; his boast that he had "worked with Lieutenant Baker in setting up the arrests" of the leftist protesters at the Highland Park swimming pool in 1948 suggests that he was acting as a private Red squad.[40] Sherman's charges about FBI involvement in UE matters are confirmed from other sources: Father Rice also worked closely with the FBI, and in 1946 the Bureau acquired yet another informant in Mary S. Beynon, a UE activist at Westinghouse's East Pittsburgh plant.[41]

Conflict in Pittsburgh's UE locals resumed with renewed intensity as the war ended. The year 1946 marked a vital turning point in the history of American labor, with a national strike wave that affected railroads, mines, steelworks, and power plants, as well as many ancillary industries; in Pennsylvania, labor militancy actually surpassed the levels of 1937. "By February 1, over a quarter of the CIO's entire membership was on strike." Throughout, radicals were blamed for inciting the conflict, but very little evidence favored such an interpretation, and some of the most actively anti-Communist unions were in the vanguard of activism. The year opened with a crippling steel strike, and in the spring the bituminous coalfields began a stoppage that lasted through December. May brought a rail strike that threatened to devastate the national economy, but it was suppressed by urgent federal action. Pittsburgh's power company, Duquesne Power and Light, was shut down by a strike that September. When the union president was jailed for refusing to obey a court injunction, the city was virtually shut down by demonstrations and wildcat strikes that affected some 25,000 workers.[42] Though industrial Pittsburgh was the most severely affected center, most areas of the state suffered some labor disruption at this time; in February, for example, most public transportation in Lancaster County was shut down in a dispute that severely damaged the region's economy.[43]

The electrical manufacturing industry found itself on the industrial battle-front, as UE struck the major companies: Westinghouse, General Electric, and the electrical division of General Motors. The conflict lasted from January through May, with Westinghouse the longest holdout, but UE won a significant victory there: 65,000 workers were involved at Westinghouse, with 18,000 at the East Pittsburgh plant alone.[44] In Philadelphia, 10,000 demonstrators fought police at City Hall during a protest against legal attempts to prevent mass pick-eting. Though the strike involved little violence in Pittsburgh, there were tense scenes at the picket lines, where the speeches of union leaders to mass meetings were recorded by state police, presumably secretly, and were subsequently read over in search of remarks that could be regarded as subversive or as inciting violence; known leftists were identified, appropriately enough, in red-pencil underlining.[45] Most of this editorial work and commentary was done by Raymond D. Evans, who later joined Sherman as an incorporator of ABC.

Conservatives saw the UE conflict as a leftist plot designed to cripple American industry, and in April HUAC's chief counsel charged that it was specifically targeted at atomic bomb production.[46] Praising the work of law enforcement agencies and the State Police in opening picket lines, Father James Cox declared in a radio broadcast that "if it had not been for the prompt action of sheriff Walter Monaghan of Allegheny county who called upon our great governor Edward A. Martin for the protection of East Pittsburgh from the machinations of Communists, we might have had the first important step in bringing the Russian system into the USA. The good people not only of Allegheny county but of all the state and the nation are with Sheriff Monaghan and Governor

Martin! Russia will never take over this arsenal of democracy we call Pittsburgh."[47]

The conclusion of the 1946 strikes left UE a prime political target for the Republican Right. Encountering UE protesters at Erie during his 1946 senatorial campaign, Edward Martin pledged support for anti-Communist elements within the CIO, "to aid them in purging and removing the PAC element which is trying to overthrow our country."[48] The following year, Governor Duff suggested that the union's criticisms of Truman's foreign policy could only be inspired by Communist subversion.[49] Another Republican enemy in these years was HUAC's John McDowell, who blamed the union for having defeated him in 1940. He waged a lengthy war against union leaders in his newspaper, the *Wilkinsburg Gazette*, and characteristically described Tom Fitzpatrick as that "blythsome breathe of Muscovy, acting as current Commissar of the comrades who hold Local 601 in bondage."[50] McDowell's defeat in 1948, which owed much to UE activism, removed one of the union's harshest critics.

More immediately threatening was pressure from within the labor movement itself, both in UE and in the larger CIO, where anti-Communist UE leader Harry Block was a powerful force (Block would also be a key figure in the emerging ADA). In the steel industry, leftist organizers were combated by the loyally Catholic Philip Murray, who became steadily more involved in the anti-Communist campaign from this point. In September 1946 Murray spoke out against Communist meddling in the affairs of the CIO, and the organization's national convention that November adopted a resolution to "resent and reject" Communist interference.[51] Some months later, Murray requested CIO unions to remain neutral in the emerging schism between the ADA and the leftist PCA, but he soon abandoned this stance and allied wholeheartedly with the Right. In 1947 Pennsylvania's CIO Industrial Union state convention in Harrisburg debated a resolution excluding Communists, Nazis, or Ku Klux Klansmen from office in the state CIO council.[52] The motion's main supporter was Harry Block, in alliance with steelworkers' leaders; it was fought by the Left caucus, led by Tom Fitzpatrick and Dave Davis, with the support of the Furniture Workers and the Fur and Leather Union, but it was eventually carried. By this stage, UE was in bitter opposition to the more conservative forces in the CIO, led by Philip Murray and Walter Reuther, and a few disaffected UE locals, in Philadelphia and elsewhere, now defected to the Auto Workers.

The irritation felt by Murray and other CIO leaders was intensified by the Wallace Progressive campaign, in which leftist union leaders took so prominent a role.[53] Murray had resolutely opposed the Wallace third-party movement since its origins in 1946, and in early 1948 he warned that CIO officials who supported Wallace should forfeit their positions, a partisan action that even earned the condemnation of the *Pittsburgh Press*.[54] Pennsylvania's CIO-PAC protested any suggestion that the organization as a whole was endorsing Wallace. The USWA was equally irate at the suggestion that the few workers who had come out for Wallace represented the whole organization, and it rejected suggestions by "Wallace commissars" that American workers would be the "political stepchildren" of a foreign power.[55] The USWA leadership now became a bastion of anti-Communist politics; one of the harshest critics of Left influence was William J. Hart, director of Steelworkers District 19, who introduced the motion barring Left or progressive groups from using school premises in the Pittsburgh area.[56] Hart was also president of the Pennsylvania chapter of the ACTU.

Pressure on the UE Left intensified during 1946.[57] For several years, Father Rice had been the moving force in an anti-Communist "rank and file" group within the Pittsburgh locals, but now this coalesced into a new right-wing dissident organization, the UE Members for Democratic Action. Financially aided by the steelworkers, the group was also supported by Harry Block, now the state CIO leader. Over the next three years, the dissidents struggled to take control of the union.[58] Recognizing the significance of the struggle, the Communists redoubled their efforts; after his arrival in western Pennsylvania in 1948, Steve Nelson decided to enhance the Party presence in UE, notably at Westinghouse's East Pittsburgh plant.[59] This was a daunting challenge, as Nelson knew: in the Pittsburgh area, "Westinghouse was no more to be trifled with than was US Steel."[60]

The right-wing offensive was aided by the wave of congressional hearings that now publicized charges of leftist infiltration in organized labor. HUAC had been interested in conditions in the Pittsburgh area at least since 1946, when it invited Mayor Lawrence to testify concerning Communist influence in the power strike, but scrutiny intensified during 1949.[61] This new focus reflected Tad Walter's membership in HUAC, as Walter was a good friend of Father Rice, and both men recognized the publicity potential of an investigation. Members of the rightist UE faction found a sympathetic audience in Washington when they came to petition for special HUAC hearings, which finally took place in Pittsburgh itself in August 1949 and did much to tilt the balance against the Left in UE elections scheduled a few days afterward.[62] These hearings led to criminal charges, as Congress voted Fitzpatrick, Emspak, Matles, and others in contempt. The men were convicted in federal court in early 1951, and Matles was eventually stripped of his U.S. citizenship, though the decision was reversed on appeal.[63]

Throughout, the media showed their commitment to the anti-Left cause, particularly the *Pittsburgh Press*, which acted as a house organ for the ACTU. In 1948 a *Press* story headlined "UE Men Here Met with Reds, Trial Told" reported the claim of a former infiltrator into the local Communist Party; the story was timed to have its impact shortly before the November elections, in which UE-linked Progressives hoped to win labor votes.[64] In response, the Left argued that it was in fact the rightist groups who were agents of an international conspiracy, namely, the Roman Catholic Church, and that the ACTU was "undemocratic and authoritarian in the last degree."[65] In this view, rightist UE leader James B. Carey was as much a puppet or front man on his side as the alleged leftists were said to be on theirs: Carey was a Catholic and a close friend of Father Rice and USWA official David McDonald.[66] Harry Block went further, asserting that Carey was "on the payroll" of Murray and the CIO.[67] If challenged with supporting a one-man dictatorship in the USSR, Communists retorted that though Stalin's regime never faced electoral challenges, neither did Philip Murray's within the CIO or the steelworkers union: in his own way, each man had his cult of personality.[68]

By 1949 the Left-Right conflict within UE was degenerating into actual physical battles. The most notorious incident occurred in April, when a Communist-sponsored meeting at Pittsburgh's North Side Carnegie Music Hall was to be addressed by New York Smith Act defendant Henry Winston.[69] Two hundred anti-Communist pickets appeared at the head of a crowd estimated at some 5,000, and over half the pickets were drawn from the now Right-dominated Westinghouse Local 601. The strongly Catholic tone of the protest was indicated by the presence of Father Rice, while Catholic War Veterans mobilized under banners proclaiming "Uncle Sam's Vets Against Stalin's Stooges." The protest turned into a melee in which leftists were attacked; cab drivers refused to carry them from the scene, and police did little to protect the Communists.[70] In one telling incident, right-wing activist Mike Fitzpatrick pointed out his leftist brother Tom to the anti-Red protesters. The UE conflict was a major factor in the inability of Communist or progressive groups to meet in public, and shortly afterward, fears of mob violence caused the early termination of a regional conference of the IWO in downtown Pittsburgh.[71]

Veterans organizations continued to be involved in the internecine strife. In August 1949 the issue of Communist penetration in UE was raised at the state convention of the American Legion when a leader of the Disabled American

Veterans remarked on the recent appearance of the Local 601 Left before HUAC. He declared that "the Westinghouse Corporation is one of the most powerful war-making industries in the country and yet these four communists themselves alone would be able to cripple that electrical industry which has much to do with the making of the atomic bomb. . . . If we who have fathers and brothers and sisters in Westinghouse, we veterans, would see that those men and women would attend the meetings, all those Communists would be thrown out of office overnight and they would never return. . . . [I]f we veterans and veterans organizations become active we can do more than all the Dies Committee and the House Un-American Activities Committees combined."[72]

National events now intervened. The new Taft-Hartley Act demanded that all union officeholders must swear that they were not members of the Communist Party and must disavow "any organization that believes in or teaches the overthrow of the United States Government by force or by any illegal or unconstitutional methods." Union leaders considered noncompliance with the political test, but by 1949 the CIO leadership accepted the process, and the confrontation with the left-wing unions could no longer be delayed. In September 1949 UE held a decisive convention at which Emspak, Matles, and Fitzgerald won election to the highest offices, systematically defeating candidates supported by the UE Members for Democratic Action. These results showed that the union could not be "reclaimed" from within, and that November the CIO federation began a purge of UE and other leftist unions. UE and the Farm Equipment and Metal Workers were both expelled in 1949, and the following year the same measures were taken against nine other unions. With the eleven unions together accounting for a fifth of the CIO's total membership, or between 800,000 and one million workers, this action marked "the climax of a self-dismemberment unparalleled in American labor history."[73] By far the most significant victim was UE, but others included the Food, Tobacco and Agricultural Workers Union, the United Public Workers, the American Communications Association, the International Fur and Leather Workers Union, and the United Office and Professional Workers. Murray dismissed them all as "pinks, punks and parasites."[74]

The split set the stage for a furious battle for control of the electrical workers' locals, in which UE had to compete for bargaining rights with the new anti-Communist International Union of Electrical Workers (IUE), which had the powerful support of "the CIO, the government, the Catholic church, the electrical corporations, and the media."[75] Through the first half of 1950, a series of ballots in the electrical plants attracted public attention and involvement with an intensity rarely found even in normal political elections, and the Pittsburgh region was particularly affected, with the crucial Westinghouse locals due to vote in April. IUE fought entirely on the Communist issue, often portraying the "UE" initials as a hammer-and-sickle logo. The implication was that electrical corporations would lose future defense contracts if the government could not trust the loyalty of the unions in the plants, so that employment would be lost. Typical IUE leaflets bore titles like *Ten Long Years of Communist Rule* and *The Communist Party Thanks You for Your UE Dues.*[76] The Communist Party was stigmatized for its cynical role after the Nazi-Soviet pact, when UE leaders were producing antiwar propaganda. In addition, the Catholic Church made little secret of its central leadership role in organizing the anti-UE vote, as parish priests read ACTU statements from pulpits and got out the vote through letters and house calls.[77]

UE was not to be defeated by simple Red-baiting, and the union fought back with what was in many ways a repetition of the Progressive electoral campaign of 1948, emphasizing what the organization had done for black workers and women.[78] A populist counterattack on IUE stressed that union's Catholic backing; UE was fighting for religious freedom and against theocracy, a view that ensured Masonic support for the old union. The image of Catholic domination was made more plausible by some IUE propaganda cartoons depicting sinister characters labeled "UE" that looked exactly like stereotypical anti-Semitic portraits of Jews, with hooked noses, beards, and horn-rimmed glasses. In response to the canard about losing defense contracts, UE explained that the plants it organized had far more defense work than, say, the steelworks of Phil Murray's USWA. UE also produced supporting statements from a range of specialized groups that included Catholics and Westinghouse Veterans, all affirming their support for the union. A victory for IUE was presented as a return to company unionism, backed by "CIO big shots" like Phil Murray and Bill Hart. Sensing a tight battle, local Democratic congressmen remained strictly neutral in the fray, realizing that backing the wrong side could lead to electoral ruin that fall.[79]

The IUE won at East Pittsburgh, but only by a margin of 100 votes out of over 11,000 cast, and a runoff was scheduled for early June. The intervening weeks were politically torrid, with all the electoral dirty tricks that characterized the machine politics of the era. At the East Pittsburgh works, for example, "through the Democratic machine, Philip Murray arranged to get hold of the main gates in Westinghouse for gate meetings today and Wednesday. The UE was refused permits and the CIO was given permits for all the days at the main gates. . . . Philip Murray arranged for the National Guard in full uniform with rifles and bayonets, followed by armored cars mounted with machine guns, to parade through East Pittsburgh to a noon gate rally where Judge Musmanno, dressed in Navy uniform, spoke for the IUE and against the UE."[80] Musmanno's speech on this occasion was appropriately purple, denouncing UE leaders as "traitors who would dance on the graves of the sainted martyrs who we honor on Memorial Day." If not actual Communists, they were part of that army of "hypocrites and moral swindlers who can be classed as fellow-travellers."[81] The state commander of the VFW wrote to every veteran in western Pennsylvania denouncing UE as Communistic: "Giving the Commies control of your union means the beginning of the end of our nation and all you fought to retain for your loved ones."[82]

The crucial need to discredit the Left may have contributed to ABC's decision to "surface" Matt Cvetic that February, as well as to new HUAC hearings into UE during the same month.[83] The political context helped shape Cvetic's testimony, in that it was important to show that the relatively small number of known Communists could in fact have established such critical influence in a mass organization like UE. To this end, Cvetic often claimed remarkable successes by Party infiltrators: for example, "with eight party members, the Party was able to take over a union of 2800 members at Crucible Steel in Pittsburgh. . . . We were able to elect the president, the secretary, and several stewards in the shop, party members . . . all in about two years."[84] Cvetic had a great deal to say about conditions within UE, which was reported at length by the *Pittsburgh Press*. Among the UE-connected leftists he named were Charles Kerns, who was now dismissed by the McKeesport radio station, and Alice Roth, whom Judge Musmanno excluded from the grand jury.[85] Cvetic was made an honorary member of IUE by James Carey and was summoned to address a mass meeting of Westinghouse workers, at which he appeared with local CIO leaders.[86] IUE stewards at Westinghouse were all issued copies of Cvetic's testimony for the information of any worker who asked to read it, and the testimony was read over station WMCK.

Cvetic's revelations damaged left-wing groups in other unions, including the USWA, where the leadership was only too pleased to have the opportunity to remove leftists from senior positions in locals.[87] Even more sweeping was the effect on the Hotel and Restaurant Employees Union (AFL). Communists had long enjoyed support in this union; in Pittsburgh the AFL's Central Labor Union had tried in 1940 to purge the Left leadership, but it was promptly restored by a vote of the membership.[88] Over the next decade, conflict focused on Local 237, in which the Left faction was led by Nick Lazari and George Nichols, both of whom were named by Cvetic.[89] It has been suggested that Cvetic's interest in the hotel and restaurant union reflected a payment of personal debts, in that through much of the 1940s, he was living rent-free in the William Penn Hotel, ostensibly in a gesture of patriotic support by the management; on the other hand, local Communists asserted that he was serving the interests of the hotel employees by spying on their unions.[90] Whatever the reason, Cvetic's appearance contributed mightily to right-wing attempts to purge their enemies, as Local 237 was embroiled in its own election fight in March 1950, in which the anti-Communist slate won a resounding victory.[91]

Ultimately, with so much powerful support, the anti-Communist IUE secured victory in several of the most important plants, including East Pittsburgh, but the older UE retained its hold in such important facilities as Lester, Erie, Lancaster, and Sunbury. While Local 601 was lost, UE did hold on to the other major Pittsburgh area local, 610, at plants in Wilmerding and Swissvale. Erie presented a fascinating case, where UE Local 506 was traditionally moderate: it included many Catholic workers of Polish and Italian origin, and local president John Nelson was himself a devout Catholic who could confidently sign the non-Communist affidavits demanded under the Taft-Hartley Act.[92] One might think that this would have been natural ACTU territory, but the history of labor relations here was very different from that in Pittsburgh, and Father Rice was regarded as an outsider, so that Nelson's Local 506 voted to remain within the old union by a 60–40 margin. By the mid-1950s UE retained 20,000 members in western Pennsylvania alone (significant centers included the General Electric plant at Erie, with 8,000 workers, Westinghouse's facility at Sunbury, with 1,100, and Sylvania's at Emporium, with 1,100), while Local 610 in Pittsburgh still had 5,000 members.[93]

Though UE had suffered a critical defeat, it was not eradicated. Over the next few years, UE generally did better than its right-wing rival in preventing the electrical employers from taking advantage of the chaos in the union by cutting incentive rates, and the Left-Right conflict reignited periodically as individual plants either drifted toward UE affiliation or defected to the Right. In one instance that attracted national attention, the Sylvania plant at Emporium originally swung toward the anti-Communist IUE during the 1950 elections, but a few years later dissatisfaction with that union induced the workers to restore bargaining rights to UE, and the propaganda war was bitter. IUE once more warned workers that "the Communist Party would like to use you to help them to political power" and that "the Communist Party has long boasted that 'UE is our union.'" James Matles was named as "one of the most dangerous Communists in the United States," and workers were told that "the only good Communist is a dead one. Let's run the rascals out of your hometown." On the other hand, UE focused successfully on the poor showing of its rival in defending workers' rights at East Pittsburgh. The restoration of the UE closed shop left anti-Communist protesters in an untenable position, and some now petitioned a sympathetic Senate committee for assistance.[94]

Surviving left-wing strength led to repeated efforts to destroy UE over the next decade. James Carey urged the electrical corporations to dismiss left-wingers, and in 1953 the manufacturers adopted the Cordiner Doctrine of firing employees who either admitted to Communist sympathies or failed to clear themselves of such charges made before congressional committees.[95] As late as 1954, Harry Sherman claimed to know the names of "hundreds" of active Communists in the local unions, information on whom he passed to the FBI.[96] Attempts to purge UE were justified by charges of sabotage and espionage, which were plausible to the extent that many electrical plants held at least some defense contracts, and by 1959 five contractors whose workers were organized with UE had $142 million in defense contracts among them.[97] The Emporium plant was involved in radar and ballistic missile early-warning systems, and UE's victory here was examined in a Senate document purporting to investigate the scope of Soviet activity in the United States. Pittsburgh firms with UE employees were making "secret sonar, radar and atomic devices for the Defense Department."[98] In 1952 a *Saturday Evening Post* series on Red espionage in industry focused on activities at the Sylvania Company's Mill Hall plant.[99]

Throughout, the federal government intervened forcefully. In 1951 Dave Davis was prosecuted as one of Philadelphia's Smith Act defendants, suggesting to the public that his union position in Local 155 had been a weapon in an ongoing attempt to promote the revolutionary overthrow of the United States.[100] In October 1952 HUAC devoted its attention to UE activities in the Philadelphia area, where Local 155 claimed some 7,000 members; nine of the witnesses summoned refused to testify on grounds of potential self-incrimination. The press publicized claims such as "Party Ran Union," and as so often before, allegations were substantiated by ex-Communist officials, in this case Thomas Delaney and Samuel DiMaria, who now supported IUE.[101]

In 1953 western Pennsylvania received two visits from Senate committees, one in June, from Senator McCarthy's own Permanent Subcommittee on Investigations, and the second in November, from the Senate Internal Security Subcommittee (siss).[102] Almost obligatory by this stage, the McCarthy hearings produced two newly surfaced FBI undercover agents, Joseph and Mary Mazzei. The siss hearings grew out of Senator Butler's proposed law to exclude from defense-related industries anyone suspected on "reasonable grounds" of involvement in espionage, sabotage, or subversion, a controversial measure as the subversive label could be applied on the basis of hearsay or unproven accusation. The subcommittee held three days of hearings in Pittsburgh itself, presenting such familiar witnesses as Matt Cvetic and William H. Harris, "research specialist" for the American Legion's Americanism Committee. The star performers were undoubtedly the Mazzeis and their attorney, Harry Sherman, who appeared as a trio, with Sherman unabashedly prompting his clients at every stage, frequently volunteering information to correct or supplement their testimony. Joseph Mazzei again told his tales of a Communist Party arming for insurrection and terrorism, and he was the principal source for allegations that Communist agents were using UE as a shield for their activities in this crucial region, photographing and mapping industrial sites.[103] This led the Senate committee to conclude that the situation in Pittsburgh represented "a serious potential danger to the security of this nation." The vision of Pittsburgh as a nest of Communist spies supported by a death squad sounds like one of Harry Sherman's darker fantasies, and this may indeed have been the source of the tale.

The siss hearings were as inquisitorial as any of their kind. The committee focused on a number of individuals who were summoned and interrogated and who duly took the Fifth Amendment on most issues. At that point, Cvetic and Mazzei would be called to testify that they had seen the witness at a particular Communist meeting or knew of his or her sympathies from some other source, in what was virtually an instant public trial and conviction. By this stage, witnesses before congressional committees had few remaining legal protections and so had little alternative but to remain silent in the face of accusation. This treatment was meted out to several familiar names from UE's recent conflicts, including Tom Fitzpatrick, Thomas Quinn, Allan McNeil, Mike Vuletich, Frank Panzino, Stanley Loney, and Harold Briney.[104] Further eroding the pretense that these inquiries were an investigation rather than a kangaroo court, Loney's counsel was served with a surprise subpoena when he refused to answer questions about his own politics.[105] In 1954 Fitzpatrick, Panzino, and two others were dismissed from the East Pittsburgh works.[106]

Erie was a special focus of concern in the SISS hearings, as the most important UE bastion in western Pennsylvania.[107] Since 1950 the *Erie Times* had investigated Red activity in local unions, with the assistance of the local American Legion and (presumably) the FBI.[108] As a result, charges of Communist sympathies or associations were made against several UE officials, including steward Alex Staber and the editor of Local 506's *Union News*. The major target was local president John Nelson, which was odd in view of his devout Catholic beliefs, though neither Mazzei nor Cvetic doubted his Communist allegiance. Nelson was subjected to a vicious interrogation by SISS's chief counsel, who called him a saboteur and a clandestine Communist. In one memorable dialogue, Nelson's resort to the Fifth Amendment was followed by the question, "Now, as a hard-core Communist, what do you think of the Butler Bill?" Nelson became the first person fired under the Cordiner Doctrine, and despite overwhelming support from union members, the constant pressure of criticism and investigation contributed to his early death in 1959.

The familiar cycle of investigations, subpoenas, infiltrators, and resorting to the Fifth Amendment continued throughout the 1950s. In 1955 Mary S. Beynon "surfaced" in order to tell her stories of Red activity at Westinghouse and to identify remaining Communist sympathizers, while Attorney General Herbert Brownell formally identified UE as a subversive-influenced organization.[109] In 1957 SISS was again examining "Soviet activity" in the Pennsylvania labor movement, this time with the excuse that technicians in Philadelphia's five radio stations were organized through the American Communications Association, and "in this day and age, when the Soviet threat to the free world is as great as it is, we feel that present-day American Communists should not be astride our vital communication lines."[110]

The last major congressional investigations occurred in 1959, when SISS investigated Communist activities at UE's Lester local, while Walter's HUAC returned to investigate "Problems of Security in Industrial Establishments" in Pittsburgh.[111] Walter's visit gave the newspapers another opportunity to proclaim that "Reds Control UE Here, Probe Told," and again, these charges were dramatized by the appearance of newly revealed FBI infiltrators.[112] This time the defectors were Harv and Mary Golden, who had been undercover since 1946, and the papers printed the now-standard accounts of "My Secret Life in the FBI."[113] But the charges had become stale and attracted little public attention compared to the earlier bombshells of Cvetic and Mazzei, while not even the most alarmist warnings could make UE seem anything like the serious menace it had been portrayed as a decade previously. If not broken, it was at least marginalized. Moreover, leftist witnesses were now able to speak more forthrightly in their own behalf, armed with newly acquired legal protections. The star of the 1959 hearings was Thomas Quinn, a long-standing target of anti-Communist labor investigators, who declared memorably that "I'm not contemptuous of Congress, only of this committee."[114] Significantly, the press was at last prepared to criticize HUAC's treatment of witnesses, so that the *Pittsburgh Post-Gazette*, never a friend of the Left, noted that "in at least one line of questioning [the committee] grossly overstepped the bounds of justice and fair play."[115] With the labor Left effectively beaten, it was doubtful if the political benefits of future investigations would outweigh the costs.

Defense concerns ostensibly justified the constant official vigilance over leftist penetration into industry, even when the linkage to military matters was tenuous indeed. In other areas the justification for purging a profession was presented in subtler ideological terms, with the suggestion that Communists were planning to subvert the nation through the respected institutions that formed public opinion. Both the legal profession and the clergy would be attacked for their "pink" members, but, as we shall see in Chapter 6, by far the sharpest such attack fell upon the educators, so that between 1952 and 1954, the teachers and college professors of Pennsylvania experienced McCarthyism at its purest and most vindictive.

TEACHING AMERICANISM

THE PURGE OF THE TEACHING PROFESSION

It takes only one bad teacher to start an Alger Hiss or a William
Remington on his way to the betrayal of a nation.
—Elmer Christine, Pennsylvania VFW[1]

It was in the area of education that Pennsylvania experienced the most vigorous purge of the sort familiar from later stereotypes of the "witch-hunt,"
in which careers were destroyed because of a political deviation a decade or
more in the past. Ordinary citizens faced the deadly dilemma that livelihoods
could be salvaged only by turning informer against friends and family. The
experience of teachers and professors before the congressional committees
indicates the difficulties faced by all of those charged with subversive connections. Under the legal provisions operating at the time, witnesses called before
such bodies effectively had to choose between total silence and a humiliating
self-abnegation.

Red influences in the schools and colleges had been a persistent nightmare of
the state's conservatives for a generation. In 1927 the American Legion secured
the dismissal of two professors at West Chester State Normal College, ACLU
members critical of U.S. policies in Nicaragua.[2] In the public schools also, accusations of Communist infiltration led to repeated controversies. In the mid-
1930s rightists claimed that Philadelphia's school system had been infiltrated by

Communists, atheists, and sexual liberals, and the school issue was taken up by patriotic organizations like the American Legion, the Sons of the Revolution, and the Daughters of the American Revolution (DAR). Activists in this controversy went on to form the core of Philadelphia's extreme, anti-Semitic Right, under the leadership of local celebrities like Bessie Burchett. Burchett's 1941 book *Education for Destruction* was a tirade against conspiratorial Communism and one-worldism and the infiltration of these dangerous ideas into schools, unions, and liberal pressure groups.[3] Concern about subversive influences in education became a divisive issue in state politics. In 1937 the Pennsylvania Federation of Teachers largely drafted a new teacher tenure law, which was intended to prevent arbitrary dismissal for partisan reasons, but the legislation came to be seen as a defense against removal for espousing radical views. As reshaped under the conservative governor Arthur James (1939–43), the law provided a probationary period for new teachers and allowed dismissal for conduct that "flagrantly violates the moral standards of the community," a phrase that some districts took to include radical politics.[4]

Once again, activities by patriotic groups like the American Legion and the DAR foreshadowed the debates of the McCarthy years. In 1940 a legion demonstration in Philadelphia was told that "while we slept, [Communists] invaded our classrooms until now the college faculties are saturated with those who call themselves liberal."[5] Over the next few years, the legion's annual state conventions regularly went on record against Red influences in the schools and urged that "the positive side of Americanism" be given greater prominence in education. In 1941 a legion-sponsored bill attempted to ban the use of leftist textbooks in state schools. The legion supported loyalty oaths for all teachers and employees of state-funded institutions, and unsuccessful bills to this effect were introduced in 1935 and 1941, with the support of the DAR. In 1944 the Pennsylvania DAR passed a resolution denouncing "false doctrines" in history textbooks. Concern about the Philadelphia schools reached a new intensity in 1941 when that city's teachers' union fell apart over charges of Communist domination. In response, the legion's state convention, meeting at Altoona, urged the creation of "a joint legislative committee for [the] purpose of investigating subversive activities and Communistic teachings and books in our public school system."[6] The Pechan Act of 1951 was thus the culmination of a long process.

Despite the occasionally hysterical tone of attacks from the Right, Communism did indeed have a significant foothold in sections of the profession, and leftist activism in the teaching unions was an open secret from at least the mid-

1930s. Communism had a particular appeal for many of the articulate young people entering the profession during the Depression years, who saw education as a means of promoting social improvement. Paradoxically, some of the most convincing testimony for these impulses comes from the later congressional hearings, which were seeking to show how teachers had gullibly fallen under the sinister influence of foreign agents. It was in this uncongenial context that some teachers were able to describe eloquently their real political motivations. For Principal Benjamin D. Anton, the decisive influences came in the late 1920s: "As an auxiliary principal, I served in some thirty-odd schools throughout the city. Some were new buildings that were overcrowded. . . . Some were old buildings, firetraps, some were buildings that had classrooms with no windows, some that had classrooms in the basement for children, and I was so moved and disturbed by these conditions that I said to myself if I ever have a chance to improve and correct conditions in education in Philadelphia I will do that, and I had that opportunity through work in the Teachers' Union."[7]

The process of radicalization accelerated in the mid-1930s. A new generation of younger teachers would form a significant element in the city's Communist clubs over the next decade, especially in the professional Benjamin Franklin section.[8] One group of a dozen or so met at the home of Sidney and Genevieve Fox, a gathering that included some of the leading activists in union affairs; the cohort would later attract the intense interest of anti-Communist investigators, initially from within the public school system, and later at the congressional level.[9] Apart from their regular work within the school system, Communist teachers contributed their efforts to the Philadelphia School of Social Science and Art, a Party-linked institution that sought to extend educational opportunities to the masses.[10]

The Philadelphia teachers were galvanized by the disasters of the Great Depression and the threat to living standards. Union militancy concentrated in the American Federation of Teachers Local 192, which enjoyed great success until it was crippled by disputes over Communist influence within the national union.[11] At least from 1935, Communists within Local 192 were accused of operating as a well-organized caucus in order to win elections, and union officials became notorious for their close adherence to the Communist Party line; within a few weeks during June 1941, for example, the local flip-flopped from vehement opposition to war to total support. The union became heavily politicized, seeking to concentrate members' efforts on issues like the Spanish Civil War rather than simple labor issues. This resulted in vituperative internal debates and falling membership, to say nothing of frequent bad publicity, so that

Pittsburgh and other locals protested against Red influence. In 1939 the election of a new right-wing president of the national union led to an investigation of several left-wing locals.[12] Matters culminated in the expulsion of anti-Communist leaders from Local 192 in June 1941, followed closely by the revocation of the local's union charter. A new union was established, Local 3 of the Philadelphia Federation of Teachers, led by the activists who had fought the Communist leadership, and its charter specifically excluded from membership those "whose political actions are subject to totalitarian control such as fascist, Nazi or Communist." Meanwhile, Local 192 eventually reorganized as a local of the CIO's more sympathetic State, County and Municipal Workers, which was itself attacked for Communist sympathies. Renamed the United Public Workers of America, this organization was forced to leave the CIO as part of the general housecleaning of 1950.[13] By 1953 the old Local 192 was known simply as the Teachers' Union of Philadelphia, an independent splinter group with some 200 members, which constituted only a tiny minority of the 8,000 teachers employed in the Philadelphia schools.[14] Lacking significant union connections, and without the numbers required for serious influence within the city, the Teachers' Union was desperately vulnerable to a Red-hunting inquisition.

The legal environment for teachers became steadily more difficult nationwide, with well-publicized antisubversive inquiries into the schools and colleges already under way in states like California, Washington, and Illinois by 1947.[15] In 1949 Pennsylvania's Public School Code authorized "termination of the contract of a professional employee for advocating or participating in un-American or subversive doctrines," but it left vague the means by which an ideological stance might be determined or proved.[16] The following year, the dismissal of Allegheny County teacher Dorothy Alberts showed that the courts were willing to accept a broad interpretation of such laws. Alberts was the sister of Communist activist Nathan Alberts, and she served as publicity director for the CRC. Identified as a Communist by Matt Cvetic, she was summoned before the superintendent of schools and was soon dismissed by the school board.[17] She took her case through the courts, arguing that although she had been a Communist, she lacked the guilty knowledge that the organization had any subversive intent. This argument was viewed scornfully by the state's supreme court, and her dismissal was upheld.

The crucial legislative change for Pennsylvania's educators was the Pechan Act of 1951, which the Teachers' Union opposed so staunchly. The law created an inquisitorial procedure: "Any appointing authority may at any time upon written complaint, investigate any person, including teachers and other employees of the public school system, appointed or employed by him, to determine whether he is a subversive person." Evidence of subversive character might include involvement in sabotage, espionage, or attempts at such, or knowingly associating with spies or saboteurs; it could involve "treason or sedition or advocacy thereof" or "advocacy of revolution or force or violence to alter the constitutional form of government of the United States or the Commonwealth of Pennsylvania." It certainly included support for the Communist Party or any of its affiliates. The mere fact of passing a law with such extensive provisions for assuring the loyalty of educators suggested that they were a suspicious class of citizens. To be consistent, opponents argued, why not require all bankers to certify "that they are not embezzlers, lawyers that they are not ambulance-chasers, doctors that they are not abortionists, businessmen that they have not violated the anti-trust laws?"[18]

Despite such objections, support for the law was overwhelming. Pechan himself saw no difficulties with the measure, on the grounds that "I don't know why anyone should object to an oath of loyalty. I get a thrill when I take my oath." He saw his law as a thorough success and dismissed public protests as "yowling and laments by various leftist groups and eggheads." In fact, he regretted that he had not gone further, and in 1953 he sponsored a new bill that would mandate the dismissal of any state or public employee who took the Fifth Amendment before an investigative body.[19] Governor Fine agreed wholeheartedly with Pechan's approach. Addressing the VFW in July, he discussed the loyalty law in the context of measures being undertaken to prevent sabotage: "Sadly enough, one of the most insidious developments in recent years has been the growth of a liberal pro-communist attitude among some of our school teachers. These people are free to hold such attitudes and beliefs, but they must not be permitted to wield that kind of influence over our children. A majority of our teachers obviously agree with this viewpoint. I know they join with me in calling for appropriate legislation removing subversive influences from our schools."[20] He had only contempt for the bill's critics, "addicts of civil rights" like ADA: "We heard about academic freedom, freedom to pollute the minds of our children too immature to understand, and freedom to corrupt youth with alien philosophies and ideologies."[21] On Loyalty Day in March 1952, the governor personally led 2,000 state employees in a public oath-taking.[22]

The initial effects of the new loyalty codes were limited, at least in rooting out active Communists, and the main victims were non-Leftists who objected to the principle of the oath, often on religious grounds.[23] In the first year of operation, direct casualties of the Pechan law included three teachers, two of whom were Quakers, as well as a social worker and a nurse; a member of the Philadelphia City Planning Commission also resigned in protest. The social worker was Helen Corson, hitherto employed by the state Department of Public Instruction, who defined herself as a Christian pacifist and declared, "My objection to the oath is that I feel its effect will be to curb freedom of thought and expression; a curb which we expect in Communist countries but which is directly contrary to the spirit and practice of Democracy." Her stance was echoed by one of the teachers, Paul W. Goulding of Nazareth, who wrote that "in spirit . . . the oath is one of several instruments by which we are being 'persuaded' that totalitarian regimentation must be met by totalitarian, 100 percent 'Americanism.' "[24] In each case, the individual in question was unanimously agreed to be loyal to the established order and wholly free of subversive ties.

State courts upheld the loyalty law in the *Fitzgerald* case of 1954, which arose from perhaps the most tragic single incident resulting from the program. The plaintiff was a nurse employed by Philadelphia General Hospital, who was recognized to be "utterly opposed to Communism and in all respects loyal to the principles of our government," but she refused to take the loyalty oath on conscientious grounds and was duly dismissed. The Pennsylvania Supreme Court agreed that she had violated the provisions of a properly enacted piece of legislation and had no excuse for her resistance. The court stated that "no employee of a government agency, whether teacher, nurse or anyone else, should be allowed while in such employ to disseminate disloyal and seditious doctrines or encourage their spread by membership in a subversive organization."[25]

Though the act did not immediately succeed in flushing out active Communists, it was more effective than its critics acknowledged, making it difficult for leftist teachers to evade public notice by remaining discreet about their political opinions. Nor could the oath simply be taken with mental reservations. Recent court decisions made it impossible to pretend that the language of the oath did not apply to the Communist Party, so that any Party member taking the oath ran a real risk of perjury. That left two options: either one resigned from the school system, as Sidney Fox did the night before he was due to swear, or one left the Party prior to swearing. Forsaking the Party might be a tactical measure of self-defense, undertaken solely to preserve a livelihood, but this was still a dangerous course. Any continued participation in Communist activities—even though not strictly as a Party member—could still be counted as a violation of the act, in that the teacher still "advocated" subversive doctrines.

With whatever reservations, most of the main Left activists in the Philadelphia schools officially resigned from the Party and took the loyalty oaths in the spring of 1952, but their action did not end the political threat. Philadelphia public school superintendent Louis Hoyer now summoned thirty or so Teachers' Union members into his presence to be "individually interrogated" about their political beliefs or affiliations; all had taken the oaths and had formally renounced Party membership. All refused to answer the superintendent's questions fully, and by the following year all were suspended on grounds of incompetence, which was established by their failure to respond. This action was legally dubious, in that the teachers' tenure act provided no such definition of "incompetence."

For both Left and Right, the question now was how far the investigation into Red teachers was likely to go. For conservatives, the purge reinforced suspicions that the Philadelphia schools were a hotbed of subversion that should have been cleared out long ago; the Un-American Activities Committee of the VFW denounced the Philadelphia Board of Public Education for "being lax in its duties and false to the taxpayers who have entrusted their children to its care."[26] On the other side, the move against Communists created panic among the old anti-Communist leaders within the teachers' unions, who had fought against Local 192 and were now organized in the mainstream Philadelphia Federation of Teachers. They feared that a possible congressional investigation could go on to taint anyone with a vaguely liberal past, so that by late 1953 even the long-time anti-Communists were desperately seeking out and destroying any potentially embarrassing materials.[27]

In November 1953 Philadelphia earned the dubious honor of a direct visit from HUAC. The committee held televised hearings at the U.S. Courthouse at 9th and Chestnut and for three days examined the leading officers of the Teachers' Union, including the current and former president as well as successive union secretaries and several executive board members.[28] Committee members present included the chairman, Harold Velde of Illinois, Kit Clardy of Michigan, and the inevitable Francis Walter; the staff counsel was Robert L. Kunzig. The date was significant, as the years 1953 and 1954 represented the only period in the committee's history that Republicans held both the White House and the House of Representatives, and the anti-Communist militants were at the height of their ambitions; also about this time, the McCarthy committee in the U.S. Senate had begun its hearings into subversion in the army. The very week of the hearing, the headlines were full of new accusations harking back to the 1948 spy trial of Harry Dexter White; once again juxtaposing images of espionage and subversion in high places, the *Philadelphia Inquirer*'s reports of the school investigations were adjacent to headlines about spy investigations.[29] Only a week before, the SISS had held its own hearings in Pittsburgh to investigate subversion and espionage in defense-related industries. The Philadelphia investigation was accordingly a matter of great media interest, with dozens of reporters unable to squeeze into the cramped courtroom.[30] Witnesses pleaded for relief from the lights required for the television cameras and the repeated use of flash photography, "with the men in front gyrating and contorting to get their pictures, and the lights glaring and the heat of the whole situation."[31] The committee was prepared to restrain the flashbulbs, but a request to prevent broadcasting was "going a little too far."[32]

The Philadelphia hearings neatly encapsulate the common pattern of congressional exposés in these years. As usual, the parade of witnesses began with friendly and informative testimony from a defector who had known Communism from the inside, and who was now prepared to paint in the darkest possible terms Communist cynicism, ambition, and tyranny. In this instance, the voluble, friendly witness was Dr. Bella Dodd, who had had an impressive career as a union activist since the mid-1930s, and who from 1944 was an open Communist, serving on the Party's national committee. By 1949 she was disenchanted with Communism and was expelled from the Party, and in 1952 she joined the Catholic Church. In her appearance in Philadelphia, she offered a two-hour jeremiad wholly in keeping with the views of the HUAC members. Chairman Velde was effusive, praising "the dignified and sincere and learned manner in which you have outlined the Communist conspiracy, with emphasis on the conspiracy in the field of education."[33]

A friendly speaker like Dodd was rhetorically important in providing a sharp contrast to the remainder of the twenty or so witnesses called on this occasion, mainly teachers, who refused to answer virtually any question concerning their political beliefs or activities and constantly referred to the advice of the attorneys who accompanied them. Observers would presumably ask why a witness like Bella Dodd (or Matt Cvetic or Joe Mazzei) could be so honest and forthright, while others appeared evasive, secretive, and downright shifty. Dodd was succeeded on the stand by Harry Fruit, a math teacher at Germantown High School, who was alleged to have served as secretary of the West Philadelphia club, Section 8, but who took his Fifth Amendment privileges on virtually every question on matters other than his employment history. Fruit's testimony set the tone for the proceedings, in which committee members repeatedly asked about membership in a number of leftist organizations, and witnesses refused to answer on the grounds of their Fifth Amendment rights.

The dialogues, if they can be called that, assumed a formulaic, even ritualized character, for legal reasons that can be understood if we examine the case of a specific witness like Louis Ivens. Ivens was a 1949 graduate of Temple University who by 1953 was teaching social studies at Stetson High School. The committee asked him about his political record, alleging that Ivens had been a member of the Communist Temple Club while at college; that from 1945 to 1948, he had been a member of American Youth for Democracy; that he had served as press director for the Party's District 3 in 1947; that in 1948 he was a member of the same district's Section 6; and that he had participated fully in the usual run of Party meetings, rallies, and commemorations. Ivens was reluctant to admit the specific allegations, and the question then arises why witnesses like him did not simply admit that they had been members of a given club, that they had contributed to a particular committee or spoken at a given street corner, all at a time when such activities had been quite legal. Why did he not say, in effect, "I was a member of a legal political party, and it's none of your business"?

The problem was that admitting one point could easily build a wider case, as the witness had no idea what testimony might be available to the committee from other sources, from defectors or informants, who could use one's presence at a meeting to suggest that one had been participating in some kind of criminal conspiracy. Even if the witness in question had never done anything that he or she considered criminal, the possibility was always there that an informant might generate an accusation, and perhaps a perjury charge. As witness William G. Soler stated, "I have invoked the privilege because such an answer might tend to incriminate me, in a sense that some stool pigeon or some informer might have baseless charges against me, of which I know nothing."[34] Who knew how many of one's friends might be long-term informants, local equivalents of Matt Cvetic or Joe Mazzei just waiting for the appropriate moment to surface?

The question of association was uniquely sensitive. A witness might have no qualms about admitting Party membership or declaring that he or she had served in a given club or section and joined the usual range of Party fronts, but the most cooperative witness would then immediately face questions about whether he or she had known other named individuals, or would be asked to name other members who had been present at particular meetings. The committee would ultimately be satisfied only by a willingness to name names, and the potential betrayal of friends and colleagues transformed the moral dimensions of testifying. The frankest witness would soon blanch and would then face the dilemma of taking the Fifth Amendment or facing a contempt charge. Fifth Amendment rights against self-incrimination had been severely limited by the 1951 *Rogers* case, which concerned a woman who had readily agreed to discuss her own political activities but refused to identify others. The U.S. Supreme Court determined that the witness had "waived her privilege of silence when she freely answered criminating questions relating to her connection with the Communist party," so that she could not refuse to answer later questions about associates (it was not clear how past membership in a legal organization was "criminating").[35] Thereafter, though a blanket refusal to testify was legally acceptable, selective refusal could lead to contempt charges. The constrained atmosphere that now prevailed may have cost the committee much in terms of its notional investigative role, as witnesses during the late 1930s had faced no such traps and had been quite garrulous.[36]

The Pechan law posed other legal dangers, as investigating committees examined whether the teachers had taken oaths in good faith. Had they abandoned their Party membership merely to retain their jobs, or worse, had they concealed current Party membership?[37] Either circumstance could mean a perjury prosecution. In any case, teachers were among thousands of Communists hemorrhaging from the Party about this time for a variety of reasons, including a justifiable fear of official repression. Of the first dozen of Philadelphia's "red teachers" who appeared before the HUAC in 1953, at least nine had already severed their Party affiliation, usually two or three years previously. Unfortunately, the fact of having resigned from the Party in 1951 or 1952 could be portrayed as a calculated measure to pass the loyalty tests, as some of the "resigned" continued to attend Communist Party meetings.[38]

Perjury charges might also be invoked against the many witnesses who had in the previous decade held some kind of federal or military employment. To gain a job or a security clearance, they would have been directly asked about their Communist affiliations, which they would have had to conceal. Party membership in 1942 or 1943 was not a crime, but concealing it was. This was the situation facing Teachers' Union president Francis Jennings, who in the early 1940s had been president of the Young Communist League and an active member of the American Student Union and the Philadelphia Youth Congress. He had also at this time spent a few months as a low-level employee at the Philadelphia Navy Yard, namely, "an under-operator of mimeograph equipment, duplicating machines."[39] However menial, this job might have entailed a declaration on a loyalty document, so that Jennings would be accused of concealing his Communist affiliations.

These legal dilemmas led witnesses into what appeared to be remarkable contortions, being prepared to discuss their political views in, say, September 1952, but resorting to the Fifth Amendment when asked identical questions about their views six months or a year earlier. The following dialogue occurred during the follow-up hearings on the Philadelphia schools, held in Washington in February 1954:

> Mr. SCHERER (Rep. Gordon Scherer, Ohio): On the day you took that loyalty oath were you a member of the Communist Party?
>
> Mrs. Eleanor FLEET: No; of course not.
>
> Mr. SCHERER: Were you a member of the Communist Party the day before?
>
> Mrs. FLEET: I refuse to answer this on the grounds of the fifth amendment.[40]

These legal niceties posed particular problems for Louis Ivens, who was prepared to be more open in describing his politics than were other witnesses. Indeed, he went far enough to run legal risks; in this situation, neither honesty nor frankness were anything like the best policy. He was prepared to declare "I am not a communist," which led inevitably to the question "Have you ever been one?"[41] The dialogue then proceeded as follows:

> Mr. IVENS: May I finish my statement?
>
> Mr. CLARDY: No. Just answer that question. Have you ever been one?
>
> Mr. IVENS: I refuse to answer that question for the same reason. But I would like to finish a statement in respect to the chairman's words a few moments ago. I stated I was not a Communist. A couple of years ago I also signed the loyalty oath of Pennsylvania—
>
> Mr. WALTER: When?
>
> Mr. IVENS: In 1952, affirming the fact—
>
> Mr. VELDE: Were you a Communist at the time?
>
> Mr. IVENS: When I signed that oath, I affirmed that I was a loyal citizen of my state and this Commonwealth and of the country, and I say it again today.[42]

But Ivens had opened the door sufficiently to place him in serious danger.

Mr. KUNZIG: Were you a member of the Communist party at the time you signed the Pennsylvania loyalty oath?

(At this point Mr. Ivens conferred with Mr. Levitan [his counsel].)

Mr. IVENS: No.

Mr. KUNZIG: Were you a member of the Party the day before?

(At this point Mr. Ivens conferred with Mr. Levitan.)

Mr. IVENS: No.

Mr. KUNZIG: A month before?

(At this point Mr. Ivens conferred with Mr. Levitan.)

Mr. IVENS: No.

Mr. KUNZIG: A year before?

(At this point Mr. Ivens conferred with Mr. Levitan.)

Mr. IVENS: No.

Mr. KUNZIG: Two years before?

(At this point Mr. Ivens conferred with Mr. Levitan.)

Mr. IVENS: I invoke the privilege, Sir.

The implication is that Ivens had quit the Party about 1950, but if he admitted the fact of resignation, he would then be conceding previous membership and opening himself to all manner of questions about his own activities and those of everyone he had ever known. These questions would be based on sworn testimony available to the committee, but from sources unknown to Ivens. He protested at the use of unknown accusations, only to be told, "Let me disabuse your mind that you are being accused of anything. You were called here to give us some information relating to Communist activities in the Philadelphia area. This is not a court of law. You are not being accused of a thing. This is a congressional committee." And if criminal penalties were not involved, why should the witness fear such things? What did he have to hide? The witness should be grateful for the opportunity to explain himself, and Representative Clardy professed himself "sorry, and indeed amazed, that you do not understand why we are doing this, instead of bringing someone to name you first." Once the various doors were closed, Ivens had little opportunity but to go through the charade of endless denial, knowing that refusing to answer made him look like a potential traitor. He even refused to answer the question whether he had used an alias: "I do not recall it, but to be on the safe side, I invoke the fifth amendment."[43]

Ivens's response to the questions was unusual, in that throughout he continued to protest aspects of the proceedings that other witnesses had long since given up fighting explicitly. He began by asserting his First Amendment rights:

> I do not think that this committee should inquire into my private associations. . . . [F]reedom of association has long been an American tradition. It has been one of the cornerstones of our liberty and freedom, and I feel that I should not answer questions about my past associations, my private associations, my beliefs, or my thoughts during that period. (At this point Mr. Ivens conferred with Mr. Levitan.) And also, in addition to that, I would also refuse to answer that question by invoking the fifth amendment. I do not intend to answer any questions which might tend to incriminate me.

A complex legal dynamic was at work here. Ivens, like many others in a similar predicament, felt that the First Amendment should have been sufficient to refuse testimony, but HUAC had long ago rejected this view, and the courts supported the committee; the issue was effectively buried in the Hollywood Ten hearings. As Clardy declared, "We do not recognize validity in any other amendments applying to refusing to answer. . . . [W]e recognize only the fifth amendment in that respect."[44] This was a politically important point, because it meant that uncooperative witnesses, by refusing to testify about unspecified damning acts with which they were about to be charged, were placed in the position of being not free speech martyrs, but probable felons. "Taking the fifth" had already acquired disreputable connotations during congressional hearings of the late 1940s, and this stigma became worse during the Kefauver hearings into organized crime during 1951–52.

The committee was anxious to avoid mention of the First Amendment, and when Ivens tried to invoke it later in the proceedings, he was lectured by Chairman Velde: "We have had these harangues before your appearance today and, while we would like to give the witness every privilege, we get a little tired and weary of all these excuses."[45] A later witness attempted briefly to revive the theme, with similar results. Samuel M. Kaplan refused to answer on the grounds of "the first amendment, which has been thoroughly discussed today; the ninth amendment of the Constitution, which I think you all know; and the fifth amendment, since it might tend to incriminate me." Committee counsel Robert Kunzig then asked, "You refuse to answer that on the grounds of the fifth amendment?" Kaplan pointed out, "I have mentioned three, sir," but again to no avail. The only teacher to rely entirely on the First Amendment was Goldie Watson, who was cited for contempt of Congress.[46]

Following the Ivens exchange, other witnesses generally responded with blanket refusals to all politically related questions, which incidentally had the effect of permitting the committee to make any statement they wished in the form of an unchallenged question. If a witness was asked whether he or she had served as the secretary of a particular club or section, denial was useless, even if the allegation was spurious. The record thus showed the question asked and not rebutted, so the question became first a charge and then a statement of fact. A sequence of such questions/allegations apparently spelled out a subversive political record, as in the interrogation of teacher Estelle N. Thomas:

> Mr. KUNZIG: I will ask you first, were you a member of the first district of the Communist Party?
>
> Miss THOMAS: All these questions are cloaked in the same robe. I refuse to answer that question on the same ground.
>
> Mr. KUNZIG: I will ask you secondly whether you were a member of the Sam Lee Club of the Communist Party?
>
> Miss THOMAS: Same answer, same reason.
>
> Mr. KUNZIG: This was in the period of time 1943, approximately?
>
> Miss THOMAS: Same answer, same reason.
>
> Mr. KUNZIG: Are you acquainted with Dave Davis and his wife, Sophie?
>
> Miss THOMAS: Fifth amendment.
>
> Mr. KUNZIG: Did you know that Dave Davis was arrested by the FBI in connection with his Communist Party activities?
>
> Miss THOMAS: I refuse to answer that question.[47]

One rare outbreak of resistance came from former teacher Sarah Welsh Wepman, who had left the school system in 1945 and presumably had no further concerns about her career. She openly derided questions of the "Have you stopped beating your husband" variety, and when asked about her Party membership, she replied, "Well, I would like to go into that testimony, but I am not going to. I would like to see that testimony placed before a court of law to see how it stacks up. I am not going to answer that question because you have had one self-confessed spy here today who, incidentally, needed a good course in enunciation because I couldn't hear half of what she said back there."[48] The "spy," of course, is Bella Dodd. With the exception of a few such sparks, the remainder of the three days of testimony was sadly predictable, as was the committee's critical review of the witnesses: "The committee is in possession of sworn testimony which leaves no room for doubt that the witnesses who were subpoenaed could greatly enlarge our knowledge of subversive activities. But the witnesses refused to talk. Instead they say nothing. One can only draw the conclusion that although many witnesses have emphasized that they are not today members of the Communist party, they did not wish to help destroy the Communist conspiracy."[49]

Such a condemnation raised the question of the judicial or inquisitorial nature of the proceedings. Committee members often declared that they had nothing to do with the dismissal or persecution of alleged subversives, and technically they were right. When one Philadelphia teacher announced that the investigation had cost her her job, destroyed her livelihood, and led to her receiving death threats, HUAC chairman Velde asserted that "the committee has never as far as I am concerned and never will attempt to interfere with any-body's livelihood in any way whatsoever."[50] In reality, publicizing a subpoena almost demanded that the prospective witness's employer take action against him or her, lest future investigators inquire why that institution continued to employ suspected subversives. For all the committee's assertions of confiden-tiality, the reasons for the subpoena usually tended to leak, together with the knowledge of whether a given witness would be cooperative or not. Though congressional committees had no formal power to accuse or judge, the fact of being a witness was sufficient to incur severe penalties against any individual. As the committee boasted, "No innocent people would be put on the stand."[51]

If all the witnesses were judged guilty by the mere fact of their appearance before the committee, sanctions would be expected from their employers, and these were soon forthcoming from the Philadelphia school system. By the end of the year over thirty teachers had been suspended on grounds of "incompe-tence," not only on the basis of their refusal to answer the superintendent's questions about political allegiance, but now also on the fact of having taken the Fifth Amendment before HUAC. The local media were overwhelmingly hos-tile to the teachers: a *Philadelphia Inquirer* headline read "Evasive Teachers Blasted by Velde for Failure to Aid War on 'Red Conspiracy.'"[52] The *Philadel-phia Jewish Times* "shuddered" at "the undeniably stupid attitude of the school-teachers who were called to the witness stand." While the paper regretted their suspension following the hearings, the real issue was why the board of educa-tion had waited so long: "They should have been dismissed before this com-mittee had them in the corner."[53]

Accused teachers sought to mobilize support on their behalf, and in Feb-ruary 1954, the Communist-sponsored Citizens Committee to Defend the Schools held a mass meeting at the Adelphia Hotel.[54] This meeting itself gave added ammunition to congressional inquisitors, as the fact of having been pres-ent was regarded as damning evidence of subversive inclinations. The protest would often feature in the questions asked by HUAC during its second wave of hearings in mid-February, and as before, witnesses generally pleaded the Fifth Amendment.[55]

The February hearings closely followed the November precedent, with a comparable parade of experienced teachers whose careers now lay in ruins. However, two confrontations illustrate both the attitudes of the investigators and the impossible legal situation in which the witnesses stood. In the first category was an outburst from Congressman Walter, when he suggested, improbably, that witness Bessie Stensky was expressing amusement at the proceedings. He lectured her on how distasteful it was "to see Americans, at least people who enjoy the birthright of American citizens, flaunting the Constitution in the faces of the duly elected representatives of the Government."

> Mrs. STENSKY: I don't feel I am flaunting the Constitution. I feel I am protecting it.
> Mr. WALTER: You feel it is funny —
> Mrs. STENSKY: I haven't been laughing.
> Mr. WALTER: This isn't any funnier than it was to the boys in Korea who died there, I can assure you of that.

An enraged Walter then launched an attack that raised one of the most sensitive unspoken issues in the proceedings, namely the ethnic background of the witnesses. After asking Mrs. Stensky to spell her name, he continued:

> Mr. WALTER: You were born in the United States I take it, Mrs. Stensky?
> Mrs. STENSKY: Yes I was. Philadelphia.
> Mr. WALTER: Were either of your parents born in Russia?
> Mrs. STENSKY: Both.
> Mr. WALTER: Well, it is indeed significant that of the Philadelphia witnesses, so called, every single one of them was either the son or the daughter of a mother or father born in Russia. I suppose that is a mere coincidence but I think that is the fact — isn't it, Mr. Kunzig?
> Mr. KUNZIG: All but one.
> Mr. WALTER: Excuse me, I apologize. 39 out of 40.[56]

Walter's rage had made him cross a dangerous threshold, and the subject returned later when Stensky's counsel, Harry Levitan, asked him to "reconsider that statement about the immigrant parents of many of the people who have been before you." Walter grasped at the opportunity, with a conventional remark about the fine achievements of America's immigrant populations, but then dug himself even deeper into trouble when he continued: "It just struck me when I learned her name as being very strange, and more than a mere coincidence that so many of the people from Philadelphia came from Russian families. I am not talking about immigrants as such. But I am just wondering whether or not there is brought to this country Old World ideologies that are kept alive, that is all. No, I won't of course, remove from the record anything I have said, because that is the way I feel."[57] A name like Bessie Stensky was not unusual in contemporary Philadelphia, and certainly not in Walter's home constituency. Such names were common among the accused teachers, over two-thirds of whom were Jews.[58] The xenophobic theme recurred once more when witness Sarah Crome expressed her resentment of a slur on her ancestors who "left Czarist Russia to get away from religious, political and economic oppression and persecution."[59] An exasperated Walter repeated that no such slur was intended and cut off further debate with a rapid dismissal of the witness. When the matter was brought up yet again, he asserted that "the next thing you know, somebody will charge me with being anti-Russian."[60] That he did not acknowledge the issue as anti-Semitism indicates that he was either stunningly naive or thoroughly disingenuous.

The second exchange that illustrated the inherent flaws of the proceedings involved Dr. Wilbur Lee Mahaney, whose case showed that not even the most transparent honesty would suffice in this setting: one had to be prepared to betray. Mahaney was an able scholar who held a doctorate from the University of Pennsylvania and had taught history and social studies at the West Philadelphia High School since 1929. He amazed the committee by his willingness to admit that he had been a Party member from 1935 to 1946 and to discuss his beliefs and activities without resorting to constitutional protections.[61] Nevertheless, Mahaney found himself in difficulty for refusing to reveal the names of the individuals who had recruited him twenty years before, although the key protagonist was long dead. Mahaney stood not on the Fifth Amendment, but on the principles of decency: "To be an informer as to the friends you might have or acquaintances that you might meet along the pathway of life is contrary to every tenet of the American way of thinking." "You are asking me to violate one of my most deep-seated convictions and one which you might say I have held since I was old enough to remember, the sacredness of human relationships and especially of 'speak well of the dead.'"[62]

On this first occasion, Mahaney was allowed to get away with this refusal, though with the specter of a contempt charge duly raised, but the questioning then turned to the closely related topic of identifying his colleagues and acquaintances in the Party and the Teachers' Union, and here, too, he demurred on the grounds of conscience.[63] Throughout the proceedings, Mahaney returned to this answer, perhaps becoming overconfident as the committee failed to press him when he repeatedly cited the same grounds for refusing to answer. However, grounds of confidentiality and decency had no legal force, and Mahaney finally reached the point at which he was specifically directed to respond to questions about other individuals. He refused, and in May 1954 he was cited for contempt of Congress by a unanimous vote of the House of Representatives, 346-0. The following month, he was dismissed from the Philadelphia school system and took a job selling encyclopedias.[64]

In July Mahaney agreed to appear once more before the committee to answer fully, conceding that his earlier position had been "unduly squeamish," "a very serious and grave mistake." He now named names freely, giving full details, for example, on those who had been with him when he attended the meetings at the home of Sidney and Genevieve Fox, and he told his story at length to the FBI.[65] HUAC members on this occasion praised his "very courageous position."[66] The failure of Mahaney's principled stand demonstrates why open declarations of political loyalty were not possible in this environment: one either had to become a straightforward informer or deploy constitutional privileges in a way that made one appear subversive.

Mahaney's fate epitomizes that of the other accused and suspended teachers. In early 1954 the school superintendent took steps to dismiss them formally for their continued "incompetence," in hearings that refused to admit testimony about their teaching credentials or their loyalty. The superintendent stated that the fact of being "in a position to be called before the Committee" of itself amounted to proof of incompetence; indeed, the school board's counsel declared in one case that "the only charge here is her appearance before the Velde Committee."[67] By June, twenty-seven teachers were terminated. Though one was allowed to take retirement, the others were dismissed outright, most to begin a long period of fruitless job-hunting, personal frustration, and grave health problems.[68] The HUAC hearings all but killed the Teachers' Union, which dissolved in 1955.

The movement against leftist teachers was based on the deep-rooted idea that intellectuals were using their skills to subvert the young in their charge, and this idea became one aspect of a general distrust of "eggheads" in these years.[69] In 1948 HUAC member John McDowell asked, "Where do they get this stuff that

Communism comes out of the slums and out of poverty and out of oppression? We have had a constant parade of those accused of being Communists who were doctors of law, doctors of philosophy, high government officials, colonels, majors, captains, lieutenants."[70] Librarians were almost as suspect as teachers, because of their ability to place dangerous ideas in public settings. One typical victim of the anti-Communist movement was Sonia Gruen, a former employee of Pittsburgh's Carnegie Library, who lost her job at the United Nations because of her refusal to answer questions from a Senate committee concerning her political beliefs.[71] Suspicion about subversive books led to a number of local attacks on libraries and their staff. One such conflict erupted in the conservative community of Mount Lebanon, where in early 1953 a woman protested about the library's holdings, naming Left-leaning authors like Louis Adamic, Agnes Smedley, and Anna Louise Strong, while criticizing the absence of "Americanist" and patriotic authors like John T. Flynn. She won the support of Matt Cvetic, and others pointed out that the library in Sewickley had a special section on "Americanism."[72] In this instance, a special committee of residents formed to investigate the allegations found no substance in the charges of subversion, and the controversy faded.

The state's colleges and universities also attracted the attention of anti-Communist militants, not surprising in view of the influence of liberal and Popular Front politics among intellectuals in the late 1930s. In 1947 the Americanism Committee of Pennsylvania's American Legion warned that "some of our schools, particularly our colleges and universities, have been infiltrated by these enemies of democracy. Their propaganda is not only persistent but clever."[73] To combat this, the legion needed to support "wholesome indoctrination of our youth at all age levels so that they grow up in a healthful democratic atmosphere."[74] In 1951 the American Legion called for the state assembly to initiate a general investigation of state-funded institutions, and many local institutions were affected. The local legion district charged in July that the Pennsylvania State University was a hotbed of subversion, and a local inquiry was initiated.[75] The evidence proved to date back largely to the late 1930s and involved support for the anti-Franco cause in the Spanish Civil War, as well as the presentation of plays and concerts said to contain Communistic propaganda, but the final detonator was a recent appearance by CRC member Carey McWilliams. In this instance, even the legion recognized the weakness of the charges, and it publicly commended university president Milton Eisenhower (brother of the general) for his efforts in combating subversion. There were many other such outbreaks. At Muhlenberg College, legionnaires led a successful effort to ban the films of alleged subversive Charlie Chaplin. At Lycoming College, a professor of philosophy and social ethics who became chairman of the local county Progressive Party was dismissed from the institution.[76] Student organizations also suffered, and in 1947 Temple University banned the local chapter of American Youth for Democracy.[77]

As in the schools, the passing of the Pechan law proved to be a turning point. During 1951 the measure was strongly opposed by college faculty, including 1,500 educators from state institutions of higher education; among the most active were Harold Stassen, president of the University of Pennsylvania, who was a conservative Republican leader in his own right, and Milton Eisenhower.[78] One would have thought that the latter's views should have carried some weight, as one of the state's U.S. senators, James Duff, was a close ally of Dwight Eisenhower and was engaged in a close fight to carry the state for him in the coming presidential election. The measure passed despite the opposition, however. It dictated that by the first of May 1952, "any state-aided institution of learning not a part of the public school system" must file a report describing its procedures to determine whether it had any subversive persons in its employment, and, further, "the report also shall unequivocally set forth that the institution has no reason to believe that any subversive persons are in its employ." The burden of detection and removal was thus placed firmly on the respective institutions, with the overt threat of the removal of state funds.[79] The law did not explicitly demand an individual oath or statement from each employee, a concession obtained by the lobbying of Milton Eisenhower, but some institutions interpreted the measure in these terms and created standards even more stringent than the law required. Colleges also established special ad hoc loyalty committees of administrators and legal counsel, which summoned suspected subversives to explain themselves.

The investigative process can be observed at the conservative campus of Penn State, where Left activism was at a minimum. During the 1940s the only political upsurge of any significance involved a campaign inspired by religious groups to picket barbers who refused to serve African Americans, and the town of State College apparently had only one known and active Communist. Nevertheless, the Pechan Act did find one near-martyr here in Wendell MacRae, the publications production manager in the college's Department of Public Information, who refused on moral grounds to comply with loyalty procedures.[80] MacRae himself had impeccable credentials, as a Marine Corps veteran active in the American Legion, a Republican Party member, and a Presbyterian involved in the YMCA and other community activities, none of them of even a vaguely subversive character. However, he believed that "it is basically un-American to force men to swear or state they are not subversive when no charges have been brought against them."[81] It was hypocritical for a Pennsylvania Presbyterian to sign an oath rejecting political violence, when it was "an American tradition, and a Pennsylvania tradition as well, to resist oppressive and tyrannical legislation." The United States was founded by an act of armed revolutionary violence, making MacRae "a native-born beneficiary of the freedom thus secured by revolutionaries."[82] Refusing to sign the necessary declaration, MacRae was promptly dismissed, but in this case the story had a favorable outcome. MacRae attracted considerable community support and was defended by the local branch of the American Federation of Teachers, while a subsequent interview was taken as confirmation of his political loyalty, and he was reinstated within a few months. The case is unusual in that MacRae was actually able to make the kind of political and historical declarations that many might have wished to use before HUAC or comparable bodies, but which they were legally unable to do.

Most cases in these years had a quite different outcome, especially after HUAC let it be known in 1952 that the nation's higher education system would be the next target for inquisition.[83] In light of recent events, there was little doubt about the tone of this investigation, and college faculty were rightly alarmed. At Penn State, one group sent a manifesto to Milton Eisenhower, warning that "the investigations may not be motivated primarily by a genuine desire to find real subversives but rather to make political capital out of the situation. If this is the case, attempts to appease the investigators will only encourage them to heightened calumny and slander." The state's various state-related colleges should present a united front, and their presidents should respond with "forthright watchfulness rather than a policy of subservient and frightened appeasement."[84] The writers also warned of the importance of communicating well with the media, so that HUAC members would not be able to slant coverage as they had been wont to do.

This well-thought-out proposal underestimated the real fear prevailing among university administrators, and "appeasement" is a fair description of their customary response.[85] Temple University presented an egregious example when the HUAC subpoenaed Dr. Barrows Dunham for its forthcoming hearings in October 1952. Dunham was a professor of philosophy and head of the department, who had been a Communist Party member in the peak Popular Front years, from 1938 through 1945. The FBI had had a file on him at least since 1942, and bureau interest became intense following his Left-leaning book *Man against Myth* in 1947; information about Dunham's activities was sought from informants, including students in his classes.[86] Naturally concerned about the HUAC summons, Dunham reported to the university vice president, who advised him to take the Fifth Amendment on all questions. Ultimately, he was not called in the October hearings, but he did appear some months later and refused to answer any questions, even standard ones about his date of birth or career history.[87] A frustrated committee promptly dismissed him. Shortly afterward, Dunham received a letter from Temple's president informing him that by refusing to answer HUAC questions, "you have deliberately created a doubt as to your loyalty status," and he was suspended forthwith. A formal hearing followed that May, at which Dunham spoke willingly about his own past but refused to name names or even to discuss his knowledge of celebrated Party leaders like Sam Darcy. He was dismissed, and the act was confirmed by the university's trustees. In their view, Dunham had improperly claimed the privilege against self-incrimination, and equally disturbing was his hostile attitude toward HUAC, which represented "not intellectual freedom but intellectual arrogance."[88] In May 1954 both Dunham and Wilbur Mahaney were cited for contempt of Congress. Though Dunham was acquitted the following year, Temple refused to reinstate hm; throughout the process, moreover, university authorities cooperated closely with the FBI.[89]

Another case in which a university went beyond the standards of the Pechan law occurred at Jefferson Medical College in Philadelphia, where an internal loyalty inquiry lasted from June through November 1953. Three professors were singled out, all of whom admitted leftist pasts but were judged to be "loyal." One professor stated that he had abandoned the Party after the war: "I saw my duty and my loyalty to my country and I thought my continuing in the CP would possibly involve disloyalty." Like Mahaney, he drew the line at naming names, and this was fatal. As his dean told him, "You must aid and assist in uncovering those who have not left. . . . [W]e would like to have evidence that you have broken, other than to say that you have, and the best evidence you can possibly give is to become an informant."[90] Ultimately, the three faculty members were permanently dismissed in November, in an act memorably oversimplified by the *Philadelphia Inquirer* in the headline, "Ordered Dismissed as Result of Five Month Inquiry in Red Activities." Significantly, the final decision came two weeks after the HUAC inquiry into the Philadelphia teachers, so public sensitivity to threats of "un-Americanism" was acute. Another factor was concern about the continuation of state and federal aid to the institution, which depended so heavily on research funding.[91]

Pittsburgh institutions also suffered from anti-Communist wrath. One of Matt Cvetic's prime targets was Marion Hathaway, a professor in the University of Pittsburgh's School of Social Work. A leading figure in the 1948 Progressive campaign in western Pennsylvania, she had since quit the Party over the issue of Communist domination. Judge Gunther still denounced her publicly, arguing that the university should lose all state funding if it failed to dismiss her, but she counterattacked with the support of Congressman Eberharter. Hathaway resigned from Pitt in 1951, but fortunately her career survived, and even flourished, in her new appointment at Bryn Mawr.[92] Less successful was Eben Matlis, a veteran of Students for Wallace, who was employed as a statistician in the Coal Research Laboratory of Carnegie Tech. He rode out early post-Cvetic inquests into his politics but was dismissed after the university acquired unspecified new information in 1952.[93]

Attacks on universities and eggheads were not always successful, even when backed by the heavy guns of the traditional anti-Communist crusaders. The limits of repression were suggested in 1952 when Cvetic made his address to the American Legion convention and devoted most of his harangue to the misdeeds of composer Roy Harris, then composer-in-residence at the Pennsylvania College for Women in Pittsburgh. Harris had been associated with several groups subsequently identified as Communist-inspired, and, most damaging, his Fifth Symphony, a 1943 work, was dedicated to "the heroic Russian people." If Harris could not actually be dismissed, then at least his work could be kept from public performance, and Musmanno led an unsuccessful attempt to prevent the symphony from being presented. The VFW and other "patriotic" groups announced plans to protest its performance, but the effort crumbled when Mayor Lawrence announced his own plans to attend, and testified on Harris' behalf before the legion's Americanism commission. By early 1953 Harris had vindicated himself in the eyes of his critics, and a sizable majority of legion posts in Allegheny County had declared themselves convinced of his loyalty.[94] Recognizing a losing issue, even Musmanno now withdrew his portrayal of Harris as a symphonic subversive. Though the judge advised the audience to maintain a silent protest at the performance, Harris's work received five minutes' applause and four curtain calls.[95]

The process of congressional investigation in these years fully justifies the term "inquisition" so often applied to it. In the schools and colleges, as in the factories, radicals were subjected to a legal process in which traditional rights and protections were forfeited, and in which any hope of vindication rested on appeasing the whims of political adventurers. The burden was placed on the suspect to prove innocence, which in the vast majority of cases was all but impossible. Even the language of legality was suspended: as one of the Philadelphia teachers was scolded, "You are not here as a defendant and are not charged with anything."[96] The fact of being called as a witness meant guilt, which must then be purged by whatever means necessary, and with whatever damage to others that might entail. When Herman Thomas was asked about the ethics of naming individuals who might have resigned from the Party, he had no qualms: "Under the law now, any one can if they want show their true, loyal American citizenship, approach any of these committees and pour their heart out, and I think confession is good for the soul."[97] The idea that one's stigma could only be purged by passing it on to others belonged to the thought world of ritual purification, however, not justice.

7

THE STRUGGLE FOR THE ETHNIC COMMUNITIES

> The peoples realize the fact that the Soviet Union is the main pillar of
> peace, and realize that the policy of Wall Street is the main prompter
> of a world war. — *Narodni Glasnik*, Pittsburgh Croatian-language
> newspaper, February 21, 1949[1]

Beyond the schools and factories, the most intense anti-Communist activism
occurred within the ethnic communities. The elaborate network of community organizations founded by eastern and southern European groups in Pennsylvania served as a solid foundation for anti-Communist campaigning. Even
where there was no direct military or political threat to a homeland, firm
Catholic loyalties mobilized other groups like the Irish, and ethnic background
is often difficult to separate from religious affiliations in these matters. The
story is somewhat more complicated than it initially appears, however. The
various groups were rarely homogeneous in their politics, so we cannot safely
assume that (for example) Poles, Italians, Slovaks, or Croats were automatically
and uniformly anti-Communist zealots. Many were, as were most of their
leading organizations and publications, but in each case, there was a sizable
minority that rejected the communal orthodoxy. The state's various ethnic
organizations can be located along a political spectrum in which Poles and
Ukrainians would be almost united in anti-Communism, followed closely by
the Italians; other groups were far more divided, however, and the South Slavs
in particular had a substantial leftist following. For all their claims that the
respective leaderships spoke for their communities on political and social
questions, ethnic organizations were often sharply divided on ideological mat-

ters. During the 1940s the left wing of the eastern European groups was mobilized through the ASC, which for a few years enjoyed real popularity and influence. Indeed, when a Pittsburgh-area state representative demanded in 1947 that the governor call a special legislative session to confront the Red menace, he remarked that "at this rate, the Communist are taking over our various organizations, especially fraternal and labor." Note that the threat to the fraternal (that is, ethnic) groups is actually given precedence over the labor issue.[2]

The vigor of the anti-Red movement in an ethnically heterogeneous state like Pennsylvania owed much to these internal divisions within the organizations themselves, as established leaderships, often Catholic and conservative in ideology, struggled to suppress left-wing dissidence and to prove that they were bastions of loyal Americanism. If established leaders failed, then the anti-Left reaction could easily turn into a xenophobic campaign against the immigrant groups themselves, as had occurred in the 1920s. Though the ethnic press of the 1950s expressed a visceral anti-Communism, that orthodoxy was the result of several years of internal struggle, and it had only been achieved by invoking the full force of government and the mainstream media, at both state and federal levels.

In the early twentieth century, Pennsylvania became a region of great ethnic diversity. Between 1880 and 1920 the state's thriving industries served as a major attraction for immigrants arriving from the nations of eastern and southern Europe. Table 5 shows the numerical strength of the major groups, though census evidence fails to make the subtler but important distinctions between subnational ethnic groups; the category "Yugoslavs," for example, includes Croats, Serbs, and Slovenes, to name only the major elements. The era of immigration was marked by a tremendous upsurge of institutions designed to assist the economic, moral, and spiritual needs of the different ethnic communities. Each group had its network of fraternal and social institutions, which served as the critical building blocks of social life at the community level, and each usually had its distinctive press.[3] Often the various structures were allied under one common umbrella organization, and some communities were dominated by one pre-eminent group like the Polish National Alliance, the Sons of Italy, or the Serb National Federation. Potentially, such a structure could provide a political base of real strength.

Though officially eschewing party labels, these groups tended to be domi-

Table 5. National Origins of the Largest Foreign-Born Populations in Pennsylvania, 1930

Country of Origin	Population
Italy	226,000
Poland	167,000
England/Scotland/Wales	132,000
Russia	116,000
Germany	111,000
Czechoslovakia	111,000
Ireland*	98,000
Austria	50,000
Yugoslavia	40,000
Lithuania	37,000
Hungary	34,000
Other	118,000
Total	1,240,000

Source: U.S. Census, 1930.
*Includes both the Irish Republic and Northern Ireland.

nated by the most conservative social and political forces. As such, it was natural that they would provide rock-solid foundations for anti-Communism during the Cold War years. Moreover, most of the leading immigrant groups came from countries that had recently fallen under Communist domination or stood in imminent danger of doing so in the late 1940s, so it is not surprising to find the ethnic federations providing some of the most implacable enemies of Communism, broadly defined. By the late 1940s anti-Communism of the most militant shades had a firm foundation among those ethnic groups with roots in eastern Europe, communities for whom the name of Yalta was an abomination, and who saw American liberals as despicably soft on the Communist menace. Ethnic grievances were often expressed in religious terms. For Catholic Croats the central martyr figure was Archbishop Stepinac, arrested by the Communist Yugoslav government in 1946, while many Slovak Americans campaigned for Msgr. Joseph Tiso, who had led a pro-German statelet and was executed in Czechoslovakia in 1947. Emphasizing the defense of clerical leaders served to combine nationalist appeal with Catholic loyalties and cemented the alliance between the ethnic pressure groups and the Catholic Church.

Societies and newspapers associated with these eastern European groups sometimes presented themselves as a virtual resistance movement in exile.

This can be illustrated by the Poles, whose leading newspapers included the Scranton-based *Polish-American Journal* (the old *Republika-Gornik*), "serving the interests of fifty thousand Americans of Polish descent living in Lackawanna County, Pa." The paper was edited from 1944 to 1983 by Henry Dende, a vigorous force in the Polish American community, who was a militant enemy of Communism and un-Americanism years before such views became so firmly fixed in the social orthodoxy.[4] No issue of his *Polish-American Journal* in these years failed to include a tirade against Communism abroad and its sympathizers on American soil. This activism became all the more apparent at times of international crisis like the fall of Czechoslovakia in 1948, when the front pages filled with complaints about the appeasement of Stalin, repeated references to Yalta, and calls "to halt at once the vicious red program of world enslavement."[5] Week by week, the headlines from Poland were alarming: "18 Poles Condemned in Communist Purge," "Strikes are Banned by Red Government," "4000 Poles Interned in Red Camp," "Fight on Church to be Continued by Warsaw Reds," and "Russia Holds 500,000 Poles in Jails, Camps."[6]

Americans were urged to be vigilant against such an enemy. The firm American commitment to containing Soviet expansion was greeted with delight, and President Truman's speech on this issue in 1948 was praised as a "monumental and historic pronouncement."[7] In 1950 a wordy cartoon depicted a GI asking, "Why am I fighting in this hellhole of Korea?" The answer was "Because *you* are fighting for survival! Because *you* are fighting to save your liberty and your whole way of life! Because *you* are fighting against being enslaved by Soviet Communism and the police state! . . . And all the rest of us *who believe in freedom* are, each in his small way, also fighting with *you*!!!!"[8] The same militant themes are apparent from newspapers like the Catholic-dominated *American Slav*, published in Pittsburgh by the Slav Fraternal Athletic Association.

Vigilance overseas had to be matched by combating the domestic Red threat, and throughout these years the *Polish-American Journal* reported enthusiastically on efforts to suppress American Communists and fellow travelers. Firmly opposed to Communists abroad, the *American Slav* denounced leftist speakers like Louis Adamic wherever they appeared on American soil.[9] The paper was harsh on naive PARFISTS, the "Passive Allies of Russia Firsters."[10] Polish organizations sponsored some of the earliest expressions of Cold War militancy. In 1945 a Pulaski Day rally at Philadelphia's Independence Hall was warned of "bloody Joe Stalin and his degenerate Dillingers," while Polish Army Day in Pittsburgh in 1947 provided an opportunity to call for universal peacetime conscription in the United States.[11] Polish events, particularly those with a church focus, provided a warm welcome to speakers like Judge Musmanno.[12]

Polish anti-Communism is epitomized by Blair F. Gunther, the cofounder of ABC, who has been aptly described as a "professional Pole." A key figure in the Polish National Alliance (PNA) at both state and national levels, he served as president of the society's Local 38 in Pittsburgh, where he was associated with the newspaper *Pittsburgczanin*. Gunther was a loyal follower of long-standing PNA president Charles Rozmarek and became censor of the national organization in 1947.[13] He also was a significant figure in state politics. Appointed an Allegheny County judge in 1942, succeeding his father-in-law in the office, he was elevated to the state Superior Court in 1950. At least from 1944, anti-Communism was the motivating force in Gunther's political career. He served as the first president of the ASC in 1942, but observing the growth of Communist influence at the group's 1944 convention, he turned violently against the Left in ethnic organizations. Shortly after the Cvetic appearance before HUAC, a laudatory newspaper piece claimed that "by this time, the judge was in full cry against Communists. He made thousands of speeches, public and private, exposing and denouncing them. He appeared before congressional committees, wrote letters to the papers, organized committees, swung the powerful PNA into the fight, hounded Commies in their tracks. He even set up a counter-espionage and developed a card index system. He worked confidentially with government agencies." Gunther even posed as a Communist himself to attend the Party's meetings. Though he was often mocked for his obsession, the events of 1950 seemed to prove him correct: "Now the payoff has arrived."[14] Gunther's militant anti-Communism was expressed through a series of pressure groups that he founded, including the Committee to Stop World Communism, as well as ABC. He also ran an exposé radio program in the Pittsburgh region.[15]

Other groups were equally passionate. The chief Ukrainian newspaper was the Catholic *America*, published in Philadelphia; just as for the Poles, denunciations of Red persecutions abroad merged easily with attacks on fellow travelers on American shores.[16] In 1956 the paper headlined new reports on the horrors of Soviet concentration camps and forced labor.[17] The message was that "Bolshevism [Is] the Worst Barbarism": "Millions upon millions are subjected to unspeakable miseries in the wastes of bleak Siberia in forced slavery, thousands upon thousands had lost their lives through the communist cruelty and sadism. Of all the victims, the Ukrainians seemed to be the greatest sufferers. The Communists had robbed them from their country, their history, religion and all, and subdued the once glorious nation to the most abject slavery and barbarism."[18] Other headlines from this era claimed "Communists Will Follow New Party Line Like Sheep" and "Russian Communist Megalomania in Superlative Degree."[19] Declaring that Communist ideology must never be permitted to gain ground in the United States, an editorial praised the U.S. Senate's investigators for their revelations of the secrets of American Communism.[20] Foreign and domestic themes were neatly combined in July 1956 following the suppressed uprising of the workers in Poznan, Poland. *America* commented sarcastically on the contrast between reactions to this affair and to the Rosenberg executions, noting that "the voices which were so voluble in upholding convicted traitors are silent when innocent men, women and children are shot down by machine guns and run down by tanks. The 'liberal' and leftwing protesters have had a chance to prove their sincerity. They failed."[21]

East European groups generally placed themselves on the political Right, but some were notably more extreme than others. This was particularly true for groups whose national aspirations had led them to support Axis collaborationism, and who had under the Nazis gained some degree of national autonomy. For at least some elements among the Croats and Ukrainians, anti-Communism shaded into a right-wing extremism marred by totalitarian ideas. The point is illustrated by the Slovaks, who were well represented in Pennsylvania's industrial regions, where they had a diverse network of newspapers and fraternal organizations of all political shades.[22] One of the many organizations aspiring to speak for the community was the Slovak League of America, headquartered in Middletown.[23] The league pledged to "fight against [Communism] with all the means at its command until the dread plague . . . is wiped off the face of the earth." This was uncontroversial enough in terms of contemporary rhetoric, but the group also idolized Father Tiso's Slovak puppet state, which had introduced anti-Semitic laws to Aryanize the economy.[24] Through the 1950s, league publications advocated an independent anti-Communist Slovakia and denounced any Slovaks who drifted too far toward liberal or socialist views. The group was in turn denounced for its "ranting" by the mainstream Slovak National Alliance.[25]

Italian Americans were just as passionately concerned about the European struggles. Fears of Communist rule were nearly realized in the crucial Italian elections of April 1948, and this nightmare galvanized the fraternal organizations who were so influential in Pennsylvania (in Philadelphia alone, perhaps 10 percent of the population claimed Italian ancestry). Philadelphia's two major Italian newspapers each followed the lead of a different family faction; the main voice for the Sons of Italy was *Ordine Nuovo*, dominated by the powerful Republican voice of Judge Eugenio Alessandroni, while *Libera Parola* looked to the Democratic interest of state senator Anthony Di Silvestro. Though the two sides differed on most aspects of politics, they united on the desperate need to keep Italy from going Communist, and tensions were all the greater following the Prague coup in 1948.[26] For a few months, Italian American concern with affairs in their homeland reached heights not seen since the Ethiopian war of the previous decade.

From mid-1947, anti-Communist politics entered ever more vigorously into the columns of the *Ordine Nuovo*, with a series of features denouncing Italian Communist leader Palmiro Togliatti as a tool of the Comintern as well as "a great adventurer, a confidence-man, and a ridiculous clown."[27] The message was presented simply and aggressively, in the language of the Italian Catholic Right: "Our brothers in Italy are engaged in the struggle against the sinister forces of Communism."[28] The winter of 1947–48 was a time of genuine panic, with fears that the Communists would launch an outright coup, and as the April election approached, *Ordine Nuovo* made repeated appeals to the Italian electorate to resist Communist temptations.[29] The defeat of the Left in those elections was greeted with triumphant assertions of the reborn spirit of immortal Italy and the traditions of imperial Rome.

Di Silvestro's Democratic *Libera Parola* often differed from *Ordine Nuovo* in its approach to Italian affairs, but the underlying anti-Communism was identical.[30] One 1947 vote of confidence against the Italian Communist Party was said to demonstrate the "cretinism which characterizes the aping of Russian Communism," and Togliatti was freely compared with Mussolini.[31] Coverage of Italian politics increasingly dominated the front page of *Libera Parola* as the 1948 election, "Italy's Date With Destiny," drew near. The prospects were grim: if the Communists won the election, the Western Allies would probably decide that the time had come for "a march on Rome," leading to European war. If the Communists lost, they would attempt a coup d'état, with the same result.[32]

Though Italian Americans observed this crisis from a distance, they were not helpless, as their numbers and economic power gave them a real say in shaping the political attitudes of their relatives and friends in the homeland. The mobilization of American support for the anti-Communist cause was apparent in Pittsburgh's main Italian newspaper, *Unione*, which normally concerned itself strictly with the activities of local community organizations and fraternal lodges. From February 1948, though, the paper adopted the suggestion of the *Pittsburgh Press* that, to confront Communist propaganda, all Italian Americans should begin a correspondence campaign with Italian relatives.[33] Over the next two months, this campaign became a central activity of the paper and the groups it served; readers were invited to copy and send a form letter declaring that "we are confronting the most tyrannical and overbearing totalitarian government, that of Moscow. Russia has already drawn the whole of eastern Europe into its sphere of influence and now, the signs are clear, the aims of Moscow are directed towards Italy."[34] Each front page in these nervous weeks focused on the central theme of "Italy in Danger," and the sense of relief at the Communist electoral defeat was as apparent in the pages of *Unione* as in the Philadelphia papers. Like Poles, Slovaks, and Ukrainians, Italians were fighting the Red threat on two continents simultaneously, and this international outlook profoundly affected their attitudes toward American politicians. The firm line by the American government and labor unions meant that the Democrats did not have to face an urban electorate that coming November trying to explain why Rome, like Prague, had slid into the Communist bloc. To the contrary, this success was to be trumpeted in ethnic constituencies. When President Truman campaigned in Scranton in 1948, his advisors outlined some powerful themes for his speech: "To be stressed: aid to Italy and all of Europe. The Displaced Persons legislation and its anti-Catholic, anti-Jewish nature. The fight of the administration against Communism and hopes to free Poland and Czechoslovakia from Soviet control just as we helped Italy escape it."[35]

Not all American ethnic groups concerned about their homelands necessarily shared the militant anti-Communist consensus, and the conservative fraternal organizations by no means spoke for every member of their respective constituencies. During the 1940s leftist and Communist militants developed a distinctive presence within the respective networks, especially among the eastern Europeans, and in a couple of instances they threatened to become the dominant force. From its earliest days, American Communism had represented a polyglot force with support in diverse ethnic communities. At least ten nationality commissions operated within the western Pennsylvania Party, seeking to mobilize Serbs, Croats, Slovenes, Slovaks, Poles, Russians, Ukrainians, Italians, Greeks, and Jews, and there was, in addition, a Negro commission. Communist influence also operated through the IWO.

Within each ethnic group, Communists established their own organizations and newspapers, while also penetrating the major mainstream structures. Even among the Poles, who would later be among the staunchest of anti-Communists, the Communists advanced their views through "progressive" organizations like the Kosciuszko League of Detroit, the Polonia Society (an iwo affiliate), Leo Krzycki's American Polish Labor Council, and, above all, the asc. Communist activism in the Polish community had been pioneered in the 1930s by Boleslaw Gebert, who was closely connected with Soviet intelligence.[36] Left influences became still more pronounced during the war years, when Communist forces in Europe and elsewhere were valued American allies and were praised by most elements of the American political consensus. Between 1942 and early 1944 the ussr was the only Allied power with significant land forces in the field against the Nazis, and the regular news media frequently praised figures like Stalin and Tito. Riding this wave of prestige, the iwo tried to portray itself as the authentic voice of the ethnic groups; in 1945 the group made an unsuccessful bid for membership in Philadelphia's Metropolitan Council for Equal Job Opportunities, which would have placed it on terms of equality with the naacp, the ajc, the Federation of Churches, and the major labor organizations.[37]

Communist views gained greater public sympathy among the Jewish community during the war years, though adherents never constituted more than a small minority. Sympathy for Communism was encouraged by adulatory coverage of the Soviet role in fighting the Nazis at just the time when Jewish papers like the Philadelphia *Exponent* were beginning to report the extermination of European Jewry. Put together, these facts made an excellent case for seeing the Soviets as the best, if not only, hope of Jewish survival in Europe. After 1945, Left Jewish groups stood out as militant opponents of any soft treatment of Germany or any slackening of denazification. During the struggle to establish the state of Israel, moreover, the major villain for the Jewish community was Great Britain, and anti-British boycotts and pickets were common in Pennsylvania cities throughout these years. Moderate papers like the *Exponent* offered caricatures of a devious and aggressive Britain of a sort rarely found in the mainstream American press, though (ironically) commonplace at this time in the Soviet and European Communist papers. In contrast, eastern European states like Czechoslovakia were acknowledged for the assistance they rendered to the new Israel. Great Britain might have been America's crucial ally against Communism, but for Jews in the 1940s (as for the Irish), it was an evil empire in its own right.

Communists enjoyed visibility through the Jewish People's Fraternal Order and the American Jewish Labor Council, both of which were admitted to Jewish federations at local and national levels. In Philadelphia both groups were included in major institutional networks like the Jewish Community Relations Council and the Philadelphia council of the ajc.[38] Not until the spring of 1949 were these groups expelled from the AJC, and the Left continued to be well represented in local affiliates. The leadership of the Philadelphia AJC was strongly progressive and Left-liberal, and Communists were active in the city's local branches and speakers' programs. In Pittsburgh the Communist Left was well represented in the Yiddisher Kultur Farband, founded in 1944, which operated a substantial Jewish Community Center.[39]

The spread of Communist influence is suggested by the groups of Yugoslav origin, the Croats, Serbs, and Slovenes, who were numerous in the Pittsburgh area: by the late 1940s, there were about 70,000 Pennsylvanians of Yugoslav stock. South Slav radical traditions dated back at least to the 1920s, when Pittsburgh's Serbian and Croatian clubs were organizational centers for leftist Westinghouse workers; a Croatian fraternal hall at Chalfant retained this role for UE radicals through the 1940s.[40] During the Second World War, Yugoslavia's Communist partisans became heroic figures, as Tito's followers led a genuine war of liberation against the Nazi occupiers. Whether or not one admired Tito, at least he clearly did not owe his power to Soviet tanks. Between 1942 and 1944, Communist militants reinforced their influence in the ethnic networks, a foothold that would become controversial in the different atmosphere of the Cold War years. South Slavs gave the local Communist Party some of its most active militants, including Croat Steve Nelson (Mesarosh), and Croats were the largest single ethnic grouping within the ASC. Workers of Yugoslav origin were disproportionately likely to support the left-wing UE in the divisive union ballots in 1950.

Another leading Croat Communist was Anthony Minerich (or Majnerich), who had been prominent in Pennsylvania's unemployed movement of the Depression years and was a major figure in the Party's ethnic press. By the 1940s he edited the Croat language paper *Narodni Glasnik* (People's Voice), which had a national circulation of 5,000–10,000.[41] The paper was formerly the *Radnichi Glasnik* (Worker's Herald), but the new title was chosen to reflect the inclusive sentiments of the Popular Front era. *Narodni Glasnik* was part of a network of ethnic Communist papers based in western Pennsylvania; in fact, all were published from the same Pittsburgh address, 1916 East Street, which served as home base for the triweekly Serbian *Slobodna Rec* (Free Expression), which had some 5,000 subscribers. *Slobodna Rec* was an important leftist voice in its own right and was close to the new Yugoslav regime. Three of its editors during the 1940s returned to Yugoslavia to take up official positions: these included Srdjan Prica, who by 1949 was the director of the American department of the Yugoslav Foreign Ministry, and Nicholas Drenovac, leader of the

Serbian Left in the United States. Another editor later joined the Yugoslav staff at the United Nations.[42] Through the war years, the Serbian and Croat press undertook vigorous propaganda in favor of the Tito partisan resistance in Yugoslavia, seeking to discredit the rightist Cetniks. The Language Press office at East Street was also the base for the Slovak *Ludovy Dennik* (People's Daily).[43] This had originally been published in Chicago with its sister paper, *Pravda*, but in 1943 both migrated to Pittsburgh under the editorship of Calvin Brook (Koloman Brueck).[44] Also among the Left press was the Carpatho-Rusyn *Vistnik* (Messenger), published out of McKees Rocks. In addition, Matt Cvetic claimed that he had been invited to found a new Slovenian paper as a counterpart to the Serb and Croat products.[45]

The East Street papers shared a common political tone, which reflected Communist Party positions to a degree that would no longer have been acceptable in the English-language media at this time. *Narodni Glasnik* published dispatches from the Soviet press agency TASS and, before the Soviet split with Tito, from the Yugoslav agency TANJUG. The three also sponsored radio programs in their respective languages from station WLOA in Braddock. Apart from Minerich and Brook, these propaganda efforts were associated with some of the most prominent Communist and progressive figures in the region, including Leo Fisher and George Wuchinich. Wuchinich's remarkable career included a spell in the Office of Strategic Services, serving with Tito's partisans and, later, alongside Chinese Communist forces. Wuchinich, a Serb, was close to the Party throughout the period; he served as executive secretary for the ASC and was a field organizer for the Wallace campaign in western Pennsylvania. His wartime background aroused fears that he might make a dangerous saboteur: in 1949 HUAC remarked that "because of his military training and espionage experience, and because western Pennsylvania is a highly strategic industrial area, Wuchinich is one of the most dangerous individuals in the American Slav Congress."[46] His undeniable achievements permitted him to ride roughshod over a HUAC hearing by contrasting his own military record with those of his interrogators.[47]

Many passages in these ethnic publications would provide rich fodder for congressional investigations into Communist subversion. In June 1949, typically, the Slovak *Ludove Noviny* reported the plan by Pressed Steel to close its McKees Rocks plant, which employed 3,000 Slovaks and other Slavs, and thereby to reduce the community to a ghost town. The problem lay, the paper claimed, in the government's refusal to trade with the socialist countries: "They claim that if the government of the United States can give billions of dollars to

Chiang Kai-Shek, the German King of Greece, the German capitalists of the Ruhr, it could also take care of the workers of McKees Rocks. But there is one catch to this. The present rulers of Washington are much closer to Nazi Germans, Fascist Greeks, dictatorial Chiangs, and Turks than to our workers in McKees Rocks. One of the reasons for growing unemployment in the United States is, after all, the Marshall Plan and the Atlantic Pact."[48]

Such sentiments were frequent in the pages of the Serbian and Croat papers.[49] Some representative examples from 1947–48 include the following: "This small handful of ruthless and greedy people is threatening with a new war, is threatening with atomic bombs, and is bent upon taking away from millions of mothers what is most precious to them—their children."[50] "It seems to me that reaction in America is not much different from that of the Fascists."[51] "The principal forces against the establishment of peace in the world are just in this country. These forces are threatening a new war. They are responsible for the big armaments in our country. They are creating hysteria and warmongering and preventing a peaceful settlement of disputes between nations—in the first place, in agreement with the Soviet Union and the new democracies in Europe."[52] Convincing evidence of direct Communist influence came following Tito's schism with Moscow in June 1948, at which point the papers immediately began denouncing the Yugoslav regime as passionately as they had once praised it, with the sudden exposure of all manner of social problems arising from crime, disease, corruption, and repression.[53]

The overtly Communist papers could be dismissed as gadflies, but in these years the Left was securing a remarkable hold on at least some important mainstream ethnic organizations, notably among the South Slavs. This process is illustrated by Matt Cvetic's career within his own Slovene ethnic group. While an avowed Communist in the mid-1940s, Cvetic served successively as executive secretary of both the American Committee for Yugoslav Relief and the ASC in western Pennsylvania; the relief committee was one of many charitable bodies set up to assist refugees and displaced persons in the aftermath of the disasters of war in which the Left developed a strong presence.[54] Cvetic exploited his ethnic background within the Party, serving as secretary and then chairman of the Party's Slovene Commission, and in this capacity, he worked with other Slovene groups in New York, Detroit, Cleveland, Chicago, and Johnstown, Pennsylvania. He also served on the Party's Nationality Commission.[55] In the Slovene Commission, he reported, "one of my first assignments was to mobilize the Slovene organizations in western Pennsylvania for the national convention of the American Slav Congress which was to be held in Pittsburgh in September 1944." Among the groups to be thus "mobilized" were the lodges of the mainstream Slovene fraternal organization, Slovenska Narodna Podporna Jednota (SNPJ), or Slovene Mutual Benefit Union, as well as the American Fraternal Union and the Slovenian American National Union: "These are not Communist Party organizations, but Communist Party members like myself who were Slovenes were instructed by the Communist Party to carry the Party line into these organizations."[56] With the support of such duly mobilized groups, the Left scored major advances at the 1944 ASC convention.

Cvetic and the Pittsburgh activists were only part of the larger leftist presence within the Slovene community. There was a leftist Slovene paper, the Cleveland-based *Enakopravnost*, and by the early 1940s an energetic speaker in these circles was Louis Adamic, who had, as a U.S. Senate committee was told, "the longest record of Communist front affiliations of any persons we have studied so far." Adamic was the main organizer of the United Committee of South Slavic Americans, a body designed to support the Tito regime, prior to the Soviet-Yugoslav split. In 1942 Adamic's faction within the Slovene community led the SNPJ and other groups affiliated with an umbrella organization, the Slovenski Amerishki Narodni Svet (SANS), or the Slovenian American National Council.[57] The SANS fell under increasing Communist influence and aligned itself to the Tito government. In 1947 Cvetic was active at the Cleveland convention of the SANS, at which seven Communist Party members were elected to the executive board and committee of the organization. By this point the SANS was under serious attack as a leftist front, to the alarm of conservative members of the mainstream SNPJ, who feared that all Slovene groups would be tainted. By 1951 the SNPJ was itself listed by HUAC as "among the Communist-dominated fraternal organizations which have constituted a bulwark of financial support for the American Slav Congress."[58] Though groups like the SNPJ retained their primary fraternal mission, there was a clear Left presence, which was closely linked to the Communist Party.

Comparable trends occurred within other South Slav groups. Among Pittsburgh Serbs, leftist and pro-Tito opinion even developed a foothold in the Orthodox Church, in which radical priests sought the removal of their anti-Communist bishop.[59] Leftist advances alarmed conservative ethnic organizations, who used both the press and the courts to expose Communist infiltration. In one characteristic case, rightist members of the Serbian Progressive Club in Wilmerding complained that the group had fallen under Communist domination, which amounted to a perversion of the body's original intents. In congressional hearings, Matt Cvetic and Harry Sherman presented the club as a virtual Soviet military outpost strategically located near Westinghouse facilities and other key industries, "preparatory to military invasion of the US." The club's leaders included prominent local leftists like Mike Vuletich, said to be a leading officer of the local Communist Party, whom Sherman claimed "was in a position himself to sabotage the important war work that was being carried on" at Westinghouse Air Brake, where he was employed.[60] The courts agreed with this sinister interpretation, appointing a receiver for the Progressive Club and issuing an injunction to prevent the new regime from using its assets.[61]

The leftist trend was apparent in the mainstream Croatian organizations. Steve Nelson records how, as early as the 1920s, Communist miners distributed their propaganda through the Pittsburgh-based Croatian Fraternal Union (CFU) as well as the SNPJ, and by 1936 the CFU was participating in an "Anti-Fascist Front."[62] By the 1940s the Left dominated groups like the Council of American Croatians and the Federation of Croatian American Women, but "progressive" elements now secured a hold on the CFU, which had 100,000 dues-paying members, and controlled substantial insurance benefits.[63] The CFU's newspaper, *Zajednicar*, was traditionally nonpolitical, but in 1943 it swung strongly to the Left, and it would be denounced by rightists for its rosy picture of the new Communist Yugoslavia.[64] *Zajednicar* represented a major gain for the Left, as its circulation was around 30,000, far larger than the Party press as strictly defined.[65] This coup initiated several years of internal conflict, which culminated with the CFU's quadrennial convention in Pittsburgh in September 1947, when the Communist-connected Left scored decisive victories. Although open Communists made up only 50 of 300 delegates, the Left slate won across the board, usually by majorities of around 175 to 125, and prominent in the new CFU regime was Steve Borich, a long-standing Communist activist in western Pennsylvania. The Yugoslav government was said to be delighted at the outcome.[66] As in the case of the Serbian club, Left victory was blighted by a prompt court decision taking charge of the organization's finances and enjoining the CFU from using its funds; in 1951 the federal government listed the CFU as a Communist-influenced organization.[67]

Communist advances were alarming for the leaders of other ethnic networks. Apart from threatening their own political positions and social dominance, the growth of leftist power threatened to taint all eastern Europeans with the Communist label, raising the prospect of a xenophobic reaction comparable to that of 1919. Such a development would have been dangerous at any time, but it was critically so in the late 1940s, when most of the ethnic groups were urgently concerned with the plight of the European displaced persons, the

"DPS" who so regularly featured in the headlines of ethnic papers across the political spectrum; indeed, Blair Gunther was national chairman of the American Resettlement Committee for Displaced Persons. The respective communities were all seeking the admission of significant numbers of displaced persons to the United States, a difficult enough task given the likely reaction to any renewal of mass immigration. If the public became convinced that eastern European immigrants were additional reinforcements for the domestic Communist conspiracy, then further admissions would be doomed.

The successes and limitations of Communist policy were exemplified by the story of the ASC, formed in 1942 as an expression of Slavic pride and solidarity. Its origins could be traced to late 1938, when Pittsburgh was the setting for a Tri-state Slav Congress designed to mobilize against Hitlerism, but this effort crumbled following the Nazi-Soviet pact and the Soviet invasion of Poland. Matters changed radically following the German invasion of the USSR.[68] By 1942 international affairs were at a remarkable juncture, with most eastern European nations under threat from Nazi aggression and seeking liberation from a solid alliance comprising the Soviet Union, the United States, and Great Britain. At such a time, there was no place for internal ideological squabbles, and even the most conservative ethnic leaders were prepared to cooperate with leftists and fellow travelers in organizing a massive demonstration of Slavic unity against Fascism. This campaign found an emotional focus in the commemoration of atrocities like the German massacre of the Czech village of Lidice in June 1942.

The new movement was born with the blessing of the United States government, which saw many advantages in a patriotic pro-war front that could appeal to large sections of the industrial working class. The movement could sell war bonds, stimulate production, and discourage labor conflict.[69] At the same time, workers themselves were by far the best-placed individuals to root out sabotage, and for two years, investigative periodicals like *The Hour* had warned that Nazi sabotage in the United States was being orchestrated by Slavic émigré groups, especially Ukrainians, but also Croats and Slovaks. If cities like Pittsburgh and Cleveland were to avoid subversive infiltration, an organization like the ASC was a necessary development, and the Roosevelt administration was happy to accept Communist support in mobilizing Slav workers.

The ASC began auspiciously. A great initial gathering convened in Detroit in April 1942, under the slogan "American Slavs, Unite for Victory," with messages of support and solidarity from the White House. The new movement claimed to represent Croatians, Serbians, Russians, Slovenians, Czechs, Poles, Slovaks, Carpatho-Rusyns, Bulgarians, Byelorussians, Ukrainians, and Macedonians, with a "nationality vice-president" for each group. In light of later charges of fellow traveling, it was striking that the president of the new organization was the militantly anti-communist Blair F. Gunther, representing the PNA. This ethnic solidarity was reproduced in many local assemblies. In June 1942, 50,000 Slavs met at Pittsburgh's Kennywood Park to celebrate American Slav Day and to hear speakers like Gunther and Harold Ickes.[70] Ickes singled out leftist ASC activist Leo Krzycki for special praise. Other speakers included Communist Party member Anthony Minerich, editor of the *Narodni Glasnik* and a member of the ASC's national committee.[71] Other Pennsylvania rallies were reported in Allentown, Johnstown, Monessen, and Farrell. This triumph of Popular Front policies inspired redoubled efforts among the various "progressive" Slav organizations, many of which held their own meetings and conventions in the coming weeks; Serbian radicals, for example, held their Seventh Vidovdan Congress, and the Slovenes formed their national council, the SANS.[72]

A second national congress, a "Victory Rally," was held in Pittsburgh in 1944, and again Harold Ickes provided an address, but this time the political environment was much less congenial.[73] With Soviet forces on the verge of a decisive push through eastern Europe, the crucial political questions of the day concerned the fate of the countries they would liberate, and throughout the region, Communist and anti-Communist forces were engaged in internecine struggles for power. Particularly divisive was the Soviet establishment of its "Lublin Committee" in July 1944, evidently a Communist shadow government ready to be imposed on Poland once the Nazis had been evicted. Notions of Slavic brotherhood were poisoned by the discovery in April 1943 of the mass graves of several thousand Polish officers in the Katyn Forest, where they had been slaughtered by Soviet authorities three years earlier. Though the Soviets blamed the crime on the Germans, and the American Left affected to believe the claim, most Polish Americans were solidly confirmed in their anti-Communist opinions, and the Katyn issue was a perennial grievance in the Polish American press through the 1950s.[74] The PNA became even more resolutely anti-Communist, and in 1944 President Rozmarek formed the Polish-American Congress as a political voice for Polish independence in the face of Soviet domination.[75]

Despite Katyn and the Polish controversies, through the first half of 1944, advocates of Slavic unity hoped to re-create the earlier spirit. A massive rally was held at Kennywood Park on June 18 to celebrate the contributions to the war effort of an estimated 15 million Americans of Slavic descent, as Mayor Scully proclaimed American Slav Week.[76] Again leftist voices were much in evidence: Louis Adamic called for Tito's recognition as leader of Yugoslavia, and Matt Cvetic now joined the ASC national committee.[77] But Popular Front sentiments did not go unchallenged. By this time mainstream ethnic organizations had withdrawn from the broad Slavic front and begun an aggressive campaign against what they regarded as a dangerous and subversive rival. In January 1944 the Serb National Federation declined to participate on the grounds that the ASC "has deserted the purpose for which it was organized and has become a tool of certain radical and communistic influences, and has become particularly a tool of one Louis Adamic."[78] Gunther himself resigned the presidency and withdrew from the organization, complaining "that today the ASC is being used by Adamic and others to put across their progressive, foreign views"; he was also dismayed at the ASC's endorsement of Roosevelt's fourth-term bid. The Pittsburgh conference may also have had longer-term significance, in bringing together Harry Sherman and Blair Gunther to form the nucleus of Americans Battling Communism; accurately or not, Sherman boasted a decade later that "I, incidentally, was the one that spearheaded that attack in Pittsburgh in 1944, to expose the Communist control of that organization [the ASC]."[79]

By the end of the European war, the ASC had earned the enmity of all the major eastern European ethnic federations, including the PNA, the Catholic Slovak Union, the Lithuanian Alliance of America, the Greek Catholic Union, the Serb National Federation, and the (Hungarian) Verhovay Fraternal Insurance Association. Slovak Catholic organizations had already refused to ally with the ASC, but now that stance was shared by other secular groups. The rightist Slovak League of America withdrew from the 1944 congress, and by 1947 it had declared the ASC a "communistic front" and a tool of Soviet foreign policy.[80] The president of the mainstream Slovak National Alliance declared in 1949: "Many of our good Americans of Czech or Slovak descent were [ASC] members during the war, when the organization worked in the lines of our war effort and supported the United States government, but when the first trends of loyalty to Soviet Russia and to communism began appearing, one after another began resigning their membership and severed all connections with this organization, so that today only real Communists and fellow travelers remain."[81] In Pennsylvania, Polish American activist Henry Dende launched radio attacks on the ASC and its local Scranton affiliate: "This organization is

Communistic in nature. It is affiliated with the national American Congress which time after time was investigated by the Congressional Committee on Un-American Activities. . . . [President] Krzycki has recently spent five months in Russia, visiting Joe Stalin, and other satellite countries." Despite this, "higher officials of this local American Slav Congress here in Scranton . . . are Democrat job holders in the Lackawanna County Court House."[82]

With the mainstream groups gone, the ASC became ever more closely aligned to the Communist and pro-Soviet cause, and subsequent investigators would date its transformation into a Communist front to the 1944 meetings. Matt Cvetic claimed that at this convention, Communists "were instrumental in getting party members in most of the key positions."[83] Left influence was even more apparent in the conventions of 1946 (New York) and 1948 (Chicago), and the organization's statements closely followed Communist policies in both domestic labor disputes and international confrontations.[84] Another decisive split with the mainstream organizations came with the Yalta Conference of 1945, which many groups denounced as a political betrayal of their respective nations.[85]

By this stage the most visible leftist representatives in the national ASC were Leo Krzycki and George Pirinsky, but local affiliates were under blatant Communist direction.[86] In western Pennsylvania the group was dominated by Party activists and associates like Anthony Minerich, George Pirinsky, and Joseph Rudiak; at different times both Cvetic and Wuchinich served as executive secretary of the regional ASC.[87] ASC worked closely with Henry Wallace's Progressive campaign; Krzycki served as chairman of Wallace's Nationalities Division and vice chairman of the PCA, and another campaign leader was Vjekoslav I. Mandic, who had recently participated in the Left victory within the CFU.[88] In late 1947 Wallace's representatives cooperated with leftists like Wuchinich, Adamic, and Cvetic in seeking to mobilize the Slavic vote, while Calvin Brook organized Progressive Party activities among Pennsylvania Slovaks.[89] Joseph Rudiak himself was a Progressive candidate for local office in Pittsburgh.[90] In turn, Wallace's rhetoric closely echoed that of the ASC. At the York People's Convention that launched the third party in Pennsylvania in March 1948, the candidate's speech denounced those "engaged in building up the bogey of a Slav menace," warning that "the threat of atom bombs will not intimidate the peoples of Moscow, Belgrade, Warsaw and Prague."[91] In reaction to the recent coup in Czechoslovakia, which had created such alarm in the United States, Wallace was sanguine: "Nor can it be said that the present political situation in Czechoslovakia is less democratic than the situation in France."[92] ASC activists were much in evidence at the founding convention of the Progressive Party in Philadelphia in June, and through 1947 and 1948, the ASC's magazine *Slavic American* became a Wallace campaign sheet.[93]

In its brief period of popularity, the ASC movement offered a potentially powerful rhetoric that associated Slavic pride and ethnic consciousness with a left-wing political stance, challenging the idea that Slavic identity necessarily implied ultra-rightist or militarist views.[94] This was an important manifestation of a kind of leftist pan-Slavic Americanism, but the ideological synthesis was to be short-lived.

From 1947 the major Slavic organizations launched a counteroffensive against the Left, as long-standing resentments were brought to new heights by the takeover of the CFU and the Wallace movement's co-optation of "American Slav" rhetoric. Moreover, however effective its use of front groups, the Communist Party could never really conceal its role in the ASC, because of the penetration by Cvetic and others. Communist nationality policy was rapidly leaked to the FBI and, presumably, to the media and to rightist political groups like ABC.

One early sign of a reaction came in Pittsburgh in November 1947, when Robert Taylor of the *Pittsburgh Press* undertook a ten-day exposé of the Communist presence in the ethnic organizations, showing the reliance of the East Street papers on Soviet-bloc news services and the Communist slant of the Slovak media. Day after day, headlines announced: "Communists Try to Use Slavic Groups in US as Red Party Front," "Slavic Papers Here Receive Soviet Service," and "American Slav Congress Is Chief Party Line Front." Taylor wrote that "an intensive campaign is under way—with Pittsburgh as the center—to organize ten million Slavs in support of Communist policies, programs and objectives."[95] The series also exposed the "usual suspects" from the ASC, who would feature so regularly in investigations over the next decade, including Calvin Brook, Steve Borich, Nicholas Drenovac, and Tony Minerich.[96]

Taylor's sources probably included FBI materials, but he was also drawing on information from conservative ethnic groups. *Slobodna Rec* struck back against the criticism and "its main source of information, the *American Srbobran*," the organ of the Serb National Federation, "which has . . . joined American national reaction in strengthening the Fascist activities in this country." The ASC denounced the *Press* and its sources, among which it named Blair Gunther and Harry Sherman, with the implication that Gunther was representing the local

PNA.[97] Indeed, ABC can be seen as an organ not merely of the anti-Communist Right in western Pennsylvania, but also, more specifically, of the conservative ethnic organizations. ABC's treasurer was Paul Kazimer, the president of the *Slovak in America* newspaper, who was associated with the most conservative wing of the Slovak anti-Communist movement; he would later head the Slovak section of the Democratic Party's Nationalities Division.[98] ABC ally Walter Alessandroni was the nephew of Judge Eugene Alessandroni, one of the dominant figures in the Sons of Italy, both in Pennsylvania and in the nation at large. In addition, Judge Musmanno was in his own right a leading figure in the Sons of Italy.

In 1949 conservatives brought their complaints to a national stage through the activities of the congressional investigative committees. One opportunity came when the U.S. Senate's Subcommittee on Immigration and Naturalization held hearings on "Communist Activities among Aliens and National Groups," with a view to passing legislation that ultimately became the McCarran-Walter Immigration Act. From May onward, a succession of conservative spokesmen appeared before the committee to denounce Red influences among their particular ethnic groups. One unspoken agenda was the need to establish the anti-Communist bona fides of the eastern European groups, in order to forestall any potential backlash against refugees. In July, Andrew Valuchek of the Slovak National Alliance exposed the Pittsburgh-based press associated with Calvin Brook.[99] In September the committee received a massive report by Serb anti-Communist Dr. Slobodan M. Draskovich on the pervasive Red rhetoric in the *Narodni Glasnik* and the *Slobodna Rec*. The Croat Left was in turn denounced by Giunio Zorkin, the former head of the Croatian Peasant Party, who had fled the Tito regime and was appalled to find the Left so ensconced among his fellow immigrants to the United States.[100] Throughout, the committee singled out the ASC as an egregious front organization.

The ASC was once more excoriated in a lengthy 1949 report from HUAC, which declared that "the American Slav Congress is a Moscow-inspired and directed federation of Communist-dominated organizations seeking by methods of propaganda and pressure to subvert the ten million people in this country of Slavic birth or descent. By means of a nationalist appeal it strives to enlist our Slavic population in behalf of Russia's ambitious designs for world empire and simultaneously to incite American Slavs against the land of their adoption." Further, it is "a powerful pressure medium in behalf of Soviet foreign policy within the United States. It has never deviated from the line of the Communist Party, USA."[101] The committee's case was illustrated by a substantial body of internal letters and telegrams, many of which derived from Blair Gunther. Throughout, these investigations portrayed the leftist groups as organized arms of Soviet-bloc intelligence, and certain individuals were singled out as likely spies or saboteurs on the basis of their military records, including Steve Nelson, George Wuchinich, and others. The FBI claimed that Calvin Brook had been involved in a spy ring operated through the Czechoslovak consulate in Pittsburgh.[102]

By the end of 1949 the two investigating committees had comprehensively denounced the key leftist individuals and groups operating within the eastern European ethnic networks, but worse publicity was to come following the Cvetic defection. Much of Cvetic's account concerned the Communist affiliations of ASC and numerous other progressive ethnic groups, and all were portrayed as tools manipulated by the Communist Party. The ASC was headlined as "the top Commie Front for infiltration of nationality groups."[103] Based on what appeared to be first-hand inside evidence, the federal government now listed as subversive many of the groups targeting an eastern European constituency; by 1953 the attorney general's list of subversive organizations included the groups shown in Table 6. By 1951 the last of the three East Street papers had closed operations in Pennsylvania. Also in this year, Louis Adamic died mysteriously, in what was reported as a suicide, though the press charged that he was killed by orthodox Communists in retaliation for his pro-Tito stance.[104]

The Cvetic exposé sent shockwaves through the ethnic organizations, most of which were already nervous about the Red presence, and which now saw the worst conservative fears apparently confirmed. Jews had particular reason for alarm, given the desperate situation of many of the remaining European displaced persons and the nightmare that conservatives might resuscitate the old stereotype of the "Jewish Bolshevik." Only a month after Cvetic's testimony, conservatives in the Philadelphia AJC launched an internal coup that deposed both the executive director, John Bernheimer, and the executive secretary. Not coincidentally, the director's brother-in-law was the head of the leftist Jewish People's Fraternal Order, and Bernheimer himself acted as attorney for the Pennsylvania Progressive Party long after most non-Communists had abandoned it.[105] The conservative faction had drawn information about the supposed Communist connections of the Progressive group directly from contacts within the FBI. That August, the head of Pennsylvania's Jewish War Veterans boasted to the state's American Legion convention of his efforts to purge Communists and leftists. He pledged to assist other veterans "in making sure that

Table 6. Selected Ethnic and Fraternal Organizations Listed as Subversive by the U.S. Attorney General

American Committee for Yugoslav Relief
American Croatian Congress
American Jewish Labor Council
American Polish Labor Council
American Slav Congress
American Russian Institute, Philadelphia
Central Council of American Women of Croatian Descent (and cognates)
Croatian Benevolent Fraternity
International Workers' Order (iwo) and all its subsidiaries
Jewish People's Committee
Jewish People's Fraternal Order
Polonia Society of the iwo
Serbia American Fraternal Society
Serbian Vidovdan Council
Slovak Workers' Society
Slovenian American National Council
Ukrainian American Fraternal Union
Union of American Croatians
United Committee of South Slavic Americans

Source: *Digest of the Public Record of Communism in the United States* (New York: Fund for the Republic, 1955), 67–74.

while our boys are cutting the cancer out of the rest of the world, the Communist cancer, we will try to cut out that cancer on the home front."[106]

After the exposés of 1949–50, the leftist challenge to the ethnic organizations was decisively rolled back, to the extent that mere association with any one of the list of stigmatized organizations was sufficient to invite a searching inquiry. New immigration laws posed a devastating threat to any foreign-born adherent of radical views, who could in theory be deported or denaturalized. Though ultimately unsuccessful in many of the attempted deportations, the government's effort to remove radicals succeeded in tying up a number of the leading Left figures in Pennsylvania, often for years. In western Pennsylvania alone, principal targets included Steve Nelson, George Wuchinich, Allan McNeil, and Nick Lazari.[107]

Without these internal rivals, the established leaderships of the various ethnic federations could focus their considerable power on denouncing Communist evils and calling on the U.S. government to repeal the Yalta compromise, root out subversives at home, and roll back Communism worldwide. When the Polish-American Congress held its convention in Philadelphia in 1956, President Rozmarek's keynote speech declared that "treating the Red criminals as gentlemen was the greatest blunder of American foreign diplomacy. . . . Instead of leading them on the road to freedom, American foreign policy mismanagement abandoned to red slavery hundreds of millions of people who, when the time is right, will be forced to fight against us. . . . Annul Yalta!"[108] But vigorous anti-Soviet sentiments were not confined to the furthest reaches of eastern European revanchism, and the new consensus was shared by traditionally liberal communities like the Jews, especially after the outbreak of the Korean War. The anti-Communism of the Jewish press developed a harder edge from about 1951, with the emergence of overt anti-Semitism in the eastern European purges, the Czech Slansky trial, and the Soviet Doctors Plot. Outrage reached new heights with the execution of Jewish Communist leaders in Czechoslovakia in late 1952.[109]

With so many groups espousing the most extreme anti-Communist policies, it was inevitable that someone would seek to unite the various eastern European groups in a common crusade, a rightist response to the old Popular Front notion of "American Slavism." There were a series of endeavors such as the Assembly of Captive European Nations. In the mid-1950s the larger movement found its figurehead in Judge Gunther, who was developing national political ambitions: he was seriously regarded in 1957 as a candidate for the U.S. Supreme Court, and when this honor failed to materialize, he made an abortive bid to replace Rozmarek as national leader of the PNA. Throughout, his political stance was founded on calls for a determined and confrontational foreign policy, along with a domestic coalition of Slavic and other ethnic groups.[110] In 1956 Gunther presided over a conference that created a new National Confederation of American Ethnic Groups, which united the efforts of fifty-two nationality organizations. The group declared as its chief goal supporting "the basic principles of liberation, self-determination and full sovereignty for all peoples and nations, as opposed to the policies of unprincipled expediency which have characterized the conduct of US affairs in the field of world relations so frequently in the post-war world." Soviet action in Hungary was condemned as an example of "treachery, murder and aggression . . . ruthless repression and systematic terrorism."[111]

Though the confederation itself achieved little visibility, its activists joined the alphabet soup of radical anti-Communist and revanchist groups of the 1950s and 1960s, the best known of which were the World Anti-Communist League and the Anti-Bolshevik Bloc of Nations.[112] These found a political focus in the crusade to secure visibility for the so-called captive nations, those groups that claimed to have been suppressed by Communist tyranny. The rhetoric was politically suspect in that some would-be national groups owed their existence only to their support of Nazi policies in the Second World War, and they were often linked to the most extreme views. Nevertheless, the idea achieved recognition in July 1959, when President Eisenhower recognized Captive Nations Week, a commemoration that survived in vestigial form until the collapse of world Communism in the 1980s. The captive nations movement epitomized the role of the ethnic organizations as bastions of ultra-Right sentiment, the coldest of cold warriors, but this position had not been attained without serious leftist challenge.

CONSTRUCTING THE BEAST

THE CHURCHES AND ANTI-COMMUNISM

The advent of the atomic bomb and push-button warfare has
silenced those who once scoffed at talk of doom's day.
—Billy Graham, Pittsburgh, 1952[1]

While it is not difficult to understand why an anti-Communist consensus
should have developed in the late 1940s, there were additional reasons why particular groups should have been so hostile to Communism even before such
views became a national orthodoxy, and religious motivations must be stressed
here. Throughout the Cold War, many Americans framed their opposition to
Communism in terms of a countervailing religious ideology. One critical force
in this religious movement was the Catholic Church, which saw Communism
as a form of absolute evil, literally inspired by the devil, with which no compromise was possible.[2] Because of the pivotal role of Catholicism in Pennsylvania's modern political history, anti-Communism found firm roots in many
communities that had wholeheartedly joined the New Deal coalition. While
Catholicism had always retained a virulently anti-Communist tradition, this
had been subsumed in the 1930s into social and economic issues of more immediate concern, particularly in promoting the sound development of organized labor. After 1945, though, changes in both domestic and foreign circumstances caused the church to focus much more sharply on the perceived Red
peril and the threat of anti-Christian persecution. The consequences would be
seen in the ferocity of political conflict in the labor movement and the ethnic
organizations.

This chapter will discuss the specifically religious and even apocalyptic foundations of the intense anti-Communist sentiment found among Pennsylvania's Catholics, which had its roots in ideas of martyrdom, prophecy, and visions. It will also examine the role of anti-Communism in the Protestant evangelical movement. Though evangelicals have attracted far less attention in this context than Catholics, their distinctive religious ideas had broad influence through the crusades, revivals, and missions of the era. In this sense, the remarkable religious phenomenon of the Billy Graham crusades, which had such an impact in Pennsylvania's cities, must be seen in the context of the broader anti-Communist movement.

Throughout the post-1945 anti-Communist reaction, we repeatedly find Catholics among the most visible leaders and militants of the patriotic upsurge, and many were Democrats who had been prominent in the New Deal coalitions of the 1930s. Francis Walter was a Catholic, as were Judges Gunther and Musmanno, Joe Barr, Matt Cvetic, and many local figures of less celebrity: Bella Dodd, Elizabeth Bentley, and Louis Budenz were among many Communist defectors for whom Catholic conversion marked the decisive break with a leftist political past. Catholics were prominent in all the manifestations of anti-Communist activism, which was a mainstay of Catholic ideology long before it became a fundamental American creed. From 1946 the Knights of Columbus, the Holy Name Societies, and the Catholic War Veterans took the lead in denouncing international Communism and opposing any popular entertainment that featured real or suspected Communists.[5]

Catholic clergy were among the most active and militant anti-Communists, notably in the struggle for control of the labor unions, where political and religious rhetoric were inextricably intertwined. The ACTU was the vanguard in the attempt to dislodge the Left from the leadership of UE, and many other priests besides Father Rice were noted for their anti-Communist enthusiasm. Vito Mazzone was pastor of one of South Philadelphia's best-known Italian parishes, St. Mary Magdalene de Pazzi; he also enjoyed a reputation as a dedicated anti-Communist preacher and pamphleteer, the author of a tract entitled *Communism: The Satanic Scourge*. For Father Mazzone, Communism, or "red tyranny," was "the greatest enemy ever faced by religion in the history of mankind," as it was directed not against one particular form of belief, but "against all religions, against God Himself." Matt Cvetic tells of an encounter with another priest of the same stripe. While playing his role as a Communist in the mid-1940s,

Cvetic occasionally attended Mass in Pittsburgh to fulfill his spiritual duties, even though this risked destroying his elaborate charade. Anxious to share his secret, he told his whole story to the priest, who criticized him for having taken such a risk: his religious obligations must take second place to his role as undercover agent. The priest reportedly told him that "you are doing a noble job, and a wonderful service for God and your country."[4]

Catholic institutions emerged as reliable bases for the anti-Communist crusade. In Philadelphia, likely supporters for the ACTU movement were trained at the labor schools run through Catholic colleges like Lasalle and St. Joseph's. In Pittsburgh, Duquesne University played an active role, under the leadership of Father John Schlicht. In 1951 the school held the first of its popular annual series of "Institutes on Communism," which gave the general public an opportunity to hear about Communism from the inside, from defectors like Matt Cvetic, Paul Crouch, and Louis Budenz. Soon Father Schlicht was broadcasting in a regular weekly television slot, and each of the institute lectures was televised. The Duquesne series soon extended to dramatized trials, in which defectors or "victims of Communism" testified to real-life judges like Harry Montgomery, who rendered their verdicts against the Communist system. Meanwhile, students at Catholic colleges were fervent supporters of anti-Communist protests like the alternative May Day parades sponsored by Newman clubs in the late 1940s. With their political loyalty above suspicion, schools like Duquesne now became natural recruiting grounds for the FBI.[5]

The clerical role in anti-Communist militancy at the national level was suggested by the work of leftist journalist John L. Spivak, who in 1947 undertook his own infiltration by masquerading as a conservative Philadelphia businessman. Purporting to represent a group of loyal citizens concerned about Red infiltration in the Philadelphia unions, Spivak wrote to the U.S. Chamber of Commerce's Committee on Socialism and Communism, seeking experts who could help root out this cancer. The Chamber of Commerce referred Spivak to Father John F. Cronin of the National Catholic Welfare Conference in Washington, D.C.: "He has a long experience in research of this type and knows a great many people who have high competence to do this kind of job." Spivak says that he had to reread this letter several times, astonished at such stark proof of the intimate alliance between the Catholic Church and the most reactionary segments of American capitalism, which Marxists had long contended existed.[6] Cronin's multifaceted role in anti-Communist politics has been discussed at length by scholars like Charles Morris. It was Cronin who first introduced Nixon to Whittaker Chambers and the whole Alger Hiss case, and he provided a conduit for passing secret FBI materials to Nixon and his colleagues.[7]

By the late 1940s anti-Communism was not merely a political belief of the church, it was integrated into everyday practice and devotional life throughout the Catholic world. It is difficult to overestimate the role of religious loyalties in shaping the political and cultural outlook of ordinary believers in Pennsylvania and comparable regions. In big cities, individuals commonly identified their home areas in terms of their parishes, Sacred Heart or St. Margaret Mary, rather than secular districts like Kensington or South Philadelphia. In political terms, this intense loyalty gave a solid foundation to anti-Communism of the most extreme kind, in a state that was over a quarter Catholic, and in which Catholics generally made up 40 percent of the legislature.[8]

This militancy is also suggested by the Catholic press, which pioneered a hard anti-Communist line even before it was adopted by the secular press. Since the 1930s, some of the most extreme anti-Communist rhetoric was found in diocesan papers like the *Catholic Standard and Times* (Philadelphia) or the *Pittsburgh Catholic*, as well as in local publications like the *Register*, in the diocese of Altoona-Johnstown. The papers conveyed these ideas to an impressively large readership: the Altoona-Johnstown *Register* alone had a paid circulation of some 20,000. The stories, features, and cartoons of these years repeatedly demonstrate the omnipresence of the Communist threat in Catholic life throughout this period. In 1946 a typical *Register* cartoon showed a clerk with a photograph of Stalin on his desk and a telephone labeled "Party Line." As an arm descends to investigate his "Un-American Activities," he protests, "But I'm a loyal government worker!"; the caption is "Which government?"[9] This seems to be a familiar warning about Reds in government employment, but the date is strikingly early, well before the HUAC campaign reached its height. Similarly, a January 1948 cartoon noted the "tattletale pink" of the third-party Progressive campaign, with its "Commie Support," ten months before the actual election.[10]

Readers of the Catholic press were expected to share wholeheartedly in the concerns of Senator McCarthy. In early 1950, three days after his Wheeling speech, a *Register* cartoon depicted a Soviet spymaster sending an agent to Washington with the consolation: "Our starting pay is low, Comrade, but you can supplement your income with a government job in Washington." In the corner, a pumpkin holds a paper labeled "H-Bomb Dope." This cartoon appeared within weeks of President Truman's announcing American plans to develop a hydrogen bomb and over a year before the first successful test, at a time when there was no suggestion of an espionage threat to this program; the pumpkin reference recalls Richard Nixon's vigilance in the Hiss case.[11] In the spring of 1950, with the McCarthy campaign reaching full momentum, other cartoons denounced members of the media for their refusal to accept the charges, their "whitewash of reds" and "smearing of witnesses," and their assertions of "no Communists in Washington."[12]

The early date of such efforts reminds us perhaps of how much of "McCarthyism" predated McCarthy, and, indeed, outlived him. Recent scholars have rightly described how many ordinary Catholics of the early 1950s were dubious about McCarthy's goals and tactics and were by no means as solidly united behind him as might be thought from some of the more extreme periodicals and from leaders like Cardinal Spellman.[13] But while some Catholic hearts and minds remained untouched by the senator's appeal, it is difficult to find any doubts about the rightness of the spiritual war against Communism, or about the absolute evil that that adversary represented. When the senator chose a Catholic Day celebration in Johnstown in 1954 to announce to a crowd of some 15,000 that "there are no tactics too rough to weed out the underground influence which threatens the very heart of the American republic," he was preaching to the converted, and they had been converted well before McCarthy had begun his own movement.[14]

The fact that the Catholic Church was profoundly anti-Communist is scarcely surprising, but the deep roots of that hostility deserve emphasis: this was a theological and mystical belief, rather than just a political stance. The church had viewed godless Communism as a deadly enemy long before the Bolshevik revolution. By the late nineteenth century, it was a Catholic commonplace that the politics of the Western world were dividing into two great intellectual camps, increasingly identified as Catholicism and Communism. The Russian Revolution of 1917 made the menace acute, and in the 1930s the Catholic nightmare of a dechristianized Europe was closer than at any time since the worst periods of the French Revolution. In response, American Catholics were deeply committed to military confrontation with Communism, especially in Spain.[15]

The papacy responded to the crisis with all the ideological tools at its disposal, opposing the Red forces of Communism with the "Blue Army" of the Virgin Mary, a confrontation often discussed in terms of these colors. Central to the new Marian devotion was the memory of Fátima, the Portuguese village in which the Virgin was said to have appeared to three peasant children from 1917 onward. The Virgin of Fátima was credited with various prophecies, including one that Russia would "spread her errors throughout the world, promoting wars," but also that even that country would ultimately be converted through the Virgin's Immaculate Heart. The fates of Russia and Communism became an apocalyptic sign, intimately connected to the future of the church and the final conflict between light and darkness. The Virgin of the apparition was identified with the "woman clothed with the Sun" described in the biblical book of Revelation, who escapes the attack of the "great red dragon"; the color red naturally suggested the Communist menace. The Fátima story was cherished by Pope Pius XII (1939–58), who combined intense Marian devotion with a virulent hatred of Communism. Through his influence, the Fátima mythology gained worldwide attention, serving as the gospel of the anti-Communist crusade.[16]

In the decade after 1945, Pius aggressively promoted his twin agendas of Marian devotion and anti-Communism. In 1949 the pope confirmed a statement of the Holy Office declaring it unlawful for any Catholic in good standing to join a Communist Party or to write articles in support of Communist causes, nor could any priest administer the sacraments to those who did such things.[17] The following year the pope proclaimed that the bodily Assumption of the Virgin was a matter of faith required of all Catholics. These ideas were deeply influential in the United States. Bishop Fulton Sheen often made Fátima the subject of his popular radio programs, and a million Americans signed up for the "Blue Army of Fátima," pledging to pray for the conversion of Russia.[18] There were also widely reported American visions of the Virgin, though church authorities treated these with much suspicion, for fear of permitting the spread of eccentric doctrine. At the summit of the American church was Cardinal Spellman, lover of Fátima and an uncompromising enemy of Communism.[19]

Throughout these years, opposition to Communism became the leading emphasis of Catholic political activism, and the church's international orientation meant that American Catholics were deeply concerned with affairs in areas of the world that attracted little attention from the mainstream. Ordinary Catholics were more likely to write or demonstrate about such international matters than any other group apart from the Communist faithful themselves; both Catholicism and Communism in this period were true universal churches. The Catholic Church in North America served to disseminate European conflicts and fears substantially before these had an impact on the non-Catholic mainstream, and often before they affected legislators.

Catholic attitudes were radicalized by the rapid collapse of eastern and central European nations to Communism and the imminent likelihood that atheistic Communist regimes might soon prevail from the English Channel to the

Bering Straits.[20] The church in several nations suffered from land redistribution and confiscation of property, while the persecution of eastern European clergy began soon after the creation of Communist hegemony. In 1946 the Croat Archbishop Stepinac was arrested in Yugoslavia, ostensibly for wartime collaboration. Cardinal-Archbishop Jozsef Mindszenty was arrested in December 1948 for his opposition to the new Communist government of Hungary, and he remained a symbol of militant anti-Communism throughout the next two decades. Czechoslovakian clergy were sentenced en masse to work in the deadly uranium mines. Particularly hard hit across the Continent were the "Uniat" churches, groups who followed an Orthodox liturgy, but who recognized the supremacy of the pope. From the end of the war, Soviet policy demanded that the Uniats abandon Catholic loyalties and return to the Orthodox fold, leading to harsh persecution in the Ukraine, Romania, and elsewhere. Communist victory in China appalled Catholics, who had a vigorous missionary presence in that region, and who had seen the vast Chinese population as ripe for evangelization.

From as early as 1945, American Catholics were expressing deep concern about European developments, beginning with Poland. Catholic anti-Communist agitation intensified, as "what had previously been only one of a large number of concerns became virtually a way of life."[21] In December 1946, tens of thousands demonstrated in Philadelphia against the persecution of Archbishop Stepinac, in a gathering organized by the Catholic War Veterans and vigorously publicized by the archdiocese through the *Catholic Standard and Times*. The chairman was Judge Vincent Carroll, a long-standing anti-Communist partisan; in a keynote speech, Judge Clare Fenerty warned that America would soon pay for its willingness to cave in to Soviet wishes at Tehran and Yalta: "It will be almost miraculous if this nation does not pay with hundreds of thousands of American lives and the destruction of our cities by atomic warfare for trying to appease the unappeasable."[22] The event was supported by Catholic politicians like U.S. senator Myers, who had made the horrors of the Yugoslav regime the focus of his address to the state American Legion convention that August.[23]

The focus on Stepinac indicated the Catholic concern for leaders seen as martyrs and confessors. In the battle for control of UE in 1949, Pittsburgh clergy read from their pulpits an ACTU statement urging the faithful to vote at all costs, warning of a "moral duty to vote in this election and to vote not to uphold Communism. The leaders of the international UE support the attackers and persecutors of Archbishop Stepinac, Cardinal Mindszenty and the heroic priests and nuns and Catholic people behind the Iron Curtain. The people over there cannot vote against Communism. You still can."[24] Calling on parishioners to support IUE in the following year's union ballots, the priest of Pittsburgh's St. William's Church stated: "Our holy Father the Pope has declared that it is not lawful for Catholics to support a Communist enterprise. . . . War with the Soviet Union grows more imminent every day. . . . [T]he same vicious Communist conspiracy which dominates the UE is oppressing and jailing and killing our priests, nuns and bishops behind the Iron Curtain."[25] In most of the state, Poles moved decisively against the Left in these elections, though Italian workers were divided.[26]

The martyrdom of the eastern European clergy became a central theme of Catholic writing on Communism over the next two decades. From as early as 1946, the Altoona-Johnstown *Register* was regularly describing Red religious persecutions in terms of the mergers forced upon Uniat churches in the Ukraine, Croatia, and Slovakia and reporting efforts by Pennsylvania's ethnic groups to support their coreligionists.[27] A typical issue in September 1946 offered an anthology of stories as "One Week's Story of Red Turmoil," as well as a rave review of Hamilton Fish's hard-line tract *The Challenge of World Communism*. Stepinac's arrest that same month provided the *Register* with its central story for several issues, under headlines like "Archbishop Stepinac Case Arouses Horror in World," and even "Another Christ Before Pilate."[28] The Christ analogy would recur during the trial of Cardinal Mindszenty during early 1949, when a cartoon depicted Jesus "on trial again" before the courts of eastern Europe.[29] The identification was made possible by the cherished Catholic idea that priests perform the role of Christ in the Mass, so that an attack on the clergy reproduced the original crucifixion. Mindszenty provided the church with a personification of Catholic suffering at the hands of Communism, a real or potential martyr, and the bishop of Altoona-Johnstown designated February 6 as "Cardinal Mindszenty Day," with appropriate prayers and services. Throughout the 1950s, the cardinal possessed a de facto sanctity among American Catholics.[30]

Mindszenty's plight was the subject of weekly headlines through 1949, with linkages to other horror stories. A few weeks in early 1949 alone brought front-page headlines like "Plot to Destroy Church Is Threatened in Poland"; "Commies Step Up Persecution Tempo"; "Church in Romania Is Wiped Out" and "Reds Slay Abbot at Prison Camp"; "Priest Refuses to Break Seal of Confession, Gets Prison Term" (in Yugoslavia); and "Polish Clergy Suffering New Persecution for Their Faith."[31] Another story that February warned of the impending danger to the Chinese missions, noting, "Missioners to Stay Despite Reds' Push—1220 Priests Remain in Zone of Danger in China."[32] The persecution theme remained at the forefront of Catholic concern throughout the next decade. A 1954 survey was claimed to show "186 Heads of Catholic Sees Dead, in Prison or in Exile: Survey Reveals Fate of 4 Cardinals, 33 Archbishops, 116 Bishops, 33 Prelates."[33] Shortly afterward, it was reported that "Ten of Hierarchy, 2,000 Priests in Ukraine Victimized by Reds—Many of Clergy and Laity Martyrs for Faith."[34] When in 1963 Father Mazzone faithfully listed the new martyrs and confessors for the faith, he claimed that Communism had been directly responsible for the deaths of over fifty bishops and 30,000 priests, to say nothing of other nonlethal persecutions: "*Poland*—1000 priests deported (usually to Siberia); *Czechoslovakia*—300 secular priests jailed . . . *Hungary*— About 1000 priests and nuns jailed; 538 put to death or deported. . . . The list of thirteen forms of persecution includes being buried alive, tongues cut out, eyes put out, shot or machine-gunned, and death from torture."[35]

Tales of global persecution and aggression provided ample material for countless tracts, lectures, and sermons. Though these stories were intended to incite anger and inspire political pressure, they carried multiple religious messages. At the most basic level, the conduct of a Mindszenty or a Stepinac offered moral lessons about courage in the face of adversity, but the correctness of their stance was said to be confirmed by miraculous intervention. In 1954 a story described a case in Indochina in which the Communist Vietminh had refused to permit the movement of a shipment of consecrated hosts.[36] When the hosts eventually were transported over a year later, they were found to be in perfectly fresh condition, despite the tropical weather conditions.

The idea of defending the church against Communism permeated the laity at the parochial level.[37] In 1948, 1,000 people turned out for a lecture to the Johnstown Catholic Forum by a priest who had worked as a missionary in China. The lecturer, Rev. Theophane Maguire, presented an uncompromising picture: "The Communist menace in China, the priest said, is imminently serious and may any day explode at our backs like another Pearl Harbor, while we watch Berlin. During the course of his talk, he showed that the insurgents take their orders from Moscow. He then asked his listeners whether we would give place in our own government if they should grow stronger and organized themselves into a rebellious army." (As Maguire was speaking two weeks before the presidential elections, he undoubtedly intended his listeners to contemplate analogies with America's own Henry Wallace movement.) Maguire argued that Communist advances in China were aided by the U.S. State Department, an early use of the "Who lost China?" canard even before China was actually lost.[38]

Father Maguire's speech represented the commonplaces of Catholic political rhetoric on international issues. Some months later, Blair County's Ancient Order of Hibernians submitted a statement to the president and the state's U.S. senators demanding resolute resistance to Communist tyranny, which was so amply demonstrated by the persecution of Stepinac and Mindszenty and by the "foreign invasion" of what were now the East Bloc nations.[39] Such protests became all but obligatory for loyal Catholic gatherings, and even a meeting of the alumni of Johnstown's Catholic High School ended with an appeal to the U.S. secretary of state demanding Mindszenty's release; similar demands were formulated by Holy Name Societies throughout the diocese.[40] In this context, it is easy to see a political agenda in events that might otherwise appear purely religious in tone, as when the Johnstown American Legion post sponsored a presentation of the 1952 film *Miracle at Fátima*, which drew some 13,000 people to the Cambria County War Memorial Arena.[41]

Charles Morris remarks that Catholic anti-Communism has variously been associated with "status anxiety, as the hyper-patriotism of the ethnic outsider, as anti-Semitism, as a reflection of traditional political loyalties. . . . But these explanations typically miss the religious component of the Catholic stance. To Catholics, Stalin was the Antichrist, a satanic figure of biblical proportions."[42] In the tense international conditions prevailing in late 1949, the *Register* published a cartoon that initially seems to be a characteristic warning against complacency in the face of Red expansionism: an American sleeps peacefully despite headlines on newspapers lying around him, which read "Communism Sweeps Europe," "Pope Calls for Militant Action," and "Antichrist Gains in USA."[43] The reference to this supernatural figure of evil raises the question of how literally Catholic leaders and activists took the notion of an apocalyptic confrontation with Communism.[44] Certainly "Antichrist" is a common metaphor in the political rhetoric of the period, and it gained force from the nuclear context: popular media of the 1950s often referred to "H-Bombs" as "Hell-Bombs."

By the late 1940s the secular news media were full of images that fitted extraordinarily well with supernatural and even mystical theories: the confrontation with absolute evil, the rise of an anti-Christian superstate, the development of "hell-bombs" capable of vast fiery destruction. All these aspects of the modern world appeared to be fulfilling the requirements for the end of the world outlined in the book of Revelation and the vast body of written work erected upon that foundation; Stepinac and Mindszenty could even be presented as the martyred "Two Witnesses" foretold there. With the approach of the Holy Year of 1950, and the endless retellings of the Fátima story, Catholic papers found themselves responding to requests from readers for discussions of apocalyptic themes. In 1949 the *Register* remarked, "Of late years, probably because of the spread of persecution, a feeling has arisen among not a few that the reign of Antichrist was beginning or is close at hand. We have often received letters about the problem." Though the writer refused to confirm this belief explicitly, he did state that "one of the great prophetic signs of his coming is now perhaps evident—the Great Apostasy. Communism is responsible. . . . The rejection of Christianity is widespread. We are face to face now with real apostasy."[45] In August 1951 another front-page feature addressed "The Coming of the Dreadful Antichrist," again in response to public demands for information: "A number of letters have reached us in recent weeks asking for a discussion of the Antichrist. It is obvious that the unsettled condition of the world, with a fear of grave impending evil because of the atom bomb and the diabolism of Communist leaders, is making many persons think of this mysterious forthcoming embodiment of evil. The fact that a great apostasy—not merely a heresy but a falling into atheism—has marked our times makes some believe the era of the greatest evil is close."[46]

Imagery of hell, the devil, and the Antichrist pervade Catholic writing on the confrontation with Communism. It is often difficult to tell whether a given Catholic reference to Communism as "Antichristian" means that that ideology is opposed to Christianity or that it actively serves the Antichrist, but the two meanings are often juxtaposed.[47] Once again, articles and cartoons contextualize skepticism, secularism, and atheism with the widely recognized political danger of Soviet Communism, implying that all are essentially different elements of one continuum, equally subservient to "Antichrist." The choice facing the world was not East or West, Communism or Democracy: it was God or devil, and there was no middle way. The solution was to be found in God and the Christian religion, a point elegantly made in a cartoon published shortly after the Bikini test in March 1954, in which the United States exploded its fifteen-megaton fission/fusion bomb. With a map of the United States targeted by "hellbombs," the paper shows the location of the "only safe state," namely, "a state of grace."[48] The choice presented to the individual believer was simple: it involved choosing heaven or hell, light or darkness, Stalin or the pope.

Naturally enough, Protestant churches rarely spoke with the unanimity of the Catholics, and they included a wide spectrum of opinion about the issue of Communism. However, many Protestants similarly found divine justification for their anti-Communist opinions.

Some liberal clergy could certainly be found to support Left opinions, and HUAC was particularly contemptuous of what it labeled "Kremlin clergymen."[49] Liberal views were particularly strong among the Unitarians and Quakers, who protested early and often against the inquisitorial atmosphere of the time; rather like the obstinate Presbyterian Wendell MacRae, the Friends often recalled their own historical struggles against oppressive governments that had sought to impose conformity by intimidation. Quaker congregations and summer camps were among the few institutions to extend help to the families of purge victims. In 1951 Friends' groups in Philadelphia and elsewhere were among the most active opponents of the Pechan loyalty bill, due in part to the movement's traditional hatred of oaths as a mean of enforcing social conformity. In November 1953, at the time of the HUAC investigation into the city's teachers, the Committee on Legislation of the Philadelphia Friends gave Justice William O. Douglas the platform from which he denounced the ongoing "hysteria" and "witch-hunt."[50]

Quakers resisted demands for purges within their own ranks. The limits of the sect's tolerance were tested by the case of librarian Mary Knowles, who was cited as a Communist by informer Herbert Philbrick, and who duly invoked the Fifth Amendment before the SISS. After she was dismissed from her job in Massachusetts under DAR pressure, she took a position with the Quaker community at Plymouth Meeting. When the appointment became known, Quakers were deluged with protests from veterans' groups and the DAR, and an "Alerted Americans Group" collected signatures urging her dismissal. Francis Walter brought the appointment before HUAC and won the support of several Quakers who agreed that such an investigation did not interfere with the freedom of religion. Nevertheless, Philadelphia Quakers went on record against loyalty oaths and inquisitions, whether political or religious, and Mary Knowles retained her job. Following her conviction for contempt of Congress in 1956, the Friends responded by raising her salary.[51]

However, as with other institutions catering chiefly to a middle-class clientele, Pennsylvania's mainstream Protestant churches generally shared the political orthodoxy of the time.[52] Even within the Friends, there were some hardline anti-Communist liberals. One of the most prominent was Philadelphia's Henry C. Patterson, who from the 1920s through the 1950s was a devoted friend of African American causes and a militant advocate of desegregation; his liberalism extended to opposing the Japanese American internments of the Second World War. On Communism, though, Patterson yielded little to Judge Musmanno or Francis Walter, and he was a founding member of the far Right Council against Communist Aggression. He was a friend of Whittaker Chambers, with whom he corresponded in traditional Quaker "thees" and "thys," and told him that "I hope history may give you a place among our distinguished patriots." Alger Hiss, Patterson wrote, was "a slippery article if I ever spotted one."[53]

Other liberal assertions by religious groups in this era tended to be outweighed by the volume of anti-Communist sentiment that they provoked within their congregations. In 1953, for instance, western Pennsylvania Methodist bishop L. C. Wicke raised a political storm by denouncing Senator McCarthy and HUAC chairman Velde as "right wing subversives" who acted as if all civil laws had been suspended, as though in wartime. This drew forth the predictable response from the *Pittsburgh Press* and other critics that the confrontation with Communism basically did constitute such a wartime emergency. Bishop Wicke was attacked on similar grounds by many within his own church.[54]

The state's best known Protestant clergyman was probably Daniel A. Poling, the editor of the *Christian Herald*, who served as pastor of the Philadelphia Baptist Temple from 1936 to 1948. He was well to the political Right, a close friend of John Foster Dulles and J. Edgar Hoover and chairman of the American Legion-sponsored "All American Conference to Combat Communism."[55] He also served on the national committee of Patterson's Council against Communist Aggression. Poling's hatred of Communism was partly motivated by his passionate interest in recent events in east Asia. For Protestants, as for Catholics, the loss of China in 1949 had been a traumatic event, destroying a mission field that was one of the glories of American Christianity. Chiang Kai-Shek and his wife commanded immense respect in these circles as "the finest flowerings of the Protestant missionary tradition in the far east."[56] As a mayoral candidate in Philadelphia in 1951, Poling made fire-breathing pronouncements on foreign affairs, including proposals that the United States arm anti-Communist guerrillas in China and give all-out support for Chiang.[57]

While mainstream denominations were firmly anti-Communist, the most determined Protestant opposition to Communist incursions came from the conservative evangelicals and fundamentalists, for whom the Communist problem was only one component of a much larger threat to religion posed by modernism in society and the churches. Though fundamentalism did not command the loyalty of the state's social elite, that view was held by one extremely important family, the Pews, who were so central to the state's Republican politics.[58] In the Cold War years the family's main representative was Philadelphia's J. Howard Pew, who served as president of Sun Oil from 1912 to 1947 and was subsequently chairman of the board. Many of the family's donations went to support explicitly religious causes, reflecting J. Howard Pew's belief that "I know of no influence which is more important to the welfare of our country than that of getting the theology of our ministers straightened up so that they may be more conservative. I have found that when a minister is sound in his theology, he is also sound on his economic and social philosophy."[59]

The main target of Pew's concern was the National Council of Churches (NCC), which was formed in 1950 from the older Federal Council, and which he saw as a hotbed of liberalism indistinguishable from Stalinism: "For fifty years these groups who pretended to represent Protestantism regularly issued statements, made pronouncements and passed resolutions which were exactly in accord with the instructions that the Kremlin had issued to its workers in this country. . . . We must educate our ministers so that they may know the processes by which Communism is effected. They must be made to realize that the program of the Welfare State and other social measures which the Social Action Committees and the National Council of Churches are advocating will inevitably lead us into Communism."[60] Like other moderate and conservative Protestants, Pew believed that the NCC committed an act of simple treason in 1958 when one of its committees declared in favor of recognizing China's Communist government and admitting "Red China" to the United Nations, which Pew viewed as "an evil organization."[61]

Responding to an approach from evangelical Protestants of several denominations, in 1956 Pew pledged $150,000 a year to fund a new mass-circulation magazine, *Christianity Today*, to counter the "many so-called Christian papers [which] are but a device whereby editors can wear the livery of the church and do the work of Socialists."[62] The relationship between *Christianity Today* and the Pews was long and cordial, to the extent that one prospective publisher suggested moving its offices onto the Pew family property in Ardmore, Pennsylvania.[63] The clergy sponsoring *Christianity Today* were led by L. Nelson Bell, whose rightist political attitudes had been hardened by the collapse of the Christian missionary endeavor in China; he remained a staunch supporter of Walter's HUAC into the 1960s.[64]

Bell's son-in-law was Billy Graham, the evangelist who was enjoying huge public popularity in these years, and who "came to love [Pew] as almost a father."[65] Though in later years Graham was known as a moderate voice within the evangelical movement, his missions of the 1950s were more overtly apocalyptic than those of later years, and just as for Catholic preachers, the total evil of Communism was taken for granted.[66] This was particularly true during his Pittsburgh crusade of 1952, which coincided with the public panic over "hell-bombs"; Graham consistently presented world events in an eschatological framework, remarking that "all of the trouble with Russia began in the Garden of Eden."[67] Only a religious revival could prevent what was ultimately a spiritual rather than a political menace: "Unless this country has a revival of both morals and religion, it can't survive the onslaught of Communism."[68] Graham represented the apocalyptic strain in the evangelical approach to Communism, the diabolical inspiration of which was proved by the destruction of Christian missions in China and elsewhere. Moreover, the imminence of the end times might well be signaled by historic events like the recent return of the Jews to the land of Israel.[69]

Christianity Today and the Billy Graham movement were both supported enthusiastically by a number of traditional and fundamentalist clergy in Pittsburgh and Philadelphia; the 1952 crusade attracted the sponsorship of some 350 Pittsburgh-area churches (as well as the local Hearst newspaper, the *Sun-Telegraph*). Evangelicals were usually staunch anti-Communists, and the president of Philadelphia's Eastern Baptist Seminary argued for the necessity of a "Christian patriotism" unabashedly located on the political Right: "Christian Patriots must be known as men of the Right . . . no-one need be ashamed to be called a Rightist if he thinks right, speaks right and lives right. This is the day to come out of the grey into the white, to come out of the dark into the light, to come out of the left into the right."[70] One Graham supporter was Pittsburgh Episcopalian Samuel Shoemaker, who in the 1930s had been a close ally of Frank Buchman and the Moral Rearmament movement, and who by the 1950s was one of the nation's most respected preachers and religious writers. Shoemaker served on the organizational committee of Graham's 1952 crusade and was a contributing editor to *Christianity Today*.[71] Like the Catholics, Shoemaker integrated anti-Communism into his theological worldview, and in 1961 he received a VFW award for his "devoted efforts in combatting Communism."[72] He saw no middle way between the competing ideologies: "A materialistic American who doesn't know that our freedom stems from God is really an ally of the Communists."[73] He warned that "an atomic holocaust" could only be averted by a new Reformation, a "world wide awakening under the Holy Spirit."[74]

The evangelical Right was particularly concerned about the menace of leftist penetration into the Christian churches. This was a major political issue throughout the 1950s, as conservatives tried to expose the alleged leftist sympathies of senior members of the NCC. When HUAC threatened an investigation of the churches in 1953, Francis Walter endorsed the idea that the NCC had been thoroughly penetrated. After liberal Methodist bishop G. Bromley Oxnam appeared before the committee, Walter remarked that this showed that "the Communists are using well known and highly placed persons as dupes and the bigger the name the better for their cause."[75] The issue revived in 1960 when the U.S. Air Force produced a controversial training manual using Communist penetration of the NCC as a case study of subversion. The manual was withdrawn following protests, but not before Walter had once more asserted that its claims were largely true; meanwhile, Matt Cvetic claimed to provide documented evidence of such activity in Pittsburgh's churches. These attacks on Protestant clergy were all the more controversial stemming from Catholics, making them appear sectarian in nature and exciting Protestant fears that the McCarthyite movement was a clandestine Catholic plot to dominate America.[76] However, J. Howard Pew and like-minded evangelicals had no doubts about the Red menace within the ranks of the liberal clergy.[77] For religious conservatives, liberal activism could only be explained by subversive influences.

Conservatives might dream of purging liberal ministers, but most realized that the most effective means of defeating domestic Communism lay in new forms of evangelism, of stimulating the "new reformation" so often referred to in contemporary correspondence. In the context of the early 1950s, this activity seems to be a kind of spiritual rearmament, a counterpoint to the political and civil defense preparations of these years, and perhaps a Protestant answer to the new Marian devotion. This missionary challenge would have to transcend existing denominational and even interfaith boundaries, and it would also employ innovative means of spreading the word. The post-1945 decade witnessed several such endeavors, such as the prayer breakfast movement that mobilized Christian businessmen. More explicitly political was the Pittsburgh Experiment sponsored by Samuel Shoemaker: originating during the 1952 steel strike, this experiment tried to reconcile employers and workers across class and denominational boundaries, to foster class collaboration under the slogan of "Faith at Work."[78]

The most spectacular manifestation of the new evangelism was the wave of urban crusades launched by Billy Graham, such as the Pittsburgh event that drew a combined attendance of over 250,000 to some twenty-six meetings in September 1952, at events held in massive venues like the Hunt Armory and Forbes Field. Ultimately, 5,000 responded to the altar call. Though overt political references were not part of Graham's sermons, news coverage of the event was steeped in apocalyptic and anti-Communist rhetoric, and the organizing committee included such firm enemies of the Communist challenge as Governor Fine and Samuel Shoemaker, and a roll-call of the region's most conservative evangelicals.[79] Presumably, the astonishing response was influenced by fears of nuclear apocalypse, which resonated so closely with religious concerns and predictions. In 1961, at a time of renewed nuclear nightmares, the Graham crusade in Philadelphia drew a total attendance approaching 700,000.

Though the 1952 Pittsburgh crusade dominated the local headlines throughout the four-week campaign, this was by no means the only event of its kind in the city at this time. In the same weeks, Bishop Sheen's visit attracted some 18,000 Catholics to a series of special Masses. The city also observed its "I Am An American Day," a patriotic extravaganza of the sort that became commonplace in these years, and which drew on a movement originally founded by the American Legion in the late 1930s; the event received official blessing from President Roosevelt in 1940. The 1952 event drew 10,000 people to a public rededication to the American way of life at a celebration attended by sports and entertainment personalities together with political leaders like Mayor Lawrence. As in contemporary Loyalty Day parades, patriotic unity was expressed through military pageantry. The religious element in the Pittsburgh gathering was symbolized by the participation of a Catholic priest, a Jewish rabbi, and a Methodist pastor, and optimistic headlines proclaimed "Three Faiths Uniting for American Day."[80]

The interfaith cooperation for this event represented another powerful theme of the religious response to Communism. Just as America could only be victorious if it overcame its class conflicts, the nation's enemies must not succeed in exploiting potential divisions between Protestant, Catholic, and Jew. Through the Cold War years, religious rhetoric was marked by aspirations for interfaith harmony such as that represented by the Aaronsburg celebrations of 1949: the "Aaronsburg Story" concerned an eighteenth-century Jewish settler in central Pennsylvania who planned a town with provision for both Christian and

Jewish places of worship. The commemoration of the settlement duly emphasized this theme of religious cooperation, at a time of extreme national peril.[81]

Equally potent was the Philadelphia movement to commemorate the "four chaplains" (two Protestants, a Catholic, and a Jew) who had died when the USS *Dorchester* was lost in 1943, sacrificing their lives to save other crew members. One of the four was Clark Poling, son of Rev. Daniel Poling, whose campaign to build an interfaith monument at Temple University became both a personal crusade and a contribution to interfaith relations. The shrine included places of worship for each of the religions, and over the main entry appeared the powerful words, "Here is sanctuary for brotherhood: Let it never be violated."[82] After the monument opened in 1951, Poling reported, "practically every patriotic and religious organization of Philadelphia has made the chapel its sacred rendezvous. The American Legion launched its Back to God movement here."[83] At one such interfaith meeting in 1952, the state commander of the Pennsylvania American Legion stressed the political importance of the ecumenical effort: "Communism has only one enemy, and that is Christianity."[84]

Such events eloquently demonstrate the religious component of anti-Communism and the degree to which Communism was seen not merely as a political challenge, but as an utter evil opposed to everything good and holy. Anti-Communism was as basic a component of the emerging civic religion of the period as it was of the political consensus.

COMING IN FROM THE COLD WAR, 1956–1968

> I cannot be sure whether the authorities knew that there was then
> no internal danger from the Communists, or were so obsessed with
> anti-Communist hysteria that they could not see or think straight.
> —Father Charles Owen Rice, 1973[1]

The anti-Communist inquisition accelerated the already sharp decline of Party membership that followed the electoral debacle of 1948 and the Korean conflict, and matters deteriorated following the crises of 1956. After Khrushchev's secret speech and the uprisings in Poland and Hungary, the Soviet Union looked less like a workers' utopia than an amoral rival superpower, and by 1958 total CPUSA membership had fallen to around 8,000. In 1956 tax problems gave the federal government the excuse to seize Communist headquarters in New York City, Philadelphia, and other centers.[2] Still, this apparent collapse did not immediately end the "red issue" in Pennsylvania, and popular anti-Communist activism remained intense for several years afterward. In part this reflected continuing international tensions, which reached a perilous height between about 1958 and 1963: hydrogen bombs and intercontinental ballistic missiles proliferated in the arsenals of both major powers, and a terrifying sequence of crises and confrontations occurred in central Africa, Cuba, Berlin, and Southeast Asia. Moreover, years of propaganda about conspiratorial Communists made it difficult to believe that the domestic enemy really had been destroyed.

Cold War politics in Pennsylvania were not transformed until traditional Left-Right issues were supplanted by other political concerns that reflected fundamental changes in the state's social, economic, and demographic structure and, above all, the rise of racial politics during the 1960s. Only then could older concerns with the Communist menace be dismissed as paranoid witchhunting, though ironically, this was exactly the point at which the upsurge of popular radicalism seemed briefly to fulfill all the old Communist dreams.

Though the fall of Senator McCarthy in 1954 did not end the extreme national sensitivity to the Communist threat, two closely related developments made it much more difficult to maintain anything like the earlier panic atmosphere.[3] Grave doubts about the reliability of the various informers and defectors now became public, and partly as a result of this, federal courts over the next few years increasingly limited the power of law enforcement and congressional committees to seek out subversion.

For Pennsylvania, what Senator Kefauver called "the professional witness racket" came to grief in two scandals that came to light during 1954, both of which followed the same general pattern. In each case, "subversive" charges, substantiated chiefly by the claims of professional informants, were levied against two highly reputable individuals; in each instance, the informants were almost certainly serving the private interests of an outside party.[4] The first of these affairs, the Mullen case, swiftly escalated from a sordid local scandal to something verging on a crisis in state politics. It began when John Mullen, mayor of Clairton, reported a bribery attempt by a local coal operator who wanted permission to strip-mine the municipal park. Shortly afterward, Mullen and Judge Musmanno met at the funeral of steelworkers' leader Philip Murray, and Musmanno, acting on behalf of some friends who stood to suffer if the prosecution of the bribery case proceeded, allegedly took this opportunity to suggest that Mullen should withdraw his complaint. Mullen was outraged at such a grossly improper attempt to interfere with a criminal case, and he reported Musmanno's approach. The judge himself was then charged with hindering a witness; the arrest order was issued by James Malone, Musmanno's fellow ABC member. At this point, Joe Mazzei came forward to identify Mullen as a Communist, in an attempt to discredit the mayor's testimony against Musmanno and show that it was part of a diabolical Communist plot to smear the judge.

The incident had enormous ramifications. Mullen was a prominent figure in the USWA, a close friend of Philip Murray, and the political director of the union's political action committee. Had Communists penetrated even the conservative and heavily Catholic hierarchy of this union? Scandal now threatened the USWA, one of the pillars of the Democratic establishment in Pennsylvania, and union president David McDonald made Mullen's defense an urgent priority. On the other side, Musmanno was now a national figure, as he was advising Martin Dies on a federal law to suppress the Communist Party, the core of what eventually became the Communist Control Act. This conflict was dreadful news for a Democratic Party hoping to win major gains in the 1954 state elections.

In 1954 the SISS held closed hearings into what it viewed as a serious high-level Communist conspiracy, and at least initially, Mullen was virtually on trial for his attack on Musmanno, with staff counsel making dire threats of the consequences of perjury. However, the committee soon found that the state's leading anti-Communist paladins were deeply divided over the issue. In lengthy hearings the following year, Duquesne's Father John Schlicht spoke highly of Mullen, stressing that the steelworkers' leader had for years sponsored anti-Communist propaganda activities, and other witnesses likewise stressed Mullen's visceral opposition to Communism. Harry Sherman, on the other hand, strongly supported his own stable of witnesses, especially Mazzei and Cvetic, who adamantly viewed Mullen as a Communist. Still others, like Judge Montgomery, believed that both claimants, Mullen and Musmanno, were honest and reliable and did not know how the whole situation could have arisen.[5] Members of the old ABC group were deeply divided, with Musmanno declaring that "Mr. Malone says he is my friend. With friends like that, I do not need enemies."[6] By mid-1955 growing doubts about Mazzei's credibility contributed to a general shift of legal and media opinion toward Mullen's account of the case, leaving Musmanno tarnished by what had presumably been his failed attempt to coerce or bribe a witness.

The Mullen affair coincided with another informer-sparked scandal that originated in Erie and also came to national attention during 1954. This case concerned Edward Lamb, a wealthy businessman with a strong liberal and pro-labor record, which included work on behalf of the National Lawyers' Guild. Though anti-Communist, his experiences in the USSR in the 1930s had convinced him that the Soviet experiment was "a genuine effort at human betterment."[7] During the 1940s he built up an Erie-based media empire that included a newspaper, the *Erie Dispatch-Herald*, as well as radio and television operations, and he naturally encountered both commercial and ideological rivals. His paper engaged in a war with the very conservative *Erie Daily Times*, which delighted in exposing the local Left, while another nemesis was Paul Block, owner of the *Pittsburgh Post-Gazette*. Charges of Red sympathies now haunted Lamb, and in 1953 were raised before the McCarthy subcommittee. This was potentially ruinous for Lamb's business activities. A routine request to expand the power of his Erie television station ran into difficulties before the Federal Communications Commission, which received testimony depicting Lamb as a former Communist Party member, and in late 1954 he faced a virtual trial before the commission.

As his autobiography boasted, however, this was "no lamb for slaughter." Lamb was a well-connected multimillionaire, a major contributor to the national Democratic Party, and his legal team was headed by former U.S. attorney general Howard McGrath; he even received assistance from friends in the FBI. Lamb's team easily showed that the informers brought against him had strong vested interests in supporting the government's case, in terms of earning money or avoiding criminal penalties or deportation. The star informer was one Marie Natvig, whose fantasies were quite as extreme as Mazzei's, and whose sexual tales brought the story into the national headlines, but Lamb's attorneys progressively demolished her credibility. In early 1955 Natvig admitted that she had been lying, earning her a federal prison sentence for perjury. Other witnesses had already collapsed, reporting "constant and consistent coaching by representatives of the FCC."[8] Following so shortly upon the Senate's rejection of McCarthy, Lamb's case provoked widespread media condemnation of the informer system, which was echoed by liberal and moderate politicians like U.S. senator Duff. The affair showed how such investigations could be used as a form of extortion, in that they could be discreetly prevented for a generous price; otherwise, the usual parade of moles and defectors would be presented at a public hearing. As in the Mullen case, the suggestion was that denunciation as a Red befell anyone unwise enough to refuse to concede to political pressures.

This was a bad time for the informing profession, and several of the Pennsylvania moles and defectors were now discredited. Joe Mazzei had faced scandals for some time before the Mullen case: he had been charged with child molestation, and he was arrested for nonsupport of an illegitimate child (he claimed his troublesome girlfriend was a Communist sent to discredit his work).[9] Broader doubts now emerged about his veracity, which was so critical because of his role as a witness in the Pittsburgh Smith Act cases. In 1956 Chief Justice Earl Warren came to the conclusion that Mazzei's testimony was wholly discredited, and the Justice Department concurred that the witness was a "psychiatric case."[10] Referring to Mazzei's original claims about Red plots to poison

Pittsburgh's water supply, Warren remarked that Mazzei's testimony "has poisoned the water in this reservoir, and the reservoir cannot be cleansed without draining it of all impurity."[11]

Other defectors and informants now crumbled. Some may have had pangs of conscience, but by far the most important element in their exposure was the detective work by a small group of committed attorneys like Hymen Schlesinger.[12] One infiltrator whose contributions were celebrated at the time of his exposure was Alexander Wright, but Schlesinger discredited him by linking him to the authorship of an autobiography of "alarming obscenity."[13] Pennsylvania witnesses were faring no better than some of their nationally known counterparts, like Harvey Matusow, whose fictions were exposed in January 1955, or Paul Crouch, who had testified at length in the Pittsburgh and Philadelphia sedition trials and was now exposed as "one of the most brazen and colorful liars in the business."[14] Matt Cvetic himself was facing acute problems with alcoholism and mental illness, and in June 1955 his evidence was treated so harshly by a federal appeals court that the Justice Department officially forbade his use in future cases. One might almost say that he had been blacklisted from his livelihood.[15] Criticism of the once-idolized informers now became possible, and a Pittsburgh paper noted in early 1955 how "things become pretty much pie-in-the-sky for people like Matt Cvetic and Joe Mazzei, with a happy assist from advisers like Harry A. Sherman."[16] By 1955 even the *Post-Gazette* was skeptically calling Mazzei a "self-styled FBI Aide."[17]

Doubts about the evidence from infiltrators and turncoats contributed to the courts' willingness to challenge antisubversive campaigns. The U.S. Supreme Court played a critical role here, with a series of decisions between 1955 and 1957 that collectively caused apoplexy among the nation's Red-hunters. One early weakening of the anti-Communist arsenal came in the case of *Quinn v. United States* in 1955, which overturned the contempt conviction of UE leader Thomas Quinn in language that suggested grave misgivings about the proceedings of congressional hearings. The Court noted that "the power to investigate, broad as it may be, is also subject to recognized limitations." Tracing the history of the right against self-incrimination, the decision proceeded: "To apply the privilege narrowly or begrudgingly, to treat it as an historical relic, at most merely to be tolerated, is to ignore its development and purpose."[18]

Other important decisions arose from the Pittsburgh trials. In the 1956 case of *Pennsylvania v. Nelson*, the U.S. Supreme Court found that the federal government had effectively taken over the whole area of sedition legislation, so that state statutes like Pennsylvania's were invalidated, and with them convictions like those of Steve Nelson and his comrades. Though *Nelson* only killed the state charges, the federal Smith Act convictions were barely less vulnerable with the collapse of the Mazzei testimony, and the Court now overturned this conviction. Steve Nelson's Smith Act case was sent back to the district court for a new trial, and the cases of four of the other accused soon followed.[19] The Pittsburgh cases ultimately collapsed, and none of the accused served a day on the charges.

The U.S. Supreme Court continued to smite the Red-hunters. In early 1957 the *Watkins v. United States* case concluded that a congressional contempt citation issued following a HUAC hearing was invalid because the committee had failed to establish that its questions were asked in pursuit of a proper legislative purpose: "There is no congressional power to expose for the sake of exposure." This conceded an issue that Left and liberal attorneys had been raising for years, and the case asserted that witnesses before congressional committees were entitled to all the rights of a criminal defendant, including the right to counsel.[20] Also in 1957, the *Yates v. United States* decision required that proof of sedition involve advocacy of some future action, rather than of a general state of affairs; no longer could prosecutors establish sedition by showing that defendants wished to see a different social or political order. *Yates* left the Smith Act "a virtual shambles." The Philadelphia convictions collapsed, as a U.S. Court of Appeals set aside the convictions of four of the accused and ordered new trials for the other five.[21] Collectively such cases galvanized the congressional right wing and did much to initiate the movement to impeach Earl Warren, which would be a centerpiece of ultra-Right rhetoric over the coming decade.[22]

But it was still too early for an obituary for either American Communism or its enemies. Though the American far Left entered a period of deep crisis after the events of 1956, its enemies saw no reason to relax their vigilance. Was the Red menace really ended on American soil, or was it all the more dangerous now that the public was lulled into a false sense of security? In 1958 Congressman Walter published a series of articles in the *Philadelphia Inquirer* recapitulating the Left's defeats in recent years but warning nevertheless that "subversive peril mounts despite comrade loss." He wrote that "the past year has been one of the greatest periods of triumph for the Kremlin and its confederates throughout the free world. Within the United States, the Communist apparatus has evolved new implements of political conquest. . . . The danger of Communism is mounting—not receding."[23] As J. Edgar Hoover stated, the mere fact of declining Communist Party rolls was irrelevant: "Numbers mean nothing."

These bizarre assessments were based on two lines of reasoning. First, the reduction of Party strength was seen as almost a Darwinian function, the purging of the weaker dilettantes leaving only the convinced hard core. Still more sinister, the apparent shrinkage might be a subterfuge. For a decade, congressional investigators had delved into the concept of clandestine Party membership, the idea that "card-carrying members" were only the tip of an iceberg and that the most dedicated and valuable agents of the cause eschewed formal affiliation: "Many party members have resigned . . . because it suits the Party's purposes to have them go underground rather than to continue working as confessed Communists." The traditional FBI guess was that for every avowed Party member there were ten concealed nonmembers, but Walter was more expansive: "For every Party member, there may be hundreds able and willing to do the Party's work. Put another way, there are at this moment the equivalent of some twenty combat divisions of enemy troops on American soil, engaged in propaganda, espionage and subversion—troops that are loyal only to the Soviet Union."[24] In Walter's view, the shock troops of the Party's current campaign were found in the Emergency Civil Liberties Committee, which was then engaged in an influential public mobilization against HUAC and the FBI.[25] Meanwhile, the Soviet bloc continued its propaganda blitz through every means possible.

The perception that the Communist threat was submerged rather than extinct lay behind a series of congressional hearings about this time, which in their intensity showed little recognition of the dramatic shrinkage in the Party's popular support. Walter's HUAC gravely examined the "current strategy and tactics" of the remaining Communists in the Greater Pittsburgh area, while the SISS focused on conditions in both Pittsburgh and Philadelphia.[26] One SISS hearing in October 1959 purported to examine the "revitalizing of the Communist Party in the Philadelphia area." Such a resurrection would have come as a delightful surprise to the remaining Party activists, though a few diehards like Thomas Nabried still boasted gamely that "if you take Philadelphia, there is always a beehive of activity."[27] In reality, the committee paid little attention to local activities; it was more concerned with clandestine national meetings that happened to have been held in the city in order to plan both national and district conventions. As we have seen, HUAC's attempts about this time to recapture its former moments of glory in Pittsburgh were a dismal failure and attracted little interest. With the courts expanding the rights of witnesses and "subversive" suspects, the arrival of a congressional committee could no longer inspire anything like the terror that it did in days past.

The sense that subversion was moving deeper underground coincided with the perceived decline in the power of congressional investigators, suggesting that anti-Communist work should be pursued by the private sector as much as by the public. The result was an upsurge of militant anti-Communist and superpatriotic groups in these years. That such movements were far from new is suggested by the example of ABC at the height of the anti-Communist purges, but there were many imitators. One of the most active was the Philadelphia-based Council against Communist Aggression, founded in 1951, which subsequently changed its name to the Council for the Defense of Freedom.[28] In the 1960s it was linked to numerous far Right sects, like the American Council for World Freedom and the John Birch Society, and also to the World Anti-Communist League.[29]

The council's leadership included religious leaders like Daniel A. Poling and the Jesuit priest Dennis Comey, and the theme of "God and Country" pervaded the emerging rightist movements.[30] Many of the most visible agitators were themselves clergy, "Christian Fright Peddlers" like Rev. Billy James Hargis or Rev. Carl McIntire. McIntire had conducted a personal war against ecclesiastical "modernism" since the 1920s, and his American Council of Christian Churches was meant as a counterweight to the hated NCC.[31] He promoted his warnings of pervasive Communist subversion through the hair-raising radio broadcasts of his *Reformation Hour*, carried on some 600 stations nationwide, as well as through his newspaper, *Christian Beacon*. McIntire's political and theological views were inextricably linked in his "emphasis upon God, the Bible, the Ten Commandments, righteousness, the Devil, and our militant opposition of the Communist conspiracy." He had some following in Pennsylvania, where he purchased a Delaware County radio station as a vehicle for his ultraconservative views. This resulted in a public controversy when McIntire was criticized by the state legislature, and he responded with a series of public protests and demonstrations in Harrisburg and elsewhere. His activities caused international concern in 1963 when he acquired shortwave station WINB in Red Lion, arousing fears that overseas listeners might mistake his opinions for official U.S. foreign policy.[32] Other religious activists of this era included old Pew allies Walter Judd and Dr. Fred C. Schwarz, who coordinated anti-Communist rallies in the Philadelphia area in the early 1960s.[33] Both Schwarz and

Judd were active in the Council against Communist Aggression and its affiliates, while Schwarz founded the Christian Anti-Communism Crusade.

J. Howard Pew's largesse was extended to the John Birch Society, the most visible of the far-Right groups. Founded in 1958, the Birch Society warned that the West faced imminent defeat in the Cold War due in large measure to the efforts of clandestine Red agents within the American establishment. One of the most dangerous, according to this mythology, was the president's own brother, Milton Eisenhower.[34] The Birch cause had a particular appeal for the evangelical Right as the legendary Birch had been a missionary killed by the Chinese Communists. Pew himself served on the editorial advisory committee of the Bircher magazine *American Opinion*. Birch recruiters included Matt Cvetic, who by now had forfeited most of his connections on the respectable Right and was living off his putative record as "FBI Counterspy."[35]

The Birchers enjoyed some success in Pennsylvania. Their speakers' bureau ran a lively program, regularly offering eight or ten presentations in various parts of the state in a typical month in the mid-1960s.[36] Popular speakers included Julia Brown, "a very patriotic Negro housewife who was formerly an FBI undercover agent in Communist organizations, of Cleveland, Ohio," and Reed A. Benson, who warned his Delaware County audience that "the Communists are winning around the world. They are winning because of our ignorance—because we simply have not done our homework regarding this conspiracy which has murdered nearly seventy million people in its rise to power."[37] In addition to lectures, the movement employed diverse methods to promote its message, including the use of floats in patriotic parades and a successful campaign to "Support Your Local Police." Believing fervently in the success enjoyed by Communist infiltration over the years, Birchers themselves made great use of front groups and sought to penetrate mainstream community institutions like school boards. By the mid-1960s the society had "a pocket of strength in the communities clustered around Philadelphia" and an area of growth around Pittsburgh.[38] Bircher influence in the police became the subject of a public scandal when Philadelphia mayor James Tate placed fifteen officers on limited duties because of their recruiting activities, declaring that "they have limited their capacity and usefulness to the police department. . . . This is the way the Nazi Party began."[39]

Bircher views were echoed by the familiar patriotic organizations like the DAR, whose annual conventions in the state provided a venue for ultraconservative speakers like Rev. James D. Colbert of the Christian Anti-Communism Crusade, Kenneth Wells of Freedom's Foundation, and E. Merrill Root.[40] In

1955 Senator Martin was in traditional form when he declared that "the US stands as the one strong barrier against the Communist conspiracy to dominate and enslave the entire world"; the group regularly passed resolutions supporting the FBI and anti-Communist investigations and opposing internationalism.[41] Into the 1960s, the DAR regularly attacked any measure that would weaken or reform the McCarran-Walter Immigration Act. A resolution in 1958 placed the organization on record for the need "to destroy the ideology of international communism," which allegedly aimed to conquer the entire globe within a decade.[42] The 1960 convention attacked the World Court and the United Nations and urged the state legislature to remain vigilant in the face of one-worlders who were rewriting school textbooks in order to promote their socialistic goals.[43]

Though conservatives saw the Warren Court decisions of the mid-1950s as yet another form of liberal betrayal, there are suggestions that the public mood was becoming somewhat more tolerant, at least in condemning the more outrageous forms of anti-Left persecution. In Philadelphia the turning point was the 1956 production of the play *Anastasia*, starring Gale Sondergaard, who had been blacklisted after taking the Fifth before HUAC in 1951. The usual vigilantes came forward claiming to express public outrage, but the performance proceeded, despite picketing by the American Legion and the VFW, and the show was a hit. As David Caute observes, "A milder season lay ahead; the worst was past."[44]

Groups like the Birchers unwittingly played their part in the process of internal détente. The media scare over the Birch movement in 1961–62 did much to refocus public attention on the potential dangers from the Right, indicating the perils of an exclusive concentration on a shrunken American Communist Party. The new ultra-Right coalition attracted alarm, especially when the Birch movement spawned an even more extreme paramilitary group, the Minutemen, which in Pennsylvania was affiliated with Ku Klux Klan and neo-Nazi activities.[45] The tone of media coverage now was quite different from that received by ultra-Right or vigilante movements at the height of the Red Scare, when newspapers had defended "head-breaking" as a necessary defense against Soviet aggression. In the new environment, figures like Carl McIntire or the Birchers and Minutemen were as unacceptably extreme as Communists. In popular culture, likewise, the idea that anti-Communism might itself represent dangerous fanaticism was the theme of films like *The Manchurian Candidate*

(1962), *Seven Days in May* (1964), and *Doctor Strangelove* (also 1964), whose ludicrous General Jack D. Ripper was a devastating caricature of the anti-Communist obsession. The extreme Right was further stigmatized by association with the renascent Ku Klux Klan.

The growing skepticism about militant anti-Communism that was becoming apparent by the late 1950s explains the defensive tone of Tad Walter's justifications for HUAC.[46] The most spectacular protest against HUAC excesses occurred with rioting in San Francisco in 1962, an event that was seized upon by conservatives and evangelicals to prove the continuing Communist threat.[47] Liberal critics also found voice in a full-page advertisement in the *New York Times*, which was signed by a contingent of Pennsylvania academics and religious leaders, appealing for the committee's abolition.[48] It was also during the early 1960s that journalists begin to refer to the Red Scare as belonging to a bygone historical epoch, that of the Cold War.

In the new atmosphere, more publicity was now given to the ulterior motives that often lay behind cases of anti-Communist persecution, which could no longer simply be seen as an honest crusade. One such instance occurred when Philadelphia radio commentator William S. Gailmor used his position on WPEN to call for more effective measures of gun control in the aftermath of a series of incidents in which children had been killed or injured.[49] He was supported by the city's district attorney, and a petition for a gun control law attracted thousands of signatures, but "the bill was strongly opposed by enforcement groups and groups such as the American Rifleman's Association and the veterans groups, who not only opposed the bill but opposed me personally and in order to discredit the bill, and discredit me, dug up material about my political activities during the 1940s which were calculated to indicate that I was possibly of questionable loyalty."[50] The issue was now transferred to Gailmor's past association with groups like the Wallace for President campaign, the ASC, and the civil rights movement; among other things, he had been a leading speaker at the Progressive Party's 1948 convention in Philadelphia.[51] Though he was repeatedly cleared of Communist affiliations, the new pressures ended Gailmor's broadcasting career.

That anti-Communist purges were becoming more controversial is suggested by the rather different circumstances that now surrounded charges of subversion in the colleges. One incident occurred in 1962 at Grove City College, a conservative evangelical institution in western Pennsylvania that had been founded under the auspices of the Pew family in the nineteenth century. The particular case arose out of a conflict between two senior faculty members whose politics were diametrically opposed: historian Larry Gara, a Quaker and pacifist who had served prison terms for draft resistance, and Hans Sennholz, a contributing editor of the Bircher magazine *American Opinion*.[52] This would have been an explosive mixture in any institution, but the administration was particularly sensitive to hints of radicalism: J. Howard Pew was only one of several members of his clan to serve on the college's board of trustees. In the winter of 1961–62 two former FBI agents now serving as private detectives undertook an investigation, and shortly afterward Gara was dismissed on the absurd grounds of incompetent teaching.[53] Allegedly J. Howard Pew had ordered the dismissal, and a major scandal ensued. In contrast to the quiescence at other institutions during earlier controversies over loyalty oaths, six Grove City faculty members resigned in protest, and the American Association of University Professors undertook an investigation, despite the bitter opposition of college authorities.

Also quite different from earlier events was the scandal in 1961 at the University of Pittsburgh, when historian Robert Colodny signed a petition urging "Fair Play for Cuba." The ensuing investigation brought out his past association with alleged "front" groups like the Anti-Fascist Refugee Committee.[54] Colodny appeared before both HUAC and Senator James Eastland's SISS, and the university held hearings to determine if he was of "subversive character" under the terms of the Pechan Act. Colodny was cleared by a university investigation; significantly, he received support from quite unexpected quarters, including Father Rice and "the industrial financial elite," and "98 percent of my colleagues were in my favor."[55] A milder season indeed.

Changing perceptions of the Communist peril are indicated by the history of the civil defense movement, which was transformed from a high social priority in the early 1960s to near farcical irrelevance by the end of that decade. The Kennedy years marked the high point of perceptions of a direct nuclear threat to the state, and the Cuban missile crisis stirred commitment to civil defense to a remarkable intensity. Civil defense preparations in these years could no longer make the optimistic assumption that the United States military would be able to shoot down Soviet bombers, and the question was *when*, rather than *if*, Philadelphia and Pittsburgh would fall to nuclear missiles. Survival could only come through evacuation or bomb shelters. In 1960 a civil defense scenario assumed that residents of the southern parts of metropolitan Pittsburgh would evacuate en masse to Uniontown in Fayette County, fleeing a city "torn, smashed and seared by a sneak atomic attack," and such exercises were repeated through the early 1960s.[56]

Defense preparedness reached its height in late 1962, during the Cuba crisis. By this point 190 buildings in Pittsburgh stored survival supplies, and some shelter complexes were vast: facilities under the Federal Building and the Penn-Sheraton Hotel each claimed to be able to safeguard 8,000 residents, while the Carnegie Museum had supplies for 12,000.[57] One shelter complex in Wilkins-burg boasted accommodation for nearly 5,000; Mount Lebanon had space for 6,400, complete with an underground hospital.[58] Allegheny County had almost 3,000 shelters by this point, and notional space for 369,000 survivors. On a domestic level too, civic authorities enthusiastically sponsored nuclear drills in schools and urged each family to develop its own survival plan and shelter area. The Cuba scare resulted in the official shelters receiving unprecedented attention, and all were now fully supplied with medical supplies, water, and food, the last mainly in the form of notoriously indigestible crackers, intended "for sustaining life and for retaining vigor and good spirits."[59] The Federal Building alone was stocked with nearly 30,000 gallons of water, as well as nearly two and a half million crackers and 164 sanitation kits.[60]

After 1962 the large commitment to civil defense seemed increasingly irrelevant, as concern about global nuclear war diminished rapidly. By the mid-1960s the news media were beginning to publish what would become an enduring genre of stories that noted the remaining vestiges of the civil defense establishment as monuments of a distant bygone era. A *Pittsburgh Post-Gazette* headline asked in 1966, "Is Civil Defense Program Worth Saving?" As the *Pittsburgh Press* asked, succinctly, in 1972, "Who's Afraid of the Big Bad Boom?"[61] Meanwhile, civil defense facilities deteriorated rapidly, so that by 1969 Pittsburgh's director of civil defense stated that the city could no longer be given an effective emergency warning in the event of attack. The sirens, powered by 1951 automobile engines, were going flat, and one had already ceased to function; a 1971 newspaper headline read, "City Bomb Sirens Rust in Silence."[62] Shelters themselves were falling into disuse and were being converted into wine cellars, photographic dark rooms, indoor marijuana gardens, museums, and simple curios.[63] The question of disposing of the remaining nuclear defenses remained a matter of semiserious debate. What exactly could be done with the multimillion remaining Cuba-era crackers? They did not lend themselves to bulk feeding to animals because they were individually wrapped; moreover, experiments suggested that their dubious taste inspired consumer resistance among the zoo animals chosen for this experiment, even the bears.[64]

In state politics too, the Communist threat was diminishing, though the generation of anti-Communist activists that had come to prominence in the chilliest years of the Cold War remained significant players into the early 1960s. Congressman Van Zandt was the unsuccessful Republican candidate for the U.S. Senate seat in 1962, and Justice Musmanno narrowly failed to win the Democratic senatorial nomination in 1964.[65] As state attorney general, Walter Alessandroni was widely expected to run for the position of either governor or U.S. senator. Blair Gunther was one of Allegheny County's three commissioners, an important position in Pittsburgh-area politics and generally the stepping stone to higher office. He ran for lieutenant governor in the 1966 Republican primary but was defeated by his old anti-Communist ally Alessandroni, a macabre result given that the latter had died in an air crash some days before. Another anti-Communist with wider ambitions was Robert L. Kunzig, who gained some national visibility as staff counsel for HUAC, and who was discussed as a possible gubernatorial contender. An active player in state Republican politics into the 1960s, he masterminded Arlen Specter's first campaign as district attorney of Philadelphia. On this occasion, Kunzig was credited with pioneering the law-and-order politics that would prove so successful for conservatives nationwide over the next two decades. He held office under President Nixon as head of the General Services Administration.

The old soldiers of anti-Communism now began to fade away: Cvetic, Walter, Gunther, Musmanno, and Pechan all died between 1962 and 1969, and in 1971 even J. Howard Pew proved to be mortal when he passed away at the age of eighty-nine. Their political world was also perishing, as Pennsylvania electoral affairs were reshaped by new economic and demographic factors that cumulatively made the old obsessions as irrelevant as the fallout shelters.

The Democrats began to establish a real political hegemony in the state. With a firm hold on the politics of both Philadelphia and Pittsburgh, the party finally achieved the influence that it had glimpsed briefly during the New Deal era. After electing only one governor since 1891, Democrats now triumphed with George Leader in 1954 and David L. Lawrence in 1958, marking the first and, so far, the only occasion in Pennsylvania history in which one Democratic governor succeeded another.[66] The 1954 elections also brought some improvement in Democratic congressional representation, with the heartening defeat of a long-standing rightist (and McCarthy supporter), Representative Louis Graham, in western Pennsylvania's Twenty-fifth District.[67] In 1958 Pennsylvania Democrats finally elected more U.S. representatives than the Republicans for the first time since 1940. The year 1958 also marked other important firsts:

Lawrence was the first Catholic to sit in the governor's mansion, and African American Democrat Robert Nix was elected as U.S. representative for Philadelphia's Fourth District, which now had a black majority. In 1960 the state went for Kennedy by a slim margin, remarkable given the avalanche of anti-Catholic propaganda directed against him throughout the campaign.[68] In 1956 Democrat Joe Clark began a twelve-year term in the U.S. Senate, defeating James Duff; Clark was a strong liberal who broke with the administration's Vietnam policy as early as 1965.

The political tone of the state was distinctly liberal and pro-labor, and also sympathetic to civil rights. Both Duff and Fine had opened employment opportunities to minorities, and in 1955 the Leader administration finally adopted a state fair employment practices law, which had been a constant demand of Left and liberal groups since 1941. Leader himself denounced the Pechan law as "an unworkable, amateurish, legislative hodge-podge . . . a farcical law." His attorney general was Thomas MacBride, who had been the attorney for both Marjorie Matson and the Philadelphia Smith Act defendants; an activist liberal, he established a civil rights division in the state Department of Justice. In the 1960s Governor William Scranton presided over a notably liberal Republican administration.[69] That these attitudes reflected the public mood is indicated by the presidential election of 1964, in which Barry Goldwater suffered a defeat on a scale that was amazing in view of past Republican triumphs in the state. Lyndon Johnson took 65 percent of the vote, and Goldwater outpolled him in only four rural counties, in the sort of electoral massacre that used to be inflicted on Pennsylvania's Democrats. The outcome demonstrated the electorate's total failure to respond to apocalyptic warnings about global Communism. That the result was specifically a rejection of Goldwater's views is indicated by the comfortable victory of Republican senatorial candidate Hugh Scott in the same election.

The political realignment of the 1950s owed much to the state's parlous economic condition, with mass unemployment resulting from the collapse of traditional industries like coal and railroads; how could a state with such pressing needs be dubious about the virtues of big government and federal aid? Between 1947 and 1958, Pennsylvania slipped from second to fifth place among manufacturing states. As the Pennsylvania Communist Party observed accurately enough in 1957, "The number of unemployed and partially employed workers in Pennsylvania is among the highest in the nation. Most of the chronic unemployment is caused by permanent layoffs in coal, textile and railroad. While the area hardest hit has been the anthracite, other parts of the state, including Philadelphia, are increasingly feeling the rise of full or partial unemployment."[70] By 1958 unemployment was running at 10.5 percent, far above the national average, and all the cities were rapidly losing population. Like other northern and midwestern states, Pennsylvania's economic decline was reflected in a relative loss of political power: the state had thirty-six U.S. representatives in the 1920s, but only twenty-seven by the 1960s, and twenty-one by the 1990s. These changes echoed through the political system, weakening the power of traditional employers' groups and unions, as well as the traditional centers of population.

Pennsylvania politics were also changed fundamentally by the shifting racial balance in the major cities, which brought black issues to the center stage of public life; traditional questions of class and economic power were challenged and later supplanted by conflicts over race and interest group. African American migration into the cities reached new heights during the Second World War, while white residents increasingly moved out to swelling suburban communities. Suburban growth was often remarkable, with the emergence of whole new communities like Levittown; the population of Bucks County rose by 112 percent between 1950 and 1960, while Delaware and Chester Counties grew by a third in the same decade. The urban black population thus increased in both absolute and relative terms. Philadelphia had about 250,000 African Americans in 1940, representing about one-eighth of the population, but by 1963 that figure had increased to 550,000, or over a quarter of the whole. By 1949 the Democratic Party in Philadelphia was under enormous pressure to ensure that black candidates were chosen for political office and judgeships. In the 1950s the city's seventeen or so "Negro wards" represented a vital power base that no party could afford to ignore, and the number of such units was increasing.[71]

The racial conflicts that had once characterized southern states now arrived in Pennsylvania. During the 1950s the southern civil rights struggle attracted widespread bipartisan support in liberal northern states, where it had a particular impact upon churches and religious groups. However, the issues raised about discrimination in jobs, housing, and business opportunities were increasingly applied to northern cities like Philadelphia and Pittsburgh, where police forces were accused of racial brutality at least as severe as that prevailing in the segregationist South. Racial questions came to pervade political life. By 1955 and 1956 controversy over residential discrimination brought Philadelphia to the verge of rioting, and in 1961 NAACP attorneys filed suit in federal court claiming racial discrimination in the city's public schools.[72] The civil rights movement arrived in the city in earnest in 1963, when sit-ins and demonstrations were designed both to show solidarity with southern activists and to demand greater minority involvement in city construction projects. During 1964 the size of demonstrations swelled and the number of violent confrontations accelerated, culminating in widespread rioting in North Philadelphia in August. These events initiated a period of several years of sporadic riots and demonstrations. The city's police chief, Frank Rizzo, showed a determined resistance to minority protests that made him a populist folk hero and laid the foundations for an enduring political career: Rizzo was elected mayor in 1971 and 1975, and he was at the heart of the city's politics until his death in 1991.[73]

Political violence with a powerful racial agenda now became a fact of urban life. For two decades after the 1964 riots, the Philadelphia police force would often find itself in brutal physical conflict with black political activists, most spectacularly in a series of raids and gun battles in 1970, and again with the successive standoffs with the radical group MOVE. Between 1967 and 1971 few weeks passed without the local press reporting some riot or protest against racial injustice or police brutality, especially in the schools and colleges, and often black movements attracted the vociferous support of white radicals; in 1970 several thousand black and white activists held a "revolutionary people's constitutional convention" at Temple University. Philadelphia's racial politics were echoed in other Pennsylvania cities, and urban rioting occurred in the mid-1960s in Harrisburg, York, Erie, and Chester. In Pittsburgh the riots following the assassination of Martin Luther King Jr. in April 1968 were the worst civil disorders the city had seen since the 1870s, and order was restored with the use of several thousand National Guard troops and State Police.

The political situation briefly resembled the worst nightmares of the anti-Communist leaders of two decades past—or, indeed, the most extravagant dreams of the leftists they had persecuted—and old grievances surfaced. The American Legion joined other veterans' groups in demanding a purge of radical student groups and leftist faculty at the state's colleges and called for the enforcement of the 1950s loyalty laws; the legion's state commander sought unsuccessfully to have leading antiwar activists prosecuted on charges of treason and sedition, presumably in a rerun of the Steve Nelson case.[74] The Philadelphia police Red squad was as busy, and as intrusive, as at any time in the McCarthy years. In a startling reversal of earlier assumptions, many of the most fervent radicals were Catholic, some of them priests and nuns: Catholic clergy were among the antiwar militants prosecuted in the state's main political trial of this era, the 1972 case of the Harrisburg Seven.[75]

Political turmoil caused some liberals to revise their attitudes to the controversies of the Red Scare years, and as leaders like Father Rice became involved in civil rights and antiwar struggles, they gained sympathy for earlier victims of official repression. By the late 1960s Rice was expressing regret at aspects of his labor crusade and apologizing for his credulity in cases like the Rosenberg affair. In a remarkable 1968 interview, he discussed the "Communist problem" in Pittsburgh: he now felt that the Left leadership in UE was rooted out by "the hysteria. . . . They were wiped out in 1950, they were destroyed in the union, and good unions were destroyed in the process. . . . The destruction of the UE was tragic for the labor movement. . . . We exaggerated the communist threat out of all proportion." Perhaps responding to charges that civil rights leaders were Communist-inspired, Rice resolutely refused to call any of his former adversaries "card-carrying" Communists: "How the hell do I know? I never saw that card."[76]

The turbulent events of the late 1960s obscured the fundamental shifts in political power occurring in the state in this era, as well as the dramatic expansion of the African American role in politics and business, which was symbolized by the election of Philadelphia's first black mayor, Wilson Goode, in 1983. Conversely, the rise of Frank Rizzo marks the redefinition of white ethnic politics, often under the cover of "law and order." Black expansion into previously white residential areas created severe resentment, increasing both racial and religious tensions. The black-white divide became a religious division, as by 1970 Catholics made up over half of the nonblack population in Philadelphia; race relations in the city in these years have been aptly described as "White Catholic/Negro relations," and the same was true to a lesser extent in Pittsburgh.[77] The stage was being set for politicians to make careers out of advancing and defending the interests of their respective races.

Traditional divisions of Left and Right were now transformed.[78] In 1968 George Wallace's third-party movement briefly enjoyed great popularity in white working-class areas of northern cities, and his American Independent Party took 379,000 votes in Pennsylvania, around 8 percent of the total votes cast. Wallace had areas of strength in the Greater Pittsburgh region as well as in the suburban counties around Philadelphia: he received 80,000 votes in Allegheny County alone. Though the new Right spoke the language of anti-Communism, this was a movement of ethnicity and status far more than any traditional ideologies; comprehensive "Americanism" was as irrelevant as

Communism. The ideological Cold War politics initiated by the campaigns of Joe McCarthy and Henry Wallace ended in the critical election year of 1968, in the movements of their respective namesakes: Eugene McCarthy, the peace activist, and George Wallace, standard-bearer for an enraged white working class.

Though American Communists themselves played little direct role in the social movements of these years, their ideas enjoyed a curious afterlife. In 1954, at the height of its persecution, the Pennsylvania Communist Party issued a periodical entitled *Pennsylvania in Facts and Figures*, the cover of which bore the slogan "Labor—civil rights—Negro rights—peace—legislation," which sounds like an outline of American history in the coming two decades.[79] Though the Party itself was eclipsed, the issues on which it had campaigned most vigorously would dominate the social agenda of the 1960s, the era of the civil rights revolution and of the most successful and broad-based peace movement in American history. The political history of the 1970s was in turn shaped by the federal government's attempts to limit radical excesses, and the disastrous failure of these efforts in the Watergate crisis.

The CPUSA itself never returned to anything like its pre-1950 strength, especially after the moral collapse of 1956, but a Communist presence continued. In the 1960s Communists still attracted massively disproportionate attention from law enforcement officials and the FBI, while the real centers of radical activity had moved far to the Left of the old Communist Party, whose members were regarded as dinosaurs. Pittsburgh Communists organized a new Party paper in the late 1960s, and old specters revived briefly in 1971 when an informant surfaced to argue that a Young Workers Liberation League was actually a Party front, though few seemed to care.[80] The following year a U.S. Supreme Court decision struck down the Musmanno law that had prohibited the Party in Pennsylvania, and a Communist presidential ticket headed by Gus Hall drew 2,686 votes in the state.[81] In 1973 Pittsburgh had about 100 registered Communists, but a Party candidate for the city council easily attracted over 3,000 signatures in support of his place on the ballot. Even today, after the evaporation of the world movement and the fragmentation of the USSR, the CPUSA still has headquarters in Philadelphia and Pittsburgh, and the Pittsburgh branch responds to queries by e-mail.[82] UE also possesses an impressive Web site, though the whole union now marshals only some 30,000 workers, where once it guided the fortunes of twenty times that number.

Though the Communist Party was destroyed as an effective political force in the early 1950s, it has continued to attract sporadic attention from historians and the mass media, for whom it often possesses a romantic ambience. We have already noted the post-1975 wave of sympathetic films about the victims of McCarthyism, as well as the tendency to acknowledge the older generation of Communists as authentic precursors of the civil rights workers and antiwar protesters of the 1960s. Some of the old leftists remained active in the new and much more promising political environment, and quondam Philadelphia Party leader Walter Lowenfels became a respected poet and editor, who published much of the new poetry and protest writing inspired by Vietnam.

The new and more respectful attitude to American Communism is exemplified by a newspaper article published in 1974 about James Dolsen, then nearing ninety. Dolsen, one of the last surviving charter members of the CPUSA and an alleged Soviet OGPU agent, was an authentic monument of the American Left. He testified to the Dies Committee in 1940 and was a leading figure in the nominating petition scandal of that year. Singled out as a key villain in Matt Cvetic's testimony, he personally sold Judge Musmanno the books that would be used to convict both Nelson and Dolsen in the state sedition trials, and Nelson and Dolsen again costarred in the federal Smith Act cases. Living in West Philadelphia, Dolsen maintained his propaganda activities as well as his age and health permitted, but the 1974 feature did not portray an unrepentant villain; it painted instead an affectionate picture of a quirky hero: "With his unruly white hair and almost mischievous smile, he looks like a kindly curator of a dusty museum." Dolsen's views were also treated with some sympathy, as a stubborn idealism. Though condemning the current wave of domestic terrorism given prominence by the Patty Hearst kidnapping, Dolsen had no doubts that the Left would ultimately triumph, and his certainty was all the greater given the crisis faced by the old anti-Communist nemesis, Richard Nixon. He had "no regrets, or doubts that 'this Watergate thing' will lead to a widespread feeling that the 'capitalistic system has passed its acme of acceptance.'"[83] For a few years at least, many would have agreed with him.

10

CONSEQUENCES

Communism and anti-Communism were both primary elements of the American political agenda in the postwar years, resulting in activity by legislatures, courts, and private groups. This final chapter explores the consequences of the anti-Communist movement, in its effects on individuals as well as on the wider polity. The most significant impact was in the area of federalism, where the Red Scare led directly or indirectly to a major expansion of federal powers and a consequent decline in state jurisdiction. Both the eclipse of the old Left and the rise of new internal security structures would have lasting effects during the political conflicts of the 1960s and early 1970s.

How far-reaching were the effects of the anti-Communist repression? Though accounts of the Red Scare era often use the language of "purge" and "inquisition," American events were not marred by anything like the bloodshed that such terms imply, and they pale by comparison with other great political persecutions of the twentieth century. The direct human cost of the American Red Scare was tiny compared to that of, say, Stalin's purges of the 1930s, which claimed the lives of millions, or the less severe persecutions of the post-war Soviet Union, when thousands died in the inhuman conditions of the prison camps. In stark contrast, the political turmoil in Pennsylvania cannot be directly connected with one death, although there certainly was violence. Still, the anti-Communist hysteria can hardly be defended on the grounds that its effects were less abominable than those of one of the worst eras in human history; by the standard of Stalin, or that of Hitler's Holocaust, it is scarcely possible to criticize any act of tyranny or corruption in a Western democracy.

The Red Scare of the 1940s and 1950s might more realistically be gauged by a comparison with other events in the United States in the same period, specifically with racial conditions in the South. Though this was not a period of mass violence or pogroms like those following the First World War, the late 1940s in the South were marked by numerous lynchings, mutilations, and other atrocities, as well as casual murders by law enforcement officials, virtually none of which were punished. By the standards of contemporary Mississippi, to say nothing of the Gulag, the suppression of northern Communists was a relatively bloodless affair. Pennsylvania's post-1945 experience was a good deal less violent than some of its own historical encounters with repression, in that on this occasion at least, the commonwealth escaped both industrial massacres and mass hangings: matters had been very different forty or fifty years earlier.

The language of "purge" is further complicated when we consider the less direct physical consequences. Though courts notoriously did hand down severe sentences, these verdicts were rarely upheld. In the Pittsburgh trials, Steve Nelson and his colleagues suffered imprisonment in harsh conditions, following trials that can only be seen as flagrant miscarriages of justice, yet both the state and federal cases ultimately collapsed. Though hundreds faced legal consequences monstrously out of proportion to any presumed misdeeds they might have committed, including deportation and denaturalization, in only a handful of cases were these penalties eventually inflicted. Once again, a comparison with the segregated South is helpful; there, well-publicized atrocities like lynching were accompanied by systematic and institutionalized repression in the jails and chain gangs. Pennsylvania prisons, by contrast, never had to deal with a whole class of long-term political prisoners. Incidentally, the abominable malfeasance of the state courts in these years was not specifically designed to ensure that subversives were swiftly railroaded; however outrageous the injustices perpetrated in political cases, these were the standard procedures of police, judges, and prosecutors in normal criminal cases in those pre-Warren Court days, regardless of the race of the accused.

Yet to say that the Red Scare did not lead to mass murder is scant defense, and it says nothing about the real damage that was caused. If we take just the teachers and professors, in absolute numbers only a tiny proportion of the state's educators were dismissed as a result of the anti-Communist movement, but that dismissal was for most a life-changing trauma, the ruin of a career and the waste of perhaps decades of emotional and professional investment. Barrows Dunham, for example, a popular writer as well as a fine scholar, never received another tenured faculty position after his dismissal from Temple in 1953. The personal outcome could be disastrous, in terms of family crises and health problems. Enough victims of the purges were said to have had their lives shortened by the experience that we can hardly speak with any confidence of "bloodless" repression. Even if an assault on one's career was successfully overcome, the effort to do so always required an immense investment in time and energy, to say nothing of embarrassment. The majority of the Philadelphia teachers were reinstated some fifteen years after their original troubles began; while the reinstatement was praiseworthy, nothing could ever compensate for such a large portion stolen from a life.

Nor were the educators the worst situated of all the victims, as their cause attracted the sympathy of support groups and like-minded activists. Perhaps the greatest tragedies of all befell the industrial workers threatened with dismissal and deportation, often after decades of grueling work in the United States. Such individuals rarely attracted the notice of protest groups, and they were not the subject of hagiographical pamphlets. If they were very lucky, they found a dedicated, progressive attorney who could fend off the official assaults, but the media demonstrated little but hostility. When a retired miner in the small western Pennsylvania community of Clarksville was threatened with deportation after being identified as a Communist by Joe Mazzei and others, the *Pittsburgh Press* noted this pathetic case with a jokey headline, "Hasson Hits Snag on Commie's Tag."[1] When Joe Mazzei named a postal clerk as a Communist, the man was dismissed, only regaining his job two years later when the informant was himself discredited. The system thus vindicated itself, but only after this ordinary individual had suffered untold personal loss of prosperity and reputation. The fact that the personal catastrophe only lasted for a year or two hardly makes the man any less a victim of a political purge run out of control.[2]

Even focusing on the sufferings of accused individuals ignores the psychic consequences to the community at large. As for the electrical workers and other unions, such a perspective ignores the impact of the lingering fear and uncertainty that affected thousands of individuals, the sense that any day one's name might appear in congressional testimony, and that quite innocent events or connections from ten or fifteen years earlier could come back to destroy a career. These troubling memories would certainly have affected the 40,000–50,000 Pennsylvanians who had ever passed through the Communist Party at some stage of its development, and perhaps the hundreds of thousands who might have attended one or two meetings of what were later designated as front groups. The number of people thus exposed to risk represented an unsettlingly high proportion of the population in some communities and ethnic groups, notably the Jews of Philadelphia. Such fears were at their keenest at times like the grim years of 1953–54, when the metaphor of "inquisition" was best justified, and when individual legal protections were at their lowest ebb, the federal courts in their deepest slumber. We know in retrospect that the scare was about to diminish and that official vigilantism would soon end, but there was no reason in 1953 to suspect that this might be the case, or that conditions might not become much worse. Who knew that the country might not have to deal soon with a President McCarthy, with Judge Musmanno or Francis Walter in the governor's mansion? The basic principle of terrorism is to strike one to intimidate a hundred.

Beyond the impact on individuals, the broader effects of the Red Scare were complex. Much has been written about the consequences on national and international politics, on the constrained policy options available to diplomats and civil servants; arguably the scare did lead to a much harder American line in Cold War confrontations over the next decade, and it ensured a ready audience for the most trenchant pronouncements concerning global confrontation. In retrospect it seems incredible that as recently as 1948 a major politician like Henry Wallace could have dared raise such fundamental questions about the image of a Free World engaged in a deadly struggle with tyranny. In the late 1950s it was the Democrats who made the most play of alleged national weakness in the face of Communism, urging greater attention to military readiness, but a broad consensus concurred on the urgency of the Soviet peril worldwide. As the supposedly monolithic Communist world dissolved in the early 1960s, it was difficult for American politicians to acknowledge the emergence of a diverse range of Left voices—or to take advantage of differences between the various factions. New approaches had to wait for the end of the Vietnam War and the policy innovations of Richard Nixon.

It is harder to trace the direct impact on domestic politics. Though anti-Communism made the careers of some individuals, there was no evidence that the Red Scare was a veiled rightist putsch, much less a successful counterrevolution against the New Deal. In Pennsylvania the end of the worst years of repression in the mid-1950s coincided with a political swing, if not to the Left, then to a Democratic Party that claimed to represent the aspirations of blacks and organized labor. As Communists noted grudgingly, Pennsylvania Democrats represented "primarily a labor, Negro, small farmer and small business vote. This majority has proven it wants vigorous anti-monopoly, liberal and good government candidates to head Demo. tickets."[3] These liberal candidates included popular figures like Joe Clark, George Leader, and David Lawrence. Leftist writers of the late 1940s had been wrong to assert that the antisubversive campaigns would lead to a suppression of the unions or of liberal forces in general, but the suppression of radicalism did have its consequences. For both the unions and the ethnic organizations, the disabling of Left rivals meant a shift in power to the larger and more hierarchical organizations, which were more conservative in social as well as political terms. In the Polish community, for instance, the collapse of small left-wing sects removed any challenge to the PNA and the authoritarian political machine that dominated it. In the unions the defeat of the CIO Left made populist rank-and-file traditions suspect, while the victorious organizations were more centralized and more inclined to uncritical veneration of charismatic leaders. These unions were also more attuned to the Democratic Party at both the local and national levels.

Post-1945 campaigns against Communism had other long-term effects in matters of ethnic and religious identity and self-confidence; for all their horrors, the anti-Communist campaigns may, paradoxically, have had a kind of democratic social effect. The New Deal era had marked the rise to electoral power of Catholics, Jews, and newer ethnic groups, and this change was consummated by the triumph of "ethnic" politicians like David Lawrence during the 1950s and the Kennedy presidential campaign in 1960. This sea change in state politics coincided with the age of anti-Communist activism, and we are bound to speculate about links between the two phenomena. This period is sometimes described in terms of an "inverted nativism," in which the canards previously directed against immigrant groups by the old WASP elites were now, ironically, turned against those elites themselves. In Pennsylvania as elsewhere, the most passionate anti-Communists were often Catholics representing the Irish or newer ethnic groups, leaders like Father Rice and Judge Musmanno, while the objects of their suspicion were the traditionally privileged classes, "eggheads" with Ivy League educations, and their particular institutions, their colleges and churches. Of course, the resulting scares often targeted Jews or Catholics themselves, quite humble individuals, and Francis Walter's anti-immigrant obsession has often been noted. Nevertheless, the anti-elite rhetoric continued to flourish, and while Catholics had once been blamed for a dual loyalty to a foreign power outside the United States, now this same charge was turned against the old elites with their supposed sympathy for the Soviet Union or (scarcely less sinister) the United Nations. While older colleges were under attack for sheltering eggheads, Catholic institutions were in the vanguard of the populist movement, organizing anti-Communist labor schools and summer institutes. In consequence, anti-Communism helped to redefine notions of Americanism, American loyalty, and American citizenship in ways that were less restrictive in terms of class and ethnicity. Veterans' organizations were swift to denounce any expression of racial or religious intolerance because it gave an opportunity to Communist propaganda and further violated the principles of Americanism of a society that fully acknowledged the contributions of Protestant, Catholic, and Jew.

The most direct achievement of the anti-Communist movement was the removal of the Communist Party as a significant voice in American politics, and the issue then arises of what difference this made to later political development. This question is perhaps unanswerable in that it requires us to postulate an alternative reality, but the indications are that Communism could not have thrived, and the movement would inevitably have been devastated by internal schisms. Put another way, even if the Communist tradition had been allowed to develop as an independent political force, it would likely have collapsed anyway during the 1960s.

We may draw analogies with the experience of other countries in which a strong Communist Party of the 1940s suffered decline in the Cold War years but remained in play in national politics. In both France and Italy the respective Communist parties enjoyed a success far beyond the dreams of the American leadership, with a firm working-class foothold that regularly gave Communists some 10 or 20 percent of the ballot through the 1960s, and often more in times of crisis. However, both parties suffered serious defections from the late 1950s on, and again following the invasion of Czechoslovakia in 1968. The year 1968 was also marked by the great political upheavals throughout Europe, in which mainstream pro-Soviet Communist parties were outflanked to the Left by far more radical organizations that drew on contemporary post-Marxist and existentialist theorists, with a heavy dose of Third World romanticism. The newer groups were also prepared to contemplate the use of direct action and revolutionary violence, of the sort dismissed by the old Communists as left-wing infantilism. After 1968 their New Left rivals regarded the Communist parties as laughably establishment-oriented, and effectively as the most potent forces of conservatism among the working classes, which had themselves succumbed to embourgeoisement. Italians created the telling word

"68ism" (*sessantottismo*) to describe the influential package of New Left, feminist, and ecological themes that radicalized a generation, and that made the old Communists seem so staid and bureaucratic. This became a generational issue, as younger militants who defined themselves as Maoists, Castroites, anarchists, Trotskyists, or "True Leninists" scoffed at Communist Party members twenty or thirty years their seniors. As terrorist campaigns erupted in Italy during the 1970s, revolutionary leftists were just as likely to target Communist officials as industrialists.

The decline of mainstream Communism was if anything still more marked in countries with closer parallels to the United States, such as Great Britain, Australia, and Canada, where parties had not had the immense advantage of having led anti-Nazi Resistance movements. Though Communism in the English-speaking nations was not a mass working-class movement, nevertheless the Party was stronger in these countries than in the United States; at any given point in the 1940s, Party membership per capita was three times as large in Australia and Canada than in Pennsylvania, while the British rate was double Pennsylvania's. In all these countries, Communists came under assault in the Cold War years, with Left unions being purged or expelled, and Australian Communists narrowly survived a Catholic-inspired attempt to prohibit the Party in a 1951 referendum. However, in none of the three countries did the Party actually suffer prohibition, nor were its activities restricted to anything like the same extent they were in the United States.[4] Legal Communist parties thus survived into the 1980s, but under increasingly heavy pressure from younger and more radical movements intoxicated by "68ism," and with ever more ruinous doctrinal schisms.[5] Middle Eastern affairs were an added source of rancor, as both the Soviet Union and the New Left adopted a vehement anti-Zionism that was anathema to older Jewish activists. Party membership rolls shriveled. The old Communist infrastructures in heavy industry became increasingly irrelevant as these other countries suffered the same sort of restructuring as Pennsylvania, with a shift to a service economy. By the early 1980s the respective parties were in shreds, facing dissolution even before the terminal collapse of the Soviet bloc.

In short, the experience of other Western countries that retained legal and active Communist parties does not sound very different from conditions in the United States in the era of its own 1960s radicalism, though there were some differences. Other Western countries never lost the concept of the Left as an integral, even respectable, part of the political spectrum, and they generally had distinct parties claiming to represent organized labor, whereas the discrediting of American leftist movements and organizations in the 1950s made such an acknowledgement of class conflict all but impossible. With an avowal of socialist or Marxist sympathies regarded as eccentric, American progressives and reformers structured their ideas in terms of "liberalism," a term with connotations quite different from the European context. Whereas the European New Left remained familiar with Marxist thought and terminology, its American counterpart only gradually rediscovered these concepts in the late 1960s, and even then the ideas had relatively shallow roots outside academe. Without even a vestigial Marxist framework, American radicalism from the 1970s onward was framed in terms of ethnic and gender identity, and in the politics of interest groups rather than classes. But even if an American Communist Party had survived as a thriving entity, could it have channeled the new radicalism into a more class-oriented perspective? European parallels make this prospect very dubious.

Though political consequences are difficult to identify with any certainty, legal and constitutional outcomes were more tangible, and the most significant was a move from the primacy of state jurisdictions or private enterprise to a potent federal role. In a sense, the course of the Red Scare was a continuation of the centralizing and federalizing trends of the New Deal era, though now exploited for politically conservative ends.

A growing federal role was evident in the area of political policing and investigation. Since the industrialization of Pennsylvania in the mid-nineteenth century, internal security functions had been mainly in the hands of private groups such as detective agencies, corporate security departments, the Coal and Iron Police, and the "professional patriots," quasi-vigilante structures like the American Protective League of the First World War years. In the early twentieth century, state agencies like the State Police had come to play a greater role, but always in intimate alliance with these private networks. The emphasis on private enterprise continued through the Cold War years, when individuals like Harry Sherman and Blair Gunther played a buccaneering role in their wars against the Left, building up the intelligence data that would later be passed to congressional committees, and finding and manipulating informants. Sherman was frank about having "to do a little extra-legal work . . . including setting up our own strongarm squads" ("our" in this context referring to his allies in Pittsburgh's right-wing unions). However, matters were now very different from the nineteenth-century days of the Molly Maguires or the Homestead

Strike, in that Sherman, Gunther, and their ilk were now collaborating at every stage with a federal agency, namely the FBI, which was taking the initiative in countersubversion.

Though federal agencies had been involved in such struggles from the First World War era, a decisive change in their scale of activity can be dated to the Roosevelt years, when it was justified by national security needs.[6] In 1936 the president gave the FBI the responsibility of combating potential subversion and sabotage, a brief that extended to Communist as well as Nazi and Fascist groups, and FBI involvement in this area reached new heights in the war scare years from 1939 through 1941. During the war Communists themselves eagerly supported the use of FBI powers against likely saboteurs or subversives, including both ultra-rightists and rivals on the far Left. The stage was set for the bureau's post-1946 activism, in which Communists were targeted as part of the general vigilance against spies.

Though the FBI always held the paramount responsibility, other federal agencies participated in countersubversive efforts. By the 1930s military and naval intelligence both had interests in key plants like those of Westinghouse, and we have seen the attempt by the Civil Air Patrol to create a "loyalty police" some years later. The exigencies of war, real or imagined, transformed the environment of law enforcement. Other federal agencies now acquired important "police" or security functions, especially the immigration authorities, who wielded perhaps the most intimidating arsenal of discretionary powers. The threat of deportation or denaturalization was so significant because many of the groups likely to respond to the Communist appeal were from the generation that had immigrated to the United States in the early twentieth century, often as infants; to men and women in their middle years, their foreign birth now raised the threat of removal to a distant country of which they knew nothing. Even as significant a New Deal agency as the National Labor Relations Board became pivotal to anti-Communist efforts, as the agency responsible for calling and supervising the elections in the electrical industry. In 1954 Edward Lamb found himself facing something like a major political trial before the Federal Communications Commission.

An expanded federal role can also be seen in the congressional committees that were so active in these years. Between 1949 and 1959 alone, HUAC held five hearings with major relevance to Pennsylvania and SISS held four, in addition to investigations by other Senate bodies like the Permanent Subcommittee on Investigations and the Subcommittee on Immigration and Naturalization; some of these hearings were held in situ, like the 1953 inquisition into the Philadelphia Teachers' Union. Roughly, at least one congressional investigation into subversion in the state could be expected every year in this period. As in the case of policing, this trend had its roots in the New Deal years, and it largely originated with liberal Democrats. One influential model for later investigations was the LaFollette Committee of the late 1930s, which had examined the operation of private police structures and employers' vigilante groups in events like the Johnstown steel strike. Meanwhile, the McCormack-Dickstein Committee of 1934–35 explored the emerging pro-Nazi underworld in the United States. Each committee was criticized at the time as a politicized abuse of congressional power, in this instance, of Left-liberal interference into the affairs of political enemies on the Right; both created headlines by parading newsworthy witnesses to report on local conditions in the most dramatic terms.

By 1938 the Dies Committee represented a ground-breaking federal move into the quest for "un-American" activities, using proactive investigators to make arrests and seize documents in the cities targeted. As we have seen, the Dies operations against Communists in both Philadelphia and Pittsburgh in 1940 closely foreshadowed later HUAC concerns and methods. By the late 1940s, though "un-American" behaviors notionally included acts of the far Right, in practice this congressional mechanism was solely targeted against Communism and the Left, and local rightists were eager to attract the interest of HUAC or SISS to conditions in a particular locality. Though state counterparts to HUAC were often proposed, and were activated in some jurisdictions, such an institution never appeared in Pennsylvania because it would have been superfluous. With Francis Walter on the federal committee, who could ask for more support in the war on radicalism?

Though federal involvement assisted the Red-hunters in many areas, the opposite was true in the courts: anti-Communist campaigns flourished there, but only until federal action finally reined in the overbroad efforts of state courts and legislators. Throughout American history, most regulation of political behavior was a state function, with the federal courts intervening only when state measures appeared grossly excessive in their scope or sanctions. Since the First World War, however, the U.S. Supreme Court had largely withdrawn from the realm of defending the rights of political activists, and First Amendment protections were increasingly restricted. Though the federal Bill of Rights protected political speech, the Court acknowledged that this right could be hedged according to circumstances, so that restrictions might be placed in time of emergency or grave political threat. The famous analogy to "shouting 'fire' in a crowded theater" originated in a 1919 case arising from the arrest of a Philadelphia socialist charged with spreading antiwar propaganda. Speech could be regulated if it was seen as abusive or inflammatory, and the 1925 *Gitlow* case made speech illegal if it had any tendency, "however remote," to bring about criminal acts. A critical distinction was drawn between discussing an idea, which was permissible, and advocacy, which might be forbidden under sedition laws like the 1940 Smith Act. The *Dennis* decision of 1951 extended the notion of "advocacy" to merely envisaging an alternative social and political order. Speech was thus free, but apparently only as long as it went no further than the quiet ruminations of a church tea party. A similar reluctance to challenge political investigations led the Court to restrict Fifth Amendment rights, thus granting immense powers to investigative committees at state and federal levels. The worst manifestations of the Red Scare were made possible by the abstention of the federal courts from the defense of political defendants, above all over the First and Fifth Amendments.

Conversely, the expansion of federal jurisdiction under the Warren Court was crucial to limiting and ending the purges. The *Nelson* decision itself annexed the whole area of sedition for the federal government, in a case seen as a blow to states' rights quite as serious as the legendary *Brown v. Board of Education* case of 1954. *Nelson* did not necessarily initiate a more relaxed political climate, as in theory the federal government might itself enact harsh laws in this area, but the decision was followed shortly by others that collectively hamstrung the congressional committees and began the gradual process of extending the realm of protected speech to include forceful advocacy. In the new order, states were severely circumscribed in their powers to regulate dissidence or protest, a historic change with far-reaching effects that would become apparent in the Vietnam War era. The remarkable fact that anti-Red purges did not recommence in the mid-1960s owes much to the Supreme Court decisions of 1955–58, which were in turn a direct reaction to the excesses of the McCarthy era. Though cities and states did not go out of the business of political policing, they were now forced to behave in a quite different environment, shaped by federal initiatives and constraints. For the federal courts, as for federal law enforcement, the chief lesson of the anti-Communist movement was the familiar New Deal theme of the inadequacy of state institutions.

Pennsylvania's postwar Red Scare has not generally left much impression in public memory, except, of course, for those directly affected by the exposés and the union conflicts. The whole movement is scarcely mentioned in historical accounts of the period, and even then it receives little notice in comparison to sweeping social changes like the collapse of the old heavy industries, the closure of mines and steel mills, the move to the suburbs, and the urban redevelopment of the Pittsburgh Renaissance years. The Cold War nightmares of the time are remembered chiefly through material vestiges like the symbols denoting fallout shelters, or fading recollections of "duck and cover" exercises in schools (though Catholics have powerful memories of the bloody tales told by priests and nuns about Communist atrocities). For all the newsprint that it consumed at the time, the whole encounter with the Red menace seems to have had little impact on the social or political life of the state.

And yet, this conclusion would be misleading. The postwar Communist issue did much to reshape American political culture and helped create new political and economic orthodoxies that came to be regarded as self-evidently correct. One set of older orthodoxies all but perished in the ruin of the Depression, and the New Deal made it possible to consider other challenging options, about internationalism, workers' rights, or the role of government in society, for instance, ideas that had once been marginalized; by the mid-1940s the range of respectable political alternatives had broadened immensely. The Red Scare set limits to these options, ending, indeed stigmatizing, the more radical dreams of the progressives, or at least driving them underground for decades. At the same time, the emerging political synthesis was by no means a return to the old pre-1932 "mossbacked" orthodoxies: internationalism became widely accepted as a key American interest, and the establishment of organized labor ensured the permanence of much of the New Deal inheritance. Crucially, too, civil rights remained at the forefront of the national agenda. Across the nation, reactions to the supposed Communist menace reshaped the political parties, but in Pennsylvania particularly, the course taken by the Red Scare ensured that the Democratic Party would survive, and indeed would remain politically dominant for decades. Though often through its indirect and unintentional effects, the anti-Communist movement left an enduring political inheritance.

NOTES

ABBREVIATIONS

AHR	*American Historical Review*
BGC	Billy Graham Center, Wheaton College, Wheaton, Illinois
CT	*Christianity Today*
DU	Duquesne University, Pittsburgh, Pennsylvania
GPO	Government Printing Office
HCLA	Historical Collections and Labor Archives, Pennsylvania State University, Pattee Library, University Park
NYT	*New York Times*
ON	*Ordine Nuovo*
PAJ	*Polish-American Journal*
PEB	*Philadelphia Evening Bulletin*
PFF	*Pennsylvania in Facts and Figures*
PI	*Philadelphia Inquirer*
PP	*Pittsburgh Press*
PPG	*Pittsburgh Post-Gazette*
PPL	*Philadelphia Public Ledger*
PPV	*Pennsylvania Party Voice*
PSA	Pennsylvania State Archives, Harrisburg
PST	*Pittsburgh Sun-Telegraph*
PSU	Pennsylvania State University, Pattee Library, University Park
Truman Library	Harry S. Truman Library, Independence, Missouri
TU	Temple University, Urban Archives, Philadelphia, Pennsylvania
UP	University of Pittsburgh
YGD	*York Gazette and Daily*

1. Thomas C. Reeves, *The Life and Times of Joe McCarthy* (New York: Stein and Day, 1982), 393; Paul B. Beers, *Pennsylvania Politics Today and Yesterday* (University Park: Pennsylvania State University Press, 1980), 152. For Duff's "Hang Communists" speech, see *32nd Annual Convention of the American Legion, Department of Pennsylvania at Philadelphia, Aug. 9–12, 1950* (American Legion, Department of Pennsylvania, 1950), 73–76; Pennsylvania's Communists nicknamed the governor "Dangerous Duff": *PFF* 3, no. 1 (January 1956): 14.

2. Ellen Schrecker, "McCarthyism and the Labor Movement," in *The CIO's Left-Led Unions*, ed. Steven Rosswurm (New Brunswick: Rutgers University Press, 1992), 139–57, quote at 139. Compare Ellen Schrecker, *Many Are the Crimes* (Boston: Little, Brown, 1998); and Albert Fried, ed., *McCarthyism: The Great American Red Scare* (New York: Oxford University Press, 1997).

3. David Caute, *The Great Fear: The Anti-Communist Purge under Truman and Eisenhower* (New York: Simon and Schuster, 1978). Compare Athan G. Theoharis, *Seeds of Repression* (Chicago: Quadrangle, 1971); Richard M. Freeland, *The Truman Doctrine and the Origins of McCarthyism* (New York: Knopf, 1972); and Jeff Broadwater, *Eisenhower and the Anti-Communist Crusade* (Chapel Hill: University of North Carolina Press, 1992).

4. Fried, *McCarthyism*, 5.

5. Quoted in David H. Bennett, *The Party of Fear*, 2d ed. (New York: Vintage, 1995), 307.

6. Other historically oriented films of this era reflecting a more sympathetic attitude to the Left include *The Private Files of J. Edgar Hoover* (1977), *Reds* (1981), and *Atomic Cafe* (1982); compare the concert film *The Weavers: Wasn't That a Time?* (1982). In 1986 PBS showed a nostalgic documentary on American Communism, *Seeing Red*. For the continuing interest in the Red Scare in Hollywood, see Patrick McGilligan and Paul Buhle, *Tender Comrades* (New York: St. Martin's, 1997), and Kenneth Lloyd Billingsley, *Hollywood Party* (Rocklin, Calif.: Prima, 1998).

7. For the Rosenbergs in popular culture, see Virginia Carmichael, *Framing History* (Minneapolis: University of Minnesota Press, 1993), and Marjorie Garber and Rebecca L. Walkowitz, eds., *Secret Agents* (New York: Routledge, 1995). Among the "forgettable" Cold War features, I would include *The House on Carroll Street* (1988) and *Golden Gate* (1993).

8. Michael O'Brien, *McCarthy and McCarthyism in Wisconsin* (Columbia: University of Missouri Press, 1980); James Truett Selcraig, *The Red Scare in the Midwest, 1945–1955* (Ann Arbor, Mich.: UMI Research Press, 1982); Don E. Carleton, *Red Scare!* (Austin: Texas Monthly Press, 1985); T. Michael Holmes, *The Specter of Communism in Hawaii* (Honolulu: University of Hawaii Press, 1994); M. J. Heale, *McCarthy's Americans* (Athens: University of Georgia Press, 1998); Kevin Fernlund, ed., *The Cold War American West* (Albuquerque: University of New Mexico Press, 1998); Sharon Hartman Strom, "Making McCarthy Possible" (paper delivered to the conference, "The Cold War and Its Implications," held at Los Alamos, N.M., August 1998). Such a local case-study approach is of course not new; see Walter Gellhorn, ed., *The States and Subversion* (Ithaca, N.Y.: Cornell University Press, 1952).

9. Caute, *The Great Fear*, 216–23, 387.

10. James T. Patterson, *Grand Expectations* (New York: Oxford University Press, 1996); Michael S. Sherry, *In the Shadow of War* (New Haven, Conn.: Yale University Press, 1995); and Philip Jenkins, *Hoods and Shirts* (Chapel Hill: University of North Carolina Press, 1997), for the isolationist movement.

11. Radio script, "On the Spot," broadcast on KQV Pittsburgh, September 1946, Box 3, Father Charles Owen Rice Papers, UE Labor Archive, UP.

12. HUAC, *Exposé of the Communist Party of Western Pennsylvania Based upon Testimony of Matthew Cvetic, Undercover Agent*, Hearings, 81st Cong., 2d sess. (Washington, D.C.: GPO, 1950), 1256 (hereafter cited as *Exposé of the Communist Party*); "Nelson Hailed Red Bomb, Cvetic Says," *PPG*, April 6, 1951.

13. *Exposé of the Communist Party*, 3030.

14. John E. Haynes, *Red Scare or Red Menace?* (Chicago: Ivan R. Dee, 1996).

15. For the concept of "inquisition," see Alvah Bessie, *Inquisition in Eden* (New York: Macmillan, 1965); Cedric Belfrage, *The American Inquisition, 1945–1960* (Indianapolis: Bobbs-Merrill, 1973); Stanley I. Kutler, *The American Inquisition* (New York: Hill and Wang, 1982); Athan G. Theoharis and John Stuart Cox, *The Boss: J. Edgar Hoover and the Great American Inquisition* (Philadelphia: Temple University Press, 1988); and Griffin Fariello, *Red Scare: Memories of the American Inquisition* (New York: Norton, 1995). Lillian Hellman, *Scoundrel Time* (Boston: Little, Brown, 1976); Richard Hofstadter, *The Paranoid Style in American Politics* (Chicago: University of Chicago Press, 1979); Robert K. Murray, *Red Scare: A Study in National Hysteria, 1919–1920* (Minneapolis: University of Minnesota Press, 1955). Though Murray's classic book concerns the first Red Scare, it clearly owes much of its inspiration to events at the time it was written, in the Pennsylvania of the early 1950s.

16. Allen Weinstein and Alexander Vassiliev, *The Haunted Wood: Soviet Espionage in America* (New York: Random House, 1999); Harvey Klehr, John Earl Haynes, and Kyrill M. Anderson, *The Soviet World of American Communism* (New Haven, Conn.: Yale University Press, 1998); Sam Tanenhaus, *Whittaker Chambers* (New York: Random House, 1997); Harvey Klehr and Ronald Radosh, *The Amerasia Spy Case* (Chapel Hill: University of North Carolina Press, 1996); Harvey Klehr, John Earl Haynes, and F. I. Firsov, *The Secret World of American Communism* (New Haven, Conn.: Yale University Press, 1995); David J. Garrow, *The FBI and Martin Luther King* (New York: Penguin, 1981).

17. Richard Gid Powers, *Not without Honor* (New York: Free Press, 1995). Compare Ethan Bronner, "Rethinking McCarthyism, If Not McCarthy," *NYT*, October 18, 1998.

18. George Seldes, *Witch Hunt: The Technique and Profits of Redbaiting* (New York: Modern Age, 1940). Compare George E. Novack, *Witch-Hunt in Minnesota* (New York: Civil Rights Defense Committee, 1941); Bert Andrews, *Washington Witch Hunt* (New York: Random House, 1948); and Carey McWilliams, *Witch Hunt: The Revival of Heresy* (Boston: Little, Brown, 1950).

19. George Sacks, *The Intelligent Man's Guide to Jew-Baiting* (London: Victor Gollancz, 1935). Seldes, *Witch Hunt*; "Call on Wealthy to Come Across for Red-Baiting," *The Worker*, October 28, 1945; Eugene Dennis, *The Red-Baiters Menace America* (New York: New Century, 1946); Victor J. Jerome, *A World "Christian Front"? . . . The Anti-Social Ethics of Red-Baiters* (New York: New Masses, 1947); George Morris, *The Red Baiting Racket and How It Works* (New York: New Century, 1947). For a recent attack on the "Red-baiting" concept, see Billingsley, *Hollywood Party*.

20. "51 Here on Wallace Sponsor List," *PP*, February 8, 1948; "More Protest Printing of Petition Names," *PP*, April 17, 1948. The names were published from April 11 through April 30, 1948.

CHAPTER 2

1. HUAC, *Investigation of Communist Activities in the Philadelphia Area*, 83d Cong., 1st and 2d sess. (Washington, D.C.: GPO, 1954), 3943 (hereafter cited as *Investigation of Communist Activities in the Philadelphia Area*).

2. Philip Jenkins, "Spy Mad: Investigating Subversion in Pennsylvania, 1917–18," *Pennsylvania History* 63 (1996): 204–31; Charles H. McCormick, *Seeing Reds* (Pittsburgh: University of Pittsburgh Press, 1997); M. J. Heale, *American Anti-Communism* (Baltimore: Johns Hopkins Press, 1990); Joel Kovel, *Red Hunting in the Promised Land* (New York: Basic Books, 1994).

3. Steve Nelson, James R. Barrett, and Rob Ruck, *Steve Nelson: American Radical* (Pittsburgh: University of Pittsburgh Press, 1981); McCormick, *Seeing Reds*. For the history of American Communism, see Vivian Gornick, *The Romance of American Communism* (New York: Basic Books, 1977); Guenther Lewy, *The Cause That Failed* (New York: Oxford University Press, 1990); Fraser M. Ottanelli, *The Communist Party of the United States* (New Brunswick, N.J.: Rutgers University Press, 1991); Harvey Klehr and John Earl Haynes, *The American Communist Movement* (New York: Twayne, 1992); Harvey Klehr, John Earl Haynes, and F. I. Firsov, *The Secret World of American Communism* (New Haven, Conn.: Yale University Press, 1995); Harvey Klehr, John Earl Haynes, and Kyrill M. Anderson, *The Soviet World of American Communism* (New Haven, Conn.: Yale University Press, 1998); Ellen Schrecker, *Many Are the Crimes* (Boston: Little, Brown, 1998).

4. "Five Hurt, Eleven Jailed, as Police Swing Clubs in Battle," *PP*, March 6, 1930; "Score Injured as Police and Radicals Clash," *PI*, May 1, 1932; "Poor Girl Who Turned Radical to Face Judge with 25 Others for Sentencing," *PP*, December 19, 1935; Harvey Klehr, *The Heyday of American Communism* (New York: Basic Books, 1984).

5. Philip Jenkins, *Hoods and Shirts* (Chapel Hill: University of North Carolina Press, 1997); Carl I. Meyerhuber, *Less Than Forever* (Selinsgrove, Pa.: Susquehanna University Press, 1987).

6. Paul Lyons, *Philadelphia Communists, 1936–1956* (Philadelphia: Temple University Press, 1982), 20.

7. Ibid., 64. Compare "3,000 at Red Rally in Reyburn Plaza," *PEB*, May 1, 1940.

8. Matthew Cvetic, *The Big Decision* (Hollywood, Calif.: The Big Decision, 1959), 1; typescript report of May Day meeting held at North Side Carnegie Hall, Pittsburgh, May 4, 1947, "Communist Party Meetings," Michael A. Musmanno Papers, DU. Several such reports in the Musmanno Papers clearly derive from infiltrators, presumably Matt Cvetic.

9. Heale, *American Anti-Communism*, 122–30. Examples included the Rapp-Coudert Committee in New York and the Tenney Committee in California. Jack B. Tenney, *Red Fascism* (Los Angeles: Federal Printing, 1947), 558–99.

10. The scope of FBI infiltration into Pennsylvania Communism is indicated by the regular reports sent by J. Edgar Hoover to President Truman's military adviser, Harry Hawkins Vaughan, which are found in the President's Secretary's Files, Boxes 167–69, Truman Library. See, for instance, Hoover's reports on Philadelphia in letters to Vaughan on December 6, 1945, March 7, 1946, June 21, 1946, November 12, 1947, and March 4, 1948. Among other sources, the FBI certainly had informants within the Left-dominated National Maritime Union. Reports on Pittsburgh are found in letters to Vaughan on November 13, 1947, and January 27, 1948. Evidence of well-placed informants within the Phila-

delphia organization also emerges from the Current Intelligence Summaries frequently sent by Hoover to John R. Steelman, in White House Confidential Files, Box 21, File 3, Truman Library.

11. "Communist School Activity Revealed in Heart of City," *PPG*, December 30, 1938. The *Post-Gazette* series by Vincent Johnson included "Workers' School Dyed Deep Red, Not Mere Pink," January 2, 1939; "Violent Revolution, Reds Aim for America," January 3; "Open and Secret Reds Lead Workers' School," January 4; "Red School's Purpose to Get Party Members," January 5; "Reds Avoid Queries on Communist Logic," January 6; "Reds Guard Secrets against Inquisitive," January 7. See also Johnson's testimony in U.S. House of Representatives, Special Committee on Un-American Activities (Dies Committee), *Investigation of Un-American Propaganda Activities in the United States*, Hearings, 76th Cong., 1st sess. (Washington, D.C.: GPO, 1940), 11–12:7605–7 (hereafter cited as *Investigation of Un-American Propaganda Activities*). Evelyn Shuler, "Philadelphia War Plants Sabotage Victims, Ask US to Hunt Wreckers Within," *PPL*, June 5, 1940. For anti-Red mob activity in these years, see "Red Students Routed by Bricks, Stench Bombs," *PPG*, May 23, 1939.

12. *Investigation of Un-American Propaganda Activities*, 11–12:7664–71; *Digest of the Public Record of Communism in the United States* (New York: Fund for the Republic, 1955), 286; Alexander Kendrick, "Philadelphia Raids Bare Reds' Foothold in Key Industries," *PI*, April 3, 1940; August Raymond Ogden, *The Dies Committee* (Washington, D.C.: Catholic University of America Press, 1945).

13. "Ex WPA Teacher Seized Here as Agent of OGPU," *PST*, March 25, 1940; "Dies Aides Sent to Round Up All Key Reds Here," *PST*, March 26, 1940; Raymond Z. Henle, "WPA Red Classes Here Aired by Dies," *PPG*, March 29, 1940.

14. *Investigation of Un-American Propaganda Activities*, 11–12:7335–451, 7476–86; "$5200 Price for Papers, Couple Say," *PPG*, March 29, 1940.

15. "Propagandist Writer for Reds Jailed in Second Libel Charge," *PPG*, April 1, 1940; "Author, Foe of Coughlin, Arrested on Libel Charge," *PP*, March 26, 1940.

16. "43 Indicted in Probe of Communists," *PPG*, July 6, 1940; compare "Dies Reveals Danger Here of Sabotage," *PPG*, November 20, 1939.

17. U.S. Senate, Committee on the Judiciary, SISS, *Subversive Influence in Certain Industrial Plants: Eastern Pennsylvania*, Hearing, 83d Cong., 2d sess., and 84th Cong., 1st sess. (Washington, D.C.: GPO, 1954–55), 1–6 (hereafter cited as *Subversive Influence in Certain Industrial Plants*).

18. "Press First Published Names of Red Signers," *PP*, February 15, 1954.

19. "Schools Seek Way to Oust Reds," *PEB*, July 5, 1940; Evelyn Shuler, "Post Office Aides Helped Red," *PPL*, July 12, 1940; "Fire Cops Now, Red Foe Asks," *PEB*, July 18, 1940; *Digest of the Public Record of Communism*, 430; "Gillies Willies," *Pittsburgh Bulletin Index*, September 26, 1940.

20. *Digest of the Public Record of Communism*, 380; "Names of 36 Fired by Relief Board," *PEB*, October 20, 1941; "Relief Board Fires Fourteen More Accused of Red Activity," *PEB*, November 10, 1941.

21. Quoted in Michael A. Musmanno, *Across the Street from the Courthouse* (Philadelphia: Dorrance, 1954), 179.

22. "Names of Pittsburghers on Communist Petitions" and "Communist Hits Printing of Names on Red Petitions," *PP*, June 11, 1940; Evelyn Shuler, "Reds Nominee Petitions Under Fire in State," *PPL*, July 3, 1940; "43 Indicted in Probe of Communists," *PPG*, July 6, 1940;

Evelyn Shuler, "Many Frauds Honeycomb Red Petitions," *PPL*, July 6, 1940; "Thirty Found Guilty in Red Trial," *PPG*, November 1, 1940.

23. The quotation from the Jefferson professor is from *Academic Freedom: Some Recent Philadelphia Episodes* (Philadelphia: Greater Philadelphia Branch of the ACLU, [1954?]), 18. For Communists in the war years, see Lyons, *Philadelphia Communists*, 23, and Maurice Isserman, *Which Side Were You On?* (Middletown, Conn.: Wesleyan University Press, 1982), but also see George Sirgiovanni, *An Undercurrent of Suspicion* (New Brunswick: Transaction, 1990).

24. Robert A. Hill, *The FBI's RACON* (Boston: Northeastern University Press, 1995), 221. The *Inquirer* quote is from Oliver H. Crawford, "Party Has Lost Place in Union Leadership but Is Alert for Action," *PI*, October 15, 1945. This story was part of a weeklong investigative series by Crawford in the *Inquirer* on "Communists in Philadelphia"; other installments included "Union Eclipse Mars Mother Bloor's Party," October 16; "Racial Equality Group Bars Troublesome Reds," October 17; "Party Fails to Capture Support of Youth Here," October 19; and "Party Expects to Thrive on Next Economic Crisis," October 20.

25. Crawford, "Union Eclipse Mars Mother Bloor's Party," *PI*, October 16, 1945.

26. Maximilian St. George and Lawrence Dennis, *A Trial on Trial* (New York: National Civil Rights Committee, 1946); Henry R. Hoke, *It's a Secret* (New York: Reynal and Hitchcock, 1946); O. John Rogge, *The Official German Report* (New York: Thomas Yoseloff, 1961). The anti-Nazi spy scare was reflected in films like *Confessions of a Nazi Spy* (1939), *Saboteur* (1942), *Waterfront* (1944), and *The House on 92nd Street* (1945), which together created the genre later continued in anti-Communist features like *I Was a Communist for the FBI* (1951).

27. Letters of PFC John C. Friedrich to CO, Troop A, S-4, Philadelphia, August 10–11, 1944, Philadelphia Transit Strike file, State Police Archives, RG 30, PSA.

28. The structure of the Pennsylvania Party is outlined in "CPUSA—Organizational Apparatus," 34–43, and "CPUSA—1948—Charts," both in the FBI files, Box 167, President's Secretary's Files, Truman Library. Compare Lyons, *Philadelphia Communists*, 51–57; the quotation about Philadelphia neighborhoods is from 54–55.

29. HUAC, *Current Strategy and Tactics of Communists in the United States, Greater Pittsburgh Area*, 86th Cong., 1st sess. (Washington, D.C.: GPO, 1959), 327; HUAC, *Exposé of the Communist Party of Western Pennsylvania Based upon Testimony of Matthew Cvetic, Undercover Agent*, Hearings, 81st Cong., 2d sess. (Washington, D.C.: GPO, 1950), 1345–52 (hereafter cited as *Exposé of the Communist Party*).

30. "CPUSA—Organizational Apparatus," 34–43.

31. *Investigation of Un-American Propaganda Activities*, 11–12:7438.

32. *Exposé of the Communist Party*, 1235, 1243, 2366.

33. *Subversive Influence in Certain Industrial Plants*, 1–35.

34. Ibid., 39–46, quote at 44.

35. Lyons, *Philadelphia Communists*, 63.

36. *Exposé of the Communist Party*, 1252.

37. Ibid., 1203.

38. *Investigation of Communist Activities in the Philadelphia Area*, 6783.

39. *Exposé of the Communist Party*, 1253. Cvetic is far from being an unimpeachable witness, in that he made false accusations against specific individuals and exaggerated his own importance within the Party; nevertheless, his accounts of Party structure and "everyday" life and activities can easily be verified from other sources.

40. Nelson, Barrett, and Ruck, *Steve Nelson*, 304–5; *Investigation of Un-American Propaganda Activities*, 11–12:7476–86, 7591–605.

41. For Louis Ivens, see *Investigation of Communist Activities in the Philadelphia Area*, 2919–22; compare 3008.

42. "Red Peace Fake Here Designed to Get Party Funds," *PI*, June 26, 1950. For the Lenin rally, see J. Edgar Hoover to Harry Hawkins Vaughan, March 4, 1948, in President's Secretary's Files, Box 167, Truman Library.

43. *Investigation of Communist Activities in the Philadelphia Area*, testimony of Robert J. Rutman, 3008–10, and Bessie Stensky, 3982. "Peace Festival Lures 1,000 to Bucks County Meadow," *PEB*, August 27, 1951.

44. *Exposé of the Communist Party*, 1294.

45. *Investigation of Communist Activities in the Philadelphia Area*, 2891–92.

46. *Exposé of the Communist Party*, 1277.

47. Dr. Bella Dodd, in *Investigation of Communist Activities in the Philadelphia Area*, 2896–97.

48. These three instances are all discussed below, in Chapters 6, 7, and 3 respectively.

49. HUAC, *Trial by Treason: The National Committee to Secure Justice for the Rosenbergs and Morton Sobell* (Washington, D.C.: GPO, August 1956), 78–82; "Vets Fight DA's Move to Drop Spy Fund Case," *PI*, November 13, 1953; John F. Neville, *The Press, the Rosenbergs, and the Cold War* (Westport, Conn.: Praeger, 1995); Marjorie Garber and Rebecca L. Walkowitz, eds., *Secret Agents* (New York: Routledge, 1995).

50. HUAC, *Trial by Treason*, 81, 107–8; compare *Subversive Influence in Certain Industrial Plants*, 21–23.

51. *Subversive Influence in Certain Industrial Plants*, 21; Wilson Record, *Race and Radicalism* (Ithaca, N.Y.: Cornell University Press, 1964). Gerald Horne, *Communist Front? The Civil Rights Congress, 1946–1956* (Rutherford, N.J.: Fairleigh Dickinson University Press, 1987).

52. *Exposé of the Communist Party*, 2455.

53. Ibid., 2447. The term "FEPC law" here indicates a measure prohibiting racial discrimination in hiring and employment; the acronym recalls the federal Fair Employment Practices Committee created by President Roosevelt. The demand for FEPC legislation was a focus of political controversy in the decade after 1945. See Louis C. Kesselman, *The Social Politics of FEPC* (Chapel Hill: University of North Carolina Press, 1948); for the Pennsylvania FEPC, see Gibson H. Gray, *The Lobbying Game* (Tyler, Tex.: n.p., 1970).

54. "Philadelphia Delegation Meets Race Hate," *The Worker*, May 23, 1948; "Mundt Bill Protests Mount in Pennsylvania," *The Worker*, May 23, 1948.

55. "Trusts Plot Fascism in Trial of Twelve," *The Worker*, September 26, 1948.

56. *Exposé of the Communist Party*, 2509. Compare 2478, 2500–501.

57. "Labor Youth League US Arm of Russia's Young Red Alliance," *PP*, March 5, 1950; *Exposé of the Communist Party*, 1275–84.

58. *Exposé of the Communist Party*, 1277, 1281.

59. See, for example, *Exposé of the Communist Party*, 2396–97, 2403.

60. These quotes are all from ibid., 2404–8.

61. Ibid., 2417–24.

62. Ibid., 2459–60. Compare Gerald Horne, *Black Liberation/Red Scare* (Newark: University of Delaware Press, 1994).

63. For police brutality, see, for example, "Philadelphia's Scottsboro: The Nick Williams Case," *The Worker*, April 28, 1946. *The Worker* was the Sunday edition of the *Daily Worker*, which was published in local editions. All references here are to the Pennsylvania edition. Sherman Labovitz, *Being Red in Philadelphia* (Philadelphia: Camino Books, 1998), 51–54.

64. Hill, *The FBI's RACON*, 221.

65. "A Changing Community," *PPV* 1, no. 1 (July 1956): 8–10.

66. Nelson, Barrett, and Ruck, *Steve Nelson*, 315–16; *An Open Letter from Ben Careathers to Judge Michael Angelo Musmanno*, Communist Party pamphlet in Musmanno Papers, DU.

67. *PPV* 1, no. 1 (July 1956); Crawford, "Party Expects to Thrive on Next Economic Crisis," *PI*, October 20, 1945.

68. Richard J. Walton, *Henry Wallace, Harry Truman, and the Cold War* (New York: Viking, 1976).

69. The "Pennsylvania Dutchman" quote is from Mary Hamilton, "A Pennsylvania Newspaper Publisher in Gideon's Army," *Pennsylvania History* 61 (1994): 18–44, quote at 21; McKinley C. Olson, ed., *J. W. Gitt's Sweet Land of Liberty* (New York: Jerome S. Ozer, 1975). For the Fast connection, see Gitt to Alfred C. Caplin, January 19, 1949, and Howard Fast to Gitt, July 7 and July 27, 1948, Box 2, "Correspondence," Josiah W. Gitt Papers, HCLA.

70. "Civil Rights," *YGD* editorial, March 15, 1950. Gitt's alarm about the threat to civil liberties is indicated by the *York Gazette and Daily*'s editorials on the Peekskill riot of 1949, significantly entitled "À la Hitler," August 31, 1949, and "It Can Happen Here," September 2, 1949.

71. "Wallace Gives Priority to Civil Rights," *YGD*, March 8, 1948; "US Controls on Steel Demanded by Wallace," *PI*, March 8, 1948.

72. "PAC Scores Two Labor Leaders for Support of Wallace" and "Four Left-wing Pittsburghers Help Spark Drive for Wallace," *PP*, January 12, 1948; "51 Here on Wallace Sponsor List," *PP*, February 8, 1948; "Director of Wallace Group Here Draws $300 Monthly," *PP*, August 5, 1948.

73. "51 Here on Wallace Sponsor List," *PP*, February 8, 1948.

74. "Third Party Opens at York Today," *The Worker*, March 7, 1948.

75. Curtis D. MacDougall, *Gideon's Army* (New York: Marzani and Munsell, 1965), 1:200–201, 217; flyer for "Grass Roots Rally," Bellevue Stratford Hotel, Philadelphia, March 9, 1947, in Box 1, John Frederick Lewis Papers, URB 38A, TU.

76. Anna W. Pennypacker "Pennsylvanians Launch Third Party," *The Worker*, March 14, 1948; "Wallace Calls for Marshall Dismissal," *New York Herald Tribune*, October 20, 1948; Charles Grutzner, "Wallace Hits ERP as Biggest Steal," *NYT*, October 21, 1948.

77. John M. McCullough, "30,000 Wallace Faithful Near Hysteria at Rally," *PI*, July 25, 1948.

78. Joseph H. Miller, "Wallace Third Party Rejects ADA Plan to Repudiate Reds," *PI*, July 23, 1948; Joseph H. Miller, "Convention Ends with Rap at Anti-Reds," *PI*, July 26, 1948.

79. Joseph V. Baker, "Progressives Support Negroes for Office," *PI*, July 25, 1948.

80. "Penna. Delegates Back Coal Seizure," *PI*, July 24, 1948.

81. Joseph H. Miller, "Convention Ends with Rap at Anti-Reds," *PI*, July 26, 1948.

82. "Gitt Pledges Unity to Elect Liberals, Defeat Reaction," *The Worker*, September 26, 1948.

83. *Exposé of the Communist Party*, 1234–35.

84. Ibid., 1237–38; Adamic to Gitt, June 1, 1948, and Gitt to Victor H. Blanc, July 27, 1948, Box 2, "Correspondence," Gitt Papers; Hamilton, "A Pennsylvania Newspaper Publisher," 32–33.

85. *Subversive Influence in Certain Industrial Plants*, 17–18; "More Names Revealed by Cvetic in Red Probe," *PP*, March 14, 1950.

86. *Subversive Influence in Certain Industrial Plants*, 39–46.

87. Lyons, *Philadelphia Communists*, 152; Labovitz, *Being Red in Philadelphia*, 55–56; Howard Fast, *Being Red* (Boston: Houghton Mifflin, 1990).

88. Parker La Moore, "France and Italy Examples," *PP*, November 21, 1947.

89. MacDougall, *Gideon's Army*, 1:218–19.

90. *Exposé of the Communist Party*, 2502–3, document of September 1948.

91. Nelson, Barrett, and Ruck, *Steve Nelson*, 303.

92. "US Court Annuls Ban on Red Probe Protest at Independence Square," *PI*, November 1, 1947; "Hecklers Break Up Rally at Independence Square," *PI*, November 2, 1947.

93. MacDougall, *Gideon's Army*, 1:216–17; Albert Kahn and Arthur Kahn, *High Treason* (New York: Lear, 1950), 285–86.

94. "More Names Revealed by Cvetic in Red Probe," *PP*, March 14, 1950; "Crowd Cheers Rainey," *The Worker*, October 10, 1948.

95. Nelson, Barrett, and Ruck, *Steve Nelson*, 300–301.

96. "The Peace of the World," editorial, *YGD*, June 30, 1950; "The Korean Conflict," *YGD*, July 5, 1950.

97. Gitt to Rebecca P. Elliott, August 31, 1950, and Gitt to Dr. Sidney Bloom, November 3, 1950, Box 2, "Correspondence," Gitt Papers; Hamilton, "A Pennsylvania Newspaper Publisher," 38–39. For the Pennsylvania Progressive Party in 1952, see President's File—Official File, 1441, Truman Library.

98. "New Crusade Urged at May Day Mass," *PI*, May 2, 1938; "McDevitt Predicts Ouster of US Reds," *PI*, May 2, 1940

99. "May Day Rally in Philadelphia Strengthens UE Strike," *The Worker*, May 5, 1946; Norman Anderson, "Mayday Returns to Philly's Reyburn Plaza," *The Worker*, May 9, 1948.

100. "Korean War GI's Parade Here," *PI*, April 29, 1951.

101. "Pro-Red Group Hails Lowenfels," *PI*, November 13, 1953.

CHAPTER 3

1. Statement of Principles Adopted by the Nationalities Division of the Pennsylvania State Democratic Committee at Harrisburg, Pa., September 7, 1950, ser. 1, Folder 2/5, Political Offices and Affiliations, Henry Dende Papers, MSS 54, Balch Institute for Ethnic Studies, Philadelphia, Pa.

2. Philip S. Klein and Ari Hoogenboom, *A History of Pennsylvania*, 2d ed. (University Park: Pennsylvania State University Press, 1980); Paul B. Beers, *Pennsylvania Politics Today and Yesterday* (University Park: Pennsylvania State University Press, 1980).

3. Joseph F. Guffey, *Seventy Years on the Red Fire-Wagon* (privately printed, 1952); James A. Wechsler, "How Industrialists Use GOP as Anti-Union Club," *PM*, August 14, 1944.

4. Russell F. Weigley, Nicholas B. Wainwright, and Edwin Wolf, eds., *Philadelphia: A Three Hundred Year History* (New York: W. W. Norton, 1982).

5. John Gunther, *Inside USA* (New York: Harper, 1951), 656–57; J. Roffe Wike, *The Penn-*

sylvania Manufacturers' Association (Philadelphia: University of Pennsylvania Press, 1960), 232–36, 245. For the 1944 campaign, see "Martin Charges All Communists Back Roosevelt," *Philadelphia Record*, September 26, 1944.

6. James Michener, *Report of the County Chairman* (New York: Random House, 1961), 76; Ann Hawkes Hutton, *The Pennsylvanian: Joseph R. Grundy* (Philadelphia: Dorrance, 1962).

7. Wike, *The Pennsylvania Manufacturers' Association*, 248.

8. Ibid., 238–39.

9. Ibid., 174–75; for Flynn, see his *While You Slept* (New York: Devin-Adair, 1951).

10. Gunther, *Inside USA*, 658–59.

11. Wike, *The Pennsylvania Manufacturers' Association*, 334–36; "Political Notes," *Time*, October 28, 1946, 25–28.

12. John L. Spivak, *Pattern for American Fascism* (New York: New Century, 1947), 28.

13. "Penna CIO Bars Commies as Officers," *Steel Labor*, May 1947, 11.

14. Melvyn P. Leffler, *The Specter of Communism* (New York: Hill and Wang, 1994).

15. Athan G. Theoharis, *Seeds of Repression* (Chicago: Quadrangle, 1971); Athan G. Theoharis, ed., *Beyond the Hiss Case* (Philadelphia: Temple University Press, 1982); Kenneth O'Reilly, *Hoover and the Un-Americans* (Philadelphia: Temple University Press, 1983); Athan G. Theoharis and John Stuart Cox, *The Boss* (Philadelphia: Temple University Press, 1988); Thomas G. Paterson, *Meeting the Communist Threat: Truman to Reagan* (New York: Oxford University Press, 1988); William W. Keller, *The Liberals and J. Edgar Hoover* (Princeton, N.J.: Princeton University Press, 1989); Tom Engelhardt, *The End of Victory Culture* (New York: Basic Books, 1995).

16. Edward Martin speech at Bloomsburg, Pa., October 23, 1946, Boxes 2–3, "Campaign Material: Campaign of 1946," Campaign Materials, 1930–60, Papers of Edward Martin, MG 156, PSA; "Taylor Calls on Guffey to Reveal Stand on Wallace," *PI*, September 21, 1946. For the CIO-PAC, see James C. Foster, *The Union Politic* (Columbia: University of Missouri Press, 1975).

17. "Platform of the Republican Party of Pa.," 1946, Martin Papers.

18. "Taylor Charges Sly PAC Trick," *PI*, September 17, 1946; "Taylor Calls on Guffey to Reveal Stand on Wallace," *PI*, September 21, 1946. The materials from Martin's speeches are found in Boxes 2–3, "Campaign Material: Campaign of 1946," Campaign Materials, 1930–60, Martin Papers.

19. *Digest of the Public Record of Communism in the United States* (New York: Fund for the Republic, 1955), 440.

20. George Sokolsky, "1946 Strikes Planned to Sabotage US," *PI*, September 23, 1946.

21. Unsigned article, "The Biggest Issue," Campaign File, Box 1, 1946 election, Papers of James H. Duff, MG 190, PSA.

22. Arthur Sears Henning, "Pennsylvania Voters Mirror Sagging GOP," *Chicago Tribune*, May 18, 1947. This account of the 1946 election is drawn from Philip Jenkins, *Hoods and Shirts* (Chapel Hill: University of North Carolina Press, 1997), 218–24.

23. Address to Republican Party meeting at Weirton, W.Va., October 12, 1948, Box 3, Campaign Materials, 1930–60, Martin Papers.

24. "30,000 Messages Sent to Martin," *PI*, April 29, 1951; William G. Weart, "MacArthurs Hailed in Lehigh Valley," *NYT*, September 22, 1951.

25. "Philadelphia Reaction to Ouster Mixed," *PI*, April 12, 1951.

26. Beers, *Pennsylvania Politics*, 191.

27. Robert Kenneth Carr, *The House Committee on Un-American Activities, 1945–1950* (Ithaca, N.Y.: Cornell University Press, 1952); Joseph C. Goulden, *The Best Years, 1945–60* (New York: Atheneum, 1976).

28. Allen Weinstein, *Perjury: The Hiss-Chambers Case*, updated ed. (New York: Random House, 1997), 28–34; John McDowell, "The Country Editor in Washington," *Wilkinsburg Gazette*, August 20, 1948; Sam Tanenhaus, *Whittaker Chambers* (New York: Random House, 1997).

29. "McDowell Whipping Up Red Alarm to Get Re-Elected, Nelson Says," *PP*, September 23, 1948.

30. "Turn McDowell Out," *PPG*, October 22, 1948.

31. Advertisement in *PPG*, April 22, 1948.

32. For the "Hitler" remark (by Nathan Alberts), see typescript report, "Re. Communist mass meeting, Carnegie Library, North Side Pittsburgh, Pa.," February 28, 1948, "Communist Party Meetings," Michael A. Musmanno Papers, DU; clip file on John McDowell, Box 3, Papers of Local 601, 1949–52, UE Labor Archive, UP; "Rep. McDowell Convicted in Political Mock Trial," *PPG*, October 27, 1948.

33. "Congressman Van Zandt Urges People to Stop Using Word Democracy," *Centre Daily Times* (State College, Pa.), March 31, 1953.

34. James E. Van Zandt, "America's First Military Defeat," *The Cross and the Flag*, July 1955, 10. The printed version of the address gives "not" for "now" in the last line, which is clearly erroneous in the context.

35. Gunther, *Inside USA*, 659; Wike, *The Pennsylvania Manufacturers' Association*, 240–48.

36. "Truman Invites Gov. Duff to Join Democratic Party," *Philadelphia Daily News*, February 2, 1950.

37. Beers, *Pennsylvania Politics*, 152.

38. Carton 13, "Communism," "1947–51" file, Official Papers, 1947–51, Duff Papers.

39. *32nd Annual Convention of the American Legion, Department of Pennsylvania at Philadelphia, Aug. 9–12, 1950* (American Legion, Department of Pennsylvania, 1950), 73–76.

40. "Reds Intolerable in US, Duff Says," *PI*, November 20, 1953.

41. *30th Annual Convention of the American Legion, Department of Pennsylvania at Philadelphia, Aug. 18–21, 1948* (American Legion, Department of Pennsylvania, 1948), 177.

42. Ibid., 179.

43. Terry Radtke, *The History of the Pennsylvania American Legion* (Mechanicsburg, Pa.: Stackpole, 1993), 74–76.

44. "Loyalty Day program," Allegheny County VFW, April 28, 1961, Folder 10, Box 3, Records of Samuel M. Shoemaker, MS Group 269, BGC Archives.

45. James H. O'Hara to Musmanno, March 25, 1955; for the Sunbury meeting, Musmanno to Mario Tedeschi, May 3, 1954; both in Musmanno Papers.

46. Compare "VFW Council to Pay Honor to Minister," *PPG*, April 23, 1961.

47. Radtke, *History of the Pennsylvania American Legion*, 74–76.

48. The biographical sketch of Van Zandt appeared in successive volumes of the *Pennsylvania Manual*. For the political circle of Van Zandt, Martin, and Dague, see the Paul H. Griffith Papers in the Truman Library.

49. Radtke, *History of the Pennsylvania American Legion*, 71–73.

50. *34th Annual Convention of the American Legion, Department of Pennsylvania at Philadelphia, Aug. 6–9, 1952* (American Legion, Department of Pennsylvania, 1952), 66–67.

51. For Earle's "apoplectic" attitude, see Spivak, *Pattern for American Fascism*, 43; Duff to Major General Richard K. Mellon, August 21, 1950, "Defense 1948–50" file, Official Papers, 1947–51, Duff Papers. Correspondence of Earle and Truman, February-March 1947, in President's Official File, 263, Truman Library.

52. *28th Annual Convention of the American Legion, Department of Pennsylvania at Philadelphia, Aug. 21–24, 1946* (American Legion, Department of Pennsylvania, 1946), 31–32; Donald F. Crosby, *God, Church, and Flag* (Chapel Hill: University of North Carolina Press, 1978), 10.

53. *29th Annual Convention of the American Legion, Department of Pennsylvania at Pittsburgh, Aug. 7–9, 1947* (American Legion, Department of Pennsylvania, 1947), 112–13.

54. *30th Annual Convention of the American Legion, Department of Pennsylvania at Philadelphia, Aug. 18–21, 1948* (American Legion, Department of Pennsylvania, 1948), 59–64.

55. "Walter of the Un-Americans," *PFF* 3, no. 1 (January 1956): 17; U.S. Senate, Committee on the Judiciary, SISS, *Subversive Influence in Certain Industrial Plants: Eastern Pennsylvania*, Hearing, 83d Cong., 2d sess., and 84th Cong., 1st sess. (Washington, D.C.: GPO, 1954–55), 16–17. Also see Francis E. Walter Papers, Library of Congress, Washington, D.C.

56. Walter Goodman, *The Committee* (New York: Farrar, Straus, Giroux, 1968), 331, 370–72, 435 for the Rayburn quote.

57. Nationwide, the Democrats held 242 congressional seats in 1944 and 188 in 1946.

58. *A History of UE-Local 601, 1939–45* (East Pittsburgh: Local 601, UERMWA, 1946); "Bosses Use State Police Power against Workers," *Union Generator* (UE Local 601 newspaper), April 10, 1946, 2.

59. "Ex-Rep Gray Bolts Guffey," *PI*, September 21, 1946; Kenneth J. Heineman, "A Catholic New Deal," *Pennsylvania Magazine of History and Biography* 118, no. 4 (1994): 363–94.

60. Michael P. Weber, *Don't Call Me Boss* (Pittsburgh: University of Pittsburgh Press, 1988); Jenkins, *Hoods and Shirts*.

61. Radio speech, October 20, 1946, ser. 1, Folder 1/11, Dende Papers.

62. "Spot Survey of Pennsylvania in Anticipation of the 1950 Election," (1949), 8–9, in President's Secretary's Files, Box 60, Truman Library.

63. For national divisions, see Steven M. Gillon, *Politics and Vision* (New York: Oxford University Press, 1987); Mary Sperling McAuliffe, *Crisis on the Left* (Amherst: University of Massachusetts Press, 1978); Clifton Brock, *Americans for Democratic Action* (Washington, D.C.: Public Affairs Press, 1962). For CPAC, see Steve Fraser, *Labor Will Rule* (New York: Free Press, 1991), 510–16, and Foster, *The Union Politic*. Philadelphia events can be traced through the ADA Papers at Temple University; see especially Box 1, John Frederick Lewis Papers, URB 38A, TU. Hal Libros, *Hard Core Liberals* (Cambridge, Mass.: Schenkman, 1975), 14–16.

64. Martin's comment is from his radio broadcast over a statewide network, WHP Harrisburg, October 5, 1946. The activities of local PCA branches are reflected in telegrams and protests sent to the federal government over issues like price control, conscription, and official repression; many examples can be found in the Presidential Files—General Files, Truman Library.

65. For the split with Philadelphia's CPAC, see, for example, Eleanor B. Davis to John F. Lewis, August 21, 1946; Michael Harris to John F. Lewis, September 9, 1946; Lewis to Edward Schultz, October 23, 1946, all in Box 1, Lewis Papers; Oral History interview with Johannes

U. Hoeber, September 12, 1966, and interview with William L. Batt, July 26, 1966, both in Truman Library. For Myerson, see "Four Left-wing Pittsburghers Help Spark Drive for Wallace," *PP*, January 12, 1948; Anna W. Pennypacker "Pennsylvanians Launch Third Party," *The Worker*, March 14, 1948. *Progressive Citizen* 1, no. 1 (February 1947). For the struggle within the American Veterans Committee, see Goulden, *The Best Years*, 63–64.

66. The quote about "the largest . . . chapter" is from the Oral History interview with Hoeber, 67; Gillon, *Politics and Vision*, 37–38.

67. Libros, *Hard Core Liberals*, 23.

68. Eleanor Bontecou, *The Federal Loyalty Security Program* (Ithaca, N.Y.: Cornell University Press, 1953).

69. "Il Cremlino di Filadelfia," *Libera Parola*, November 1, 1947.

70. Joseph H. Miller, "Wallace Third Party Rejects ADA Plan to Repudiate Reds," *PI*, July 23, 1948.

71. Gillon, *Politics and Vision*, 26–27.

72. *Digest of the Public Record of Communism*, 440. Meade's charges were presented in a special newspaper, *Voice of the People*, under the banner headline "Who Is the ADA?"; Johannes U. Hoeber, "New Broom in Philadelphia," *New Republic*, December 5, 1949. The quote about Dilworth is from Gillon, *Politics and Vision*, 78; Dilworth's reply is from Joe Alex Morris, *The Richardson Dilworth Story* (New York: Mercury, 1962), 72–73. For the "progressive reaction," see Sherman Labovitz, *Being Red in Philadelphia* (Philadelphia: Camino Books, 1998), 63–64.

73. Statement on the Mundt-Nixon Bill, H.R. 5852, Committee on Democratic Rights of the Philadelphia Fellowship Commission, June 8, 1948, Philadelphia Fellowship Commission MSS, Balch Institute for Ethnic Studies, Philadelphia, Pa.

74. "Statement by Albert R. Pechan—State Senator from Butler-Armstrong Counties, as Requested by INS," 1953, Papers of John S. Fine, MG 206, PSA. From 1948 to 1951, the most active civil liberties group in the Philadelphia area was the Citizens' Council on Democratic Rights, which in 1951 affiliated with the ACLU; see Greater Philadelphia ACLU Papers, URB 7, TU.

75. Robert Griffith, *The Politics of Fear*, 2d ed. (Amherst: University of Massachusetts Press, 1987); David M. Oshinsky, *A Conspiracy So Immense* (New York: Free Press, 1983); Thomas C. Reeves, *The Life and Times of Joe McCarthy* (New York: Stein and Day, 1982); Richard M. Fried, *Nightmare in Red* (New York: Oxford University Press, 1990).

76. Republican Party platform, adopted Pittsburgh, September 9, 1950, Campaign Materials, 1930–60, Box 3, Martin Papers; Robert Bendiner, "Anything Goes in Pennsylvania," *Nation*, October 28, 1950, 385–88.

77. Newspaper release, October 21, 1950, reporting rally in Peoria, Illinois, Box 3, Campaign Materials, 1930–60, Martin Papers.

78. *32nd Annual Convention of the American Legion, Department of Pennsylvania at Philadelphia, Aug. 9–12, 1950* (American Legion, Department of Pennsylvania, 1950), 136.

79. *34th Annual Convention of the American Legion, Department of Pennsylvania at Philadelphia, Aug. 6–9, 1952* (American Legion, Department of Pennsylvania, 1952), 29.

80. David Caute, *The Great Fear: The Anti-Communist Purge under Truman and Eisenhower* (New York: Simon and Schuster, 1978), 38.

81. "Myers Defends Policies," *PI*, October 8, 1950. Compare Richard M. Fried, *Men Against McCarthy* (New York: Columbia University Press, 1976), 112–13.

82. "Shoot Stalin, Put All Communists in Jail—Musmanno," *YGD*, October 6, 1950.

83. "Statement of Principles Adopted by the Nationalities Division of the Pennsylvania State Democratic Committee at Harrisburg, Pa., September 7, 1950," ser. 1, Folder 2/5, Dende Papers.

84. The importance of Korean affairs was repeatedly emphasized by both successful and unsuccessful candidates interviewed in the immediate aftermath of the congressional elections in the state. See "Candidates Explain Outcome," *U.S. News and World Report*, November 17, 1950, 37. For the 1950 election, see Greg Mitchell, *Tricky Dick and the Pink Lady* (New York: Random House, 1998).

85. Kenneth Hechler, "The 1950 Elections," in Box 92, George M. Elsey Papers, Truman Library.

CHAPTER 4

1. "Statement by Albert R. Pechan—State Senator from Butler-Armstrong Counties, as Requested by INS," 1953, Papers of John S. Fine, MG 206, PSA.

2. Philip Jenkins, *Hoods and Shirts* (Chapel Hill: University of North Carolina Press, 1997).

3. Les K. Adler and Thomas G. Paterson, "Red Fascism," *AHR*, 75 (1970): 1046–64.

4. Guy Oakes, *The Imaginary War* (New York: Oxford University Press, 1994).

5. "McDevitt Predicts Ouster of US Reds," *PI*, May 2, 1940.

6. "Defense 1948–50" file, Official Papers, 1947–51, Papers of James H. Duff, MG 190, PSA.

7. George R. Acheson to James Duff, July 22, 1950, and letter of Duff to local government authorities, August 1, 1950, ibid.

8. *32nd Annual Convention of the American Legion, Department of Pennsylvania at Philadelphia, Aug. 9–12, 1950* (American Legion, Department of Pennsylvania, 1950), 73–76.

9. "State Open to Red Attack, Duff Says," *PP*, August 31, 1950.

10. Duff to Vincent A. Carroll, August 1950, "Defense 1948–50" file, Official Papers, 1947–51, Duff Papers.

11. Michael A. Musmanno, *Across the Street from the Courthouse* (Philadelphia: Dorrance, 1954), 84–85.

12. Speech by Ross Leffler, "If War Comes," May 1950, Governor's Committee on Civil Defense, "Defense 1948–50" file, Official Papers, 1947–51, Duff Papers; Douglas Naylor, "34 Key Posts Filled Here in Civil Defense," *PP*, August 9, 1950; "Seven Thousand Needed for City's Civil Defense," *PP*, August 17, 1950.

13. Harry E. Sharkey to Governor Duff, January 29, 1948; Harry E. Sharkey to Senator Francis Myers, January 29, 1948; news release, from state Civil Air Patrol, n.d. [ca. January 1948], all in Box 2, "Correspondence," Josiah W. Gitt Papers, HCLA; Walter Lowenfels, "Industry Backs Labor Spy Ring in Pennsylvania Factories," *The Worker*, March 21, 1948.

14. John S. Fine, "Governor Fine Says," *Keystone Defender* 1, no. 1 (March 1952): 1.

15. Fine speech to Amvets convention at Harrisburg, July 22, 1951, p. 5, Box 1, William W. Wheaton files, Fine Papers; John S. Fine, *A Record* (Harrisburg: Commonwealth of Pennsylvania, Governor's Office, 1954).

16. "Statement by Albert R. Pechan—State Senator from Butler-Armstrong Counties, as Requested by INS," 1953, Fine Papers. For the long-standing interchange of information

between the State Police and the Justice Department, see, for example, J. Howard McGrath to T. McKeen Chidsey, September 29, 1949, in Box 118, J. Howard McGrath Papers, Truman Library.

17. *Digest of the Public Record of Communism in the United States* (New York: Fund for the Republic, 1955), 264.

18. Box 1, William W. Wheaton files, Fine Papers; compare *Civil Defense for Schools* (Harrisburg: State Council of Civil Defense/Dept. of Public Instruction, 1952). The list of films and pamphlets is derived from successive issues of the civil defense newsletter, *Keystone Defender*.

19. "Two Counties Hold Alerts," *Keystone Defender* 1, no. 4 (June 1952): 7.

20. "Defense Head Comes Up with New Horror Hoax," *The Worker*, December 9, 1951.

21. "Mothers Protest Effects of A-Drills on Kids," *The Worker*, February 4, 1951.

22. Steve Nelson, James R. Barrett, and Rob Ruck, *Steve Nelson: American Radical* (Pittsburgh: University of Pittsburgh Press, 1981), 377, for the reservoirs. The sabotage manual story is from Ralph Schapell, "The Termites Within," *Keystone Defender* 1, no. 3 (May 1952): 1–2. James H. Dolsen, "Pittsburgh Paper Reveals Frameup Techniques," *The Worker*, March 11, 1951.

23. "If Washington Is Destroyed, What Then?," *Keystone Defender* 3, no. 12 (February 1955): 1.

24. "Hot Reception Awaiting Any Red Bombers Here," *PST*, May 18, 1952.

25. "Tighter City Air Defense Still Snarled," *PPG*, September 5, 1952; "Sirens to Wail October 15 in Statewide Air Raid Test," *PP*, October 4, 1952, 2. The general shift to missile defenses during the 1950s is described in Christopher J. Bright, "Nike Defends Washington," *Virginia Magazine of History and Biography* 105 (1997): 317–46.

26. James McCarthy, "Vital Records on Microfilm Go Underground in Unused Pits to Protect against War Loss," *PST*, May 20, 1951; Herbert G. Stein, "Plant Records Go Underground," *PPG*, January 30, 1961.

27. Douglas Smith, "Industrialists Here Know What to Do If A-Bombs Wipe Out Capital," *PP*, January 17, 1960.

28. HUAC, *Exposé of the Communist Party of Western Pennsylvania Based upon Testimony of Matthew Cvetic, Undercover Agent*, Hearings, 81st Cong., 2d sess. (Washington, D.C.: GPO, 1950), 1195–1205 (hereafter cited as *Exposé of the Communist Party*). Compare Herbert L. Packer, *Ex-Communist Witnesses* (Stanford: Stanford University Press, 1962).

29. Matthew Cvetic, *The Big Decision* (Hollywood, Calif.: The Big Decision, 1959), 21.

30. Daniel J. Leab, "Anti-Communism, the FBI and Matt Cvetic," *Pennsylvania Magazine of History and Biography* 115 (1991): 535–81.

31. Tony Smith, "Henry Wallace Met Commie Leaders Here, Cvetic Tells Probers," *PP*, February 22, 1950; "Plan Told for War on US," *PST*, February 23, 1950; Tony Smith, "FBI Agent Lists Reds for Spy Probers," *PP*, February 20, 1950; William Theis, "Infiltrate Mines, Mills, Party Told," *PST*, February 22, 1950. Compare Jim Tuck, *McCarthyism and New York's Hearst Press* (Lanham: University Press of America, 1995), and Edwin R. Bayley, *Joe McCarthy and the Press* (Madison: University of Wisconsin Press, 1981).

32. "Pro-Commie Papers Launch Bitter Attack on Cvetic," *PP*, February 24, 1950.

33. James Moore, "Cvetic a Traitor, Fifth Column Snarls," *PST*, February 20, 1950.

34. Tony Smith, "25 in Congress in Red Front Donation List," *PP*, February 25, 1950.

35. Tony Smith, "Absence of Papers Hides Names of Donors to Red Front," *PP*, March 19,

1950; "House Leaders Accused by Ex-FBI Man," *PP*, March 25, 1950; Tony Smith, "Search Fails to Locate Cvetic File Naming Congressmen for Probers," *PP*, March 26, 1950.

36. Tony Smith, "New Charges Pile Up on District Reds," *PP*, March 15, 1950.

37. See, for example, "Four Left-wing Pittsburghers Help Spark Drive for Wallace," *PP*, January 12, 1948; "51 Here on Wallace Sponsor List," *PP*, February 8, 1948; "House Probers Eye Reds Here, Quiz Two," *PST*, March 20, 1949; C. Edmund Fisher, "District Commie Boss Mum, Faces Contempt Citation," *PPG*, September 15, 1949.

38. Matt Cvetic (as told to Pete Martin), "I Posed as a Communist for the FBI," *Saturday Evening Post*, July 15, 1950.

39. For the pervasive impact of Cold War thought on popular culture, see Margot A. Henriksen, *Dr. Strangelove's America* (Berkeley: University of California Press, 1997); H. W. Brands, *The Devil We Knew* (New York: Oxford University Press, 1993); Steven M. Gillon and Diane B. Kunz, *America During the Cold War* (Fort Worth, Tex.: Harcourt Brace Jovanovich, 1993); Fred Inglis, *The Cruel Peace* (New York: Basic Books, 1991); Stephen J. Whitfield, *The Culture of the Cold War*, 2d ed. (Baltimore: Johns Hopkins University Press, 1996); Paul S. Boyer, *By the Bomb's Early Light* (New York: Pantheon, 1985); J. Fred Mac-Donald, *Television and the Red Menace* (New York: Praeger, 1985).

40. *34th Annual Convention of the American Legion, Department of Pennsylvania at Philadelphia, Aug. 6–9, 1952* (American Legion, Department of Pennsylvania, 1952), 83–94; "Amvets Here Cite Cvetic for Exposé," *PP*, February 26, 1950.

41. Cvetic, *The Big Decision*, 12.

42. Leab, "Anti-Communism, the FBI and Matt Cvetic," 575.

43. Ibid., 555–56.

44. Steve Nelson, *The Thirteenth Juror* (New York: Masses and Mainstream, 1955). A vast amount of information on the Pittsburgh prosecutions is found in the Michael A. Musmanno Papers, DU, which contain extensive press clippings and ephemera as well as a trial transcript.

45. Sherman rejected any suggestion that Musmanno had been a prime mover in ABC. See Transcript, Testimony on Reports of Subversive Activities in the Pittsburgh Area, SISS, Committee of the Judiciary, U.S. Senate, June 16, 1955, 619, Boxes 62–63, "The Mullen Case," Musmanno Papers.

46. Mel Fiske, *McCarthyism in the Courts* (New York: Provisional Committee to Free Steve Nelson, 1953), 11.

47. David L. Rosenberg, "The Red Scare in Pittsburgh," *Jewish Chronicle of Pittsburgh*, July 9–16, 1992, 2; Art Shields, *Pittsburgh: Peace on Trial* (reprinted from *Masses and Mainstream*, published by the Committee to Defend the Pittsburgh Frame-Up Victims, 1951), 12.

48. Michael P. Weber, *Don't Call Me Boss* (Pittsburgh: University of Pittsburgh Press, 1988).

49. Musmanno, *Across the Street from the Courthouse*, 73–74; Michael A. Musmanno, *Verdict!* (Garden City, N.Y.: Doubleday, 1958).

50. Frank M. Matthews, "Justice Musmanno Says, Can Do More in Senate," *PPG*, April 15, 1964; "Musmanno, Andrews Again Trading Insults," *PP*, August 14, 1951.

51. John Troan, "Mount Lebanon Engraver Exposed by Cvetic Duped Reds Ten Years," *PP*, March 6, 1950; "Man Who Posed as Communist Tells of Spying," *PPG*, March 7, 1950.

52. "ABC Officials Warn of Olive Branch of Deception," *PST*, March 12, 1950.

53. Nelson, Barrett, and Ruck, *Steve Nelson*, 315.

54. "Three Fired, Others Jittery, over Cvetic's Red Label," *PST*, March 19, 1950.

55. Nelson, Barrett, and Ruck, *Steve Nelson*, 315.

56. "Alleged Red on Staff at Tech Lab," August 9, 1951.

57. "Radio Station Bars Speaker Named as Red," *PPG*, March 15, 1950.

58. Matson to Herbert M. Levy, May 6, 1950, Marjorie Matson Papers, UP.

59. James H. Dolsen, "Red-Baiters Try to Heat Up Anti-Communist Fever," *The Worker*, August 5, 1951.

60. "More Names Revealed by Cvetic in Red Probe," *PP*, March 14, 1950; "FBI Aide Puts Finger on Alberts," *PPG*, April 26, 1950; Nelson, Barrett, and Ruck, *Steve Nelson*, 314.

61. Hymen Schlesinger to ACLU, May 2, 1950, "In re Schlesinger," Matson Papers.

62. "Mundsinger Strikes Out, Westinghouse," *Trafford-Pitcairn News*, March 2, 1950.

63. *Digest of the Public Record of Communism in the United States* (New York: Fund for the Republic, 1955), 418; "Red-Tainted Woman May Be Kept Off Jury by Judge Musmanno," *PPG*, March 7, 1950; Musmanno, *Across the Street from the Courthouse*, 41–46; "Musmanno Lashes Court for Red Stand," *PP*, June 7, 1950.

64. "FBI Aide Puts Finger on Alberts," *PPG*, April 26, 1950; compare Nelson, Barrett, and Ruck, *Steve Nelson*, 313–14.

65. "Nine Seized in Riots at New Kensington," *PST*, March 20, 1950; *Digest of the Public Record of Communism*, 322–23.

66. Musmanno, *Across the Street from the Courthouse*, 173–78; "County Bar Resolution Aimed at Red Attorney," *PPG*, May 6, 1950; Ralph S. Brown, *Loyalty and Security* (New Haven, Conn.: Yale University Press, 1958), 115.

67. Weber, *Don't Call Me Boss*, 420n; Matson to Duff, October 21, 1947, Carton 13, "Communism," "1947–51" file, Official Papers, 1947–51, Duff Papers; ACLU folders, Matson Papers; "Musmanno Blisters Civil Liberties Union for Defending Reds," *PP*, June 5, 1950.

68. Weber, *Don't Call Me Boss*, 283–86; *Digest of the Public Record of Communism*, 380, 440.

69. Harold Spencer, *In Danger: The Right to Speak for Peace* (Philadelphia: Pennsylvania Committee to Defend the Pittsburgh Six, 1952); Musmanno, *Across the Street from the Courthouse*, 76–88; Jeffrey Zaslow, "When the Red Scare Hit Pittsburgh," *Pittsburgher Magazine*, March 1980, 61–72; Griffin Fariello, *Red Scare* (New York: Norton, 1995), 194–98, 204–12.

70. Nelson, Barrett, and Ruck, *Steve Nelson*, 319.

71. Robert Louis Benson and Michael Warner, eds., *VENONA: Soviet Espionage and the American Response, 1939–1957* (Washington, D.C.: National Security Agency, 1996), 49–50, 105–8; *In the Matter of J. Robert Oppenheimer* (Cambridge, Mass.: MIT Press, 1971), 194–96; Nelson, Barrett, and Ruck, *Steve Nelson*; Cedric Belfrage, *The American Inquisition, 1945–1960* (Indianapolis: Bobbs-Merrill, 1973), 18–21; Jacob Spolansky, *The Communist Trail in America* (New York: Macmillan, 1951), 154–61.

72. Musmanno, *Across the Street from the Courthouse*, 104.

73. Howard Rushmore "Plot to Cripple Nation Headed by Steve Nelson," *PST*, February 26, 1950. Compare "Commie Leader Here Unmasks Self as FBI Agent for Nine Years," *PP*, February 19, 1950.

74. "Nelson Gave M-Day Orders to Reds Here," *PP*, February 27, 1950.

75. Walter and Miriam Schneir, *Invitation to an Inquest* (Garden City, N.Y.: Doubleday, 1965), 70–77.

76. Box 1, Papers of UE Local 601, UE Labor Archive, UP. A contemporary Philadelphia

exposé of a Communist "peace petition" movement in the Oxford Circle area made the gratuitous observation that Harry Gold had lived nearby, presumably seeking to link Communism and espionage; see "Red Peace Fake Here Designed to Get Party Funds," *PI*, June 26, 1950.

77. Shields, *Pittsburgh: Peace on Trial*, 14; "Fight Opens to Jail Red Leaders Here," *PP*, March 10, 1950; "DA to Prosecute Reds Here—IF," *PP*, March 11, 1950.

78. Weber, *Don't Call Me Boss*, 296–98; Paul B. Beers, *Pennsylvania Politics Today and Yesterday* (University Park: Pennsylvania State University Press, 1980), 117–36.

79. Musmanno, *Across the Street from the Courthouse*, 53–68.

80. "Reaction Mixed over Opening of Reds Office," *Pittsburgh Daily Reporter*, October 1, 1950; "Bill Outlawing Reds Offered," *PPG*, August 7, 1951.

81. Belfrage, *The American Inquisition*, 151.

82. Musmanno, *Across the Street from the Courthouse*, 47.

83. Phillip Bonosky, "Pittsburgh Experiment," *Masses and Mainstream*, August 1950, 27.

84. Shields, *Pittsburgh: Peace on Trial*, 3; Nelson, Barrett, and Ruck, *Steve Nelson*.

85. "Two Commies Convicted of Sedition," *PP*, July 31, 1951; "Eight Month Red Trial Here Cost Taxpayers More than $54,000," *PP*, August 31, 1951; Frank Shenkel, "Guilt of Two Here Death Blow to Pennsylvania Reds," *PST*, September 2, 1951.

86. Belfrage, *The American Inquisition*, 152.

87. "High Court Hears Fight for Teacher," *PST*, October 1, 1952. Bell has aptly been described as "one of the most conservative figures of modern times"; in 1944, as lieutenant governor under Edward Martin, he had accused the Roosevelt administration of seeking to build a new order "on shifting sands brought from Germany, Italy and Russia" (Beers, *Pennsylvania Politics Today and Yesterday*, 168. Thomas P. O'Neil, "Attack on FDR Gives a Preview of GOP Campaign," *Philadelphia Record*, May 20, 1944).

88. The *Dennis* case is discussed in Samuel Walker, *In Defense of American Liberties* (New York: Oxford University Press, 1990), 187–88; Peter L. Steinberg, *The Great "Red Menace"* (Westport, Conn.: Greenwood Press, 1984); and Stanley I. Kutler, *The American Inquisition* (New York: Hill and Wang, 1982).

89. *Digest of the Public Record of Communism*, 196–205; Sherman Labovitz, *Being Red in Philadelphia* (Philadelphia: Camino Books, 1998). "FBI Seizes Six Philadelphia Red Leaders," *PI*, July 30, 1953; "$175,000 Bail Set for Six Seized as Top Penna. Reds," *PI*, July 31, 1953; "Judge Allows All Testimony Given by Budenz," *PEB*, May 3, 1954; "Red Trial Hears City Librarian," *PEB*, July 26, 1954; "Judge at Red Trial Refuses to Subpena [*sic*] Records of FBI," *PEB*, July 27, 1954; "Face Jail Terms of Five Years—Ask New Trial," *PEB*, August 13, 1954.

90. *34th Annual Convention of the American Legion, Department of Pennsylvania at Philadelphia, Aug. 6–9, 1952* (American Legion, Department of Pennsylvania, 1952), 150–51, 168–69.

91. "Reds Here Open New Purge of Party's Rolls," *PP*, March 31, 1953.

92. James McCarthy, "Wouldn't Hesitate to Kill, Red Quoted," *PST*, March 27, 1953; "Reds School Bared in Culture Center," *PST*, July 23, 1953; U.S. Senate, Committee on the Judiciary, SISS, *Subversive Influence in the United Electrical, Radio and Machine Workers of America (UERMWA), Pittsburgh and Erie, Pa. (Investigation Relative to Legislation Designed to Curb Communist Penetration and Domination of Labor Organizations)*, Hearings, November 1953, 83d Cong., 1st sess. (Washington, D.C.: GPO, 1954), 5–40.

93. Ingrid Jewell, "Plot to Kill Senator McCarthy Linked to District Red Leader," *PPG*,

June 19, 1953; "Knew of Reds' Death Plot, Says McCarthy," *PST*, June 19, 1953; "Exposé Surprises Rep. Fulton," *PP*, November 16, 1953.

94. Michael A. Musmanno, *Justice Musmanno Dissents* (Indianapolis: Bobbs-Merrill, 1956), 423–42, quote at 431.

95. "District Man Links Reds, Civil Rights," *PPG*, December 10, 1954; "Undercover Agent Tells of Work against Reds," *PPG*, January 4, 1955; "Can't Tell Commie from FBI Aide Here," *PP*, December 4, 1955.

96. "Truitt Fails to Testify at Inquiry," *PPG*, November 1, 1955.

97. "Can't Tell Commie from FBI Aide Here," *PP*, December 4, 1955.

98. "Witness Says He Joined Reds at FBI Request," *PEB*, May 10, 1954; Labovitz, *Being Red in Philadelphia*, 99–105; U.S. Senate, Committee on the Judiciary, SISS, *Subversive Influence in Certain Industrial Plants: Eastern Pennsylvania*, Hearing, 83d Cong., 2d sess., and 84th Cong., 1st sess. (Washington, D.C.: GPO, 1954–55), 16–17 (hereafter cited as *Subversive Influence in Certain Industrial Plants*). Thomas testified that "Congressman Walter, being the wonderful American that he is, certainly doesn't tolerate the doings of the Communist Party, and at one time or another has attacked the Communist Party. Also for his sponsorship of the McCarran-Walter bill, which the Party vehemently worked against." Compare HUAC, *Trial by Treason: The National Committee to Secure Justice for the Rosenbergs and Morton Sobell* (Washington, D.C.: GPO, August 1956), 78–82.

99. *Subversive Influence in Certain Industrial Plants*, 37–53. For a later informer in this area, Harry G. Walter, see John G. McCullough, "Red Spy Net Operated Here, Probe Is Told," *PEB*, July 16, 1957.

100. Nelson, Barrett, and Ruck, *Steve Nelson*, 318.

101. Typescript report of meeting held at 440 Wood Street, Pittsburgh, May 26, 1947, quoting Andree Hudson, "Communist Party Meetings," Musmanno Papers. That November the FBI believed that the Philadelphia-area Communist Party was on the verge of going underground: J. Edgar Hoover to Harry Hawkins Vaughan, November 12, 1947, President's Secretary's Files, Box 167, Truman Library.

102. *Subversive Influence in Certain Industrial Plants*, 8–9.

103. Paul Lyons, *Philadelphia Communists, 1936–1956* (Philadelphia: Temple University Press, 1982), 156–57.

104. Harv Golden, in HUAC, *Current Strategy and Tactics of Communists in the United States, Greater Pittsburgh Area*, 86th Cong., 1st sess. (Washington, D.C.: GPO, 1959), 329–30.

105. *Subversive Influence in Certain Industrial Plants*, 43.

106. Ibid., 14–15.

107. *Digest of the Public Record of Communism*, 284.

108. Brown, *Loyalty and Security*.

109. "More Hysteria," *PEB*, August 22, 1951.

110. "Red Hangover," *Harrisburg Evening News*, August 22, 1951.

111. "Anti-red Bill Foes Blasted by Musmanno," *PP*, August 23, 1951.

112. *Digest of the Public Record of Communism*, 406; Musmanno, *Across the Street from the Courthouse*, 181–85; "Bill Outlawing Reds Offered," *PPG*, August 7, 1951.

113. "Demand Public Hearing on Loyalty Oath Bill," *The Worker*, March 11, 1951.

114. *Digest of the Public Record of Communism*, 376–80. The pioneering state "loyalty" measure in this area was Maryland's Ober Act of 1949. See Walter Gellhorn, ed., *The States and Subversion* (Ithaca, N.Y.: Cornell University Press, 1952).

115. Clark Byse, "A Report on the Pennsylvania Loyalty Act," 1014 *University of Pennsylvania Law Review* (1953), 480–508; Loyalty Procedures, 1952, Folder 2, Robert Wallace Brewster Papers, 1949–65, University Archives, PSU.

116. "Labor Leaders Blast State Loyalty Oath Bill," *PP*, August 14, 1951; "Friends and Foes Throng State Capitol on Loyalty Bill," *PEB*, December 11, 1951. The intensive work of the Teachers' Union in opposing the Pechan bill is evident from the large correspondence in the Teachers' Union Papers, Boxes 7–9, URB 36, TU. See, for example, Hiram Andrews to Francis Jennings, December 13, 1951, in Box 8.

117. "How Democracy Can Undermine Itself," *Philadelphia Sunday Bulletin*, August 26, 1951.

118. Beers, *Pennsylvania Politics Today and Yesterday*, 176. The "steamroller" quote is from Francis Jennings to "Fellow Veterans," November 12, 1951, Box 8, Teachers' Union Papers.

119. "Musmanno Objects to Loyalty Bill," *PST*, August 22, 1951.

120. *Digest of the Public Record of Communism*, 418.

121. The York and Lancaster measures are found in ibid., 457, 461.

122. "Two Red Leaders Ousted in Fight on Tube City Law," *PPG*, August 4, 1950; Nelson, Barrett, and Ruck, *Steve Nelson*, 314–15.

123. *Digest of the Public Record of Communism*, 486–87. For the Jamieson bill, see Greater Philadelphia ACLU Papers, 7/I/106–7, URB 7, TU; Ned Behney, "City Council Eyes Harsher Anti-Red Law," *Philadelphia Daily News*, September 27, 1950.

124. *Digest of the Public Record of Communism*, 95.

125. Nelson, Barrett, and Ruck, *Steve Nelson*; David Caute, *The Great Fear: The Anti-Communist Purge under Truman and Eisenhower* (New York: Simon and Schuster, 1978), 552. In fairness, it should be said that most of the teachers felt they did receive good representation, generally at reasonable fees.

126. Caute, *The Great Fear*, 98.

127. Jack Sirott case, 1953–54, Folder 1, Brewster Papers.

128. Letter of Arthur Reede to Sirott, July 15, 1953, Brewster Papers.

129. Richardson Dilworth described Kunzig as "a two-bit copy of Gerald L. K. Smith": Dilworth to George A. Penglase, September 24, 1951, Box 7, Teachers' Union Papers.

130. "Cvetic Tells of Red Queen's Commie Ties," *PP*, June 27, 1950; the quotation is from "Kick Alleged Reds Off Dole, State Demands of Court," *PP*, August 28, 1950. Nuss's brother wrote a response to the hysterical denunciation in Bonosky, "Pittsburgh Experiment," 25–33.

CHAPTER 5

1. HUAC, *Exposé of the Communist Party of Western Pennsylvania Based upon Testimony of Matthew Cvetic, Undercover Agent*, Hearings, 81st Cong., 2d sess. (Washington, D.C.: GPO, 1950), 1242 (hereafter cited as *Exposé of the Communist Party*).

2. Ibid., 1240.

3. U.S. Senate, Committee on the Judiciary, SISS, *Subversive Influence in Certain Industrial Plants: Eastern Pennsylvania*, Hearing, 83d Cong., 2d sess., and 84th Cong., 1st sess. (Washington, D.C.: GPO, 1954–55), 22 (hereafter cited as *Subversive Influence in Certain Industrial Plants*).

4. Ralph Schapell, "The Termites Within," *Keystone Defender* 1, no. 3 (May 1952).

5. Ronald W. Schatz, *The Electrical Workers* (Urbana: University of Illinois Press, 1983), 115–16; David J. Saposs, *Communism in American Unions* (Westport, Conn.: Greenwood Press, 1959).

6. Paul Lyons, *Philadelphia Communists, 1936–1956* (Philadelphia: Temple University Press, 1982), 59–60; August Meier and Elliott Rudwick, "Communist Unions and the Black Community," *Labor History* 23 (1982): 165–97; Elizabeth Fones-Wolf, "Industrial Unionism and Labor Movement Culture in Depression Era Philadelphia," *Pennsylvania Magazine of History and Biography* 109 (1985): 3–26; Oliver H. Crawford, "Union Eclipse Mars Mother Bloor's Party," *PI*, October 16, 1945; "Ex-Red Tells Jury of Plot to Organize Dockers Here," *PEB*, June 14, 1954. Compare Lisa McGirr, "The Black and White Longshoremen in the IWW," *Labor History* 36 (1995): 377–402.

7. *Exposé of the Communist Party*, 1242–44.

8. Steve Nelson, James R. Barrett, and Rob Ruck, *Steve Nelson: American Radical* (Pittsburgh: University of Pittsburgh Press, 1981), 21–22.

9. Ibid., 299–301; *Exposé of the Communist Party*, 1249, for the hotel workers.

10. *Exposé of the Communist Party*, 1248, 1348.

11. Ibid., 1241–42.

12. Nelson, Barrett, and Ruck, *Steve Nelson*, 310.

13. *Exposé of the Communist Party*, 1242.

14. *Subversive Influence in Certain Industrial Plants*, 16–21; also see Chapter 2 above.

15. Alexander Wright, of course, proved to be an FBI informant. "PAC Scores Two Labor Leaders for Support of Wallace" and "Four Left-wing Pittsburghers Help Spark Drive for Wallace," *PP*, January 12, 1948; "51 Here on Wallace Sponsor List," *PP*, February 8, 1948; "Director of Wallace Group Here Draws $300 Monthly," *PP*, August 5, 1948. Note, however, that even in such a left-wing union as UE, support for Wallace was personal rather than institutional; see Robert Zieger, *The CIO, 1935–1955* (Chapel Hill: University of North Carolina Press, 1995), 274.

16. Walter Lowenfels, "Thousands Hear Wallace Speak in Pennsylvania," *The Worker*, October 24, 1948.

17. "Penna. Delegates Back Coal Seizure," *PI*, July 24, 1948.

18. "Wallace Wins Support of 22 Union Leaders," *PP*, February 17, 1948.

19. *Subversive Influence in Certain Industrial Plants*.

20. Zieger, *The CIO, 1935–1955*.

21. Douglas P. Seaton, *Catholics and Radicals* (Lewisburg, Pa.: Bucknell University Press, 1981); Patrick J. McGeever, *Rev. Charles Owen Rice: Apostle of Contradiction* (Pittsburgh: Duquesne University Press, 1989); Charles J. McCollester, ed., *Fighter with a Heart* (Pittsburgh: University of Pittsburgh Press, 1996); Kenneth J. Heineman, *A Catholic New Deal: Religion and Reform in Depression Pittsburgh* (University Park: Pennsylvania State University Press, 1999); Kenneth J. Heineman, "A Catholic New Deal," *Pennsylvania Magazine of History and Biography* 118, no. 4 (1994): 363–94; Steven Rosswurm, "The Catholic Church and the Left-Led Unions," in *The CIO's Left-Led Unions*, ed. Steven Rosswurm (New Brunswick: Rutgers University Press, 1992), 119–37; "AFL and CIO Urged to Oust Communists," *PPG*, September 2, 1941.

22. Ronald L. Filippelli and Mark McColloch, *Cold War in the Working Class* (Albany: State University of New York Press, 1995), 13; Schatz, *The Electrical Workers*, 188–217.

23. Filippelli and McColloch, *Cold War in the Working Class*, 112, 128.

24. *A History of UE-Local 601, 1939–45* (East Pittsburgh: Local 601, UERMWA, 1946).

25. WMCK radio schedule, March 20–27, 1950, Papers of UE Local 601, 1949–52, UE Labor Archive, UP; George Lipsitz, *Rainbow at Midnight* (Urbana: University of Illinois Press, 1994).

26. Nelson, Barrett, and Ruck, *Steve Nelson*, 309.

27. Filippelli and McColloch, *Cold War in the Working Class*, 51–64.

28. Typed memoranda and copies of newspaper articles including "Memo re Statement of Michael Fitzpatrick," September 27, 1945, and "Big Mike Moves Over against Reds," Strike Reports: Westinghouse Strike, 1946, Bureau of Crime, State Police Archives, RG 30, PSA.

29. HUAC, *Hearings Regarding Communist Infiltration of Labor Unions, Part 2: Security Measures Relating to Officials of the UERMWA-CIO*, December 5–6, 1949, 81st Cong., 1st sess. (Washington, D.C.: GPO, 1950), 846–47.

30. Oral History interview with Harry Block, 1967, 34, HCLA.

31. "Thirty Found Guilty in Red Trial," *PPG*, November 1, 1940.

32. Petition, 1940, for the "removal of Communists from representation of Local 601," Margaret Darin Stasik Papers, UE Labor Archive, UP; Schatz, *The Electrical Workers*, 192–93.

33. Filippelli and McColloch, *Cold War in the Working Class*, 54–57; Nelson, Barrett, and Ruck, *Steve Nelson*, 312; "The Country Editor," *Wilkinsburg Gazette*, September 21, 1950. For Catholic activism in other unions, see "Power of Reds in Labor Unions Faces Vote Test," *PP*, December 15, 1940, and "Firm's Action in Discharging Girl Is Upheld," *PP*, January 28, 1941.

34. U.S. Senate, Committee on the Judiciary, SISS, *Subversive Influence in the United Electrical, Radio and Machine Workers of America (UERMWA), Pittsburgh and Erie, Pa. (Investigation Relative to Legislation Designed to Curb Communist Penetration and Domination of Labor Organizations)*, Hearings, November 1953, 83d Cong., 1st sess. (Washington, D.C.: GPO, 1954), 16–19 (hereafter cited as *Subversive Influence in the UERMWA*).

35. Typed memoranda and transcripts of newspaper articles including "Return Papers, Attorney Told," January 19, 1945, and "Sherman Suit Ousted by Jurors," March 29, 1945, Strike Reports: Westinghouse Strike, 1946, Bureau of Crime, State Police Archives.

36. *Subversive Influence in the UERMWA*, 34, for the conflict with McNeil, and 119, for the Kultur Farband affair.

37. Ibid., 27–28.

38. Transcript, Testimony on Reports of Subversive Activities in the Pittsburgh Area, SISS, Committee of the Judiciary, U.S. Senate, June 16, 1955, 625, Boxes 62–63, "The Mullen Case," Michael A. Musmanno Papers, DU. This document will hereafter be cited as SISS, Mullen Transcript.

39. Ibid., 633.

40. *Subversive Influence in the UERMWA*, 8.

41. "Testimony Hits Role of Schlesinger," *PP*, March 10, 1959.

42. The quote is from Zieger, *The CIO, 1935–1955*, 223. See also Ronald L. Filippelli, ed., *Labor Conflict in the United States: An Encyclopedia* (New York: Garland, 1990), including his chapters "Pittsburgh Power Strike of 1946," 421–23, and "Steel Strike of 1946," 509–10.

43. Strike Reports: Conestoga Transportation Company, 1946, Bureau of Crime, State Police Archives; "Lancaster AFL Wins Victory in General Strike," *The Worker*, February 24, 1946.

44. Strike Reports: Westinghouse Strike, 1946, Bureau of Crime, State Police Archives.

45. "Transcripts of Victrola Records," March-April 1946, ibid.; Philip Conti, *The Pennsylvania State Police* (Harrisburg: Stackpole, 1977).

46. "Union Official Hits Red Charge," *PP*, April 25, 1946; "Red Plot Charged in Electric Strike," *PPG*, April 25, 1946; compare Michael P. Weber, *Don't Call Me Boss* (Pittsburgh: University of Pittsburgh Press, 1988), 226.

47. Summary of Rev. James A. Cox's talk over radio station WJAS, April 7, 1946, Strike Reports: Westinghouse Strike, 1946, Bureau of Crime, State Police Archives.

48. Joseph H. Miller, "Martin Asks Truman to Oust Red Employees," *PI*, September 21, 1946.

49. Thomas Fitzpatrick to Duff, October 10, 1947, Carton 13, "Communism," "1947–51" file, Official Papers, 1947–51, Papers of James H. Duff, MG 190, PSA.

50. John McDowell, "The Country Editor in Washington," *Wilkinsburg Gazette*, n.d., in clip file on John McDowell, Box 3, Papers of UE Local 601, 1949–52.

51. Curtis D. MacDougall, *Gideon's Army* (New York: Marzani and Munsell, 1965), 1:175; *Exposé of the Communist Party*, 1244; "CIO Warns Communists: Don't Meddle in Unions," *Steel Labor*, December 1946, 2.

52. *Subversive Influence in Certain Industrial Plants*, 13–15; William Jacobs, "Union Left Wing Loses Convention Battle on Subversive Elements," *PP*, April 25, 1947; William Jacobs, "Reds Voted Out as State's CIO Parley Ends," *PP*, April 26, 1947; C. Edmund Fisher, "State CIO Votes to Put Ban on Reds," *PPG*, April 26, 1947; "Penna CIO Bars Commies as Officers," *Steel Labor*, May 1947, 11.

53. Harry Block emphasized the Wallace campaign as a decisive factor in the CIO decision to move against UE; Oral History interview with Harry Block, 29.

54. Stephen Fischer, "How Murray Came Home to the ACTU," *Daily Compass*, November 29, 1949; "Mr. Murray Goes Too Far," *PP*, February 9, 1948.

55. "Steel Union Bars Affiliation with Wallace, Official Says," *PI*, July 26, 1948.

56. "City Called Number One Target of Communists," *PP*, March 20, 1950; Sam Hood "Board Backs Ban on Red Use of Schools," *PP*, March 22, 1950; "Board Bans: Resolution Adopted Closing Doors to All Communist Meetings," *PPG*, March 22, 1950; "Board Unanimously Fires Miss Alberts as Teacher," *PPG*, May 18, 1950. For the USWA in this era, see Paul F. Clark, Peter Gottlieb, and Donald Kennedy, eds., *Forging a Union of Steel: Philip Murray, SWOC, and the United Steelworkers* (Ithaca, N.Y.: ILR Press, 1987).

57. David M. Oshinsky, "Labor's Cold War," in *The Specter*, ed. Robert Griffith and Athan Theoharis (New York: Franklin Watts, 1974), 116–51.

58. "State CIO Leader Maps Purge of Communists in Electrical Union," *PP*, August 12, 1946; "UE Challenged as Communist," *PP*, October 7, 1946. Compare "ACTU Leader Outlines Union-Splitting Methods," *The Worker*, June 20, 1948; Schatz, *The Electrical Workers*; Seaton, *Catholics and Radicals*, 197–202; Rosswurm, "The Catholic Church and the Left-Led Unions."

59. *Exposé of the Communist Party*, 1246; Schatz, *The Electrical Workers*, 196.

60. Nelson, Barrett, and Ruck, *Steve Nelson*, 309.

61. Lawrence declined the invitation: Weber, *Don't Call Me Boss*, 226.

62. Statement of William H. Peeler, 1951, "Leaflets, 1951–55," Papers of Thomas J. Quinn, UE Labor Archive, UP.

63. HUAC, *Hearings Regarding Communist Infiltration of Labor Unions, Part 1: Local 601, UERMWA*, 81st Cong., 1st and 2d sess., *Part 2: Security Measures Relating to Officials of the*

UERMWA-CIO, December 5 and 6, 1949, 81st Cong., 1st sess. (Washington, D.C.: GPO, 1950).

64. "UE Men Here Met with Reds, Trial Told," *PP*, October 2, 1948.

65. "Catholics Seek Control of UE, Says Matles," *PP*, March 25, 1947.

66. Stephen Fischer, "Carey Once Tried to Take on ACTU—He's Part of It Now," *Daily Compass*, November 30, 1949. Carey was "a very good friend" of Harry Sherman: SISS, Mullen Transcript, 627–33.

67. Oral History interview with Harry Block, 18.

68. Radio script, "On the Spot," broadcast on KQV Pittsburgh, September 1946, Box 3, Father Charles Owen Rice Papers, UE Labor Archive, UP.

69. Nelson, Barrett, and Ruck, *Steve Nelson*, 303–4.

70. "Violence Flares at Commies Rally," *PP*, April 3, 1949; "250 at Meeting Chased Jostled by Angry Crowd," *PPG*, April 3, 1949; "Reds Claim Police Shirked Duty at Rally," *PPG*, April 4, 1949; *Storm Trooper Attack on North Side Communist Meeting Threatens Rights of Every American*, Communist Party leaflet, 1949.

71. Nelson, Barrett, and Ruck, *Steve Nelson*, 304–5.

72. *31st Annual Convention of the American Legion, Department of Pennsylvania at Pittsburgh, Pa.* (American Legion: Department of Pennsylvania, 1949), 61–62; George N. Craig, "Labor Sets an Example," *American Legion Magazine*, April 1950.

73. Filippelli and McColloch, *Cold War in the Working Class*, 1.

74. William Jacobs, "CIO Leaders Hurl Epithet in Final Kick at Left-Wing," *PP*, November 2, 1949.

75. Filippelli and McColloch, *Cold War in the Working Class*, 167; Stephen Fischer, "Murray Lauds Holy Fight of New Electrical Union," *Daily Compass*, November 29, 1949; Charles Owen Rice, "Catholics Lead in Labor's Anti-Communist Drive," *Our Sunday Visitor*, April 23, 1950.

76. *Ten Long Years of Communist Rule*, IUE pamphlet, 1950, in Box 4, Papers of UE Local 601, 1949–52.

77. "Red-baiting" file in ibid.

78. This account is drawn from the abundant election materials in the Papers of UE Local 601, 1949–52.

79. *Memo to Defend the UE Committee*, April 14, 1950, 1, in ibid.

80. James Matles to "UE General Vice-Presidents," May 29, 1950, Box 1, ibid.

81. Box 1, ibid.; Michael A. Musmanno, *Across the Street from the Courthouse* (Philadelphia: Dorrance, 1954), 290–95.

82. Letter of Glynn Brotherson, n.d., Box 5, Papers of UE Local 601, 1949–52.

83. Filippelli and McColloch, *Cold War in the Working Class*, 143–46.

84. *Exposé of the Communist Party*, 1351.

85. "Cvetic Tells How Nelson Lost UE Fight," *PP*, February 27, 1950; "Red-Tainted Woman May Be Kept Off Jury by Judge Musmanno," *PPG*, March 7, 1950; "Radio Station Bars Speaker Named as Red," *PPG*, March 15, 1950.

86. Art Shields, *Pittsburgh: Peace on Trial* (reprinted from *Masses and Mainstream*, published by the Committee to Defend the Pittsburgh Frame-Up Victims, 1951), 8–9; "City Called Number One Target of Communists," *PP*, March 20, 1950.

87. "Union to Probe Charge That Chief Is Red," *PP*, September 9, 1953; "Oakmont Steel Union Leader Charged as Red," *PST*, September 20, 1953.

88. For the Communist sympathies of Hotel and Restaurant Workers president Carl Hacker, see U.S. House of Representatives, Special Committee on Un-American Activities (Dies Committee), *Investigation of Un-American Propaganda Activities in the United States*, Hearings, 76th Cong., 1st sess. (Washington, D.C.: GPO, 1940), 11–12:7594; "Communists Hold Lenin Day at Rally," *PPG*, January 24, 1938. For the union in Philadelphia, see "Union Charges Reds Are Seizing Power," *PEB*, February 26, 1938.

89. "51 Here on Wallace Sponsor List," *PP*, February 8, 1948; "Two in AFL on Carpet as Reds," *PST*, February 24, 1950.

90. Daniel J. Leab, "Anti-Communism, the FBI and Matt Cvetic," *Pennsylvania Magazine of History and Biography* 115 (1991): 550; James Moore, "Hotel Manager Tells How He Aided Cvetic," *PST*, February 21, 1950.

91. "Hotel Union Waging Hot Election Drive," *PP*, March 9, 1950.

92. Schatz, *The Electrical Workers*, 204–17.

93. *Subversive Influence in the UERMWA*, 65.

94. U.S. Senate, Committee on the Judiciary, SISS, *Scope of Soviet Activity in the United States: Communist Activity in Labor*, Hearing, 85th Cong., 1st and 2d sess. (Washington, D.C.: GPO, 1958), 8–9 (hereafter cited as *Communist Activity in Labor*).

95. Schatz, *The Electrical Workers*, 239.

96. SISS, Mullen Transcript, 630.

97. "Reds Control UE Here, Probe Told," *PP*, March 11, 1959.

98. *Communist Activity in Labor*, 27–28; "District Union Commie-Led, Probers Claim," *PP*, March 3, 1954.

99. Filippelli and McColloch, *Cold War in the Working Class*, 154–57.

100. "UE Local 155 Demands End to FBI Harassment," *The Worker*, September 30, 1951.

101. HUAC, *Communist Activities in the Philadelphia Area*, Hearings, October 13–16, 1952, 82d Cong., 2d sess. (Washington, D.C.: GPO, 1952); "Former Aid [*sic*] Says Party Ran Union," *PEB*, October 13, 1952; "Five Witnesses Defy US Probe of Communists," *PEB*, October 14, 1952; "Red Clique Ran Big Philadelphia Union, Ex-Communist Tells Probers," *Camden Courier-Post*, October 14, 1952; "Ex-Communist Tells of Plans to Help Russia," *PEB*, October 15, 1952; "Probers to Dig Deeper into Red Underground," *PEB*, October 16, 1952; *On the Un-American Front* (UE Local 155 newsletter), October 1952; *What Is McCarthyism?* (New York: United Electrical, Radio and Machine Workers of America, 1954).

102. U.S. Senate, Committee on Government Operations, Permanent Subcommittee on Investigations, *Communist Party Activities, Western Pennsylvania*, Hearing, June 18, 1953, 83d Cong., 1st sess. (Washington, D.C.: GPO, 1953); David M. Oshinsky, *Senator Joseph McCarthy and the American Labor Movement* (Columbia: University of Missouri Press, 1976).

103. *Subversive Influence in the UERMWA*, 39, 117.

104. "District Union Commie-Led, Probers Claim," *PP*, March 3, 1954. For John Nelson, see HUAC, *Problems of Security in Industrial Establishments, Greater Pittsburgh Area*, 86th Cong., 1st sess. (Washington, D.C.: GPO, 1959), 447–52. Stanley Loney case, Papers of M. Y. Steinberg, UE Labor Archive, UP.

105. *Subversive Influence in the UERMWA*, 78.

106. "Communist Affiliations Cost Four Area Workers Their Jobs," *Independent*, October 10, 1957.

107. *Subversive Influence in the UERMWA*, 127; Schatz, *The Electrical Workers*, 239–40.

108. *Subversive Influence in the UERMWA*, 48–54. The *Erie Daily Times* was owned by the Irish Catholic Mead family.

109. U.S. Senate, Committee on Government Operations, Permanent Subcommittee on Investigations, *Subversion and Espionage in Defense Establishments and Industry*, Hearing, January 3, 1955, 83d Cong., 2d sess. (Washington, D.C.: GPO, 1955); "Undercover Agent Tells of Work against Reds," *PPG*, January 4, 1955; "UE Branded as Pro-Red by Brownell," *PPG*, December 21, 1955.

110. *Communist Activity in Labor*, 4961–64; the remark is from chief counsel Robert Morris.

111. U.S. Senate, Committee on the Judiciary, SISS, *Revitalizing of the Communist Party in the Philadelphia Area*, Hearings, 86th Cong., 1st sess. (Washington, D.C.: GPO, 1959), 74.

112. HUAC held three related hearings on the Greater Pittsburgh area: *Current Strategy and Tactics of Communists in the United States*, *Problems of Security in Industrial Establishments*, and *Problems Arising in Cases of Denaturalization and Deportation of Communists*, 86th Cong., 1st sess. (Washington, D.C.: GPO, 1959). "Reds Control UE Here, Probe Told," *PP*, March 11, 1959.

113. "Testimony Hits Role of Schlesinger," *PP*, March 10, 1959; "FBI Spy Beaned as Commie," *PP*, March 10, 1959; Mary Golden, "My Secret Life in the FBI," *PST*, April 12, 1959.

114. "Reds Control UE Here, Probe Told," *PP*, March 11, 1959; Lester Sullivan, "Sparks Fly as Quinn Steals Probe Show," *PST*, March 12, 1959.

115. "Unfair Play," *PPG*, March 12, 1959.

CHAPTER 6

1. Quoted in Michael A. Musmanno, *Across the Street from the Courthouse* (Philadelphia: Dorrance, 1954), 237.

2. Terry Radtke, *The History of the Pennsylvania American Legion* (Mechanicsburg, Pa.: Stackpole, 1993), 35–36.

3. Bessie R. Burchett, *Education for Destruction* (Philadelphia: privately printed, 1941); "Red Teaching Laid to Philadelphia Schools," *PI*, May 5, 1936.

4. James Sanzare, *A History of the Philadelphia Federation of Teachers, 1941–73* (Philadelphia: Health and Welfare Fund, Local 3, The Federation [of Teachers], 1977), 5–6; *PFF* 2, no. 3 (1939): 5. For comparable events in the New York schools at this time, see Lewis Lerman, *Winter Soldiers* (New York: n.p., 1941).

5. "McDevitt Predicts Ouster of US Reds," *PI*, May 2, 1940.

6. Thomas Fullerton Armstrong, "The Public Educational Programs of Selected Lay Organizations in Pennsylvania" (Ph.D. diss., Temple University, 1948), 84–98. The "false doctrines" resolution is discussed in pages 183–86. For the Altoona convention, see page 97.

7. HUAC, *Investigation of Communist Activities in the Philadelphia Area*, 83rd Cong., 1st and 2d sess. (Washington, D.C.: GPO, 1954), 2996 (hereafter cited as *Investigation of Communist Activities in the Philadelphia Area*).

8. Ibid., 2926, 2934, 2961.

9. Ibid., 3966–67, 6785–87.

10. Ibid., 2935, 3963–65.

11. U.S. House of Representatives, Special Committee on Un-American Activities (Dies Committee), *Investigation of Un-American Propaganda Activities in the United States*, 76th

Cong., 1st sess. (Washington, D.C.: GPO, 1940), 11:6857–911 (hereafter cited as *Investigation of Un-American Propaganda Activities in the United States*).

12. Sanzare, *A History of the Philadelphia Federation of Teachers*, 4–30.

13. *Investigation of Communist Activities in the Philadelphia Area*, 2893–97.

14. Ibid., 2939.

15. Edward L. Barrett, *The Tenney Committee* (Ithaca, N.Y.: Cornell University Press, 1951); Vern Countryman, *Un-American Activities in the State of Washington* (Ithaca, N.Y.: Cornell University Press, 1951); Walter Gellhorn, ed., *The States and Subversion* (Ithaca N.Y.: Cornell University Press, 1952); Stuart J. Foster, *Red Alert!* (New York: Peter Lang, 1998).

16. *Academic Freedom: Some Recent Philadelphia Episodes* (Philadelphia: Greater Philadelphia Branch of the ACLU, [1954?]), 28–30; compare *Digest of the Public Record of Communism in the United States* (New York: Fund for the Republic, 1955), 430.

17. "More Names Revealed by Cvetic in Red Probe," *PP*, March 14, 1950; "Board Unanimously Fires Miss Alberts as Teacher," *PPG*, May 18, 1950; Musmanno, *Across the Street from the Courthouse*, 224–26.

18. Clark Byse, "A Report on the Pennsylvania Loyalty Act," 1014 *University of Pennsylvania Law Review* (1953), 480–508.

19. "Statement by Albert R. Pechan—State Senator from Butler-Armstrong Counties, as Requested by INS," 1953, Papers of John S. Fine, MS 206, PSA. For the 1953 bill (S. 94), see the correspondence in Box 7, Teachers' Union Papers, URB 36, TU.

20. Address by Governor Fine to VFW, Ben Franklin Hotel, Philadelphia, July 12, 1951, B. Wheaton file, Fine Papers.

21. *34th Annual Convention of the American Legion, Department of Pennsylvania at Philadelphia, Aug. 6–9, 1952* (American Legion, Department of Pennsylvania, 1952), 30.

22. Paul B. Beers, *Pennsylvania Politics Today and Yesterday* (University Park: Pennsylvania State University Press, 1980), 175–76.

23. Loyalty Procedures, 1952, Folder 2, Robert Wallace Brewster Papers, 1949–65, , University Archives, PSU.

24. Byse, "A Report on the Pennsylvania Loyalty Act."

25. *Digest of the Public Record of Communism*, 380.

26. Quoted in Musmanno, *Across the Street from the Courthouse*, 238. "VFW Official Keeps Children from School, Assails Board," *PEB*, November 17, 1953.

27. Sanzare, *A History of the Philadelphia Federation of Teachers*, 15–16.

28. Philip Arthur Steinberg, "Communism, Education, and Academic Freedom" (D.Ed. diss., Temple University, 1978).

29. "FBI Director Says White Transfer Hampered Bureau in Spy Inquiry," *PI*, November 18, 1953. The story appeared next to "Probers Told Teacher Trained at Red School."

30. "Scores Unable to Gain Entrance to Red Inquiry," *PI*, November 17, 1953.

31. *Investigation of Communist Activities in the Philadelphia Area*, 2954.

32. Ibid., 2914.

33. Ibid., 2886–910; Velde's quote is from 2910. Compare Bella V. Dodd, *School of Darkness* (New York: P. J. Kenedy, 1954).

34. *Investigation of Communist Activities in the Philadelphia Area*, 2969.

35. Carl Beck, *Contempt of Congress* (New Orleans: Hauser Press, 1959), 102–3, 132–33; Victor Navasky, *Naming Names* (New York: Viking, 1980).

36. Compare, for example, the testimony of the Pittsburgh witnesses in *Investigation of*

Un-American Propaganda Activities in the United States, vols. 11–12, discussed in Chapter 2 above.

37. *Investigation of Communist Activities in the Philadelphia Area*, 2966–67.

38. Ibid., 3936.

39. Ibid., 3917, 3924–25.

40. Ibid., 3916.

41. Ibid., 2917–18.

42. Ibid.

43. Ibid., 2918–19.

44. Ibid., 2915–17.

45. Ibid., 2918.

46. Beck, *Contempt of Congress*, 132–33.

47. *Investigation of Communist Activities in the Philadelphia Area*, 2926.

48. Ibid., 2928.

49. Ibid., 3020 (Velde).

50. Ibid., 2931.

51. Ibid., 2957.

52. "Evasive Teachers Blasted by Velde for Failure to Aid War on 'Red Conspiracy,'" *PI*, November 19, 1953.

53. Esther Klein, "The Publisher Speaks Out," *Philadelphia Jewish Times*, November 27, 1953, 1.

54. *Investigation of Communist Activities in the Philadelphia Area*, 3922.

55. Ibid., 3935, 3939.

56. Ibid., 3979–80.

57. Ibid., 3985.

58. Murray Friedman, ed., *Philadelphia Jewish Life, 1940–1985* (Ardmore, Pa.: Seth Press, 1986), 14.

59. *Investigation of Communist Activities in the Philadelphia Area*, 4004.

60. Ibid., 4009.

61. Ibid., 3942–69.

62. Ibid., 3943–44.

63. Ibid., 3945, 3949.

64. Ibid., 6780.

65. Ibid., 6773–98, quotes at 6776, 6791.

66. Ibid., 6793.

67. *Academic Freedom*, 32.

68. David Caute, *The Great Fear: The Anti-Communist Purge under Truman and Eisenhower* (New York: Simon and Schuster, 1978), 555. However, former Teachers' Union president Francis Jennings went on to enjoy an exceptionally productive career as the author of several major historical works on Native Americans and the colonial era. See, for example, his books *The Invasion of America* (Chapel Hill: University of North Carolina Press, 1975) and *The Ambiguous Iroquois Empire* (New York: Norton, 1984).

69. Richard Hofstadter, *The Paranoid Style in American Politics* (Chicago: University of Chicago Press, 1979).

70. Musmanno, *Across the Street from the Courthouse*, 230.

71. Chester Potter, "Ex-Librarian Shuns Red Queries," *PP*, July 1, 1953.

72. Mary Carey, "Seeing Red," *Mount Lebanon Magazine*, December 1995, 46–49.

73. Ellen Schrecker, *No Ivory Tower* (New York: Oxford University Press, 1986); compare Kenneth O'Reilly, ed., *McCarthy Era Blacklisting of School Teachers, College Professors, and Other Public Employees* (Frederick, Md.: University Publications of America, 1989); Charles Howard McCormick, *This Nest of Vipers* (Urbana: University of Illinois Press, 1989); Lionel S. Lewis, *The Cold War and Academic Governance* (Albany: State University of New York Press, 1993); and Robert E. Summers, *Freedom and Loyalty in Our Colleges* (New York: H. W. Wilson, 1954).

74. *29th Annual Convention of the American Legion, Department of Pennsylvania at Pittsburgh, Aug. 7–9, 1947* (American Legion, Department of Pennsylvania, 1947), 432.

75. Michael Bezilla, *Penn State: An Illustrated History* (University Park: Pennsylvania State University Press, 1985), 258–59; Edwin W. Tomkins to C. S. Wyand, July 23, 1951, Fine Papers.

76. Radtke, *History of the Pennsylvania American Legion*, 83; for Lycoming, see Albert Kahn and Arthur Kahn, *High Treason* (New York: Lear, 1950), 293.

77. Fred R. Zimring, "Academic Freedom and the Cold War" (D.Ed. diss., Columbia University, 1981), 127–28.

78. Summers, *Freedom and Loyalty in Our Colleges*; *Teachers' Union News*, October 1951, published by the Teachers' Union of Philadelphia, Local 556, UPW.

79. For comparable developments elsewhere, see, for example, *Academic Freedom "Redefined"* (New York: College Chapter, Teachers Union Local 555, UPW-CIO, 1949).

80. "Summary Analysis of the Loyalty Procedures of the Pennsylvania State College as Applied in the Case of Wendell MacRae," Folder 6, MacRae Case, 1952, Brewster Papers; compare "Before the Loyalty Review Board of Pennsylvania State College in re Wendell MacRae," August 26, 1952, ibid.; Bezilla, *Penn State*, 256–60.

81. "Summary Analysis," Brewster Papers.

82. "Before the Loyalty Review Board," ibid.

83. HUAC, *Communist Methods of Infiltration: Education*, Hearings, February-June 1953, 83d Cong., 1st sess. (Washington, D.C.: GPO, 1953).

84. Typescript, unsigned draft from "Our Organization" to "Dear President Eisenhower," Folder 3, "Academic Freedom 1953," Brewster Papers.

85. Schrecker, *No Ivory Tower*.

86. There is a detailed account of the Dunham case in Zimring, "Academic Freedom and the Cold War." Barrows Dunham, *Man Against Myth* (Boston: Little, Brown, 1947), *Giant in Chains* (Boston: Little, Brown, 1953), and *Heroes and Heretics* (New York: Knopf, 1963). For Dunham's speech during the Philadelphia transit strike, see letters of PFC John C. Friedrich to CO, Troop A, S-4, Philadelphia, August 10–11, 1944, Philadelphia Transit Strike file, State Police Archives, RG 30, PSA.

87. HUAC, *Communist Methods of Infiltration: Education*, 117–19.

88. *Academic Freedom*, 10–12.

89. Beck, *Contempt of Congress*, 102–3; Zimring, "Academic Freedom and the Cold War."

90. *Academic Freedom*, 18.

91. Ralph S. Brown, *Loyalty and Security* (New Haven, Conn.: Yale University Press, 1958), 117.

92. "Four Left-wing Pittsburghers Help Spark Drive for Wallace," *PP*, January 12, 1948; "Pitt Instructor Hits Back," *PPG*, March 22, 1950; Marion Hathaway to Adele Margolis, July 23, 1951, Box 7, Teachers' Union Papers.

93. Somewhat different in character was the 1954 attack on Bela Gold, a faculty member at the University of Pittsburgh, and his wife, Sonia, who taught at the Pennsylvania College for Women. In this case the issue was not left-wing sympathies, but Sonia Gold's involvement in the "spy ring" allegedly connected with Harry Dexter White. See "PCW Teacher Called Red Spy," *PP*, November 18, 1953, and "Sonia Gold Quits as PCW Teacher," *PST*, July 30, 1954.

94. Brown, *Loyalty and Security*, 374–75. For Cvetic's attack on Harris, see *34th Annual Convention of the American Legion, Department of Pennsylvania at Philadelphia, Aug. 6–9, 1952* (American Legion, Department of Pennsylvania, 1952), 86–87; Musmanno, *Across the Street from the Courthouse*, 328; and Michael P. Weber, *Don't Call Me Boss* (Pittsburgh: University of Pittsburgh Press, 1988), 286.

95. Frank M. Matthews, "Justice Musmanno Says, Can Do More in Senate," *PPG*, April 15, 1964.

96. *Investigation of Communist Activities in the Philadelphia Area*, 2957.

97. U.S. Senate, Committee on the Judiciary, SISS, *Subversive Influence in Certain Industrial Plants: Eastern Pennsylvania*, Hearing, 83d Cong., 2d sess., and 84th Cong., 1st sess. (Washington, D.C.: GPO, 1954–55), 35.

CHAPTER 7

1. Quoted in U.S. Senate, Committee on the Judiciary, Subcommittee on Immigration and Naturalization, *Communist Activities among Aliens and National Groups*, Hearing, 81st Cong., 1st sess., on S. 1832 (Washington, D.C.: GPO, 1949), 669 (hereafter cited as *Communist Activities among Aliens and National Groups*).

2. Letter of Peter Bender, State Representative, Swissvale, to Governor James Duff, October 10, 1947, Carton 13, "Communism," Official Papers, 1947–51, Papers of James H. Duff, MS 190, PSA. Bender was of Yugoslav American origin.

3. John E. Bodnar, Roger Simon, and Michael P. Weber, *Lives of Their Own* (Urbana: University of Illinois Press, 1982); John E. Bodnar, *Steelton—Immigration and Industrialization, 1870–1940* (Pittsburgh: University of Pittsburgh Press, 1990); John E. Bodnar, ed., *The Ethnic Experience in Pennsylvania* (Lewisburg, Pa.: Bucknell University Press, 1973); Sally M. Miller, *The Ethnic Press in the United States* (New York: Greenwood Press, 1987).

4. Radio speech, October 20, 1946, ser. 1, Folder 1/11, Henry Dende Papers, MSS 54, Balch Institute for Ethnic Studies, Philadelphia, Pa.; Jan Kowalik, *The Polish Press in America* (San Francisco: R and E Research Associates, 1978).

5. "Finns Now—Who's Next?," *PAJ*, March 7, 1948; compare "PA Congress Head Censors America for Fall of Czechs," in ibid.

6. "18 Poles Condemned in Communist Purge," "Strikes Are Banned by Red Government," *PAJ*, March 14, 1948; "4000 Poles Interned in Red Camp," *PAJ*, March 21, 1948; "Fight on Church to be Continued by Warsaw Reds," *PAJ*, July 4, 1948; and "Russia Holds 500,000 Poles in Jails, Camps," *PAJ*, January 7, 1956.

7. "The President's Speech," *PAJ*, March 21, 1948.

8. "Question and Answer," *PAJ*, September 23, 1950 (all emphases in the original).

9. "Adamic Lecture Raises Red Issue; Begany Speaks for US Democracy," *American Slav*, December 1948, 29–31.

10. "Meet the Parfist," *American Slav*, September 1948, 1–2.

11. "Call on Wealthy to Come Across for Red-Baiting," *The Worker*, October 28, 1945; "Universal Training Backed by Falcons," *PP*, November 24, 1947.

12. "Judge Musmanno Assails Reds in Local Address," *Shamokin News Dispatch*, February 4, 1952.

13. Donald E. Pienkos, *PNA Centennial History* (Boulder, Colo.: East European Monographs/Columbia University Press), 170, 375–76.

14. Kermit McFarland, "Traveling Judge," *PP*, November 14, 1943; Kermit McFarland, "When It Comes to Commies, Gunther Is a Gumshoe," *PP*, March 19, 1950.

15. "Gunther Will Direct Anti-Red Air Show," *PAJ*, April 16, 1949.

16. Alexander Lushnycky, ed., *Ukrainians in Pennsylvania* (Philadelphia: Ukrainian Bicentennial Committee, 1976).

17. "60 Percent in Con-Camp Are Ukrainians," *America*, May 14, 1956.

18. "Bolshevism the Worst Barbarism," *America*, January 13, 1956.

19. "Communists Will Follow New Party Line Like Sheep," *America*, April 5, 1956; "Russian Communist Megalomania in Superlative Degree," *America*, October 4, 1956.

20. "Exposure of Communism in USA," *America*, January 13, 1956.

21. "Sympathy, But Not for Poznan Workers," *America*, July 19, 1956.

22. M. Mark Stolarik, *Growing Up on the South Side* (Lewisburg, Pa.: Bucknell University Press, 1985), and *Immigration and Urbanization* (New York: AMS Press, 1989).

23. Joseph Pauco, ed., *Sixty Years of the Slovak League of America* (Middletown, Pa.: Slovak League of America, 1967), 112–19.

24. Pauco, *Sixty Years of the Slovak League*, 73–86. Joseph Pauco, "Dr. Joseph Tiso: Christian Democrat," *Slovakia* 7, no. 2 (June 1957): 37–50; Milan S. Durica, "Dr. Joseph Tiso and the Jewish Problem in Slovakia," *Slovakia* 7, no. 3–4 (1957): 1–22.

25. In 1957 *Slovakia* devoted a special commemorative issue to the tenth anniversary of the death of Tiso, "executed on the gallows by the Benes-Gottwald Communist-dominated government" (7, no. 1 [March 1957]). For its "ranting," see *Communist Activities among Aliens and National Groups*, 381.

26. "La III Guerra Mondiale In Pieno Svolgimento," *ON*, January 24, 1948.

27. A. Bilotti, "Perche Gli Italiani Sappiano Chi E' Palmiro Togliatti," *ON*, September 20, 1947; "L'Ecatombe dell'Armir Dopo la Cattura," *ON*, October 11, 1947.

28. George J. Spatuzza, "Appello agli Americani di Origine Italiana," *ON*, November 15, 1947; "Sons of Italy Cheer Proposal to Fight Reds to the Death," *ON*, November 15, 1947; A. Bilotti, "Le Fasi Attraverso Cui E Passata la Politica Italiana," *ON*, September 27, 1947.

29. "Esistono in Italia le Precesse per un Colpo di Stato?," *ON*, December 5, 1947; "Appello ai Giovani Americani Combattere il Comunismo Perche' Vuol Rendere Schiavi della Materia Bruta," *ON*, December 20, 1947; "Sconfiggere la Brutale Tirannia Comunista," *ON*, April 3, 1948; "Dio Salvi L'Immortale Italia dal Comunismo Distruttore," *ON*, April 17, 1948; "Le Forze Anti-Cristiane Sconfitte in Italia," *ON*, April 17, 1948.

30. "I Repubblicani e l'Italia," *Libera Parola*, May 3, 1947.

31. "I Comunisti d'Italia," *Libera Parola*, October 18, 1947; "Da Mussolini a Togliatti in Italia," *Libera Parola*, September 20, 1947.

32. "L'Appuntamento con Destino in Italia," *Libera Parola*, April 10, 1948.

33. "Un Editoriale del *Pittsburgh Press* Incitante gli Italo-Americani a scrivere lettere in Italia a Parenti e Amici per Smentire le False Accuse dei Comunisti," *Unione*, February 20,

1948. Compare Ronald L. Filippelli, *American Labor and Postwar Italy, 1943–1953* (Stanford: Stanford University Press, 1989).

34. "La Nostra Patriottica Campagna Per L'Invio di Lettere in Italia," *Unione*, March 5, 1948; front page of *Unione*, March 19, 1948.

35. "L'Italia in Pericolo," *Unione*, March 12, 1948; "Schiaccante Vittoria Demo-Cristiana in Italia," *Unione*, April 23, 1948. The themes for the Truman speech in Scranton are from notes in Library Clippings, Box 168, Pennsylvania file, Democratic National Committee Papers, Truman Library.

36. *Communist Activities among Aliens and National Groups*, 9, 471–73. Louis F. Budenz, *Men without Faces* (New York: Harper, 1950), 55–66; Jacob Spolansky, *The Communist Trail in America* (New York: Macmillan, 1951), 58–68.

37. Oliver H. Crawford, "Racial Equality Group Bars Troublesome Reds," *PI*, October 17, 1945.

38. Paul Lyons, "Philadelphia Jews and Radicalism," in *Philadelphia Jewish Life, 1940–1985*, ed. Murray Friedman (Ardmore, Pa.: Seth Press, 1986), 107–24.

39. Michael A. Musmanno, *Justice Musmanno Dissents* (Indianapolis: Bobbs-Merrill, 1956), 423–42.

40. Ronald W. Schatz, *The Electrical Workers* (Urbana: University of Illinois Press, 1983), 190, 196.

41. HUAC, *Report on the ASC and Associated Organizations* (Washington, D.C.: GPO, 1949), 51–57 (hereafter cited as *Report on the ASC*); *Communist Activities among Aliens and National Groups*, 613–16.

42. "Local Editors Make Journeys to Yugoslavia," *PP*, November 18, 1947; *Communist Activities among Aliens and National Groups*, 50, 615–19; HUAC, *Exposé of the Communist Party of Western Pennsylvania Based upon Testimony of Matthew Cvetic, Undercover Agent*, Hearings, 81st Cong., 2d sess. (Washington, D.C.: GPO, 1950), 1199.

43. *Communist Activities among Aliens and National Groups*, 475–77; *Exposé of the Communist Party*, 1204–21.

44. *Report on the ASC*, 60–62. *Ludovy Dennik* was subsequently replaced by the *Ludove Noviny*, or People's News.

45. *Report on the ASC*, 62–63; *Communist Activities among Aliens and National Groups*, 371–73; "Reds Offered Cvetic $4,000 to Start Paper," *PP*, May 28, 1952.

46. *Report on the ASC*, 54; Steve Nelson, James R. Barrett, and Rob Ruck, *Steve Nelson: American Radical* (Pittsburgh: University of Pittsburgh Press, 1981), 306; "Cloak and Dagger," *Bulletin Index*, June 22, 1946; "Slav Congress Loses Red Line Spokesman," *PP*, March 2, 1949.

47. "Ex Army Spy Defies Probers," *PP*, June 11, 1953; George Wuchinich, "As a Veteran Sees It," *Slavic American*, Fall 1947, 9–10.

48. Quoted in *Communist Activities among Aliens and National Groups*, 373.

49. Ibid., 603–713.

50. *Narodni Glasnik*, May 9, 1947, quoted in ibid., 611.

51. *Slobodna Rec*, May 27, 1947, quoted in ibid.

52. *Narodni Glasnik*, December 1, 1948, quoted in ibid., 610.

53. Ibid., 663–70.

54. *Exposé of the Communist Party*, 1196; Robert Taylor "Yugoslav Relief Organizations Keep Close to Red Party Line," *PP*, November 20, 1947.

55. *Exposé of the Communist Party*, 1201–6.

56. Ibid., 1204; see below for the 1944 ASC convention.

57. *Communist Activities among Aliens and National Groups*, 56; Louis Adamic, *Laughing in the Jungle* (New York: Harpers, 1932); Ivan John Molek, "Slovene Immigrant History, 1900–1950" (Dover, Del., 1979; typescript in Balch Institute for Ethnic Studies, Philadelphia, Pa.), 264–345; *Shall Slovenia Be Sovietized? A Rebuttal to Louis Adamic* (Cleveland: Union of Slovenian Parishes of America, 1944).

58. *Exposé of the Communist Party*, 1212; compare Molek, *Slovene Immigrant History*, 271.

59. Robert Taylor "Serbian Bishop under Attack for Resistance to Reds," *PP*, November 22, 1947.

60. U.S. Senate, Committee on the Judiciary, SISS, *Subversive Influence in the United Electrical, Radio and Machine Workers of America (UERMWA), Pittsburgh and Erie, Pa. (Investigation Relative to Legislation Designed to Curb Communist Penetration and Domination of Labor Organizations)*, Hearings, November 1953, 83d Cong., 1st sess. (Washington, D.C.: GPO, 1954), 23 for "military invasion," 83, 184–86.

61. *Digest of the Public Record of Communism in the United States* (New York: Fund for the Republic, 1955), 418.

62. Nelson, Barrett, and Ruck, *Steve Nelson*, 22.

63. *Communist Activities among Aliens and National Groups*, 629; *Report on the ASC*, 72, 84–88; Ivan Cizmic, *History of the Croatian Fraternal Union of America, 1894–1994* (Zagreb, Croatia: Golden Marketing, 1994), 245–47.

64. *Report on the ASC*, 72.

65. *Communist Activities among Aliens and National Groups*, 613–16, puts the paper's circulation at 100,000.

66. Robert Taylor, "New Croatian Group Led by Alien Radical—Borich Also Writes for Commie Press," *PP*, November 19, 1947; *Communist Activities among Aliens and National Groups*, 625; Cizmic, *History of the Croatian Fraternal Union*, 265–94.

67. "27 Groups Here Named in New Subversive List," *PP*, March 12, 1951.

68. Spolansky, *Communist Trail in America*, 58–68.

69. Kermit McFarland, "Traveling Judge," *PP*, November 14, 1943; Kermit McFarland, "When It Comes to Commies, Gunther Is a Gumshoe," *PP*, March 19, 1950.

70. "Slavs Hear Ickes in Pittsburgh," *American Slav*, July 1942, n.p.

71. *Report on the ASC*, 15.

72. *Communist Activities among Aliens and National Groups*, 630–36.

73. *Second American Slav Congress: Sept. 23–24, 1944, Carnegie Music Hall, Pittsburgh, Pa.* (Pittsburgh: American Slav Congress, 1944).

74. See, for example, recurrent stories in the Scranton-based *PAJ*.

75. Pienkos, *PNA Centennial History*, 151–85.

76. *Second American Slav Congress*.

77. *Voice of the American Slav*, May-June 1944; Louis Adamic, *1944 . . . Crucial Year: The Need of Dynamic Unity in the Immigrant Groups* (New York: United Committee of South Slavic Americans, 1944); *Exposé of the Communist Party*, 1200.

78. *Report on the ASC*, 18.

79. Transcript, Testimony on Reports of Subversive Activities in the Pittsburgh Area, SISS, Committee of the Judiciary, U.S. Senate, June 16, 1955, 627, Boxes 62–63, "The Mullen Case," Michael A. Musmanno Papers, DU.

80. *Report on the ASC*, 18–19.

81. *Communist Activities among Aliens and National Groups*, 374.

82. Radio speech, October 20, 1946, ser. 1, Folder 1/11, Dende Papers; compare Leo Krzycki, *What I Saw in the Slavic Countries* (New York: ASC, 1946).

83. *Exposé of the Communist Party*, 2366.

84. *Report on the ASC*, 23–24; *Rally to Win the Peace: American Slav Congress, New York, Sept. 20, 21, 22, 1946—Manhattan Center* (New York: ASC, 1946).

85. See, for example, Pienkos, *PNA Centennial History*, 164–76; "Serbs Are Betrayed at Yalta," *The American Serb* 2, no. 2 (February 1945): 1; "Charges Tito Has Betrayed Yugoslavia," *The American Serb* 2, no. 7 (December 1945): 1.

86. George Pirinsky, *The Struggle for Peace and Democracy in USA* (New York: American Slav Congress, 1947).

87. *Exposé of the Communist Party*, 1209–10. For Rudiak, see "51 Here on Wallace Sponsor List," *PP*, February 8, 1948; "Testimony Hits Role of Schlesinger," *PP*, March 10, 1959.

88. "Director of Wallace Group Here Draws $300 Monthly," *PP*, August 5, 1948.

89. *Exposé of the Communist Party*, 1237–38; *Communist Activities among Aliens and National Groups*, 373.

90. File on the Progressive Party, 1949, Papers of M. Y. Steinberg, UE Labor Archive, UP.

91. *Report on the ASC*, 30.

92. Anna W. Pennypacker, "Pennsylvanians Launch Third Party," *The Worker*, March 14, 1948.

93. See, for example, Leo Krzycki, "Henry Wallace: Champion of Peace," *Slavic American*, Fall 1947, 3–4; "Slavic Americans Help Found the Progressive Party," *Slavic American*, Summer 1948, 4–7.

94. *Exposé of the Communist Party*, 1224.

95. Robert Taylor, "Communists Try to Use Slavic Groups in US as Red Party Front," *PP*, November 16, 1947, for the "intensive campaign." Other articles by Taylor in this series included "Slavic Papers Here Receive Soviet Service," November 17; "Local Editors Make Journeys to Yugoslavia," November 18; "New Croatian Group Led by Alien Radical— Borich Also Writes for Commie Press," November 19; "Yugoslav Relief Organizations Keep Close to Red Party Line," November 20; "Communist Nations Trying to Lure American Slavs Back to Homeland," November 21; "Serbian Bishop under Attack for Resistance to Reds," November 22; "American Slav Congress Is Chief Party Line Front," November 23; "Slav Congress Is Always on the Moscow Line," November 24; "Pro-Commie-Slav Congress Now Tries to Hide Membership," November 25.

96. Robert Taylor, "Pro-Commie-Slav Congress Now Tries to Hide Membership," *PP*, November 25, 1947.

97. *Communist Activities among Aliens and National Groups*, 637–38 for the quote from *Slobodna Rec*, 676 for the ASC response.

98. Art Shields, *Pittsburgh: Peace on Trial* (reprinted from *Masses and Mainstream*, published by the Committee to Defend the Pittsburgh Frame-Up Victims, 1951), 13.

99. *Communist Activities among Aliens and National Groups*, 371–73.

100. Ibid. By the early 1960s Draskovich was a national figure in the emerging John Birch Society; see J. Allen Broyles, *The John Birch Society* (Boston: Beacon, 1964). For Zorkin, see Cizmic, *History of the Croatian Fraternal Union*, 288–89.

101. "House Probers Eye Reds Here, Quiz Two," *PST*, March 20, 1949; *Report on the ASC*, 1–2.

102. "Pittsburgh Number One Sabotage Target for Reds, Court Told," *PP*, January 8, 1952.

103. Tony Smith, "25 in Congress in Red Front Donation List," *PP*, February 25, 1950.

104. For the death of Adamic, see "Adamic Shot Dead, Threat Is Disclosed," *Washington Post*, September 5, 1951. For the movement against the ethnic organizations, compare Arthur J. Sabin, *Red Scare in Court* (Philadelphia: University of Pennsylvania Press, 1993).

105. Paul Lyons, "Philadelphia Jews and Radicalism," in *Philadelphia Jewish Life, 19402–1985*, ed. Murray Friedman (Ardmore, Pa.: Seth Press, 1986), 107–24. For the Progressive Party, see the correspondence with J. W. Gitt in 1950–51, in Box 2, Josiah W. Gitt Papers, HCLA.

106. *32nd Annual Convention of the American Legion, Department of Pennsylvania at Philadelphia, Aug. 9–12, 1950* (American Legion, Department of Pennsylvania, 1950), 71.

107. Nelson, Barrett, and Ruck, *Steve Nelson*, 306–7.

108. "Polish American Congress," *American Slav*, June 1956, 2–5.

109. "Anti-Semitism Rampant behind Iron Curtain," *Jewish Exponent*, December 21, 1951, 27; "Jewish Leaders Hit Anti-Semitic Purge," *Philadelphia Jewish Times*, December 5, 1952, 2.

110. "'Peace at Any Price' Blasted by Gunther," *American Slav*, December 1956, 4–6.

111. Press release, National Confederation of American Ethnic Groups, ca. 1956, Box 3, Folder 1, American Latvian Association of the United States, MSS 23, Balch Institute for Ethnic Studies, Philadelphia, Pa.

112. Scott Anderson and Jon Lee Anderson, *Inside the League* (New York: Dodd, Mead, 1986).

CHAPTER 8

1. "Billy Graham Predicts End of World Near," *PP*, September 20, 1952.

2. Martin Marty, *Modern American Religion: Under God Indivisible, 1941–1960*, vol. 3 (Chicago: University of Chicago Press, 1996).

3. Donald F. Crosby, *God, Church, and Flag* (Chapel Hill: University of North Carolina Press, 1978), 16–18.

4. Vito Mazzone, *Communism: The Satanic Scourge* (Philadelphia: Community Press, 1963), 59; Matthew Cvetic, *The Big Decision* (Hollywood, Calif.: The Big Decision, 1959), 69–78, quote at 77.

5. For the labor schools, see Oral History interview with Harry Block, 1967, 20–22, HCLA; "A Good Movement: Philadelphia Sets an Excellent Example with an Anti-Communist School," *PPG*, December 11, 1935. For Duquesne, see "Louis Budenz to Lecture at Duquesne," *PST*, September 21, 1952, 21; "Scripts from TV Programs *The Case against Communism*, programs 1–5," Institute on Communism, University Archives, DU. I am very grateful to Dr. Joseph Rishel for sharing his work in progress on Duquesne in this period.

6. John L. Spivak, *Pattern for American Fascism* (New York: New Century, 1947), 62–66; see Harvey Klehr, John Earl Haynes, and F. I. Firsov, *The Secret World of American Communism* (New Haven, Conn.: Yale University Press, 1995), for Spivak's possible role as an important clandestine member of the Communist security apparatus.

7. Compare Charles R. Morris, *American Catholic* (New York: Times Books, 1997), 246–50; Crosby, *God, Church, and Flag*, 47–52; Marty, *Modern American Religion*, 354–75; John E. Cronin, *Communism: A World Menace* (Washington, D.C.: National Catholic Welfare Conference, 1947).

8. Paul B. Beers, *Pennsylvania Politics Today and Yesterday* (University Park: Pennsylvania State University Press, 1980), 359. By the late 1970s the Catholic proportion of the state legislature was approaching one-half. James T. Fisher, *The Catholic Counterculture in America, 1933–1962* (Chapel Hill: University of North Carolina Press, 1989).

9. "Which Government?," *Register* (Altoona-Johnstown, Pa.), December 8, 1946.

10. "It's Getting to Be a Party Line," *Register*, January 11, 1948.

11. Cartoon, *Register*, February 12, 1950.

12. "With Men Who Know Tobacco Best," *Register*, April 23, 1950; "Smog over Washington," *Register*, May 21, 1950.

13. See Crosby, *God, Church, and Flag*, 96–98, 115–19, 228–51; Michael O'Brien, *McCarthy and McCarthyism in Wisconsin* (Columbia: University of Missouri Press, 1980), 176–80.

14. Thomas C. Reeves, *The Life and Times of Joe McCarthy* (New York: Stein and Day, 1982), 644; David M. Oshinsky, *A Conspiracy So Immense* (New York: Free Press, 1983).

15. James F. Connally, ed., *The History of the Archdiocese of Philadelphia* (Philadelphia: Archdiocese of Philadelphia, 1976).

16. The ideological importance of Fátima is stressed by Morris, *American Catholic*, and Richard Gid Powers, *Not without Honor* (New York: Free Press, 1995).

17. Owen Chadwick, *The Christian Church in the Cold War* (New York: Penguin, 1983), 16.

18. Morris, *American Catholic*, 229; Thomas A. Kselman and Steven Avella, "Marian Piety and the Cold War in the United States," *Catholic Historical Review*, July 1986, 403–24.

19. John Cooney, *The American Pope* (New York: Times Books, 1984).

20. This account is based on Chadwick, *The Christian Church in the Cold War*.

21. Crosby, *God, Church, and Flag*, 8–9.

22. "20,000 at Meeting Urge Release of Yugoslav Prelate," *PI*, December 2, 1946.

23. *28th Annual Convention of the American Legion, Department of Pennsylvania at Philadelphia, Aug. 21–24, 1946* (American Legion, Department of Pennsylvania, 1946), 31–32.

24. Ronald L. Filippelli and Mark McColloch, *Cold War in the Working Class* (Albany: State University of New York Press, 1995), 132–33.

25. "Red-baiting" file, Box 4, Papers of UE Local 601, 1949–52, UE Labor Archive, UP.

26. Filippelli and McColloch, *Cold War in the Working Class*, 150.

27. "Societies Join Forces against Advances by Reds," *Register*, April 21, 1946; "Eastern Rite Catholics Are Standing Firm in Face of Forced Red Schism," *Register*, January 2, 1949.

28. "Archbishop Stepinac Case Arouses Horror in World," *Register*, October 20, 1946; "Protests Pour from Whole World" and "Another Christ before Pilate," both *Register*, October 27, 1946.

29. "On Trial Again," *Register*, January 23, 1949.

30. Compare Powers, *Not without Honor*, 227–28; Crosby, *God, Church, and Flag*, 11–12. The Mindszenty case gave Hollywood the theme for its pious 1949 film *Guilty of Treason*.

31. The following stories are all from the *Register*: "Eastern Rite Catholics Are Standing Firm in Face of Forced Red Schism," January 2, 1949; "Plot to Destroy Church Is Threatened in Poland," January 16, 1949; "Commies Step Up Persecution Tempo," January 30, 1949; "120 Greek Rite Priests Arrested [in Romania]," February 6, 1949; "Reds Slay Abbot at Prison Camp," February 27, 1949; "Priest Refuses to Break Seal of Confession, Gets Prison Term [in Yugoslavia]," March 6, 1949; and "Polish Clergy Suffering New Persecution for Their Faith," March 20, 1949.

32. *Register*, February 6, 1949.

33. *Register*, December 26, 1954.

34. *Register*, October 21, 1956.

35. Mazzone, *Communism*, 83–85.

36. "Blessed Sacrament Miracle Reports," *Register*, April 11, 1954.

37. O'Brien, *McCarthy and McCarthyism in Wisconsin*, 176–80.

38. "Johnstown Forum Speaker Criticizes China Policy," *Register*, October 24, 1948.

39. "AOH Resolutions Are Protest against Communist Oppression," *Register*, February 20, 1949, 8.

40. "Windber Unit of Holy Name Society Voices Condemnation of Red-Run Persecution," *Register*, March 6, 1949.

41. Terry Radtke, *The History of the Pennsylvania American Legion* (Mechanicsburg, Pa.: Stackpole, 1993), 75.

42. Morris, *American Catholic*, 229, and 228–54; compare Kenneth D. Wald, "The Religious Dimension of American Anti-communism," *Journal of Church and State* 36 (1994): 483–506.

43. "Time to Awake," *Register*, September 25, 1949.

44. Bernard McGinn, *Antichrist* (San Francisco, Calif.: HarperSanFrancisco, 1994).

45. "The Great Apostasy and the Antichrist," *Register*, March 27, 1949.

46. "Listening In: The Coming of the Dreadful Antichrist," *Register*, August 12, 1951.

47. See, for example, "Le Forze Anti-Cristiane Sconfitte in Italia," *ON*, April 17, 1948.

48. "The Only Safe State," *Register*, April 25, 1954.

49. HUAC, *Trial by Treason: The National Committee to Secure Justice for the Rosenbergs and Morton Sobell* (Washington, D.C.: GPO, 1956), 78–82.

50. Michael A. Musmanno, *Across the Street from the Courthouse* (Philadelphia: Dorrance, 1954), 314. For the Friends and the loyalty oath bill, see extensive correspondence in Teachers' Union Papers, Boxes 7–9, URB 36, TU.

51. Cedric Belfrage, *The American Inquisition, 1945–1960* (Indianapolis: Bobbs-Merrill, 1973), 200–201, 255; David Caute, *The Great Fear: The Anti-Communist Purge under Truman and Eisenhower* (New York: Simon and Schuster, 1978), 454–55; Thomas C. Reeves, *Freedom and the Foundation* (New York: Knopf, 1969).

52. Robert S. Ellwood, *The Fifties Spiritual Marketplace* (New Brunswick, N.J.: Rutgers University Press, 1997).

53. Henry C. Patterson Papers, MS series 4, Balch Institute for Ethnic Studies, Philadelphia, Pa.; also see letter to Whittaker Chambers, July 10, 1950, Whittaker Chambers case file, ibid.

54. Quoted in Musmanno, *Across the Street from the Courthouse*, 310–12.

55. Daniel A. Poling, *Mine Eyes Have Seen* (New York: McGraw-Hill, 1959), 249; *32nd Annual Convention of the American Legion, Department of Pennsylvania at Philadelphia, Aug. 9–12, 1950* (American Legion, Department of Pennsylvania, 1950), 71.

56. Poling, *Mine Eyes Have Seen*, 212, 240–45.

57. Walter Lowenfels, "Poling Speaks for Billionaires in Backing War Against China," *The Worker*, October 21, 1951.

58. Mary Sennholz, *Faith and Freedom* (Grove City, Pa.: Grove City Press, 1975).

59. Pew to Senator John Bricker, November 13, 1956, Box 1, MS Group 8, BGC Archives.

60. Pew to Bell, May 15, 1959, ibid.

61. Pew to L. Nelson Bell, July 11, 1960, Folder 4, Box 31, Papers of L. Nelson Bell, Collec-

tion 318, BGC Archives; compare Billy James Hargis, *The Facts about Communism and Our Churches* (Tulsa, Okla.: Christian Crusade, 1962).

62. Appeal of May 23, 1956, Folder 57, Box 1, Records of *Christianity Today*, MS Group 8, BGC Archives; Marty, *Modern American Religion*, 266–68; Poling, *Mine Eyes Have Seen*, 280–81.

63. Bell to Pew, May 11, 1962, Box 1, MS Group 8, BGC Archives. Pew never obtained anything like the propaganda sheet he was seeking, and *Christianity Today* evolved into one of the most respected of American religious publications, but it is doubtful that it would have seen the light of day if not for the radical Right aspirations of J. Howard Pew.

64. Bell to Pew, August 27, 1958, Box 1, MS Group 8, BGC Archives; for HUAC, see correspondence in Folder 23, Box 29, Bell Papers; Bell to Walter Judd, July 9, 1960, Folder 4, Box 31, ibid.

65. For Pew's support of Graham's 1961 crusade in Philadelphia, see Pew to Bell, April 26, 1961, Box 1, MS Group 8, BGC Archives. Another conservative ally was Walter Judd, U.S. representative from Minnesota's Fifth District and another former China missionary; for Judd correspondence, see Folder 4, Box 31, Bell Papers. For Graham and Pew, see Sennholz, *Faith and Freedom*, 58.

66. William C. Martin, *With God on Our Side* (New York: Broadway, 1996); Marty, *Modern American Religion*, 150–53.

67. *PST*, September 8, 1952.

68. "Christianity Can Stop Reds, Billy Graham Declares Here," *PST*, September 7, 1952.

69. Paul S. Boyer, *When Time Shall Be No More* (Cambridge, Mass.: Belknap Press, 1992), 157.

70. Gordon Palmer, "Men of the Right," reprinted in *Johnson City Press-Chronicle* (Tennessee), July 18, 1962. For the emerging evangelical networks of these years, see Joel Carpenter, *Revive Us Again* (New York: Oxford University Press, 1997).

71. Samuel M. Shoemaker, ed., *Faith at Work* (New York: Hawthorn, 1958); Helen Smith Shoemaker, *I Stand By the Door* (New York: Harper and Row, 1967).

72. "VFW Council to Pay Honor to Minister," *PPG*, April 23, 1961.

73. Bill Lamkin, "Church Faces Tough Enemy," *Charlotte Observer*, March 30, 1960.

74. Edward J. Meeman, "Pastor's Book Says Sects Have a Place," *New York World Telegram*, July 9, 1960.

75. Walter Goodman, *The Committee* (New York: Farrar, Straus, Giroux, 1968), 333–41; Robert M. Miller, *Bishop G. Bromley Oxnam—Paladin of Liberal Protestantism* (Nashville, Tenn.: Abingdon Press, 1990).

76. Powers, *Not without Honor*, 251.

77. Goodman, *The Committee*, 405–7; Hoover to Pew, May 31, 1961, Box 1, MS Group 8, BGC Archives; compare Hargis, *The Facts about Communism and Our Churches*, 151; Matt Cvetic, "Communism in Our Churches," *Christian Crusade*, February 1961.

78. Shoemaker, *Faith at Work*.

79. Folders 10–17, Box 2, Records of The Navigators, MS Group 7, BGC Archives.

80. Arthur T. Moore, "Three Faiths Uniting for American Day," *PST*, September 7, 1952.

81. Arthur H. Lewis, *The Aaronsburg Story* (New York: Vanguard Press, 1955).

82. Francis B. Thornton, *Sea of Glory* (New York: Prentice-Hall, 1953).

83. Poling, *Mine Eyes Have Seen*, 256.

84. Radtke, *The History of the Pennsylvania American Legion*, 74.

CHAPTER 9

1. Quoted in "Rosenbergs Revisited," *Commonweal*, December 28, 1973.

2. David A. Shannon, *The Decline of American Communism* (New York: Harcourt, Brace, 1959); Joseph R. Starobin, *American Communism in Crisis, 1943–1957* (Cambridge, Mass.: Harvard University Press, 1972). For the loss of faith in Communism about this time by one of the former Smith Act defendants, see Sherman Labovitz, *Being Red in Philadelphia* (Philadelphia: Camino Books, 1998), 143–48.

3. Thomas Rosteck, *See It Now Confronts McCarthyism* (Tuscaloosa: University of Alabama Press, 1994); John G. Adams, *Without Precedent* (New York: W. W. Norton, 1983).

4. Edward Lamb, *No Lamb for Slaughter* (New York: Harcourt, Brace and World, 1963), preface.

5. Stenographic transcript of hearings, SISS, Committee of the Judiciary, U.S. Senate, February 3, 1954, and August 11, 1954, executive session, Boxes 62–63, "The Mullen Case," Michael A. Musmanno Papers, DU; Transcript, Testimony on Reports of Subversive Activities in the Pittsburgh Area, SISS, Committee of the Judiciary, U.S. Senate, June 10, 11, 16, 1955, ibid. (hereafter cited as SISS, Mullen Transcript). "Charge Musmanno Aid to Takers of Bribes," *The Worker*, March 1, 1953; "Musmanno Slapped Down by State Supreme Court," *PPG*, May 26, 1955; "Musmanno-Mullen Case Opinion for Record," *PP*, June 21, 1955; "Under a Cloud," *PST*, June 24, 1955; Frank M. Matthews, "Justice Musmanno Says, Can Do More in Senate," *PPG*, April 15, 1964. For Mullen as a "Labor Mayor," see Benjamin Appel, *The People Talk* (New York: Touchstone, 1982), 120–26.

6. SISS, Mullen Transcript, 589.

7. Lamb, *No Lamb for Slaughter*, 35.

8. Ibid., 167, for "coaching"; "Red Probers Approve Erie TV License," *PP*, December 8, 1953; "Turnabout Witness Jailed for Lying in Lamb Case," *PPG*, June 21, 1955.

9. "Mazzei Free on $2,000 Bail," *PST*, June 19, 1955; David Caute, *The Great Fear: The Anti-Communist Purge under Truman and Eisenhower* (New York: Simon and Schuster, 1978), 221–22.

10. Griffin Fariello, *Red Scare* (New York: Norton, 1995), 211; Cedric Belfrage, *The American Inquisition, 1945–1960* (Indianapolis: Bobbs-Merrill, 1973), 252–53.

11. Quoted in Caute, *The Great Fear*, 222.

12. Papers of Hymen Schlesinger, UE Labor Archive, UP, only partly catalogued at the time of writing. I am grateful to Dr. David Rosenberg for his assistance with these papers.

13. Belfrage, *The American Inquisition*, 252–53.

14. Daniel J. Leab, "Anti-Communism, the FBI and Matt Cvetic," *Pennsylvania Magazine of History and Biography* 115 (1991): 576–77; Harvey M. Matusow, *False Witness* (New York: Cameron and Kahn, 1955). Compare John Henry Faulk, *Fear on Trial* (New York: Simon and Schuster, 1964). Crouch often contradicted himself in the Philadelphia trials, and his whole reputation now crumbled: Joseph and Stewart Alsop, "US Witness in Red Trial Here Faces Perjury Probe," *PEB*, May 18, 1954, and "Crouch Explains Davis Testimony," *PEB*, June 3, 1954. See Caute, *The Great Fear*, 126–32.

15. Cvetic had a long record of drink-related problems, and his enemies publicized a 1939 case in which he had beaten his sister-in-law so badly that she was hospitalized. See *What His Ex-Wife Says About Matt Cvetic, FBI Stool Pigeon and Labor Spy* (Pittsburgh: Communist Party of Western Pennsylvania, 1950).

16. Milton K. Susman, *Pittsburgh Jewish Criterion*, February 11, 1955.

17. "Self-Styled FBI Aide to Pay Alimony," *PPG*, July 7, 1955.

18. Thomas J. Quinn Papers, UE Labor Archive, UP.

19. "US Questions Mazzei on His FBI Testimony," *PPG*, September 29, 1956; "Four Other Top Reds Included," *PPG*, October 11, 1956; "Victim of Mazzei Testimony Reinstated," *PPG*, December 7, 1956.

20. Samuel Walker, *In Defense of American Liberties* (New York: Oxford University Press, 1990), 243–44.

21. Caute, *The Great Fear*, 208; Sherman Labovitz, *Being Red in Philadelphia* (Philadelphia: Camino Books, 1998); "Court Acquits Four Communist Leaders Here," *PEB*, November 13, 1957.

22. Donald J. Kemper, *Decade of Fear* (Columbia: University of Missouri Press, 1965), 142–50.

23. Francis Eugene Walter, *Chronicle of Treason*, HUAC, 85th Cong., 2d sess. (Washington, D.C.: GPO, 1958), 3–6.

24. Ibid., 3–4.

25. HUAC, *"Operation Abolition": The Campaign against the House Committee on Un-American Activities, the FBI [and] the Government Security Program by the Emergency Civil Liberties Committee and Its Affiliates* (Washington, D.C.: GPO, 1957).

26. HUAC's hearings on the Greater Pittsburgh area were respectively entitled *Current Strategy and Tactics of Communists in the United States*, *Problems of Security in Industrial Establishments*, and *Problems Arising in Cases of Denaturalization and Deportation of Communists*, 86th Cong., 1st sess. (Washington, D.C.: GPO, 1959). U.S. Senate, Committee on the Judiciary, SISS, *Scope of Soviet Activity in the United States*, Hearing, 85th Cong., 1st sess. (Washington, D.C.: GPO, 1957).

27. U.S. Senate, Committee on the Judiciary, SISS, *Revitalizing of the Communist Party in the Philadelphia Area*, Hearings, 86th Cong., 1st sess. (Washington, D.C.: GPO, 1959), 69.

28. Anti-Communist pamphlets, Henry C. Patterson Papers, MS series 4, Balch Institute for Ethnic Studies, Philadelphia, Pa.

29. Scott Anderson and Jon Lee Anderson, *Inside the League* (New York: Dodd, Mead, 1986).

30. Dennis J. Comey, *The Waterfront Peacemaker* (Philadelphia: Saint Joseph's University Press, 1983).

31. Leo P. Ribuffo, *The Old Christian Right* (Philadelphia: Temple University Press, 1983); Brooks R. Walker, *The Christian Fright Peddlers* (Garden City, N.Y.: Doubleday, 1964); Billy James Hargis, *The Facts About Communism and Our Churches* (Tulsa, Okla.: Christian Crusade, 1962); John Harold Redekop, *The American Far Right* (Grand Rapids, Mich.: Eerdmans, 1968).

32. Benjamin R. Epstein and Arnold Forster, *The Radical Right* (New York: Random House, 1967), 7, 71–72; Walker, *The Christian Fright Peddlers*, 96–106.

33. Bell to Pew, October 17, 1961, Folder 59, Box 1, MS Group 8, BGC Archives; Pew to Bell, October 25, 1961, ibid.; Martin Marty, *Modern American Religion: Under God Indivisible, 1941–1960*, vol. 3 (Chicago: University of Chicago Press, 1996), 371–74; Robert Griffith, *The Politics of Fear*, 2d ed. (Amherst: University of Massachusetts Press, 1987), 75.

34. Seymour M. Lipset and Earl Raab, *The Politics of Unreason*, 2d ed. (Chicago: University of Chicago Press, 1978); Daniel Bell, ed., *The New American Right*, rev. ed. (New York:

Anchor, 1964); Donald Janson and Bernard Eismann, *The Far Right* (New York: McGraw-Hill, 1963); Mark Sherwin, *The Extremists* (New York: St. Martin's Press, 1963); J. Allen Broyles, *The John Birch Society* (Boston: Beacon, 1964).

35. Leab, "Anti-Communism, the FBI and Matt Cvetic," 579.

36. *Bulletin of the John Birch Society*, November 1965, 85.

37. John Birch Society handbill, SPC 359, Balch Institute for Ethnic Studies, Philadelphia, Pa.; Julia C. Brown, *I Testify* (Boston: Western Islands, 1966).

38. Epstein and Forster, *The Radical Right*, 198–202.

39. Benjamin R. Epstein and Arnold Forster, *Report on the John Birch Society* (New York: Random House, 1966), 54–55.

40. James D. Colbert, "The Crisis Hour of Liberty," *63rd Annual State Convention, The Pennsylvania State Society, DAR* (Harrisburg: DAR, 1959), 56–66; Edward Merrill Root, *Collectivism on the Campus* (New York: Devin-Adair, 1955).

41. *59th Annual State Convention, The Pennsylvania State Society, DAR* (Harrisburg: DAR, 1955), 69.

42. *62nd Annual State Convention, The Pennsylvania State Society, DAR* (Harrisburg: DAR, 1958), 49.

43. *64th Annual State Convention, The Pennsylvania State Society, DAR* (Harrisburg: DAR, 1960), 56–57.

44. Paul Lyons, *Philadelphia Communists, 1936–1956* (Philadelphia: Temple University Press, 1982), 164; the quote is from Caute, *The Great Fear*, 537–38.

45. J. Harry Jones, *The Minutemen* (Garden City, N.Y.: Doubleday, 1968).

46. Frank J. Donner, *The Un-Americans* (New York: Ballantine, 1961).

47. Hargis, *The Facts about Communism and Our Churches*; Walter Goodman, *The Committee* (New York: Farrar, Straus, Giroux, 1968), 399–418.

48. "An Appeal to the House of Representatives: Abolish HUAC," *NYT*, February 22, 1962.

49. SISS, *Revitalizing of the Communist Party in the Philadelphia Area*, 52–67.

50. Ibid., 53.

51. Joseph H. Miller, "Convention Ends with Rap at Anti-Reds," *PI*, July 26, 1948.

52. Larry Gara, *The Liberty Line* (Lexington: University of Kentucky Press, 1967); Hans F. Sennholz, *Age of Inflation* (Belmont, Mass.: Western Islands, 1979).

53. Edward P. Morgan, "Academic Freedom and a College Campus," *Presbyterian Outlook*, June 25, 1962, 2.

54. Griffin Fariello, *Red Scare* (New York: Norton, 1995), 440–43.

55. Compare Robert G. Colodny, *The Struggle for Madrid* (New York: Paine-Whitman, 1958).

56. "Volunteers End Two Week Stay in Bomb Shelter," *PPG*, June 20, 1960; "Shadyside Test Success," *PPG*, March 18, 1961; "Mock Nuclear Attack Devastates District," *PPG*, May 18, 1963; compare Barry Paris, "The Bomb and Pittsburgh," *PPG*, November 12, 1981.

57. "175 Buildings Here OK'd as Raid Shelters," *PPG*, November 24, 1962; "700 Calories a Day for Atom Survivors," *PP*, June 16, 1963.

58. Paul Maryniak, "City Still Suffering Shelter Fallout from Cuba," *PP*, September 3, 1994.

59. "Survival Food Stored Here for Emergency," *PPG*, November 9, 1962.

60. "700 Calories a Day for Atom Survivors," *PP*, June 16, 1963; Geoffrey Tomb, "County Set for A-Attack," *PPG*, April 30, 1973.

61. Jack Ryan, "Is Civil Defense Program Worth Saving?," *PPG*, January 12, 1966; Robert Stearns, "Who's Afraid of the Big Bad Boom?," *PP Roto*, December 24, 1972.

62. "Civil Defense Chief Wails for Sirens and City Turns a Deaf Ear," *PP*, April 6, 1969; "City Bomb Sirens Rust in Silence," *PP*, October 31, 1971.

63. "County Warms to Cold War Shelters," *PPG*, April 14, 1980.

64. Paul Maryniak, "City Still Suffering Shelter Fallout from Cuba," *PP*, September 3, 1994.

65. Governor Fine, dogged by charges of corruption, was eventually tried and acquitted for tax evasion: see Paul B. Beers, *Pennsylvania Politics Today and Yesterday* (University Park: Pennsylvania State University Press, 1980), 173–89.

66. M. Nelson McGeary, *Pennsylvania Government in Action* (State College, Pa.: Penns Valley, 1972); Richard J. Cooper and Ryland W. Crary, *The Politics of Progress* (Harrisburg: Penns Valley, 1982); Reed Meredith Smith, *State Government in Transition* (Philadelphia: University of Pennsylvania Press, 1963); Beers, *Pennsylvania Politics Today and Yesterday*, 231–38.

67. Graham's subcommittee had recently provided valuable help to Musmanno and Dies in their federal effort to ban the Communist Party. See Musmanno to Graham, December 31, 1954, Musmanno Papers.

68. James Michener, *Report of the County Chairman* (New York: Random House, 1961), 89–108.

69. Paul B. Beers, *The Republican Years* (Harrisburg: Patriot-News, 1971); George D. Wolf, *William Warren Scranton* (University Park: Pennsylvania State University Press, 1981); Beers, *Pennsylvania Politics Today and Yesterday*, 275–312. For Leader's views on the Pechan law, see *George M. Leader: Democratic Candidate for Governor* (official campaign biography, 1954), 13–14.

70. *PPV* 2, no. 3 (April 1957): 7; Thomas Dublin, *When the Mines Closed* (Ithaca, N.Y.: Cornell University Press, 1998).

71. Miriam Ershkowitz and Joseph Zikmund, eds., *Black Politics in Philadelphia* (New York: Basic Books, 1973); Joseph V. Baker, "Negro Democrats Vie for Row Slate," *PI*, July 13, 1949.

72. Bettye Collier-Thomas and V. P. Franklin, *A Chronology of the Civil Rights Era in the U.S. and Philadelphia, 1954–1975* (Philadelphia: Center for African American History and Culture, Temple University, 1994); compare John T. McGreevy, *Parish Boundaries* (Chicago: University of Chicago Press, 1996), 91–92.

73. S. A. Paolantonio, *Frank Rizzo* (Philadelphia: Camino, 1993).

74. Terry Radtke, *The History of the Pennsylvania American Legion* (Mechanicsburg, Pa.: Stackpole, 1993), 92.

75. John C. Raines, ed., *Conspiracy* (New York: Harper and Row, 1974); Jack Nelson and Ronald J. Ostrow, *The FBI and the Berrigans* (New York: Coward, McCann and Geoghegan, 1972); William O'Rourke, *The Harrisburg Seven and the New Catholic Left* (New York: Crowell, 1972).

76. Oral History interview with Father Charles Owen Rice, 1968, 7–10, HCLA.

77. McGreevy, *Parish Boundaries*, 91–92, 132, 175–77, 234–40; "A Changing Community," *PPV* 1, no. 1 (July 1956): 8–10.

78. Epstein and Forster, *The Radical Right*, 44.

79. *PFF*, no. 2 (November 1954).

80. "Group Plans Commie-Backed Paper for City," May 4, 1968; "FBI Informer Links City Club to Communists," *PP*, February 26, 1971.

81. "Communist Party Hopeful Seeks City Council Seat," *PP*, May 31, 1973.

82. Bill Steigerwald, "Endangered Species," *PPG Magazine*, March 13, 1994.

83. Susan Jenks, "Old School Communist," *Philadelphia Sunday Bulletin/Discover*, May 5, 1974, 19; James H. Dolsen, *Bucking the Ruling Class* (privately printed, 1984). Dolsen's library can be found in Philadelphia's Balch Institute for Ethnic Studies.

CHAPTER 10

1. "Hasson Hits Snag on Commie's Tag," *PP*, December 9, 1953.

2. "Victim of Mazzei Testimony Reinstated," *PPG*, December 7, 1956.

3. *PFF* 3, no. 1 (January 1956): 14.

4. One exception here was the Canadian province of Quebec, which suppressed all Left activities by rigorous censorship and "padlocking" premises, in a drive that may directly have inspired Musmanno's actions in Pittsburgh.

5. Reginald Whitaker and Gary Marcuse, *Cold War Canada* (Toronto: University of Toronto Press, 1994); Tom O'Lincoln, *Into the Mainstream* (Sydney, Australia: Stained Wattle Press, 1985).

6. Charles H. McCormick, *Seeing Reds* (Pittsburgh: University of Pittsburgh Press, 1997).

INDEX

Matusow, Harvey, 188

May Day celebrations, 20, 31, 42, 55–56, 168

Mazzei, Joseph, 21, 88, 115–16, 185, 187–89, 206

Mazzone, Vito, 167

Meade, Bill, 64

Mellon, Richard King, 70

Mellon family, 47–48, 70, 78, 85–86

Middletown, 147

Miller, Arthur, 11

Mill Hall, 114

Mindszenty, Jozsef, 172–76

Minerich, Anthony, 151, 157, 159, 160

Monaghan, Walter, 106

Monessen, 157

Montgomery, Harry, 78, 81, 85–86, 95, 168, 186

Montgomery County, 26, 62, 102

Morgan, Thomas, 59

Morris, Charles, 175

Mount Lebanon, 136, 196

MOVE, 200

Muhlenberg College, 136–37

Mullen, John, 185–86

Mundt Bill, 34, 65, 103

Murray, Philip, 101, 104, 107–12, 185

Musmanno, Michael Angelo: and anti-Communist legislation, 89–95, 202; and anti-Communist rhetoric, 56, 71, 140; and labor movement, 5, 112; and Mullen controversy, 185–86; political career of, 66–67, 78–79, 161, 197; religious views of, 167; and sedition trials, 81–85

Myers, Francis, 57–58, 67, 103, 172

Myerson, Joseph, 62

Nabried, Thomas, 36, 87, 190

Narodni Glasnik, 142, 151, 157, 161

National Association for the Advancement of Colored People (NAACP), 31, 34, 39, 150, 200

National Citizens' Political Action Committee. *See* Citizens' Political Action Committee

National Council of Churches, 179, 181, 191

National Guard, 112, 200

National Labor Relations Board, 212

National Lawyers' Guild, 186

Nazareth, 123

Nazi-Soviet pact (1939), 5, 20, 63, 103, 111

Nelson, John, 116

Nelson, Steve: attempted deportation of, 163; background of, 82–83, 104, 151, 155; as Communist leader in Pittsburgh, 30, 32, 77, 80; and industrial activism, 100–1, 103, 108; as possible Soviet agent, 52, 83; pro-Soviet views of, 9; and sedition trials, 83–88, 95, 188–89, 203, 205. See also *Pennsylvania v. Nelson*

New Kensington, 81, 100, 102

Nix, Robert, 37, 198

Nixon, Richard, 10, 48, 52, 168, 170, 197, 203, 207

Northampton County, 90, 101

Nuclear weapons, 31, 61, 65, 70–74, 110, 114, 153, 169–70, 175–76, 180, 195–96. *See also* "Atom spy" charge; Civil defense

Nuss, Antoinette, 96

Oakland, 28, 41

Onda, Andrew, 81, 84, 86, 101

Oppenheimer, J. Robert, 82–83

Ordine Nuovo, 147–48

Owlett, G. Mason, 48

Oxnam, G. Bromley, 181

Patterson, Henry C., 177–78

Pearl Harbor: attack on, 8, 23, 71, 174

Pechan, Albert R., 69, 92–93, 122, 197. *See also* Pechan Act

Pechan Act, 55, 65, 92–94, 119, 121–24, 137, 177, 195, 198

Pennsylvania College for Women, 140

Pennsylvania Manufacturers' Association, 48–49, 78

Pennsylvania State Police, 71, 73, 200, 211

Pennsylvania State University, 96, 136–38

Pennsylvania Turnpike, 72

Pennsylvania v. Nelson, 188, 214

Pennypacker, Anna, 37

Pew, J. Howard, 179–81, 192, 195, 197

Pew, Joseph N., 47, 51–52

Pew family, 47–48, 194–95

Philadelphia: anti-Communist demonstrations in, 41–43, 55, 172; electoral politics, 5, 45, 59–60, 63, 178; North, 26, 200; police, 192, 200; racial polarization in, 199–202; religious revival in, 182; sabotage fears in, 73; South, 26, 167; strikes in, 19, 24, 106; West, 25–26, 203. *See also* Americans for Democratic Action; Citizens' Political Action Committee; Communist Party: in Philadelphia; Progressive Party; Teachers' Union of Philadelphia

Philadelphia Evening Bulletin, 91, 93

Philadelphia Inquirer, 24, 51, 63–64, 93, 125, 132, 139, 189

Philadelphia Record, 47

Philbrick, Herbert, 177

Philco, 102

Pinchot, Gifford, 46

Pirinsky, George, 159

Pittsburgh: anti-Communist demonstrations in, 41–43, 109; East, 27, 81, 100, 102, 108, 111–14; elections in, 45, 59, 63; Highland Park, 36, 81, 105; North Side, 7, 28–30, 109; religious revival in, 180–81; racial rioting in, 200; sabotage fears in, 73, 187–88; South Side, 28, 101; strikes in, 51, 105–6; Wylie Avenue, 36. *See also* Americans Battling Communism; Communist Party: in Pittsburgh; *Pittsburgh Courier; Pittsburgh Post-Gazette; Pittsburgh Press; Pittsburgh Sun-Telegraph;* Radio stations: KDKA; United Electrical, Radio and Machine Workers of America; Westinghouse

Pittsburgh Courier, 37

Pittsburgh Experiment, 181

Pittsburgh Post-Gazette, 21–22, 40, 52, 91, 117, 187–88, 196

Pittsburgh Press: and anti-Communist attacks, 76, 80, 82, 89, 96, 148, 160, 178; and civil defense, 196; and involvement in labor conflicts, 108–9, 112; liberalism of, 47; publishes nominating petitions, 13, 23, 38

Pittsburgh Sun-Telegraph, 76, 86

Plymouth Meeting, 177

Poling, Daniel A., 178, 183, 191

Polish-American Congress, 157, 164

Polish American Journal, 145

Polish Americans, 32, 34, 60, 113, 144–46, 150, 157, 172–74

Polish National Alliance (PNA), 78, 143, 146, 157–58, 164, 208

Popular Front, 14, 17–20, 138, 151, 158

Powers, George, 22–23, 28

Progressive Citizens of America (PCA), 38, 41, 61–62, 80, 107, 228 (n. 64)

Progressive Party: and African Americans, 37–39; and colleges, 137, 140; and Communists, 37–43, 76, 81, 169, 174; and Democratic Party, 61–64; electoral strength of, 17, 26–29; and ethnic groups, 152, 159–60; and labor support, 101–2, 107–9; stigma of involvement in, 140, 194. *See also* Progressive Citizens of America; Wallace, Henry

Protestants: and Communism, 137–38, 177–83

Quakers, 34, 65, 123, 177–78

Quinn, Thomas, 115, 117, 188

Radio stations: KDKA, 77; WINB, 191; WLOA, 32, 152; WMCK, 32, 80, 103, 112

Rahauser, William, 83–84, 86

Rainey, Joseph, 39, 41

RCA, 99. *See also* United Electrical, Radio and Machine Workers of America

Reading, 18–19, 26–28, 39

Red-baiting, 12, 103

Red Lion, 191

Register (Altoona-Johnstown diocese), 169–70, 173, 175–76

Religious responses to Communism. *See* Jews; Protestants; Quakers; Roman Catholic Church

90, 213; and investigation of Philadelphia schools, 123–34; involved in labor conflicts, 108; religious beliefs of, 108, 167, 179, 181. *See also* McCarran-Walter Act

Warren, Earl, 187–88

Washington County, 27, 100

Watergate scandal, 10, 203

Watkins v. United States, 189

Watson, Goldie, 38, 130

Wepman, Sarah Welsh, 131

Westinghouse, 30, 35, 38, 74, 78, 106, 113, 154, 212. *See also* United Electrical, Radio and Machine Workers of America

White, Harry Dexter, 125, 246 (n. 93)

Wicke, L. C., 178

Wilkes-Barre, 26, 39, 94

Wilkinsburg, 52, 196. *See also* McDowell, John

Williamsport, 101

Wilmerding, 113, 154

"Witch-hunting," 11–14, 185

Works Progress Administration, 22

World Anti-Communist League, 165, 191

Wright, Alexander, 77, 89–90, 101, 188

Wuchinich, George, 77, 79, 152, 162–63

Yalta agreement, 60, 66, 144, 159, 164

Yates v. United States, 189

Yiddisher Kultur Farband, 89, 104–5, 151

York, 26–27, 38–39, 62, 74, 92, 94, 159, 200

York Gazette and Daily, 26, 37–38, 47, 72

Yugoslavia, 7, 143, 151–55, 172–73. *See also* Croatian Americans; Serbian Americans; Slovene Americans

Zajednicar, 155